Innocent in Africa

An amusing and poignant story of a teach
overnight impulse, joins her partner in The

D0120645

an

About The Author

Annette Willoughby, the eldest of five children, was born in 1940 and spent her childhood in the West Riding of Yorkshire. After qualifying as a teacher in Hertfordshire, she spent most of her adult life teaching children with special needs while bringing up her own family. She has also dabbled in antiques and traded in artistic memorabilia.

Recently starting a new phase of her life, she naturally became involved with children of the Third World when she joined her partner - an engineer on a hydro-project in the Mountain Kingdom of Lesotho.

'Innocent in Africa', her first book, is an account of her time in Lesotho and South Africa shortly after the ending of apartheid.

Latterly, she has contributed to a number of articles and reports in various publications in connection with her fascination with Lesotho.

This book is published by Authors OnLine Ltd in electronic format and may be obtained at:- www.authorsonline.co.uk

An AuthorsOnLine Book

Published by Authors OnLine Ltd 2001

Copyright © Authors OnLine Ltd

Text Copyright © Annette Willoughby

Cover design and photograph © Annette Willoughby
& Authors OnLine Ltd

Also published in large print by ISIS Publishing Company, Oxford, UK
in 2003 ISBN 0-7531-9888-6

Printed in the UK by Antony Rowe Ltd

ISBN 0 7552 0009 8

Authors OnLine Ltd
15-17 Maidenhead Street
Hertford SG14 1DW
England

Visit us online at www.authorsonline.co.uk

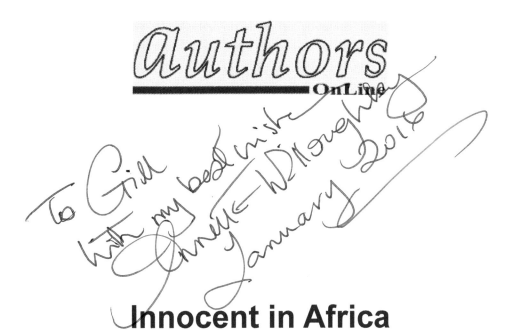

Innocent in Africa

by

Annette Willoughby

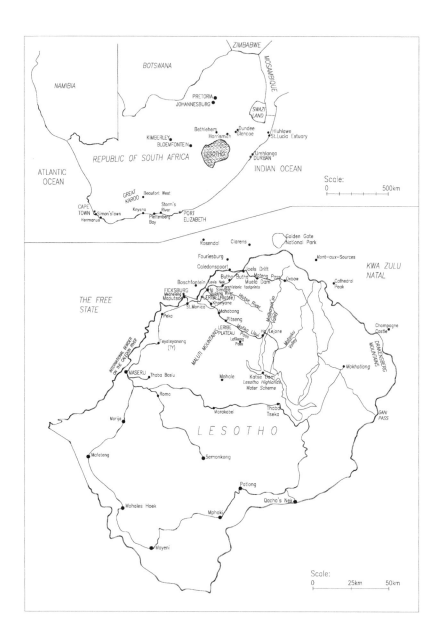

ZIMBABWE
BOTSWANA
MOSAMBIQUE
NAMIBIA
PRETORIA
JOHANNESBURG
SWAZI LAND
Bethlehem
Dundee
Glencoe
Hiluhlawe
St.Lucia Estuary
KIMBERLEY
Harrismith
BLOEMFONTEIN
LESOTHO
REPUBLIC OF SOUTH AFRICA
Umhlanga
DURBAN
INDIAN OCEAN
ATLANTIC OCEAN
GREAT KAROO
Beaufort West
CAPE TOWN
Simon'sTown
Knysna
Storm's River
PORT ELIZABETH
Hermanus
Plettenberg Bay

Scale:
0   500km

Golden Gate National Park
Rosendal
Clarens
Fouriesburg
Mont-aux-Sources
KWA ZULU NATAL
Caledonspoort
Joels Drift
Butho Buthe
Mateng Pass
prehistoric footprints
Oxbow
Cathedral Peak
Boschfontein
Levis Nek
Muela Dam
Ng Simode
FICKSBURG
Meshekeng
Maputsoa
LERIBE (Hlotse)
Hlotse River
Holse River
St.Monica
Khonyane
Mahobong
Mafika Lisiu
Pitseng
LERIBE PLATEAU
Peka
Mafika Lisiu Pass
Lejone
Mafika Lisiu Pass
Lefikeng Pass
Malaoku Valley
Champagne Castle
Teyateyaneng (TY)
MALUTI MOUNTAINS
DRAKENSBERG MOUNTAINS
INTERNATIONAL BORDER ON THE CALEDON RIVER
MASERU
Thaba Bosiu
Mohale
Mokhotlong
Roma
Katse Dam Lesotho Highlands Water Scheme
Morija
Marakabei
Thaba Tseka
SANI PASS
L E S O T H O
Mafeteng
Semonkong
Patlong
Mohales Hoek
Mphaki
Qacha's Nek
Moyeni

Scale:
0   25km   50km

iv

Acknowledgements

To my husband Barrie, without whose constructive criticism and co-operation this book could not have been written. It has been a landmark in our marriage. Neither the journey nor the book would have been achieved without him. My story belongs to us both.

To say that my biggest debt is to the people of Lesotho is also true. It is they who befriended me and welcomed me into their hearts. Chapter 28 is dedicated to the memory of Sam, our driver who took me on so many journeys.

Walter Makibi gave me the opportunity to understand the Basotho. Rose, Stephen and the family showed me how to appreciate a quality of life which has little to do with possessions and everything to do with the spirit. Solomon gave himself to his school and his music and shared it with me. I will never forget those things. Betty gave me the honour of naming her baby. Thabo and Sophie taught me how to smile. From my pupils I learnt the art of survival. Petros taught me never to give up.

I thank all the characters in my book, whom I had the pleasure to meet and contributed to the wide tapestry of this work. To Liliane with whom I shared so many adventures. To Priscilla who taught me how to laugh at myself. To Janet who gave me an education. To Peace with whom I shared poetry and to Father Brown and the Sisters who brew the best tea in Leribe. I thank Ian Judi and Bob, who made the most of a good bar stool and Noi who taught me how cook spring rolls. Also Borrie and Elsa Bornman who allowed us to exchange our marriage vows in their garden.

This book would not have been finished without the dedicated skills of my sister Marje with her keen eye and sharp pencil. Some of the reading was done by Kathy Gill, Jenny Gardner and Jan Creedy. To Imogen Olsen I owe a special debt of gratitude for her professional guidance. To all my friends and family who, through encouragement and unfailing support have seen me through my disappointments and my inadequacies in handling a computer. Thanks to Nick Carter who never gave up on me. His good sense and hard advice were what I needed most.

I owe the establishment of the Datchworth/Lesotho link to Richard Syms and the congregation of All Saints Church. The Lesotho Committee gave much of their free time to highlighting the needs of St John's Community in Ha Simone. Children from opposite ends of the world came to know each other. A seed was planted and continues to grow.

Extract from THE LOST WORLD OF THE KALAHARI by Laurens Van Der Post published by Chatto & Windus. Used by permission of The Random House Group Limited.

Poem entitled 'Africa' by David Diop (Senegal) from Growing up with Poetry by D.Rubadiri. Reprinted by permission of Heinemann International Publishers, a division of Reed Educational & Professional Publishing Ltd.

Words by Grace Nichols :- I have been unsuccessful in identifying the owners of the copyright of the work from which these words are taken. I would be pleased to include them in these acknowledgements, should they become known to us.

I readily accept that my knowledge of the culture of the Basotho people is limited and I apologise for any misunderstandings of their traditions which may be evident. All opinions expressed and, of course, errors, are entirely mine.

Author's Note

The Kingdom of Lesotho (pronounced *le-soo-too*) is a small country in South Africa and a member of the British Commonwealth. Ruled by the young King Letsie III, whose Coronation took place in November 1997, Lesotho became an independent Kingdom in 1965 after a century of being a British Protectorate.

The Basotho (people of Lesotho) emerged as a nation between 1815-1829 when Moshoeshoe the Great gathered the remnants of his tribes, scattered by Zulu and Matabele raids and established a stronghold at a place called Butha -Buthe at Mount Thaba- Bosiu, known as the 'Mountain of the Night'. From this mountain fortress, King Moshoeshoe began a policy of assisting refugees, granting them and their herds, some protection and welcoming missionaries from France to teach his people Christianity. By 1840, there were 40,000 refugees in the area and they formed the beginning of the new nation, naming their territory Basutoland.

The Boers had crossed the Orange River in the 1830's hoping to gain more land. The Basotho, under constant attack, were afraid that they might have to become integrated with the rest of South Africa. They were a proud people and wanted to be left alone to govern themselves. Tensions increased when the Boers assumed that they had grazing rights to the rich agricultural lowlands, west of the Caledon River. Eventually Moshoeshoe was forced to sign away some of his land, but the Boer settlers were unable to conquer Thaba Bosiu.

Moshoeshoe sought help from the British people, welcomed more peacemaking missionaries from France and then from England to set up their centres in the remote mountain villages. Queen Victoria intervened and a British Protectorate was set up in the Cape in 1871 .

In the build-up of tensions between Boers, the British government and his own seSotho tribes, Moshoeshoe emerged as a great diplomat, a man of integrity and dignity, who tried to resolve the problems of land in a conciliatory way, even though he was being pushed further and further out of the Orange Free State. His death in 1870, his fight for freedom of his people, had set his country on a road to learning and brought about a new era of development for Basutoland.

Today, Lesotho is still an all-black nation, fiercely independent, self reliant and proud of its long tradition of leadership under the system of paramount chiefs and its own King. It may be poor, but has succeeded in remaining politically independent of white controlled governments. Whites were never allowed to gain leases for land and even today, white people are not allowed to build homes. It is a Kingdom in the true sense of the word.

Lesotho's most contentious political aspect, is that it is landlocked by South Africa; an isolated enclave that has excluded it from the realms of travellers and tourism. It has remained a geographic island, its borders surrounded by South Africa, divided by the Caledon River to the west, the Drakensberg Mountains to the eastern and southern edge and to the north, the Maluti range.

Two thirds of Lesotho is almost impenetrable mountain. It is sometimes called 'The Mountain Kingdom' and has the highest low point in the world. Temperatures in summer can reach 35 degrees centigrade, but in winter may fall to as low as minus 8 degrees. It is entirely outside the tropics, situated at a considerable height above sea level, thus free from tropical diseases. Being in the Southern Hemisphere, the summer season lasts from November to January and the winters from May to July, when snow falls often occur.

Up in the highlands, remote villages still exist where settlements remain the same as a hundred years ago. Rondavels of rock with thatched roofs, usually set in a homestead which houses an entire family, are built close to the caves where, thousands of years ago, the San Bushmen once lived. Their spectacular cave art appears in many places;

Symbolic mystical messages are carved into the caves, alongside skeletal drawings of lion, leopard, buffalo and numerous kinds of antelope. evidence that many different kinds of wild animals once lived there. For at least 25,000 years nomadic hunter gatherers lived in the mountains and the valleys of the present Lesotho.

But long before the time of early civilisations, long before the mountain ranges were thrown up by volcanic activity, Lesotho was a flat arid land, interspersed with inland lakes and rivers. This was dinosaur country. 250 million years ago, enormous mammal-like reptiles and birds roamed this land. Abundant fossil remains and footprints now make Lesotho a prime target for scientists interested in the evolution of life on earth. No wonder it has been called ' Roof of Africa' and is recognised as a historical site of great evolutionary importance.

The flat topped mountains are still home to wandering herd boys with their cattle, and the hardy mountain folk, who typically wrap themselves in the garb of colourful blankets and wide brimmed conical straw hats. Transport is by donkey or the small strongly built Basotho pony, fit to trek over high pasture and deep mountain gorges.

Lesotho's most important natural resource is water. Up in the highlands, the source of the Orange river, known as the Senqu River, starts its journey down the mountains. The water is pure and fresh and has supported the lives of the inhabitants for thousands of years. They call it the 'white gold'.

This is a country with a rich and savage heritage; those who discover it find fascination and mystery, some say magic. The journey of a lifetime brought us here to Leribe, a small town built on the Hlotsi River (pronounced *Shlotsi*) near the South African border. Moshoeshoe himself was born in the foothills of the Leribe district.

Founded in 1876 by an Anglican missionary, the town of Leribe suffered repeated siege during the 1880 Gun War and relics of a monument to a European soldier dressed for battle in the main street, is all that is left of a white military presence. An Anglican Mission still flourishes today and brings a Christian unity to the people here.

Their language is seSotho (known locally as 'Sotho) but English is widely known and is taught in their schools. At primary level, English is the medium of instruction and children grow up with English as their second language and an inherent love of England, the country they are a part of.

Life for the Basotho goes according to climate, rainfall and ancestral spirits. Their culture is rich and fascinating, their ancient tribal traditions barely relative to the life of the modern westerner. To understand them as a people is surely a vital link towards unity in a broken world.

CONTENTS

Chapter   **Page**

    Foreword   x
1   Sweet Suburbia and beyond.   1
2   Snow in South Africa   7
3   The Mountain Kingdom   18
4   The Camp.   22
5   Grandmothermania   30
6   Au Revoir   35
7   Lesotho for real   39
8   A Basotho Maid   44
9   Life by the Side of the Road   54
10 The New South Africa   65
11 Late Developers   69
12 Does Queen Elizabeth have any Sheep?   74
13 A Festival of Cherries   79
14 Umhlanga   85
15 Midsummer Christmas   92
16 Priscilla and the Buffalo   109
17 Brave Faces   120
18 The Choir   126
19 Katze Dam   132
20 Walter and the Dinosaur   140
21 Proposals   150
22 Gooseplucking   160
23 The Medicine Man   174
24 Bending the Rules   179
25 A Wedding and a Birth   191
26 Rainbow Nation   203
27 The Concert   211
28 Death of Sam   224

    Bibliography   226
    Glossary   229

FOREWORD

African Music.

It was a small unheated room, with nothing more pretentious than a few plastic chairs and a broken ceiling fan. People filed in slowly, huddled in blankets and warm coats; drab shapes squeezing themselves into rows of small seats. It was a cold night. Through the smoke haze, a guitarist tuned up. Some of the men shared a can of beer as they waited for the evening to begin. A quiet buzz filled the room. Women stared from under gaudy scarves and frizzy plaited hair. No one spoke to us. I could feel them asking why we were there- the only white people in the room, but no words came.

Two policemen stood silently near the door, wearing blue uniform overcoats with .38 Police Specials in full view. They too waited and watched as more people packed into the small space between the chairs, spilling over into the aisles. An air of excitement rippled through the swelling ranks.

The tall lead singer closed his eyes and began strumming his guitar, soft and low. His accompanist was a beautiful South African girl in a scarlet silk blouse, which glowed like fire. She had strong features and a handsome profile, like a bronze statue. She moved in a way that was smooth and sexy, to the rhythm. Sure and purposeful in her playing, she thumbed the strings of her guitar with expert fingers, following the arousing beat of her partner. A black youth stroked the drums. A middle aged hippie character, drifted into the music with the soft shush of a tambourine, like the swirl of tobacco smoke in a bar. The players didn't speak to one another. Eyes closed, they took up the rhythm and started to play.

A huge lady, cocooned in a scarlet blanket, shuffled to a seat in the back row and went to sleep. Another, dressed in a shiny silver coat, greeted her friends loudly and sat on a chair between the two standing officers of the law. The frothy pinkness of her skirt spilled onto their uniforms. Like sleeping lizards, they remained unperturbed - one eye on the door. Suddenly there was a commotion and a crunching of boots and bodies. One of the policemen twitched. Two sleazy looking characters were trying to get in. I couldn't tell what they were shouting, but the response from the doorman was clear, 'no money, no come in'.

Augustine was officiating. He had greeted us with a huge smile and seated us on the cleanest of the white plastic chairs, with a great flourish. Broad and handsome, his shoulder fitted exactly into the doorframe and one very large boot stood against the steel grill. Gatecrashers were par for the course tonight. The lead guitarist was Augustine's brother, of whom he was extremely proud. A few heavy characters were not going to spoil his evening.

Otherwise known as Mister Mafia, Augustine was perfect for the job. Taxi driver, organiser, football team manager - the man who could fix a bank note to a donkey's elbow. In Leribe, nothing happened that he didn't have a slippery hand in. Born and bred in the town, it was his personal consortium who had provided the chairs for the dignitaries to sit in, that important day, five years ago, at the grand official opening of Nelson Mandela Road, the first tarred highway up to Katse Dam; the road which had taken eight years to build and had opened up the way to the Lesotho highlands. Although his name wasn't on the contract, everyone knew that Augustine built Nelson Mandela Road.

Now the music was getting louder and more urgent, the crowd eager; bass guitar and hypnotic beat of African rhythm vibrating through the soles of my feet. Suddenly the lady in the back row woke up and smiled. She really was quite young after all and her eyes grew alive with the music. Her blanket fell to the floor. She stood up and started to gyrate, with an easy graceful movement, smiling broadly and uncaring about her large shape, almost knocking one of the policemen into a corner.

The deep throaty voice of the lead singer sang in seSotho, a language that I never imagined I would hear - because I am a Yorkshire girl. From now on, this small town overlooking the Maluti mountains was my home; a speck on the map of South Africa, in a country known as The Mountain Kingdom.

A young man, wearing a scruffy jersey got to his feet and started to dance. His body rippled like flowing water. Oblivious of everyone, he danced in front of the crowd, every muscle in his sinewy shape swinging and turning in complete harmony with the beat. People around us got to their feet. The lead singer played crazily, his fingers flying.

The girl in the voluminous coat, whose buttons were stretched to breaking point, threw herself into the fray next to a huge guy wearing a trench coat and long woollen scarf. Together they gyrated, so wonderfully fluid and sensuous. Coats of all shapes and sizes danced. Some with wild ecstatic gestures, knocking over chairs as if nothing must get in the way of their passion, others in some small space between heaving hips and bosoms, as if their lives depended on it. Big ladies with big bottoms shook and wriggled from their shoulders to their feet. Belts and braces stretched alarmingly. In between the pulsating bodies, shone seductive flashes of scarlet silk.

Their faces lit up when they smiled. Several came up and shook hands when the music stopped. Their eyes shone. We did not understand a word they were saying. One man embraced us, sweeping me off my feet in a torrent of dancing fervour. Augustine patted us both on the back in a gesture of approval, speaking in English.

"Thank you for coming *Ntate, 'M'e* - we do good music eh!"

It was a charming welcome to their world. They loved us because we had joined in. We were strangers to their town but it didn't matter whether you were black or white, old, young, toothless or penniless, sober or drunk. It was Saturday night in the back room of the Leribe Hotel and we were a long way from home.

Bright stars lit the way as we drove back to the camp, the music still throbbing in our ears. Tonight we had experienced our first taste of hospitality -Lesotho style. In that small music filled room, torn garments went unnoticed, empty pockets and empty stomachs were forgotten; no one saw the cracked walls or the peeling paint. Current fashion as we know it, was meaningless; price tags irrelevant. Those lucky enough to own a coat kept it on. The spirit of the Basotho people had captured our hearts.

AFRICA

Africa my Africa
Africa of proud warriors in the ancestral savannahs
Africa of whom my grandmother sings
On the banks of the distant river
I have never known you
But your blood flows in my veins
Your beautiful black blood that irrigates the fields
The blood of your sweat
The sweat of your work,
The work of your slavery
The slavery of your children

Africa tell me Africa
Is this you this back that is bent
This back that breaks under the weight of humiliation,
This back trembling with red scars
And saying yes to the whip under the midday sun,
But a grave voice answers me
Impetuous son that tree young and strong
That tree there
In splendid loneliness amidst white and faded flowers
This is Africa your Africa
That grows again patiently obstinately
And its fruit gradually acquires
The bitter taste of liberty.

David Diop (Senegal)

Chapter 1

Sweet Suburbia and Beyond.

The deep purring of the engines droned on. Cabin lights were out and my neck ached from being scrunched up against the window. A large man in the next seat had over-spilled his airspace and lolled into mine. An intense quiet reigned. At 35,000 feet, three hours from Johannesburg, the stark reality of the journey began to sink in. I was actually on my way to South Africa.

Four unforgettable days of activity had brought me to this point. Gradually, as waves of exhaustion brought the first respite, anxiety began to recede. In its place, a feeling of great excitement. There was no going back.

Propelled into the inky darkness, my head rest became a feather pillow, and sleep played tricks in my mind. Then another pitch black night where no star shone, came from memories long ago in another place.

Cradled in gentleness, soothed by the singing of lullabies, someone held me and protected me from the thing they called war. The eldest of three sisters, I remember being taken by my mother, from my warm bed into the dark shelter – because the siren had sounded from the pit. Coal industries and steel factories were known targets of bombing raids in the West Riding of Yorkshire and running for safety in the blackout scared the wits out of hundreds of ordinary families.

The slag heaps of Bentley Colliery were the mountains of my childhood Even in the daytime, through the half light of slate skies, a heavy mist rose from the coal tips. The acrid smell of smoke stung the nostrils and grime from pit chimneys relentlessly smeared soot across the rooftops.

Muck was part of life. Porridge tasted of it, clean washing smelled of it. The sound of heavy boots crunching on the yard and the slack sliding from the sacks into the coal bunker, belonged to the miner and his family. In every colliery village, men walked home in the early morning, through the back streets of a million terraced houses. Sleeping children were woken by the sound of the night shift coming off. Women peered through net curtains to see if their man was on his way.

My grandfather arrived home from the pit, black from head to toe. He took off his boots, knocked the coal from each one on the stone step, enough to fill a shovel, before placing them on clean newspaper by the scullery door. After the long tiring night shift, we children were shooed outside while the soaping ritual took place.

The back yard playground boasted a brick air raid shelter, an outside lavatory, furnished with the Doncaster Gazette hung in squares on a nail behind the door, and a square patch of dirty grass - the size of a twopence ha'penny stamp. Against the wall leaned a great iron mangle with rubber rollers.

We waited for the steam to drift out of the scullery window as my Grandmother poured jugs of boiling water from the copper into a wide stone sink. Dirty water came splashing onto the stone flags around the grate, and we knew that he would soon come and shout us.

"You can come and kiss me now bairns," yelled a hearty voice, "where are my beautiful girls?" And we would run into his arms.

*   *   *   *   *

The adjacent passenger turned over, shifted his gut about ninety degrees, moved his head and released my shoulder, until now pinned into a six hour crease. A thread of cotton light of the palest blue coming from the east, made running stitches onto the black sky. The thread became wider as the aircraft sped alongside, keeping a steady distance, like a flight of geese over a Norfolk marsh. Soon, a quiet line of pale yellow light, criss-crossed the tinges of blue, hemming under and over, as delicate as lace on a pillow. Luminous pencils of light, constantly changing; purple, pink, gold, ran along - folding, plaiting, stitching a tangle of colours onto the last traces of darkness.

Suddenly came the first glimpse of the sun, pushing back the edges of the night, spreading like fire through the cabin. The red ball rose fast, bleeding through the sky, filling the aircraft with orange light, scorching the faces of sleeping passengers. Blinds were thrown back. Children awoke. Daybreak erupted across the heavens; shining, perfect, as each new morning gone before.

In my excitement, I reached for my diary. '30th June 1996 – have just seen the sun rise over Africa.'

The Ivory Coast, the Great Zambezi River, the Kalahari Desert – I pictured the blots beside the magic names of Africa in my school atlas; the elephants, lions and snakes scribbled in Indian ink in the margin next to the page of Equatorial Rain Forests - images conjured up by previous pupils of 3A at Percy Jackson Grammar School. Africa was about as unknown in the fifties as the North Pole today. How would we ever know if the countries of our dreams truly existed?

Was Johannesburg really the 'City of Gold'? Was South Africa really a Rainbow Nation? The thrilling prospect of my journey stretched every nerve in my body. The Maluti Mountains of Lesotho, at that moment, meant no more than a tiny pink dot on the map of the African Continent.

*   *   *   *   *

What if he wasn't there? I hardly dare to think about it. Still clinging to the hope that he would come to meet my flight – I went over the previous four days in my mind yet again, just to be sure.

Last Tuesday, one of my students had been taken ill, allowing me a free morning. Walking up the High Street alone, for no other reason than to search the library for maps, a poster for a bargain holiday caught my eye in a travel agent's window - nothing special. I went inside. Addressing the girl behind the counter, I heard this voice came out of my mouth.

"How much is the fare to Johannesburg?"

"When do you want to go?" came the smart request from young lady, looking at me with great directness.

"On Saturday," came the commanding voice inside me. That was four days away. In a blinding flash, with the rare conviction which comes once in a lifetime, my future was sealed. If the girl had answered me, telling me the cost of the fare, I would still be sitting in my garden waiting for my lovely man to come home.

"You will have to book your ticket within the next twenty four hours if you want to travel on Saturday; by four o'clock tomorrow."

"That's perfect," the calm voice answered. "Thank you."

My spontaneity was having a field day, as though nothing mattered except an air ticket to the southern hemisphere and filling myself with typhoid vaccine. Moments later, passing the local jewellers shop, my unsteady legs took me inside. The bell on the counter rang and my friend Theresa emerged from her little office behind the dark glass panel where she worked.

"Theresa - I'm going to South Africa on Saturday!"

Her glasses fell off her nose and her mouth fell open.

"What will Barrie say?"

"He doesn't know I'm coming! Don't even know where to find him! I've got three days to get ready!"

The listed injections for South Africa were Typhoid, Hepatitis B, Tetanus and Polio. On an emergency appointment, the surgery nurse administered all four together in one afternoon. Lying on the couch, mobile phone in one hand and sharp needle dug into left buttock, I yelled happily at the girl at South African Airways.

"Yes, I would like to confirm my single ticket to Johannesburg on Saturday. Yes, I know it's almost four o'clock. Couldn't ring any sooner! When am I coming back? I don't even know *if* I'm coming back!"

The hallway became awash with suitcases and trolley wheels. My whole wardrobe was thrown onto the bed, while trying to guess the right things to wear in South Africa in mid July. There was always the possibility that the typhoid would get to me before there was time to contact Barrie, to ask him if he would come to the airport to meet me.

Reaching someone by phone in Lesotho requires a small miracle. The highly- strung telecommunications system works successfully if it isn't prevented by snowfalls, heavy rains, tribal warfare or strikes. One of those is applicable most working days. Barrie's job in Lesotho was up in the mountains on a huge contracting site and his office situated in a small town called Leribe. His company helped me to locate him, but with difficulty, as there was a major strike on and he had been sent to another part of the site for safety reasons. Threats against staff were taken seriously and it took many persistent attempts to track him down. Two whole days in fact.

Barrie had no idea what my plans were. His plans were always logical informed choices. He had taken his departure to Lesotho, leaving behind a contented gardener with watering can to match. His overseas assignment offered a three week unaccompanied posting, possibly longer, with courier mail address in case of emergencies.

From his office in a remote mountain hideaway, caught up in the furore of hundreds of striking tunnellers, his reply was somewhat sharp.

"How on earth did you manage to find me?"

"Nine attempts Barrie - I'm coming to Johannesburg on Saturday.... can you meet me off the night flight, early Sunday morning? "

"What!......Christ Nettie - do you realise Lesotho is hundreds of miles from Johannesburg! We're up in the mountains.... where the heck do you think we're going to live!"

"I'm sorry there's not much time. Decided to quit my job and come. Don't worry darling – I know you'll think of something by Sunday!"

*　　*　　*　　*　　*

It was March 1993 when we met. Buying and selling antiques were my bread and butter. My life was full of auction house bargains, overdrafts and parking fines.

One of my best investments had been the purchase of an old Citroen van, found in a scrap yard while looking for bits for cast iron stoves. It was underpinned in rust and farmyard manure, but it looked like a fighter and it was cheap. Despite having no spare wheel, it ran for two years on the circuit of antique markets and village fairs. Its girth was wide enough to carry brass fenders and crumbling oak pews and once brought home a sort of plough, collected from some genteel residence in the country. The hunt for a bargain had come to be a lifeline.

"Do you always live life on roller skates?" shouted a man's voice next to me during a wild afternoon in a Force 8 gale, while restraining the flapping canvas of a friend's makeshift stall at a Hertfordshire village country fair. Dashing around from one venue to another, collecting other people's rubbish and selling it, was more of an addiction than a job.

"Don't you ever stop?"

"Never. It's called paying the bills."

Without realising, I must have plunged down that slippery slope of resenting a man in my life, without noticing. There was no time for serious relationships.

Attired in a suit and matching tie, unmistakably English, Barrie arrived in my life. He was tall and slim, with singing blue eyes, and an attractive north country accent. If I had fallen for a gentleman farmer with wax jacket and green wellies - no one would have been surprised - but an engineer in a city suit! It was like running into a barn door at a hundred miles an hour. I stopped running and fell in love.

The measure of my success had always depended on single handed energy, the R.A.C. and working round the clock seven days a week. Things changed after that. The Citroen hurtled between Hertfordshire and South London until we could no longer stand the strain of being apart. We made a joint decision to close my shop in Hertford and emigrate south of the Thames. Sadly, my basement heaven 'Memorabilia Enchantica' in the bistro end of St Andrews Street, went under the hammer. Treasured possessions went to the highest bidder, antiques were converted to cash and I left a life I loved. My friends told Barrie amusing stories of my ability to attract other people's junk, but it wasn't sufficient to put him off. He whisked me off to the depths of Croydon and bought me a mountain bike.

My two adult teenagers, a son and daughter, wished us both the best of luck in our middle life romance. We couldn't have asked for more. They were quite glad to have escaped the French polishing lessons and carpentry manuals piled in date order up the stairs. Walnut cabinets and Victorian commodes were crammed into the hall downstairs and the lounge was filled with paint pots and school desks carved with the names of illiterate children who knew how to etch in pine.

"Mum - the kitchen table's gone…is it Auction Day at the Castle?"

That was my daughter. My son wouldn't register the table was missing until his plate of bacon and eggs hit the floor. James went through life in a dream. If a snake charmer moved in he wouldn't notice.

Auctions were treasure troves. Tables moved out – pianos moved in. There was never enough space. In 1994 Magnolia Cottage was finally sold. Our family floundered for a while, then within months each had found a new life and we were three points of a triangle but in close touch. It's what Dr Spock calls 'moving on'.

Barrie and I found a lovely Victorian house in Beckenham in March 1995. With a mortgage to pay, my skills as a teacher of children with special needs, once more became a priority .With a spot of re-training, employment was plentiful.

In Croydon, a new centre for excluded school pupils had recently opened and the aim was that the students would be returned to mainstream school, once their problems had been identified. I took a job as a peripatetic teacher and was constantly meeting kids who had fallen off the ladder of progress and for whom failure was the norm. After a time of systematic readjustment, and a change in attitude, some students were successfully re-integrated. Learning about this special kind of help for young people, and how to restore self esteem to the sorry pupil who had reached the bottom rung, was as therapeutic to me as to the student.

Kent was new and fascinating. Beckenham is close to Downe House, the home of Charles Darwin; a short distance from the lovely Standen House - enriched by William Morris interiors and the architecture of Philip Webb, and within sight of the rustic beauty of Chartwell and Penshurst Place. We shared summer days in Canterbury amongst the splendour of monastic buildings and medieval stained glass.

Weekend cycling, never before part of my itinerary, became first a hazard then a pleasure, depending on which co-ordinates of the Ordnance Survey Barrie had selected. The wide open vistas of the Weald, rolling into the chalk cliffs of the North Downs stole my heart unawares. Dappled lanes of rosy Kentish villages, oast houses reminiscent of hop fields, ancient forests of oak and ash, bluebells at Brasted Chart, now were seen from the saddle. I conquered the sore butt, yet never learnt how to mend a puncture.

Our lives together were just beginning. After a year's engagement, our wedding blessing was planned for April 1997 in a Hertfordshire village, where our paths had first crossed. My children and I had lived in the parish of Datchworth for fifteen years; a pleasant village of green meadows, an ancient whipping post and a claim to an entry in the Domesday Book.

It was my spiritual home. Barrie's parents were laid to rest in the old churchyard, where, every spring, the cherry blossom grew in circlets around the ancient tree trunks, like pink coronets. On a visit to see Mrs King, the Church Warden, in the spring of 1996, we requested that our names be entered in the Register of Forthcoming Marriages at Datchworth All Saints.

Then something happened which blew our plans overboard. The company Barrie worked for, offered him work in Southern Africa.

"The company have asked me to go to Lesotho for a few a few weeks, to work on a hydro-project up in the mountains." he announced one evening.

"Where's Lesotho?" I started, quite taken by surprise. He was used to travelling half way round the world on engineering business.

"It's a small country, landlocked by South Africa. It'll be cold this time of the year. Never mind it won't be for long."

Attempts to organise his leaving date so that the roses we had bought for our beloved garden would be planted before he left, were thwarted. Our bikes hung sadly from racks in the cellar. We were facing our first separation. On 8th June, Barrie flew from London Heathrow on a night flight to Johannesburg, and I cried.

"For heavens' sake," sighed my sister down the phone, "he's only gone for three weeks!"

*   *   *   *   *

My isolation in the plane began to worry me. Around me families were preparing to holiday in the Winelands of the Cape or climb Table Mountain without ropes. Early arrivals by lone passengers with single tickets and hardly any luggage might look suspicious. Johannesburg Immigration might put me back on the next flight to Heathrow. The worst scenario was that he might never know that I came.

When a stewardess in bright red lipstick approached with a breakfast tray, my appetite shrank. Hiding behind a paper plate of cheese spread and warm muffins did nothing to disperse my worries and I joined the toilet queue in the hope that sanity would return via an empty bladder. If he wasn't there that was one thing. If he wasn't pleased to see me that was another.

A single ticket, a new Estee Lauder night cream, a dose of typhoid and a three hundred pounds overdraft at the bank - the only evidence of my actions. Having spent the last few days like a headless chicken, leaving an excellent job overnight, organising the whole of my life into a carrier bag and boarding a Boeing 747 to South Africa, on the strength of a three minute phone call to a country that I had never even heard of, seemed to touch on insanity. Yet in my heart, I knew it was right.

Collecting my suitcase off Flight SA 233, the passenger exit loomed in front. A little black man in a uniform stood smartly by the door into the arrivals area. It was 7.30am South Africa time.

Chapter 2.

Snow in South Africa

"Nettie! Over here!"

He was there, waiting at the side of the barrier. He had seen me first. My lungs were bursting with anticipation.

"You crazy woman!" was all he could say through his tears, "You came all this way to see me!"

We hugged each other and cried, getting in everybody's way as they tried to manoeuvre loaded trolleys around us. Bashed by feet and metal wheels, we stood, holding each other, for a long time, hardly noticing the chaos. As his arm went round my shoulders, a wave of exhaustion hit me. My 'last -a -whole- day' mascara had exceeded it's life expectancy and my 'feel good factor' had diminished to a shadow.

"Thanks for coming down from the mountains to meet me," I said, swallowing hard while admiring his tanned look. Seeing his familiar face and neatly trimmed beard, I could see where the sun had caught the laughter lines in his face.

"Darling, you won't believe me when I tell you…."

"With you Nettie – I can believe anything, but come on, lets go find the car ….I've forgotten where I parked it in the rush to meet the plane."

Glued at the hip, Barrie and I walked out of Johannesburg Airport to a new South African morning into a steely blue sky. Feeling the bitter temperature cut through my light clothes, I realised that winter in South Africa meant it was not slightly chilly, but extremely cold.

"I hoped you'd be there… are you angry?" I said, finding my voice at last.

"Left Leribe at 4.00am. I was one of the first cars through the border. The guard was still asleep. Oh, its so good to see you, honey."

"Beats weekend biking eh?"

"No, I'm not angry…..but you really gave me the shock of my life. I've heard of spontaneity, but this takes the biscuit. Had a hell of a job finding us somewhere to live in such a short time."

"Not much planning," I teased him, "sorry about that."

"Don't be sorry," he laughed, and planted a kiss firmly on my cheek.

"A regiment of elephants couldn't have stopped me once my mind was made up. There didn't seem much point in cooking for one! Where are we going to live?"

"A place called Fouriesburg, it's on the South African side. It's a four hour drive. Journeys are measured in hours – not miles. The company have lent us a house belonging to a French couple, who've gone on holiday."

As we searched the vast Johannesburg car park, I began to feel light headed after my long anxious flight. My maiden journey to South Africa would be indelibly printed on my mind. We were both suffering from a sense of disbelief and kept grinning at one another stupidly.

"Let's get on the road. We've a long way to go."

He turned to speak to the black security guard at the exit gate, who offered us some directions, in a very strong South African accent.

"*Dankie*" said Barrie confidently, with a glance at the route map sitting on the dashboard. Soon we were out on the Freeway.

"Fouriesburg is a small town south of Bethlehem, near a place called Clarens, which is in the Golden Gate National Park. I've been there already, it's very beautiful. Ostriches in the park - and baboons. Saw them playing on the hillsides. Hope you like Fouriesburg. Quite a few ex-pats living there. The strike's just started and it looks like being a long struggle. Might have to move to the camp, but for the moment, I'll be travelling over the border into Lesotho to the office and have to be away very early in the morning. Hope you'll be able to fill your time – the days are going to be a bit lonely."

"I'll start jogging and learn to cook."

"Don't bank on it. You can't just go anywhere you like and it's not like shopping in Sainsbury's."

"I won't then. I'll stay home and read books on South Africa. You don't have to worry about me." His eyes wrinkled at the corners into a smile and he reached for my hand. "Wait 'til you see Lesotho, then you'll really know what this country's like."

*   *   *   *   *

The city of Jo'burg is only a hundred years old. It grew out of the discovery of the gold reef in 1887 when thousands of mining entrepreneurs descended on the land to seek their fortune. Today, it is similar to any other anonymous western-style centre; regarded by some as a brash fast growing and ugly city, surrounded by advertising hoardings showing the range of its huge hi-tech industry; by far the largest city in South Africa. In the last official census of 1985, the population was put at three million: two million whites and a million blacks. But the figures were inaccurate. No allowance was made for the numbers who lived in the black townships which ring the city. Today, the 'City of Gold' holds around six million people – of all colours and creeds.

Once off the Freeways, the landscape changed. Everything was brown and bare. How drab the fields looked. There were hardly any trees. The rocky terrain was even more barren and vast than I had expected. Apart from the tarmac road, there were no buildings of any kind, except low barn- like structures and one or two farm houses. There was no other vehicle in sight.

"We could be the only people on the planet" I commented, puzzled at seeing neither people nor buildings. A single straight road went on mile after mile, up a hill, then another and another; Villiers, Frankfort, Reitz. This was the road to Bethlehem.

Brown earth rolled past, endlessly bounded by fences enclosing mile after mile of yellow stalks with spiky leaves. It was maize at the end of the harvest; the staple diet of the black people. Small herds of cattle dotted the horizon and in the blue distance across the plains - the mountains. Now and again, the winter sun washed over burnt umber land and picked out strips of water that sparkled with life.

Then, out in the middle of nowhere, a black woman walked by the side of the road, carrying a bundle of extremely long branches, tied together - not under one arm, but on her head. Her brightly coloured dress reached down to the ground and she wore a scarf to protect her head. The road ahead was empty.

"Oh look Barrie! I can't believe I'm seeing her – am I really only twelve flying hours away from London, with all those anoraks and denims! Her back is so straight, she walks with such purpose."

The sight of her caught me remembering my childhood picture books. The woman, so innocent of my delight, was the beginning of my fascination with Africa. From this moment, I had fallen under its spell. The magic had pierced my skin. Although a familiar sight to any African, it touched my heart like a dream resurrected in some distant age.

Barrie held my hand and smiled. He knew it was a first for me and was glad to share in my delight.

Further along the road - another young woman, carrying not only heavy branches on her head, but in a blanket tied around her waist, the curved rounded shape of a small child, resting against her back. Her tread was measured and lithe. Her hands were free and as she walked into the fresh wind, her feet kicked up small clouds of dust. She had nothing on her feet.

The frontiers of my previous travels related to no more than a Dutch canal and a rather nice walk in the pine forests of California. Even the view from the top of the Empire State building in New York which had affected my vocal chords like grapes in a wine press, didn't allow for this – seeing a legend come true.

"You often see people walking alone for miles along tarmac roads," said Barrie seeing my expression. The only public transport is a strong pair of feet."

Soon after that, a short distance from the road and heading out into the open landscape, a group of women appeared, most carrying something on their heads, with the balance of disciplined acrobats; some with water pots, others with branches. Their tall figures were wrapped in woven shawls and blankets, but there was no distinguishing mode of dress, except a patchwork of rich reds and browns like the earth, folded and tied like kite trails from thin narrow hips. There was nothing ahead except the low sky and a sea of biscuit dry maize.

*   *   *   *   *

Fouriesburg is a small town in The Free State (formerly Orange Free State) quite close to the Lesotho border and surrounded by mountains. We set out to find Fouvie Street with dogs barking at us from every street end and gatepost. It was a sprawling neighbourhood – more the size of an English village. Most of the houses were set in large gardens with high fences and steel bars at every window. The address we were searching for was in the newer end of the village, next door to the Police Station. Every building was single storey - it was like bungalow-land with dogs. No flowers grew in the gardens; the lawns in front of the residences were brown and bare and at the gates, the tenacious bull terriers sat, waiting for the next pair of ankles along the walkway. So far I wasn't impressed. Turning a corner into a modern street, with a built up road, the fences not so high and the outlook very pleasant, Barrie drew up to a gate and took out a bunch of keys.

"Here we are - 22, Fouvie Street," he said, "reminds me of the chalets up in the Swiss mountains."

The house was quite attractive - Scandinavian style with sloping roofs in an unusual arrangement, with enormous windows and odd shaped corners. Barrie parked the car in the drive, and locked the gate. Opening up the solid wooden front door, we trod respectfully and spoke in whispers, almost as though the family who lived there were still inside. A picture of a black lady stared down at us from the wall. This was to be our first South African home.

We woke to a canary yellow light and a mountain outside every window. Like shafts of dazzling crystal, golden rays filtered through the white lace curtains, bouncing off glass surfaces and making rainbows everywhere. It was such a pretty house, with sloping ceilings and odd shaped rooms arranged on one level. The floors were tiled and the furniture mostly wooden. A beautiful African pot stood on a table and a cluster of carved heads made from deep rich ebony wood glowed with unseeing eyes from the white plastered wall. Narrow burglar bars, fitted to every window - gave a stark reminder that this was South Africa.

Our house was situated in a valley with long sloping views upwards. From the kitchen window we could see bare brown earth stretching away into the distance, turning to pale greens and yellows, and then reaching into the blue and purple shades of the Maluti mountains. The tapestry of skies changed constantly throughout the day. The mornings were bright golden yellow, midday was the blue of willow pattern china and in the late afternoon, the skies would turn pink and red and copper orange, like a fire on a Christmas hearth. Watching the sun go down from my kitchen window was sheer joy.

We were blissfully happy those first few days; exploring Fouriesburg, hearing the sound of new languages around us and getting used to living amongst different nationalities. Most of our neighbours were Afrikaners, (white South Africans, mainly Dutch by descent). There were a few French, German and Swiss families who were here working on contracts like ourselves; the Portuguese families who lived in one area, and the Africans who lived on the hill.

Up on the highest ridge, overlooking Fouriesburg, silhouetted against the winter sunshine, the houses of the black township clustered along the skyline. During the daytime, many people walked up and down a long wide track into the centre of town usually carrying their packages on their heads. It could be a water container, a cardboard box or a huge water melon. The women walked with an air of detachment and regality, attractive in their colourful dresses with scarves tied round their heads and from a distance seemed to float over the horizon. In the town, they gathered on the grass verges in the bright sunshine and sat together, calling out their greetings to one another like a battery of hens, selling apples and oranges and boxes of fruit.

Small children played games in the dust. At about five o'clock, the women would call out their goodbyes loudly, arrange their burdens on their heads - piling several boxes one on top of the other, and start their steep journey.

Along the main street, the garden boys would emerge from the big houses, stamping the mud from their boots and carrying cabbages with earth clodden roots. They were the labour force of the white families whose ample lifestyle afforded perhaps two garden boys and a maid. They gathered on the verge and chatted, perhaps smoking or chewing tobacco. It was the first time I had heard the phrase, 'garden boy' and realised that it referred to a man or a boy who was employed to look after a garden belonging to a white family. The maids looked after the children and worked in the house. In the late afternoon, large groups congregated together on the edge of Fouriesburg, treading the worn paths up to the township.

The difference between the houses of blacks and whites was staggering and in the struggle to understand such a new concept my eyes were opened for the first time.

Just before nightfall, the distant mountains turned a deep blue and a sprinkling of early stars glowed like carriage lamps in the sky.

During that first week in Fouriesburg, the temperature began to fall and at night registered minus three degrees. Sunset was around half past six. It was strange getting used to the early nightfall, after recently enjoying the long warm light evenings in England. At four o'clock the balmy afternoon temperature dropped quickly and we were glad of our one electric heater. We lived on *papayas* for the first few days, as the one and only shop had just had a boat load delivered. The house had no television. On the house radio, I roamed the airwaves every day, listening for an English voice and almost shrieked for joy when the voice of the World Service at five o'clock broadcast news from London.

Companionship arrived in the form of the maid from the house next door. Her name was Dentle and she was employed to take care of an energetic toddler. She and I met, when their alsatian dog jumped the fence one day and sat outside my French window baring his teeth every time I went out of my front door. She chose not to ignore my frantic signals from inside and came to remove him.

Dentle and I had a brief and charming acquaintance. Her English was thankfully quite good, and it was the first time I had spoken to a South African whose mother tongue was Southern seSotho. She had never met an English person before, so we were mutually inclined to get to know one another. Her friendliness impressed me and her kind manner with the little boy, not to mention her handling of the dog. Her daily routine was to walk down from the mountain where she lived, to arrive at half past six and take over the running of the house while the family was at work.

Eager to learn about Fouriesburg, questions came tumbling out.

"Dentle, where can I buy bread? How far is the nearest shop? Will I be understood? Is it safe to walk round the neighbourhood by myself?"

" 'M'e I will show you everything," replied the girl, smiling.

We must have looked an unusual sight. A plump South African girl, wearing a colourful blanket and a white turban, a beautiful blond French child who ran everywhere as two year olds do, and an auburn haired English lady carrying a tapestry handbag. In the crisp midday sunshine, which brought forth bright blue skies and a freshness that made us feel good to be alive, we tramped around the town and talked like old friends.

"Most of the whites in Fouriesburg have a maid and a garden boy. It is wise to tell the garden boy to go and ring the doorbell if you want to speak to the owner, in case the dog takes a bite out of your shoes."

I was tempted to invite a conversation about what maids were paid, but decided to wait until we were better acquainted. We walked slowly up to the centre of the town.

"How will I know if a building is a shop?" I questioned. "Every building is painted white and is single storey and there are no signs outside. The only way I can tell is by the number of people sitting on the ground."

Adults and children alike in Fouriesburg seemed to favour sitting on the ground. The town was fairly busy with different nationalities shopping between the bank and the post office. It was easy to spot the Portuguese, French, Dutch, Germans and white South Africans. Most of them owned cars or *bakkies*. Traffic was sparse and any vehicle pulling up in the centre was a source of interest. There was a surfeit of blue overalls worn by workmen and gardeners; the uniform of any male servant in South Africa.

Over the supermarket entrance, where a customer might expect to see the name of the shop or trade, there was only the red Coca Cola sign, ubiquitous throughout the whole of South Africa. There was no display of goods in the window - just an open doorway.

The shop sold bundles of wood, wall to wall soap powder, moth balls, oxo cubes, long bars of yellow soap, steel wool by the acre, and candles by the wagon load. I looked around me for bread.

The lady on the till told me, "no bread today. It is coming only Thursdays and Fridays and you must come early in the morning."

I felt as if all eyes were upon me. The solution was to find some yeast and flour.

"Cabbages are cheap and spinach is good," recommended Dentle, " and so is the liver."

"Do you know what 'chops' are Dentle?" I asked, thinking of supper. She looked puzzled.

"No, it is not some word that I know."

"*Koffiehuis* is the name for instant coffee and has chicory in it," she said trying to be helpful.

"Thanks Dentle. Will I find any Ty Phoo tea……and some flour?"

"I don't know what is 'Ty Phoo' - is it the medicine? There are many kinds of flour - it depend what you want."

I was dismayed to find no cheese counter, no white overalled shop assistants, only tins of things piled on wooden pallets or tipped in a pile on the floor. 'Sell by' dates are useless, when labels are written in another language. Determined not to go home empty handed, I resorted to looking at the pictures, searching the piles for peaches and baked beans, milk in cartons - surely it would show a picture of a cow. Like a veritable detective, I spotted the words on the front of a packet - '*Lae Vet Melk*'.

Suddenly, the word 'Kellogs' loomed as if in neon lights. Suspended between bales of stringy beetroot and gigantic sacks of maize, breakfast cereals swung from floor to ceiling in a string hammock, but no choices. Cornflakes or Cornflakes.

Their system for displaying goods seemed to be on the principle of first through the door, first on the shelf. There were no price tags, Rands didn't mean anything to me and the dozens of funny little coins in my purse could have been tiddlywinks.

Approaching the black lady stacking the shelves, I asked , "do you sell ham? " She shook her head and said, what sounded like, "May" and moved away, taking her home made ladder somewhere in the region of the wood pile. The word 'cheese' was rewarded with a carton of goat's cheese. Then to my delight, came the discovery of Joko tea bags. To a Yorkshire girl in South Africa -'*Topgehalte teesakkies*' would be the key to home comforts.

"Dentle, the stars can fall from the sky, the gin and tonic well can dry up - but life without tea is unthinkable."

Dentle was wife number two to an agricultural worker. She had two children, aged five and three and would see her husband every eighth week when he came to visit the kids and bring her money. Otherwise, he lived with wife number one.

"He very kind man, he very good man," she said, gallantly defending him, "he come to give me money for the children."

I was absolutely fascinated, never having met a second wife before - when there was still a first.

"Do you know your husband's first wife ?"

"Yes, we are good friends. We speak often. Over the telephone. We both must agree on the same amount of money. If he give to one of us, he must also give to the other. We always speak together on a Monday to see if our husband is happy."

I loved the way she pronounced 'happy' as though it was spelt 'heppy' and as she went on, I tried not to look too surprised. At Dentle's house, sitting at the table with a large bowl of pineapple each, we talked. She explained how she had come to be wife number two.

"I am the wife of a respectful man. First wife has three children and I have two children, a boy and a girl. My husband, he looks after all five children. We both have a job and have our own money. The children are very fond of their father. He brings them presents when he comes home."

At last the saga came to an end. I could think of nothing to say. She made it all sound so matter of fact. There were no pieces of paper from a court; no legal documents about matrimonial access or maintenance; just a convenient arrangement which seemed to suit all parties- and a telephone call on Monday mornings.

"Is it like this in England where you live?"

There didn't seem to be a short answer. I longed to talk more to Dentle but the gathering gloom outside threatened a change in the weather. She took me to the door.

Neither of us knew quite how to acknowledge our goodbyes. Dentle - reserved and aware of her 'place' with a white lady, stood a little apart. I had to check myself, thinking of the way people kiss on both cheeks in England after first meetings. I touched Dentle's arm in a half gesture of friendship and thanked her. Dentle smiled.

"Please come again and meet my daughter, Gladys. I will bring her to the house. She like to see you. I will tell her I have an English friend."

I stepped outside into the bitter cold winter afternoon. The cup of hot *'teesakkies'* was a tempting thought now, along with the pleasure of making my first batch of bread with maize flour.

*   *   *   *   *

In the rooftop restaurant of the Maluti Lodge, wearing borrowed overcoats, Barrie walked over to speak to the restaurant manager about switching the heaters on, as it was a very cold night.

"Sorry Sir, if you are feeling the cold. We have no heaters. May I recommend the hot soup."

Other diners, like ourselves, shivered and put on their coats, ordering their springbok platters and linefish souffles, while the ample black waitress in frilly apron squeezed between the tables and lit more candles. She smiled happily when asked to describe one more delicacy. The room was full, mostly with engineers and their wives who were on the same project as Barrie, some of whom had worked there for three or four years and were regulars. The ambience was pleasant.

Maluti Lodge was one of the well known places to eat. If you ate there in the daytime, the stunning views of the mountains, towering high above the town of Clarens, was enough to turn a dish of steaming spare ribs into a banquet.

It was our first celebration since my arrival six days ago. In six days I had switched into South African mode, worn out a pair of shoes climbing rock strewn mountain paths, had tea with a Chinese lady called Chai Tin, who spoke Mandarin and painted my first picture of an African sky.

Chai Tin was one of my new neighbours. She sent me an invitation to take tea with her as a way of welcoming me to the neighbourhood. She had a most beautiful house on the edge of Fouriesburg, which had a panoramic view of the Maluti Mountains.

Across the table, Barrie looked relaxed and far less tired than after a week at his desk in Croydon.

"It's great that you're here in Lesotho Nettie, but what about your life? Are you lonely?"

"The answer is no, I'd rather be here with you. Chai Tin and I had a lot in common. She loves painting too. Between cups of tea without tea leaves and 'aah so' lots of times, we managed a respectable conversation."

I remembered being in her studio. A fleet of carved giraffes with mahogany heads had stood elegantly gazing, towards the far off hills. Chai Tin was a diminutive lady, no taller than the tallest giraffe. Everything about her was delicate. With tiny hands, she had graciously placed brushes and paint alongside a tray of shell-like china cups. Tea was poured from an exquisite porcelain tea pot. Standing by my easel, laying down the first smears of cerulean blue and alizarin crimson onto an empty palette, I hoped an 'Impressionist' sky would leap from my brush.

"In one week, England has gone from my mind," I continued. "I love it here – life is so different …….except I feel uneasy about all those houses in Fouriesburg with burglar bars. It's a bit unnerving hearing the incidents of crime people talk about. It seems strange knowing and yet not knowing."

"You just have to have your wits about you, and don't be too friendly."

"It's just that I'm not used to being on the defensive all the time."

Ordering our calamari soup and ostrich pie, we were thinking how lucky we were to be able to enjoy such sweet Saturday evening pleasures.

Having our weekend stretching before us was a good feeling, and we did not hurry to leave a candlelit table, despite the cold. Lashings of good South African wine made up for the low temperature and we were pleasantly surprised by the bill. Wine at three pounds a bottle was a rare treat. It had been a very good evening from every point of view. What did it matter if we had to eat in our coats.

"Don't worry – plenty of time to get home," muttered Barrie, casting a look outside, as a few flakes of snow swirled against the window.

We left Clarens and drove slowly towards Fouriesburg, seeing flurries of snow in our car headlights, but little realising how quickly snowfalls can arrive in South Africa. By the time we reached the outskirts of our village, some 30 kilometres away, everything was under a white canopy and the road we were travelling on had grown slippery and treacherous. Road signs, if there were any at all, had been obliterated and we were not sure of our way. It was a long way past midnight.

"I can't see any sign to Fouriesburg. In fact I can't see anything at all now," I shouted with my head outside the window. With a worried frown on his face, Barrie turned the wheel in the direction of the main road. Our predicament was emphasised by the absence of street lights. The windscreen wipers on the car were too heavy with snow and had stopped working altogether.

Inching our way forward, we soon forgot about the Maluti Lodge celebrations. When we reached the last corner of our road, the car skewed sideways into a giant cactus covered in white spears.

"Can you get out and push, Nettie? It's the only way we'll get back on the road." I obliged. Wet, shivering and white from head to toe, I opened my mouth to shout and swallowed a ball of snow.

Our wheels finally made it to Fouvie Street. Across from the house, the searchlights of Fouriesburg Police Station had transformed its prison compound into a legendary scene from the Snow Queen's palace. The security beam, picked out the icicled razor wire fence surrounding the building, diamonds of snow glittered and sparkled between spikes; a bizarre vision, in the darkness.

Our night time journey through the snow storm, engulfed us in a strange feeling of unreality, and we were heartily glad to reach the safety of our front door.

The following morning we awoke to find our car completely covered in snow. Not even the radio aerial was visible. We looked out to a pristine white world. In the garage attached to the house, we found two spades and set to work to clear a path from our door, an extraordinary thing to be doing on a July morning, we remarked to each other. Our helpful neighbour across the way, wearing what looked like an army great coat from the Boer War and knee high rubber boots, shouted over.

"It's the worst snowfall for twenty seven years."

He disappeared inside his house. Moments later, he was back.

"When it snows in Fouriesburg, the power usually goes off!"

Throwing down our spades, we went inside to assess our chances of survival. We had enough food for the time being, but the house was extremely cold and there were only a couple of small heaters. We weren't sure if the French family, whose house it was, would mind us using their own facilities, but after searching around, discovered a wood burning stove hidden under a large brightly coloured rug in the living room. Even better, there was a small amount of wood in the garage. This raised our spirits and Barrie set about lighting a fire in the grate. It burned brightly for a few minutes, then went out. He tried again and the fire sparked with flames once more, sending little puffs of smoke up the clean white painted wall in the lounge

Almost on cue, the electricity went off. Maybe there were candles in the kitchen. Things did not look too good; no stove, no heat and no light. As we looked out into the late afternoon darkness, through our burglar bars and saw more snow falling, we had to admit to a little homesickness. July in England can be quite nice! Our torch, which still had .01 of an English volt left in it, shone weakly into the gloom and then went out.

During the next few days our lives precipitated into good British survival techniques. After several more failed attempts at fire lighting, we finally got the stove to burn, found two and a half candles and I became quite proficient at making soup on the slow slow hot plate, dressed in outdoor coat and scarf and doing my Jane Fonda exercises to keep the circulation going. The temperature was below freezing and each day more snow fell. We were mobilised into action each morning because the night burning stove hadn't stayed alight beyond 3.00am and the house was like a fridge. Hot summer nights in Croydon were lost in the vanishing mists of my memory. I found my Factor 15 sun protection cream at the bottom of the suitcase and used it to grease the door handles with. It prevented the locks from icing up.

The local dustcart cleared a very treacherous pathway to the main part of the town which you could only negotiate with fishing wellies and a spade, but as families ran out of food and wood, people began to try and get to the village stores for fresh supplies. We were down to our last few pieces of wood and half a candle, with another freezing cold night ahead. Everyone we spoke to seemed to think the snow was here to stay, the road to Bethlehem was still blocked and no fresh supplies were available. Stories of vehicles getting stranded on mountain roads were rife, the store owner stated categorically that the power wouldn't come back on for six days and the village seemed set for a siege.

On day three of the snowfall, we discovered that house water supplies were cut off and the tap dribbled only a cupful or two, before finally running completely dry. The ice from the deep freeze was making a river down the middle of the kitchen floor and the equally disastrous stove had gone out. The hostile Alsation next door had been_frozen into his kennel, and his pathetic howls resounded round the neighbourhood like a lioness who had lost a mate.

Despite the cold and the lack of warm clothes, food and candles, the pioneering spirit was not dead. Inspired by his years as assistant leader of the Caterham 5th Scouts, Barrie decided it was all hands to the pump. My orders were to fill the kitchen sink, the scullery sink and the bath, with snow. And just to be sure, every other receptacle in the house. My book on mosquito bites wasn't helpful.

The French lady's beautiful cast iron pans were neatly stacked along the floor, alongside flower jugs, washing up bowls and a watering can. If my mate earned his Proficiency Badge in fire lighting, I earned mine for Emergency Aid and Best Camp Cook. I may not be able to make a fisherman's knot, but knew how to double hitch a bucket full of snow around my arm, while under emergency instructions.

There was no question of Barrie being able to go to work along snow-bound roads to Lesotho; we were completely stranded. Exactly ten days after my arrival in South Africa, I was in danger of dying from superficial bruising by miscalculating the distance between the edge of the great iron stove and my shin, while pouring buckets of ice into successive pans, to boil yet more water. In my pantry were hard biscuits, tins of meat and a pile of gently decaying bananas.

By now Barrie was well into designs for an igloo in the garden; an engineer's igloo, dug to scale. The closely packed frozen food in the kitchen freezer, left by the French family, was in danger of going bad and the only solution was to invent a natural freezer - under a pile of snow. Social niceties were going to be difficult if they came home to find their wood pile gone, the wall in the lounge besmirched with smoke and their food stocks non existent. Both of us were a bit short on humour and survival skills were becoming slightly over-stretched but Barrie was pleased when I went out to admire his garden igloo and take a memorable photograph.

The following morning, with the whole of our world still iced over and an igloo outside our window, we were surprised by a knock at the door, just as we were about to embark on our 'snow bucket' routine. On the doorstep was a smiling black girl, dressed in a multi-coloured blanket, wrapped tightly around her and a gorgeous red scarf on her head. She looked stunning against the snow.

"My name is Grace. I come to do the work. Do you have the ironing? " She paused as my face must have registered surprise at her appearance. "I was working for the Madam." Her face looked pinched with cold.

"I have no ironing, but come in and tell us how we can help."

Grace pointed to the top of mountain. She had walked a long way to reach us. It seemed most ungrateful to send her away.

Suddenly our dead telephone rang. We almost jumped out of our skin as the lines had been down for several days. Barrie answered it. It was a relief to hear a French voice at the other end of the phone asking about the state of the roads in Fouriesburg, and telling us that the main road to Leribe was now open.

"If you would like to move to a house on the camp, there is one available," said his Company boss. "Can you pack up and move today Barrie? It shouldn't be too bad now, some of the big trucks have been able to get through this morning."

Our decision was made. We would start moving house right away. Grace could help us get everything packed and restore the house to its original state of order and cleanliness and earn herself some money into the bargain. Willingly, she set about emptying the bath of snow and stared in disbelief at the giant igloo in the garden.

Her English was poor and our seSotho was non existent. With coins on the table, our theatrical mime went something like this:

Tomorrow - ten Rands for cleaning - then go home.

Day after - five Rands for walking to house - no cleaning - still snow. Go Home.

Ditto- five Rands every day until electricity back on (not sure if Grace understood).

When electricity back on - switch on fridge freezer and put food from garden into freezer - twenty Rands.

We never knew if Grace arrived each day to check if the electricity had come back on, or whether she understood what was under the pile of snow in the garden, or if the people arrived back from their holiday to find all their food eaten by the neighbourhood dogs. She may not even have understood the word 'electricity. She was however, impressed with the amount of money we left her and readily took to the mop and bucket.

Packing was never done quicker. We wrote a letter to the French absentee landlords explaining our hasty departure, said a quick 'au revoir' to Neil Diamond, who had been locked inside the stereo since the power had gone off, waved a hurried goodbye to Grace - the new custodian carte-blanche - and set off. The snow outside was beginning to turn to slush. It was two thirty and we had to make this journey across the border into Lesotho in the next few hours before dark. The distance was about 30 kilometres. In normal circumstances it should take about an hour, on a good road without snowdrifts. We were mercifully grateful that the sun was shining and the sky looked clear as we left Fouriesburg for our journey through the mountains.

With block capitals, in eyebrow pencil my diary entry read, '10th July - I'll always remember Fouriesburg for Chinese tea and baths full of snow'.

Chapter 3

The Mountain Kingdom

Soon we were crossing the South African border into Lesotho at a place called Caledonspoort. The guard in uniform peered inside the car, asked for our passports and told us to go and wait at the window. Barrie answered with the usual respectful greeting to an official, *"Ntate. "*

We joined the long queue by the border office window. It was icy cold and the wind whipped around our faces. The mountains rising steeply on both sides of the road, looked like a scene from a Christmas card and snow on the roofs of incoming vehicles told us they had come from bad weather.

This was my first border crossing. At the barrier, there was a long line of people waiting - travellers crossing from South Africa into Lesotho on foot. Dressed in shawls and blankets wrapped around them for warmth, carrying an assortment of cardboard boxes, rolls of bedding and carpet, they stared at us. Around them, a mountain of cases, heavy bags and children with the most beautiful smiles. The whole queue looked in our direction; their expressions quiet and dignified. Slowly the shuffling queue diminished and with frozen ungloved hands, they picked up their belongings and walked through the barriers into the sub- zero temperatures beyond.

It was a shock to see that people were without transport in weather like this and in my naivety, I couldn't get over the feeling that everyone was black. I felt angry with myself, yet couldn't help but look about me for the sight of another white face. There was no disrespect in my anxieties, yet perhaps a relatively mild neurosis gripped me as we crossed the border. Coming from Fouriesburg, with its multi-national enclaves of ex-pats and professionals, to this Third World Kingdom of Lesotho, as the partner of one of its workers, I was faced with a problem. Perhaps the authorities didn't hold with a white stranger entering their country with a British Passport, coming to live for an unspecified amount of time? You couldn't really call it a holiday. And tourists were not that plentiful. No one I had spoken to in England had ever heard of Lesotho.

For all I knew, the curiosity of the queue may have been down to a personal grievance because *I* was white. Though they looked physically fatigued, they *were* curious.

"Passports please," said a voice through the glass screen.

"We are in transit to Lesotho," Barrie assured him. " Our destination is L.H.P.C."

The man's tone altered and he said warmly, "Welcome to Lesotho. Enjoy your stay."

We were both given the official entry stamp. I shivered, more with excitement than cold, and we went back to our car.

L.H.P.C. was the name of the consortium Barrie worked for and was as good a passport as one needed for moving freely between countries. The building of Katze Dam in the Lesotho mountains was a world event amongst international engineering projects and the men who worked there were treated respectfully between borders.

The slow line of cars and *bakkies* in front, crossed the Caledon River Bridge - the dividing line between the two countries - towards the official entry gate into Lesotho. The footpath was interspersed with small groups of individuals crouched over stoves and fires, trading their wares on icy ground. There was another showing of papers and another uniformed guard. As he lifted the boom to let us through, I noticed for the first time, on the belt he wore round his waist, a revolver - part of the official uniform. The guard motioned us under the barrier and we entered the Kingdom of Lesotho.

The road in front of us twisted and turned between high snow- covered peaks. Below were wild sweeping valleys. The views changed every moment; first a sheer rock face, then the endless white plain, like a desert of snow broken only by a ridge of trees in the distance.

"Where are the houses?" I whispered as though inside a hushed cathedral.

"Look upwards, there – can you see them?" Along the steep rocky ridges, silhouettes of round thatched dwellings perched, some very high on the skyline.

"Exciting eh! What must it be like living up there with no electricity?"

"I can't get my breath."

"It's the altitude, we're about 1,500metres high."

My first encounter with Lesotho left me feeling completely dazzled by its beauty and without enough breath to speak. Peaks, high and dramatic; boulders etched against the steel blue sky; people living up the steepest slopes without roads or concrete buildings or cars – it was all too much. The shoulders of the escarpments looked awesome in their blanket of snow; an enchanting fairytale whiteness that might disappear if you were to blink.

Here you seemed to be closer into the mountains, as though people and mountains were friends with one another; a closeness absent in the vast open reaches of South Africa. Now and then a deep gulf appeared in the land, like a wide crack in the landscape. From the air, they must look like craters of the moon. Over the centuries, the land, eroded by extremes of weather- torrential rains and extreme heat, has split open to reveal deep sided gulleys, which zig-zag across the open fields, as if dug by a giant mole. They are known as '*dongas*'.

There were no road signs and only one road that dipped and rose, along the edge of the slopes. Like a glassy river, the ice on top shimmered blue in the late afternoon sun. Deep snow drifts banked against the rocks like a great white sea. A swarm of children sitting on an upturned cart by the side of the road waved to us. They were wearing shawls, blankets and woolly hats and minding a few skinny goats.

"Well Nettie, what do you think of Lesotho?" Barrie asked, sensing my excitement.

"It's beautiful, so dramatic! Look at those mountains! It's glorious - but where are all the people? I pointed to the group of huts sitting below a shelf of rock, high above the road ."I love it already. I would much rather be here than in Fouriesburg. Can we stop the car Let's get out!"

Barrie pulled over to the side and switched off the engine.

"Up there, to the north, the road goes up to the Moteng Pass. It's over 2,000 metres. It's the famous 'Roof of Africa' rally route. Spectacular scenery. The road climbs into the foothills of the Malutis. Perhaps we'll have chance to go up one weekend. Depends on the snow."

"There are no fences here! No barbed wire! No houses with burglar bars and no mad dogs! Fouriesburg is barbed wire crazy. These people live in freedom. This is how I imagined Africa would be!"

Suddenly we spotted a lone horseman riding through the snow, some distance from us and I felt a shiver of excitement go through me. He was wearing a scarlet blanket as bright as blood against a white veil. For a few minutes, we stood close together – unbelieving - sharing the moment of our first winter in the Malutis.

Although our tyres slipped and slithered along the downward slopes, the tracks of other heavy vehicles that day made our journey easier than we anticipated. About 4.00pm, we arrived in Butha-Buthe - an old frontier town with a feel of Wells Fargo about it, at the main camp gate of The Highlands Water Scheme. Inside the confines of high steel fences, acres of the most enormous metal sculptures lay side by side. Tunnel-boring machines and pieces of earth-moving equipment; huge rusty creatures, now snow covered and abandoned; incongruously nestling beneath the mountains.

Next to the engineering site, covering a wide area, sprawled the avenues of houses where the workers lived. It was the first time I had seen a construction site and the living quarters of engineers and their families. Now I was one of them. But the camp we were destined for, was another 20 kilometres further on.

The sun was low in the sky and there was a glorious pink glow above the rooftops. Reflections on the distant snowy peaks, flashed like crimson mirrors. Past the prison which housed short-term offenders- splashes of red uniforms, like berries, showing bright against the low walls of their compound. Without even a perimeter fence, the single storey buildings, adjoined by a row of small dwellings, looked onto a field of cabbages, tended by a few working inmates.

Further along the main road, the Butha-Buthe Hotel hailed us - a quantity surveyor's dream for demolition. A single sign pointed to the Crocodile hotel, which offered accommodation, electricity and live music. Hidden behind the main road was the shopping area and a hospital.

People were walking by the side of the road, most wrapped in blankets reaching down to the ground and wearing a hat or scarf, the men carrying a stick or pulling a donkey. Traditional dress is a blanket for the men, fastened around their shoulders; the women wear them in a different way, often tied around their waist. Piled high on top of their heads, were the usual boxes and cartons.

The town centre, cluttered with stores, small businesses and bars, trawling buses and taxis, was bustling. Rows of small wooden shacks leaned precariously against each other, their roofs held together with planks of wood or plastic sheeting, some with doorways, many open to the weather. Even though this was the middle of winter, business was brisk and people braved the waterlogged ground in an effort to buy and sell their wares. There were no concrete walkways – just mud. The stall-holders sat on wooden boxes. Ladies under makeshift shelters or umbrellas, some with a child wrapped close to them in a blanket, called out to the crowd in the hope of selling a few oranges.

"No refuse collections here," I observed, pointing to a collapsed wooden structure which was buried under a blizzard of plastic bags and rubbish.

"No money either," answered Barrie. "Hence no proper roads."

Fruit was piled high on wooden carts or wheelbarrows; a lad pulled an unwilling goat on a string; wandering sheep seemed destined for premature death under the wheels of passing traffic - of which there was plenty. It made Covent Garden Market seem like a fully regimented state occasion. Fires glowed and smoked along the perimeter of the market place. Men with old leathery faces huddled together, warming their hands.

Open-backed jeeps and trucks filled the road, honking their horns incessantly; mini-bus taxis streamed alongside, picking up passengers, parking in awkward places, creating traffic mayhem. In the general hubbub, reggae music bellowed from underneath the plastic sheeting and jumble of doorways. One stall, with its sign saying 'Soozy Woozy Cafe' looked as popular as the fish and chip shops in Margate and the lady who carried a live chicken in one hand and a child in the other made me think hilarious thoughts of

Doncaster Market in Yorkshire, where you can still buy a chicken with feathers on and carry it home on the end of a stick.

The town was founded in 1884, because the local chief refused to go into Hlotse to pay his taxes and a centre was set up here to oblige him, which then attracted local trade. People came to sell stock and crops, and this formed the original Butha-Buthe market town.

The road to the left out of Butha-Buthe into the highlands to Mokhotlong is one of the most dramatic in Lesotho. It is bleak and sparsely populated, winding up through mountain passes up to more than 3,000metres. Hiking is not recommended in the winter, but in the spring , the high passes and ravines are a great challenge for the fit climber and the scenery stunningly beautiful. The Basotho pony is probably the best way to continue up as far as Oxbow Lodge and from there you can snow or grass ski down the mountains. Mokhotlong is so remote that you have to plan a journey very carefully, taking note of the climate and the weather, before you attempt it. The people who live there have to fetch their supplies on horseback or by aeroplane from a small airstrip.

We took the lower road to the right, towards Leribe (previously known as Hlotse – pronounced *Shlotsie*) The tide of stalls receded and once again we were out on the snow-covered road between Butha-Buthe and Levis Nek. On one side, the rocky outcrops loomed high, and at times, looked as though some of the precariously perched boulders would fall on top of us.

The white road snaked along the side of a valley, crossed a river, then wound upwards again, towards the darkening sky. Silhouettes of women carrying their water pots across the bleak terrain, made me feel instant admiration for these hardy people, whose lives revolved around a village well. Some had been gathering firewood to make fires for cooking. There were precious few trees around and they must have walked a far distance to obtain such little reward. The warmth of their fires would be small recompense for such a cold night.

As we approached our destination, deep indigo clouds to the west carried the threat of more snow and the pale moon already showed like a guiding lantern. At every turn in the road, small herds of cows were being driven home by young boys, hugging their blankets around them to keep out the cold. Sleepy villages prepared themselves for the night. It was an eerie time to be out on a road in an unknown land , with the darkening night coming so quickly after the day, seeing our new country for the first time.

Tired and weary, we reached Leribe Camp just after six o'clock. The whole place was in darkness. The guard at the big gate let us in and waved us to the house next to the high wire fence, speaking in seSotho as he moved into the car headlights. The only words I recognised were 'Mr Glenn'. We were expected. The engineers were suffering from a power cut and the in-house generator, which usually brings everything back to life in seconds, had died. 'Home from home', we thought, as we lifted our luggage from the car into our new house by the light of a torch. Behind us, someone stepped out of the darkness and called out,

"Welcome to Leribe." There was a pause. A shadow loomed out of the darkness carrying a lamp. How long had it been since we had heard an English voice?

Chapter 4

The Camp.

Leribe Camp is located on Nelson Mandela Road, on the new highway to Katse Dam where the road goes up to Pitseng. It is situated on a mountain plateau at an altitude of approximately 1,700metres. A wide open landscape spreads gently up the slopes, with hardly any trees or vegetation. Looking from east to west across the nearest mountain, rows of small square houses sit along the rocky ledges - their tin roof tops shining red and rust coloured in the sun. Soil erosion in this region is obvious looking at the barren stretches of land. Razor sharp summits in strange zigzag sculptures, meet the horizon. Further away, the shades of the Malutis, soft and delicate, like Wordsworth's hills on an autumn morning, are outlined against a purple sky. Whisps of white cloud, like winter seagulls, hover over them.

On my first day in our new home, bound into the hilly landscape of snow, I felt a sense of belonging. My first African July. I walked the camp from end to end, speaking to nobody. The air was pure, the skies were clear and my lungs felt good. Feeling ridiculously happy, I hugged my excitement to myself, at the same time longing to share this new country with my friends at home. Observing the personality of my nearest mountain, I learnt its shape and saw all its contours and colours. The shiny road to Pitseng, wound its way upwards, between two craggy valleys, on its way to Katse. Looking at the broad blue sky and feeling the silence - all the time loving it, enjoying it and wanting to breathe it through my senses, I did not want to confuse it with the happiness that was England - with its own beauty and its loving people - my people and Barrie's people.

The sun slipped over our mountain sending a rosy light through the curtains at about eight o'clock, waking the birds and gilding the edges of the furniture like gold coins. On the meadow in front of our house, cows and sheep grazed in tussocky brown fields in search of the dry stalks of left-over maize. Wooden carts pulled by oxen - enormous chestnut coloured beasts, lumbered their way across the harvested *mealie* crop. Through the hazy dewiness of the morning came the sound of cowbells. The young herdsmen wore red and orange blankets tied around their shoulders. It could have been a scene from the Bible.

"You couldn't have come at a worse time of the year," offered one of our colleagues, "what with the snow and the cold. But you'll love the spring."

"We think we'll be back in England by then."

The painful finality of the remark left behind a sad feeling of emptiness. From the clawing sound of London's traffic to a third world African Kingdom, we acknowledged a favourable exchange. We had already begun to love the stars in the southern sky. They were so bright, you felt they were singing at the earth. No night sky in my lifetime had glowed with such radiance.

There were about twenty houses on our camp and a central canteen where meals were cooked for the engineers. Attached to this was a bar, a central patio area for company social gatherings and a small swimming pool. Each family had their own large garden and there was a play area for the children. It took about fifteen minutes to walk round the whole camp and longer than that to clean your shoes. Engineers don't build themselves roads. They prefer quagmires and a decent bit of grit.

The offices belonging to the Consortium were situated at one end of the camp, next to a large car park the size of the parade ground at Whitehall Palace. This was for all the company traffic which came in and out each day. Every morning the guards raised the five flags, one for each of the five countries involved in the joint venture, who were working together in the huge project made possible by the Treaty signed by South Africa and Lesotho in 1986. Known to most people as the Highlands Water Scheme, the project encapsulates the vision that will make use of the natural water resources from high in the mountains of Lesotho.

A guard in a green uniform stood on duty a few yards from my garden gate, with a gun on his shoulder, next to the double locked gates. Security was high, for this was a venture of international importance. An eight foot steel fence had been built around the entire camp and all cars had to be screened when entering and leaving.

My new neighbour was a charming lady from Thailand with a talent for oriental cooking, which she was happy to show me. Her huge mountain dog called Hercule, who liked to create a diversion every time one of the construction staff went within yards of his territory, thrived well on Thai green curry with ginger and spiced spring rolls. As a guard dog, he seemed able to differentiate between black and white visitors, even before they set foot in the camp. A small bark for whites and an on-going din accompanied by a frenzied gallop through the bushes, for blacks. Undeterred by Hercule's racist approach, the gardeners crossed his patch with lawnmower and spade, warily eyeing him. Mr Darcy's cat kept well out of Hercule's way. She was an English moggy with a proud pedigree and prowled just out of Hercule's reach.

A family from Paris were our immediate neighbours. On the other side of us lived an Afrikaner family. There were very few wives at Leribe, perhaps three or four at that time. Only a handful of people amongst the ex-pats spoke English. French was the main language on the camp. Even the television in the bar spoke French.

Barrie worked long hours in the main office, only two minutes away from home. My time was my own. With the cold wind whistling out of doors, and no transport anywhere because of the snow, I begged books on Lesotho's historical and cultural traditions and started my days of quiet reading, feasting on books as never before.

Winter in Leribe has an invigorating climate. The middle part of the day is sunny; the kind of weather you get on a crisp January day in Hyde Park in London, when families walk out to feed the ducks and children race with their packets of stale bread to the water's edge. Instead of blue-green mallards, we came to recognise the raucous cry of the *ha-di-dahs*, which flew across our village every evening in geese formation with their long necks stretching towards the setting sun, screeching out their names - so unfamiliar to our ears. And at five o'clock the sky in the west drew soft pink strands of cotton across the tops of the mountains and then came a rosy glow, just before the startling crimson ball disappeared from sight .The light changed quickly and it was dark before six.

During the night, temperatures dropped to minus five degrees. Someone told us that a man had been found dead on the road outside the camp not far away. Frozen to death. It made me think of winter in London under Westminster Bridge - where people sleep in cardboard boxes and freeze to death. The equator lies between us, but the disease is the same.

It wasn't long before the names of the gardeners, the girls in the canteen and the maids who worked on the camp, became familiar. They came and went, pushing wheelbarrows, carrying washing baskets on their heads, bringing in piles of office sandwiches perched on trays on their heads, and greeting everyone with their morning clamour .

"*Lumela 'M'e, Lumela Ntate*," their loudhailer sized voices pealing with laughter.

Sophie, the tray-clanging boss of the canteen, sharing a joke with one of the lorry drivers arriving to deliver supplies, could raise a smile from the dead. Arms akimbo, she supervised everyone on her staff with beady eye and brass windpipe. Uproarious deep toned laughter often bellowed from the steaming window of the cookhouse as Sophie prepared meals for hungry engineers. She would go and bang on the metal door of the kitchen to call someone in whom she wanted or flush out a thief at the dustbins with a torrent of abuse aimed at the mountain tops. Sophie's doctrine of food was simple. A dam cannot be built without food in stomachs - and lots of it. The bachelors or the ones whose wives were away, were noticeable by their expanding waistlines as they tended to eat in the canteen more often.

One morning, Sophie arrived at my door with a special request.

"*Lumela 'M'e*. I wish to come and pick de leaves of de aloe plant that is in your garden - I will put dem in a plastic bag to take home with me."

"Why do you want the aloe leaves, Sophie?" I asked curiously.

"It is good for my blood pressure 'M'e. Very good for swollen ankles. I will take de leaves and boil dem in a pot. Doctor, he no good. He doesn't know nothin."

Then off she clucked, balancing her tray of chicken and salad sandwiches on her head for morning snacks at the office, swinging the bag full of aloes, her body in a continuous state of wobble and glide, downhill to the offices. I was full of admiration.

Across from our house the trucks came squealing into the gravel car park bringing in the office workers to start work at seven o'clock. The office staff who were brought in by *kombi*, (taxi) in the same emphatic tone, hailed each other from one side of the parade ground to the other, loud and demonstrative.

"*U robetse joang?* " (How did you sleep?)

Ke robetse hantle, uena u robetse joang? " (I slept well, how did you sleep yourself?)

"*Ke robetse hantle*" (I slept well my friend.)

In the dark winter mornings, we could hear them arrive, greeting upon greeting until nine or ten o'clock., along with the clatter of doors and telephones. It seemed the Basotho could not go to work quietly.

The official drivers, who were responsible for transport between all the camps and drove back and forth to Jo'burg airport to bring in overseas visitors, were often in the yard between trips. There was Kenneth, Augustine, Sam and Patrick - each one of them was a friendly face and a helpful guide in learning about Lesotho. On journeys to Butha-Buthe or to Ficksburg, our two nearest towns, I asked questions about the customs and ways of the people living in Leribe and the villages beyond. They knew about the state of the roads, the police road blocks, the hi-jacks, the village funerals and the minibus accidents. They had local knowledge of the legal, the illegal and the about-to-happen. If anything newsworthy took place at the border they knew about it. No one was married without their knowledge and no one died that wasn't one of their relations. I began to realize that in Lesotho - everyone is related.

In the camp there was usually a morning flourish of mowers and spades when the gardeners arrived in their bright blue boiler suits. The volley of greetings went on most of the morning. Thabo, the head gardener, always knew where my hosepipe was hidden when it had mysteriously disappeared overnight and would find it very quickly if I gave him a tip. It was a little game we played. Nothing ever went missing for ever - but things seemed to go on a walkabout for days on end and then would suddenly turn up and you would be so pleased it seemed right to put a few rands in his pocket.

Petros, the head groundsman, arrived one morning to tell me that the road up to Katse was still blocked and some of the company staff were marooned up at the top of the mountain. Petros also held the position of camp electrician, general handyman and Inspector of Infestations. His English was exceptionally good and we had long conversations about all manner of things, especially drains and toilets.

During a morning visit to my sick washing machine, Petros, with head inside my spin dryer, asked, "would you like to see a Lesotho diamond 'M'e? I can show you one."

The question surprised me. I had heard that diamonds could still be found in Lesotho.

" Well – yes, Petros, it would be part of my education in your country. I have never seen a rough diamond."

"Tomorrow - I 'll bring someone to see you."

He was gone before I could ask anything more. The question of my temperamental washing machine seemed to have been quite overlooked. I didn't think about it again. The following afternoon, Petros arrived at my door, with a couple of people I didn't know.

" 'M'e – I've brought a lady to see you – I keep my promise."

Without further ado, the woman who was standing behind Petros, thrust her hand well down into her bosom and brought out a very small packet containing several very small pieces of glass wrapped in a bit of cloth. She spoke no English , but held them out for me to look at. She looked at Petros and said something in seSotho. I stared at the minute pieces.

"Madam, if you would like to take something for your daughter when you go to England….? It would not be very expensive to you."

Now I understood. They obviously thought I was a sitting target – to them a white lady is a rich lady.

"Petros, I couldn't tell if these were diamonds or pieces of plastic. And I don't want to buy one. Tell your friend I'm sorry."

They crept away as quietly as they had come. It was my first and only experience in the art of precious stones.

Then came the day of the rubbish collection, which meant that Henry, the camp lorry driver, backed the big truck up our road, his foot stuck on the accelerator in reverse gear, giving rise to mud revving waves that rolled the soft ground into a permanent peat bog. Collecting rubbish was an enviable position. Henry had the face of a playful Irish pixie.

"Lumela 'M'e, Ko! Ko! Bula lemati! " he called out to me loudly in seSotho which means, 'Hello Madame, knock knock, open the door'.

"Morning, Henry. Would you like a hot drink while you go through the bin? Take anything you want."

Henry liked empty glass bottles, plastic bags and old newspapers. The glass bottles were to take to the shop and swap for a full bottle of coke, thus saving him two rands, plastic bags for carrying items home from the kitchen after Sophie had cleared up and any old newspapers, to find out what was happening in the rest of the world, as he loved politics.

"I work twenty seven years in de gold mines for small wages 'M'e. Not good job – very hard .Now I have good job at home."

"Do you have a wife Henry?"

"My wife is here in Lesotho. She don't like me come home."

"Why not?" I asked him.

"She say she don't like me much." He paused thoughtfully and his snub nose wrinkled, making deep furrows on his temple. "I gone a long time in South Africa and we only four children. They good children."

Obviously, it was Henry's wish to be father of more. His simple logic caused him to grin widely. "Now we maybe have many children."

Then he would drive off in the big lorry, looking very pleased with life and churn up any bit of road which he had missed on the way in.

Among the ex-patriots on the camp, were people from France, Iran, South Africa, Mauritius, Venezuela, Switzerland, Viet Nam, Canada, Thailand and the Philippines. We were the only English couple on the camp at that time. The bar in the evenings was a babble of different languages and dialects, all talking at once and to my inexperienced ear, a fascination. Games of pool were international incidents. Altogether, thirty nationalities represented the whole project, and often, men from other camps would come to Leribe to work, which meant there was always something interesting going on in the bar, on an evening. I loved to go and listen.

Three camps were situated at strategic sites across the mountains - Leribe, Butha-Buthe and Ha Lejone, the highest camp, far higher than we were, at almost 3,000 metres. Ha Lejone, completely at the mercy of the weather, was often marooned by snow. The drivers would tell stories of trucks getting stuck on the road or occasionally one of the wives, about to deliver a baby, having to be dug out and taken at great speed to Bethlehem Hospital in South Africa - a journey of four hours in good weather. As yet no babies had been delivered in a truck. Since the beginning of the project, a dozen or more babies had been born to ladies on the camp at Ha Lejone.

From time to time, the wives visited our camp. When the road to Ha Lejone was blocked, they would be obliged to stay two or three extra nights in the visitors' house while the food they had bought in Bethlehem deteriorated. Too often, the telephones were down and getting messages through was difficult. I used to feel sorry for the ladies who were stranded on our doorstep. Not only were hi-jacks more likely on the road to Ha-Lejone, but the weather could be most unpredictable. Being an engineer's wife at 3,000 metres, was no simple matter.

During the next few weeks, I learned to shop in the local markets for fruit and vegetables, buying from the ladies on the pavement, who spent all day sitting on a cardboard box or a wooden bench, sometimes with a sleeping baby on their back, their shiny black curls just visible from inside the folds of a blanket. Fruit was priced per item, not in weight and no matter how many were paid for, there was always one or two extra, as a gift.

My friend Noi, drove me through the busy market place in Leribe, to find the best vegetables, the freshest eggs (*mahe*) and the best cuts of meat. We visited the chicken lady, who lived in a ramshackle house, with a falling down tin roof and dusty white hens running to and fro amongst the stack of wood laid in the yard. More hens pecked between the legs of the baby calves who were tied up next to the corrugated tin toilet leaning precariously against the fence. The eggs would be big and brown and fresh and the woman would shout hard at us to give her more money for the trays, because white people should pay for the trays. We tried to explain that next time we came we would bring back the trays for more eggs, but still she clamoured for more money and thrust her grubby hand inside the car until we gave her some coins. The ratty little dog snarled and yapped at our wheels until we made it outside onto the dusty track

"Why must we risk life and limb for the sake of a few eggs?" I enquired.

"The King of Lesotho owns all the chickens. He collects royalties from the farmers so it is forbidden to bring eggs into the country without paying a tax on them. These are the cheapest in the town."

A visit to the butchers was quite another experience. My friend had been many times to buy meat, so first there was a barrage of welcome once we got inside the shop - well perhaps shop was an over- statement. It was a square concrete building on the main street, sandwiched between the potato seller with his bags of *litapole* spilling out onto the dusty road - and the smoking spitting stove of the rent-a-chef man, who occupied a large area near the road. You could buy slabs of brown liver and give it to the man with the greasy apron who would throw it onto the flames to be cooked. It was cheaper than sitting inside the cafe and many of the busy stall holders in the market preferred to eat this way.

Loud groovy disco music played frenetically from a radio somewhere, so loud that, once inside the shop only sign language was possible. A long counter was arranged along one wall and meat was piled up in enormous heaps. People jostled and pointed over the glass partition and the jovial large bosomed ladies wielding knives, cut lumps off this and that throwing their pieces into a weighing machine with the manner of a hoopla player in a fairground. The long queue gyrated to the throbbing rhythm of the music. Everyone shouted at once.

Along the front of the shop was a higgledy piggledy row of plastic chairs and tables, unfinished plates of food and the odd box of bananas sitting on the floor. This was where people ate their snacks of fried liver and *mealie pap*. Cutlery, either was not provided, or was not the custom, because everyone shovelled food from plate to mouth with fingers.

The concrete floor was clean and the ladies serving meat looked very respectable, but overalls were not the custom either and you had to guess how many greasy thumbs had been wiped down the front of their cotton dresses. they smiled and shouted over the blasting music, shook my hand over the top of the counter and pointed to the offal lying in huge mounds on the metal trays. I shook my head, unable to fancy the liver from the ox, or the unrecognisable slabs of red meat with bits of bone through the middle, strewn in bleeding piles along the counter. All the slices of meat looked exactly the same.

"*Ke bokae*?" I asked. No one heard. Where were the lamb cutlets and the pork steaks and the sirloin? Homesickness flooded in for the beautifully labelled freezer packs and delicate gourmet oven-ready meals from Marks and Spencers.

Noi marched confidently round the back of the counter where she opened the door of the walk-in freezer, followed by the all-singing, all-dancing butcher, with a huge blade in his hand. Whole skinned carcasses of meat hung on hooks and my friend pointed at this one and that one whilst the butcher's knife heaved and shoved and hacked. Seven whole beef fillets emerged - well I think it was beef - which were cut from the whole carcasses and thrown on the scales. After these came the long stiff ox- tails, drawn from inside the freezer which he proceeded to cut into bits with a ban-saw. There was a young lad operating a ban-saw, at a table some feet away, whose job it was to cut through all the bones. Perhaps it had something to do with the fact that all the pieces of meat looked the same.

Noi beckoned me inside the freezer to observe closely what the butcher was cutting and asked me if I wanted a whole fillet. I had never been inside a deep freezer with a black man before. Shoulders and eyebrows held in a question mark, the arm was poised and ready. It was now or never. I felt brave enough to nod. At this the man beamed and shook my hand - with his non knife- holding one. One of the ladies came over and handed me a free bunch of carrots and a beetroot as big as a football, which I took to mean, 'come again'. I saw my friend drop some coins into the man's greasy palm, which he put into his greasy pocket .With a large flourish, he showed us to the door, holding his huge knife above his head and shouting , "H*a re tsamaeeng"* (let us go) above the din, as he guided us back through the heaving crowds to our car.

Our last sight of 'the butcher' was a swashbuckling arm waving through a cloud of dust, by the roadside, and I prayed that he didn't slice off somebody's ear in his enthusiasm. It was a relief to be going home with my fillet of something for fifteen rands, which was about two pounds in English money, my tray of fresh eggs, a free bunch of carrots and three feet of dangling beetroot stalk.

Next door to our house lived a young French couple with a baby and a visiting brother, aged about thirteen who could speak no English and was eager to learn, so I offered lessons every afternoon. Despite having no teaching books with me, Charles and I managed to occupy ourselves fruitfully with English conversation. After almost thirty years of not using my O'level French, I congratulated myself at reaching the stage of *"Bonjour, comment ça va?"* and *"ça va, merci"* and Charles progressed beyond the few English phrases he had. Every afternoon we would be joined by the two Afrikaans girls who lived along the way and together, we enjoyed many hilarious games of Scrabble on the long veranda table under the shade of the green baize roof, in the warmth of the winter sun. On subsequent days we had also the company of two ladies from Thailand who came to join in the fun, so with four languages between us, we progressed to a great exchange of words and pastimes. Experiencing other languages was very stimulating, besides giving me something useful to do. It also helped to prepare me for the bombshell, which came out of the blue a few days later.

Barrie came home one evening and said quietly during supper, "I've been offered a new contract in Lesotho. They want us to stay for another year. What do you think Nettie? Would you be prepared to stay on?"

I was totally unprepared! The unexpectedness of his words hit me like a wet sponge. For once in my life I was speechless. Sudden tears welled up in my eyes. As the impact of the statement slowly dawned on me, I spluttered, "what about our wedding? What about our house in Beckenham? What about our families….. does it mean staying in Lesotho from now on, or would we be able to go home first? I mean - it would be a huge change of plan for us.... and what about us.....you and me?"

Suddenly I was struggling to voice all manner of questions. The news had arrived so unexpectedly, yet it was no surprise when we really thought about it. The company needed someone with Barrie's experience and there was at least another year of the work to go, before the dam would be completed. We had been in South Africa for five weeks but only on a temporary basis. We both loved it - but to give up our home in England.... that would be quite a different proposition.

"Where would we live?"

"Here of course, in Leribe. The company have offered us a house - a better one. We're close to the border- you could get into Ficksburg easily and we would buy a car. You'd be independent, maybe get a job if we can get you a work permit. You could go to Bethlehem once a week with the driver... there's everything there we need shops, dentist and the like ....what do you think?"

He stopped and waited for my reply.

"Are there any more surprises?"

"No...not yet...but its not without its complications. I don't know for how long."

Chapter 5

Grandmothermania.

For the next week, my old Remington typewriter oozed letters and postcards to both our families. We could have filled a small truck with our mail to England. No electronic gadgets for me, just an old fashioned live performance on a mechanical keyboard at a rate of knots - paper streaming across the floor in cascades - mailed out as fast as the courier could carry it. Letters to change our lives from living in South London, to the Mountain Kingdom of Lesotho.

Grand readjustments were in place. It would be quite a task returning to our house in Beckenham to clear the clutter out of the cellar, completely re-organise our social calendar and appoint a tenant. After a lifetime of being the on-duty mother, nurse, babysitter, money lender and agony aunt, the feeling of leaving one's brood to fend for themselves, still rates in the same bracket as the seriously overstrung piano. Caught somewhere between an attack of guilt and an entrepreneurial parent poised on the brink of an African safari with unknown ending – I began to suffer from an acute mid-life trauma.

For Barrie it meant saying goodbye to his four grown-up children, his desk in Croydon, the 5th Caterham Scouts and the tax man. For us as a couple, it was a case of love me love my varicose veins. We were together in this, bound into a year's contract with the Lesotho Highlands Project Consortium and an unwritten contract to each other. Our English wedding would have to be postponed for another year and the trees in Datchworth churchyard would blossom without us. Our timetable had gone pearshaped, Barrie's planning programme had been replaced by a myriad of uncertainties and my hormones had completely disappeared off the chart.

The following day, one 'very high protection for sensitive skin' Sun Lotion and a monster-sized 'Doom - Death to all Mosquitoes' pack were placed on top of the bathroom cabinet, in readiness for our return. Bedtime reading became health warning manuals, lists of infectious diseases – Lesotho style and 'how to conquer homesickness in foreign climes.'

"When you come back in September, everything in your garden will be in bloom," the gardeners told us, "and the snow will be gone."

The ground was hard yet the roses looked in good shape. There was eucalyptus and willow in front, honeysuckle and vines criss-crossing the verandah, whilest peach trees spread over the back garden, still bare and autumnal.

"You will see what our climate is like," explained Petros "just a few days of warm sunshine and everything bursts into life."

A jungle of tropical palms screened us from our neightbours and and a patch of strawberry plants in one corner, struggled to survive in a bed of stones.

"Lotov, lotov, many many fruits for you, 'M'e" beamed Thabo, after explanations that we would come back soon. " Please, I am always planting de spinach vegetables when you come to Lesotho Very very good. I am de good spinach gardener when you go to England."

We offered to reward his efficiency on our return. Thabo did not have any idea about Barrie's precision gardening and gingerly, I brought up the subject of where exactly the vegetable garden was to be dug.

"I'll show him where I want it," was the reply.

The following evening, Barrie and Thabo strode over the chosen patch with serious faces. Despite language difficulties and no available string, Barrie explained where next year's spinach was to be planted and it was agreed with much smiling, arm waving and head nodding. The following day a furrow appeared on the wrong side of the garden.

By now my body clock was totally confused about what time of year it was. We had recently left an English summer, lived through part of an African winter and were going home to an English Autumn. We would return in an African spring. My internal wiring would soon be pronounced unstable and unsound.

On learning we were coming back to the camp, Sophie cooked us a celebration meal for 'de special journey of homecoming' with salt beef stew and suet dumplings - the consistency of liquid cement. Her black eyes danced with merriment as she stood side by side with Anna, the other cook, posing for the camera as a gesture of farewell. Their shiny faces, bathed in perspiration from the hot kitchen, shone like black shoe polish and with heavy forearms overpinning ample bosoms they came to bid us *'tsamaea hantle'* in the knowledge that we would soon return.

" 'M'e, we will be here to dance a welcome to you and Mr Barrie."

Colleagues warned of Lesotho's summer tropical storms, describing how hot it gets in November and December. The men from L.H.P.C. work four weeks without a break, then take four days holiday, when most families travel around South Africa.The serious listening began.

"Once you've experienced the game parks, seeing wild animals in the bush – swum in shark infested seas in Durban; watched the whales come into the beaches at the Cape….you'll not want to go home," was the conversation in the bar one evening. Invitations for adventure came flooding in and our excitement grew. An acquaintance who had been on a climbing expedition in the Bushman caves of Champagne Castle, described the beauty of the Drakensberg mountains of Natal. By now we were totally convinced that we had made the right decision.

Our English wedding would have to be postponed. Family ties would have to be loosened.There are only two basic requirements for making a bolt for it in middle age - a blind eye and a diplomatic bank manager.

It was our last Sunday in Lesotho, before leaving for England. We were all set for our journey up to Ha Lejone, a two hour drive into the mountains, to see the Malutis in the snow. It was our first experience of travelling up into the highlands. We planned to drive as far as we could, first up to Pitseng and then further, to try and reach the 'viewing platform' from where we might be able to see Katse, which is almost 4,000 metres high. The Basotho are the only African nation who have adapted to living part of the year in snow and winter temperatures have been known to drop to minus ten degrees.Two thirds of Lesotho is almost impenetrable mountain. Remote villages still exist so high up that their only food is the crops they harvest themselves; a bleak formula for survival.

We began our climb slowly in a good strong vehicle with a powerful engine, sun dazzling on snow as all four of us donned sunglasses to protect our eyes. The air was clear and fresh and put us in good spirits. On the higher slopes, the square concrete houses with corrugated tin roofs, were replaced by traditional huts known as *rondavels*. These typically African houses, round in shape, built from stones gathered from the mountainside and held together with a mixture of mud and cow dung, called '*liso*', with conical thatched roof and an opening for light. They couldn't be called windows as Basotho folk don't go in for glass. The walls of the houses were covered in a mixture of clay and mud, boldly painted in bright coloured symmetrical patterns.The designs, known as *litema,* represent many aspects of agriculture. Often the artist would combine different sized circles which symbolises life, the cycle of the seasons, wholeness, fertility and community. In Lesotho, a man's wealth is judged by the number of cattle he owns and the number of children he has.

As in most of Africa, houses are built with locally found materials, sometimes it is grass or reeds and they differ in shape from place to place. Here the rock from the mountains provides a rich source of building materials which will stand up well to the harsh weather conditions. The thick walls protect them from ice and snow and make for a cosy interior under a mud thatch. A sloping porch, also made of thatch, gives protection from the cold. Whole families live crowded but cosy lives, in the one-roomed huts. A group of huts together with their animals nearby is known as a *kraal.*

There may be as many as seven or eight in one homestead, where different generations of a family live together - parents, children, grandparents, and other members; sometimes other wives and their children. Cows were tethered beside the rondavels, with the occasional small group of goats or sheep. A few hens pecked for seeds, the stack of firewood or compacted cow dung was heaped in readiness to be burned on a good fire; home made wooden carts were in evidence and sometimes a precious horse or donkey. A horse in these villages means wealth indeed, providing essential transport into the mountains. It is a strange thing to see whole villages without the presence of a motor car. On these roads one does not see many bicycles. The Basotho ponies are strong and robust, well known for trekking through rough mountainous country.

As if they knew we were approaching, smiling children waved and came running down the hillside to see our car full of white strangers. They looked healthy, if a little thin, and their expressions revealed curiosity at our presence - their closely shaven hairstyles and fuzzy plaits, typically African. The women seemed most curious.

Our road wound upwards through Khanyane where the snow lay thick on both sides of the road.The wide sweeps of the lowlands made it possible to travel safely. We climbed slowly, passing many people on foot, dressed to suit the cold weather.

The Basotho are good horsemen, used to travelling in the mountains. Groups of riders, wearing traditionally patterned blankets pulled up high around their necks, trod the rocky hillsides Their blankets in rich earth colours; reds, yellows, browns and orange, worn with wide brimmed conical straw hats, looked dramatic against the snow. Horses were introduced into Lesotho in the middle of the last century and have been adopted as the best means of transport.

"Look at the way they ride," I exclaimed as we passed riders travelling bareback, galloping fast along hard stony tracks. The men were straight backed with their feet almost touching the ground. The horse seemed too short for a tall man. Only the men were on horseback. The women carrying their babies, bound tightly within brightly coloured rugs and blankets, walked freely and upright.

"Aren't the young women beautiful - just as I had imagined African women to be – so composed and serene."

Their bodies were supple and slim from walking long distances; the men, lean limbed and handsome with remarkable profiles.

Collecting firewood was their daily struggle. The resulting fires for their cookpot must have obliterated the pain on the back of the neck, as many soldiered on with their burden through the snow. The average life expectancy here is around fifty nine years.

I desperately wanted to photograph them, but felt afraid to approach them, it seemed rude and intrusive. My efforts to learn their language, were on the short list of things to do on the long flight to England.

Village life centres around places where water can be found. The *setibeng* is either a spring which comes out of the ground into a rock pool, or in some areas, a man- made pump. Normally it is the job of the women to fetch the water for the family. Up in the highlands, the water is clean and safe to drink as it comes from the mountain streams. For at least 25,000 years nomadic hunter gatherers have lived in these mountains, drinking the pure water from the great rivers of the Malutis. It is as healthy as the water which comes from our purification plants. In Lesotho water is known as 'white gold'.

Our car climbed higher, the road became more slippery and the views increasingly dramatic. As we looked backwards over the hairpin bends, the glaciers - like clusters of diamonds, glistened so much, even sunglasses failed to prevent the glare. On every side the views were breathtaking.

Snow can fall here anytime between May and August and in the mountain regions it can last for several weeks. In the spring of 1988, when much snow fell, the highlands of Lesotho were declared a national disaster zone; whole districts were cut off from major supply routes and scores of shepherds froze to death along with their flocks. Helicopter supplies dropped into remote villages saved many people from starvation.

At Pitseng we stopped to look at the slopes below us, dazzling and shimmering in the sun. Barrie stopped the car.

"Come on, lets get out and have a walk."

There was a loud yell as he sank up to his knees in snow." Icy winds stung our faces.

"Don't go near the edge," shrieked the voice of my Thai friend, knowing too well of the dangers. "A bus went over the edge near here! Look out!" I plunged forward up to my waist. With much hilarity, for the scene seemed to cause an increase in adrenalin all round, we threw snowballs at one another, almost burying ourselves in the soft feathery whiteness.

Just before Ha Lejone, we reached the Mafika-lisiu Pass. It had taken us more than two hours. The hairpins had begun to get ever more steeper and roadsigns offered advice on driving with care.

We were now 10,000 ft high. The curves of the road were lined with safety barriers but the height was making me nervous. The people by the roadside got fewer with only a lone herd boy on a donkey to greet us. He looked about nine and was carrying sacks of mealie up to his family, who probably lived in some remote spot hidden from view. From the car the mountains looked almost blue.

Until ten years ago, villages up here would have been cut off from the lowlands and their only mode of travel would have been on horseback. The road to Katse has made such a difference to these farmers. The boy, greeting us with a mixture of alarm and disbelief, took hold of his beast of burden and stared at us with huge inquisitive eyes. Our heavy tyres crunched on the ice. No other vehicles had passed us since early afternoon.

It was essential that our return journey took place in the light. Night time out on this road could prove fatal. Besides, my neurotic rantings about falling over the side had become unnerving for my fellow passengers.

My only previous experience of mountains in snow had been the gentle undulating slopes of the Old Man of Coniston in the Lake District and Sutton Bank in North Yorkshire. I held my breath whilst Barrie turned our vehicle round with military precision - without taking my eyes off the edge of the ravine for one second. My fear of sliding over the edge almost reached wild panic. Higher peaks in the range were turning to deep purple. The silver clouds were dotted with early stars. The day was almost gone.

"Okay honey?" said Barrie knowing that my anxieties were very real.

"Sorry to spoil things," I answered through clenched teeth. "I feel safer now."

Peat and dung fires burned outside homes with open doorways. Children waited patiently with supper bowls ready. The job of pushing wheelbarrows of fresh water in the winter fell to the village lads in bright caps and a few hefty buxom ladies. Sunday's courting couples meandered unhurriedly and ladies in blue cloaks carried home their Bibles.

Approaching Leribe an hour and a half later, the mountain appeared completely black, with pinpricks of fire here and there in the darkness. Whole villages were swallowed up into the night. Only our headlights lit the empty road. Now and then the eyes of a scavenging herd dog glowed red and reminded me of Hollywood wolves.

It was hard to imagine in a few day we would be back in the green meadows of Kent, 6,000 miles away. We felt suspended in time between two worlds.

"How do you feel about coming back?" questioned our passengers. "We will see each other again in a few weeks, there will be time for lots more journeys – but when you return the snow will have disappeared and it will be Spring."

The mountains had given me more than an attack of vertigo.

"I am curious about the lives of the Basotho people, I want to experience the seasons and the weather and the customs - not just as a sightseeing visitor- but as part of them. I want to belong."

"Sure we'll do lots of travelling, in between my work of course." chimed in Barrie, "South Africa has so much to see – perhaps some serious climbing?"

"Shall we bring the bikes?" I said laughingly.

"What on roads like these….no chance."

The thought of hunting for fossils and cave art, seeing remote places still untouched by man's progress, exploring Lesotho's wild rugged countryside had hit my imagination like a whirlwind. My days of driving up and down the M25 between north London and Kent combatting the relentless traffic had been a necessary part of life's journey. Slogging away in a classroom for years, teaching the bottom end of G5 had given me survival techniques. My Yorkshire upbringing had given me my spirit of adventure and South Africa was here now, offering blazing sunsets and mountains to climb. To emigrate from outer suburbia to a construction site 1,700 metres high on a remote mountain plateau, close to the lands once occupied by triassic creatures, in my middle prime- was as far from the quaint fashions of grandmotherhood as it was possible to be.

Excitement beckoned. But on the other side of the world, there was a very special little girl. Her name was Abigail and she was my granddaughter.

My courage may fail me when I come to say goodbye.

Chapter 6

Au Revoir.

Back in our home in South London, we wondered how, in our three and a half years together, we had managed to collect so many belongings, so much furniture and so much rubbish. My cellar full of unplanted out geraniums, divided roots and seed trays full of last years cuttings would have to go.There was my half- finished stained glass window, promised to Abigail - its pieces of green and blue glass still waiting to transform itself into my designer masterpiece. Layers of dust had almost obliterated the face of the clown and he looked sadly forlorn.

Our beloved garden was a riot of weeds, overgrown honeysuckle and leggy sunflower stalks. Barrie's favourite tomatoes hanging in over ripe bunches between the canes and my galloping Russian vine had galloped over the whole of our fence and next door's as well. My hanging baskets drooped sadly over the back porch. Only the blue trailing lobelia had survived its five week drought. We gave the whole garden a luxurious watering and gathered in the few good tomatoes, before cutting the long grass, which hadn't seen a lawnmower for six weeks.

We braved the M25 and went to Hertfordshire- strange after driving along empty roads in Lesotho where a traffic jam meant six cows and a donkey. In drizzling rain, we watched village cricket, downing pints of cider with every fallen bail. Celebratory lunches at 'The George & Dragon' in Watton, dining in style at 'The Cricketers' in Clavering, and singing songs in the back room of 'The Horns' in Burnham Green, were all respectable rituals of farewell. We were 'seen off' generously by our fellow diners, all of them eager to know what kind of a country Lesotho was.

We walked our favourite walks. The lanes of Hertfordshire were lovely in August. Gazing at the wheatfields, we watched the harvest come in and realized that we wouldn't see another for a while. The corn looked golden and ripe and the combines worked non-stop until dark. The sight of the bales scattered across acres of Hertfordshire countryside brought a lump to my throat. At Sunday Evensong we sang our favourite hymns in the church where one day we hoped to return. Hand in hand we visited our own quiet churchyard to say a few personal goodbyes. Maybe for a year….or two. The date of our forthcoming marriage, planned for next spring, was put on hold until we came back to England.

At my daughter's home, we watched as she cared for Abigail, position her into a special chair, fix her straps around her and feed her. Bath nights and hair wash nights meant lifting her gently, wrapped in a towel, then dressing her; difficult because of those stiff limbs. Spasticity of her spine caused by her cerebral palsy makes any movement awkward. Perhaps Lizzie would still be able to lift her unaided for a few years yet. After that we would have a new set of problems. At five years old, Abigail was still very light. Her legs were straight and stiff and her muscular development delayed; her sight severely impaired.

One evening, I carried her outside to sit on the grass. Together, in the garden we listened to the birds and I sang softly in her ear. Her fingers touched the tiny white daisies with fragile grace, like a sea flower touches a shell. Her skin was milky white and her cornflower blue eyes looked at me as though she could see. Apart from one or two transitory words, her only language was to blow kisses to those she loved. Her hair curled with golden strands into the nape of her neck. When she heard the sound of a bird, she turned prettily and looked up, her back resting against me. She was not able to sit by herself.

Everyone with whom she comes into contact, loves her. Undeniably, she extracts the best from people around her. Passers-by stop to talk, children stop to give and share. Adults overcome their need to rush off when they see her in the street.

We continue to pray that one day she will grow strong and walk by herself. Her eyes may never see the colour of the flowers or watch other children coming home from school. Her world is a world of voices from where she sits. Meanwhile, her beautiful smile continued to light all our days.

"We'll soon be back, my lovely girl," I whispered into her ear, as my daughter arrived to lift her inside.

Our next stop was Yorkshire. We shared our plans with all my family and - to a man - they all wished us well in our new life in Lesotho, revealing perhaps more than the usual concern and interest in such a venture, as no-one had even heard of Lesotho before.

"Laysooto, where's that?" said Auntie Edna, "never 'eard of it. What you going there for?"

When Barrie explained that it was a small Kingdom, the size of Belgium, situated in Southern Africa and it had a King and was known as 'The Roof of Africa', out came the family atlas and the spectacles and the questions.

"What yer buildin' a dam fer then, Barrie, can't they build their own dam ?"

My Auntie Edna was a great and gracious lady, but a diplomat she was not. "Anyway, put t'atlas away and let's clear t'table, we're going to 'ave ower tea. I bet they doohn't make tea in Laysooto."

Clean white tablecloth arrived on the table, "an you'll 'ave to get used to all them elephants!"

Then everyone drank our health with a bottle of Uncle Harry's best home made wine, vintage 1993, made and bottled lovingly and kept in their little garden shed, now a fully converted distillery and fishing tackle store, where my uncle spent many happy hours - away from Auntie Edna.

We drove back to Kent, having made our peace with Hertfordshire and Yorkshire, now fully committed to preparing for our imminent departure. My ideas of holding farewell parties with friends were fast disappearing under the mound of duties and the league of letters we had to write before we could hand our home over to a tenant.

It sounds much easier than it is. The probables came and went, through the front door of our delightful 'Des.Res.victorian house, with large cellar, established garden and double parking'(no pets please) one year let'.

We went through the 'mights' and the 'maybes' and the sagas of the bouncing cheques, the re-starts and the 'sorry no reference' calls. One lady rang late one night, to tell us that her new boyfriend, who was related to an Irish racehorse owner suddenly found he had a stop on his bank account, which was a mistake by the bank and would be put right the next day, but they still definitely wanted the tenancy. Out of courtesy we spared them one more day, while war was declared between the Irishman and his bank manager, only to find that the prospective tenant had disappeared quietly from town and the dear lady was left weeping tears of despair and abandonment. When she had dried her eyes, she rang to thank us for educating her to the dodges of a shenanigan middle-aged

Irishman, whose sharp practice had gone unnoticed until she had found his bankbook and his marriage certificate.

Barrie's hobby is making lists. Our precious belongings had to be packed in a trunk for two whole months while en route to Lesotho, but the question was, what had to go and what had to stay. Lists hung like flypaper to the kitchen wall.

"How do I know if I've crossed off hot water bottles !" I yelled upstairs.

My mind boggled at the choices I was expected to make.

"How do I know what we will need in the next year, in a house we don't know, in a country we've never lived in, in a climate we can't even imagine."

Possessing no sense of geography, no sixth sense when it comes to domestic or practical neccesities and an imagination which is wildly sentimental, meant we usually fell out when it came to planning. Then there was the question of who keeps which keys to which doors. My addled brain was awash with what was to go where, and with whom.

In post-war rationbook days, when things were scarce, my mother had been a collector of black treacle, dandelion tea and chunks of fairy soap. Sour milk hung in nylon stockings from underneath the stairs. My hoarding instinct was plainly inherited from her side of the family. I averaged several weird objects per week, much to Barrie's alarm. In my studio below stairs there was my collection of half sketched one boobed nudes ready for the canvas; palettes of cadmium yellows and flesh pinks at the ready; bottles of muddy turps and piles of picture frames which never seemed to fit. Catastrophic attempts at macrame lampshades hung in tangled hemp and twine - never to be unknotted; books I could never bear to part with, old clocks with no innards, brass lamps with no wicks and enough Victorian lace to curtain the royal mews. No cracked china plate was ever put in the bin, nor broken glass discarded – it was more like a disease than a hobby.

Various unwieldy pieces of rustic garden furniture adorned the patio outside and my collection of tree roots was gathering momentum. A birdcage hung over the back porch filled with late summer flowers. And I would die rather than part with my antique cast iron three legged garden table, which had two legs and a piece of wire to support its weight.

Barrie had other ideas. He possessed a consistant sense of logic and orderliness. His sound sense and good reason was what got us to Africa in the first place, and at times he couldn't sympathise with the collecters' curse.

"I think we'll order a skip," he shouted, knowing how it would galvanise me into action.

"Over my dead body!"

Pleading passionately for extra time, I crammed everything I loved into my little cave in the cellar. Every inch of space was filled to the gunnels. Then the door was padlocked until further notice.

"And this stays locked until we come back from South Africa!!" spoke my other half with conviction. I retired early and cried into my pillow.

When every room in the house looked like a battlefield and I had decided to have a bonfire, burn every list in the house, and send the air freight trunk to China, Barrie came home with a bunch of flowers and two tickets for the concert version of 'Carmen' at the Barbican. It was exactly what we needed. A few hours away from the packing, a musical evening with Spanish toreadors and a romantic evening at our favourite restaurant in Piccadilly.

My mood was transformed. Long floaty dress was whisked out of the trunk, high heels retrieved out of the ' stay in England' box, a dash of Anais Anais, an instant hairdo and I was ready for an evening of good British culture. Barrie looked dashing in silk waistcoat and bow tie which we agreed he would not be needing in our new home. Our concert seats turned out to be good ones, the show gloriously extravagant and bold, as only 'Carmen' can be and with Bizet's music ringing in our ears, we taxied across London to dine out.

Wine and candles have an extraordinary effect on me at the best of times, but because it would be our last evening in London together, and even more special because our departure to Lesotho meant leaving so many familiar things, tears were on the brink. One minute laughing over the castanets and smouldering passions of Spanish love affairs and then an emotional silence at our own imminent goodbyes and partings.

"I wish we didn't have to leave Lizzie with so much responsibility, a year is a long time," I said, aware that the waiter was watching us. "Looking after Abigail is such hard work. And what about her own life? What happens to her own future, that's what really worries me - she is so young....."

Barrie looked very thoughtful and seemed to be searching for words.

"Why don't we tell our kids we'll try and be home for Christmas. We could have a short holiday. A couple of weeks. We'll think of a way - if you're really worried."

Our sudden move to South Africa had been quite a shock all round. What it boiled down to was that my maternal feelings were having a guilt stampede. Sensing an attack of theatrical neurotica coming on, I accepted the handkerchief which was offered.

"Come on, let's take a last walk along the embankment. I love the river at night. The next big river we see, might be the Great Zambezi."

We left the restaurant, to have a last look at the familiar skyline; to say goodbye to the big city and to each other. Our next evening out together would be somewhere in the Southern hemisphere.

Chapter 7

Lesotho for real.

September is a beautiful month in Lesotho. The countryside looks as if someone has gone round with a paintbrush and added colour to the land, the trees, and the mountains. The herdboys smile and make music. The young men in the villages start their Initiation Schools, the children put on their uniforms to start the new term and the fields are burnt, ready for next year's crops. Everywhere the peach trees are in full bloom and their delicate blossoms sprinkle themselves over every hillside, like pink frilly skirts. The snow disappears from the tops of the mountains and on every bare field, pairs of oxen pull hand ploughs, turning the soil ready for the new planting.

When Barrie returned to work, in early September, the strike was in full swing and 1,800 men were laid off. The tunnelling had stopped and all the big machinery ground to a halt. Up in the highlands of Lesotho, where our men were working on site, there were outbreaks of trouble. He rang from his office, to tell me that things were bad. The Basotho labour force on the project were demonstrating their feelings by chanting rebelliously outside the main camp at Butha-Buthe and the town was rife with rumours. Pressure was mounting. Wives and children who lived on the camp were either confined to barracks or sent to stay in Bethlehem, where it was safe. The English School was closed. Nobody knew what was going to happen. Meetings were taking place round the clock and the management was locked into negotiations with the workers. The Bishops became involved, news bulletins were being broadcast on Radio Lesotho and tensions seriously increased.

I was still in London, making final arrangements to leave. Answering the phone wedged between a trunk, a pile of stacked chairs and a mountain of books, we had our last conversation before my departure.

"Yes Barrie, everything's fine….." I stopped in mid sentence as the voice at the other end sounded very serious.

"Nettie, can you cancel your ticket and wait for a week or two, things are very bad here?"

"Why? What's wrong?"

"Well there's been some shooting, several people have been killed. The strike is a bad time to arrive. It would be better if you came in a couple of weeks. The roads aren't safe - we've suffered more hi-jacks. The soldiers have been brought in. You might have to be evacuated with the other wives on camp."

He waited for my reaction.

"No, I can't do that. If you think I'm putting off my travel arrangements, just because a few trigger-happy guys are taking a pot shot at the military, you needn't think I'm going to cancel my plans. I couldn't possibly stay here any longer- besides, I've got nowhere to live."

"Well, that's what I hoped you'd say - just wanted to keep you up to date. I might arrange for you to stay in Jo'burg for a few days."

The phone went down a little shakily. I went into the kitchen and put the kettle on to make tea. On the kitchen table was a silver photograph frame with a sepia portrait of my grandmother as she was in 1918, at the age of twenty five. This lovely young woman's face looked at me, as it had hundreds of times before. The eyes were like my mother's, clear and straightforward. I had been given this photograph when I was twenty years old and had treasured it all my life.

Clara Louisa Ward, my grandmother, lived through the first world war as a young wife. She looked after our family throughout the six years of the second world war, while my father fought behind enemy lines in Germany. She would have approved of my journey to South Africa. Quietly, I drank my cup of tea and began to pack up yet another wooden crate.

Picking up the phone, I spoke to the owner of a farmhouse, somewhere in East Hertfordshire.

"I would like to confirm a booking for accommodation for Christmas, for two people."

I was going to Lesotho and that was that.

Signing our flat over to a tenant was easy compared to saying goodbye to my family. Lizzie and I had tearful hugs and kisses, with Abigail giving me plenty of smiles to take with me in my heart. As I left my daughter's house, I gave her a tiny pair of silk ballet shoes as a leaving present, just to remind God that he must make Abigail's feet into walking feet, but Lizzie handed them back to me.

"You keep them Mum, hang them on your wall when you get to your house in Leribe, it'll help you to think about us!"

We hugged each other and I left them sadly, with a lump in my throat, but knew they would be alright. Lizzie was a survivor.

"It's your turn now, Mum. It's your new life," These were generous words. I hugged her once more.

"Take good care of that little girl, and write to me often."

Precious last moments were remembering Abigails's blue eyes as we parted - she would not understand our farewell. The ribbons, which Lizzie had tied so prettily in her hair, matched her eyes and with childish dexterity, she tugged at the rope of a toy telephone and blew kisses into it. Perhaps she understood more than we knew.

Abigail - the child of a Gulf War soldier, born with a condition called microcephaly, totally dependent on others, has changed my daughter's life for ever. Abigail's father has chosen to have no part in her upbringing.

Lizzie gave me a resolute smile. "Go on Mum, you'll be late for your flight."

Barrie's departure and now mine, across the equator, seemed as natural as moving house to a different part of England. This was my turn to be an individual in my own right - not a mother, not a grandmother, nor a salaried teacher. Barrie and I were certain of our boundaries and our love. Time would be the compass. Neither of us knew then, that our commitment to South Africa, would extend well beyond our expectations.

James, my son, was at the South African Airways terminal to meet me, accompanied by his girlfriend, Claire. They had promised to see me on to the flight, my second in two months. I was over the limit with my luggage and spent the last half hour on English soil throwing shoes and books in all directions until relegated to the late queue, destined for Johannesburg with an overspill.

James picked up my heavy bags, plus the excess luggage which he handed me at the departure gate.

"Look Mum, if you packed it, then you must have wanted it .Take everything and just pay the bill. And come back safe and sound."

He gave me that look which meant he had made up his mind, steered me through the queues of waiting passengers. I could see him standing head and shoulders above the crowd, tall and strong and it seemed as if my son had become a man overnight. I waved until I could see them no longer.

All the hectic weeks of packing and storing, arranging and re-arranging were pushed to the back of my mind now. My twice weekly gymnastic sessions at the 'Fitness for the over forties' classes' with George at the Addington Leisure Centre were gone for ever.

George was my hero - one because he had the muscles of a giant and two because he never minded old ladies like me using his running machine for the odd ten minutes on Wednesdays and Fridays instead of the pounding feet of the hairy and well tattooed black belted heavyweights who regularly smashed his precious machine to pieces. Faced with a fight for flab all my life, his stay- healthy F.F.O.F classes were perfect, but I suspect I was top of George's list for effort rather than results. The Addington Leisure Centre had taught me a lot. I knew where my pectoral muscles were for a start and from sideways glances at the weight-lifting corner, I learned that 'I love Mary' could be indelibly written in the most extraordinary places.

For the second time in two months, my flight from London landed at Johannesburg airport, but this journey was very different from the first panic stricken arrival.This time, I had changed emotionally. Learning the names of African malarial areas had suddenly become more important than the squabbles of the new European Parliament headlined in every London newspaper. Once over the equator, the pilot relaxed into playing jungle music over the air and passengers emerged from the toilets wearing shirts with parrots on and khaki shorts. On the drinks list, vodka and ice was replaced by frothy concoctions with floating pineapples and our airborne breakfast was interrupted by films showing wilderness trails and elephant watering holes.

With the air of a well travelled passenger in a slightly crumpled jet-setting tracksuit, I wheeled my luggage through the exit door of the airport lounge and looked around for the face of my driver. It would probably be Sam or Kenneth. I was quite nervous.

It was nine thirty South Africa time and I paused to adjust my watch. There was no familiar face. Milling hordes of chauffeurs waiting for arrivals from London, touted for passengers. Groups going on internal flights bartered prices and I was glad not to have to cope with that.

'Fifty rands, special price for taxi with diesel' was written on a cardboard plate. One wondered what the taxi without diesel might cost.

My driver arrived at last. It was Barrie who had set off at 4.00.am. from Leribe, to meet me as a new resident of Lesotho - with excess baggage. After my eleven hour flight and a rather tearful doze, I could not have wished for a warmer welcome.

"Darling, why didn't you leave it to one of the drivers?"

"I wanted to meet you myself." I hugged him with relief. My eyes were aching behind my sunglasses as we came out of the building into the early glare of the South African sun, bursting to hear all the news .

"Is the strike finished now and everyone back at work?"

"Well, the management have taken most of the men back on, except the trouble makers and work has restarted, but the weekend I came back, there were several men killed at Butha -Buthe. Seven or eight men were shot dead." He paused and looked serious for a moment. "It was between the ring- leaders of the strike and the local military. Negotiations are still in progress, but things could suddenly escalate.This week things have been calmer. All the ladies have returned to camp and the school's been re-opened, but we've all been advised to travel daytime only - in convoy."

As we drove away from the airport, into the green countryside, we reflected on the situation and Barrie told me the hi-jack season was back with a vengeance and several cars had been stolen from the company as a result.

"Lets get going love, we've got a four hour journey ahead. Chin up, fingers crossed."

I was longing to see the mountains again. The startling green of the willows splashed colour across the land, draping their shimmering foliage like cascading waterfalls. The pink peach blossom was on the downward turn, but other colours sang out on the homesteads as we passed and it was obvious that spring had arrived in its full glory. Young ponies galloped across the skyline, life exuded a fresh new spirit. The rivers sparkled and danced. It was a wonderful September morning, with a touch of rosy mist along the far horizons. My nose had learnt to recognise the fresh zingy aura of the southern hemisphere, the smell of wide open spaces, animals on the hillsides, and lush green grass.....yes it was good to be back.

As we crossed the border at Ficksburg Bridge, one of the guards greeted us with a wave of his arm and a grin

"*Lumela 'M'e,* we thought you had gone to England for ever."

"Hi, Felix. Its great to be back in Lesotho. I have a present for your little son, I'll bring it tomorrow."

"What's that?" asked Barrie.

"His boy likes cars and I've found him an English 'Matchbox' taxi."

We smiled together, knowing how a little gift would bring much joy. But I would have to give it in secret, as we weren't supposed to offer anything which might be misconstrued as a bribe.

Then the hectic crowded market place of Maputsoe with its shouting taxi drivers and horse drawn carts clopping up the main street while music blared from every doorway; shoppers carrying everything on their heads, touts who offered to change your money for counterfeit notes, people roasing their mealie by the side of the road.

The drive to Leribe was different this time, I knew every turn and twist in the road. The mountains were green again. The mimosa was in full bloom. It sprinkled its yellow ferny branches around St Monica's Mission and the whistling herd boys brandished sticks over the rumps of their cows who chose to stroll down the middle of the road in front of the car.Young striplings played football around the *setibeng*, running like wild hares on bare feet and in the yard of one of the concrete houses, a father saw fit to *sjambok* his son in full view of his friends. Discipline was fierce in Basotho families up to the age of puberty and a child must obey his parents.

Barrie drove slowly along the dirt road to the camp, trying vainly to avoid the bumps and hollows, past the suckling calves on the rough meadow grass. We waited for the camp gates to be opened by Pirri, one of the guards in his green uniform, who cheekily saluted me with a white quill poking from his hat. Thabo emerged from the guard hut and came over.

"Hello Mrs Glenn. Mr Glenn is very pleased that the spinach is making a good grow. Every day, from England, I am making de water come."

I understood what he was saying, very well. Sophie, across at the canteen, was ranting at someone who had come into her disfavour. Hercule came tearing through the bushes, his tail flying madly, doing somersaults along the the six foot fence trying to hurl himself over the top.

Soon, I was welcomed by all our neighbours, kissed on both cheeks by the French, licked all over by Hercule and bitten on the hand by 'the buzz'. I reached for my handbag sized 'insect bite spray-on relief'. All my life, my skin has been a target for anything which flies and bites at the same time- they are entirely devoted to my anatomy. Petros came striding across the garden to greet me with a wide grin on his face and offered the traditional Lesotho handshake - hand, thumbs, hand.

"Hello Petros. Its great to be back."

"Welcome 'M'e, it is good to see you again."

It was a memorable homecoming. The afternoon was hot. On the verandah table, was a huge bunch of flowers in a bucket with a note saying, 'Welcome Home honey, September 96'. The definition of home had a very special meaning for me.

Holding my hand, Barrie led the way up the steps of our new house. He had arranged the move while I was still in England. We went inside. There was a pot of flowers in every room and some of my own pictures were already pinned to the walls.

Straight away the house gave me a good feeling. The large windows looking onto the garden made it light and spacious

"I love it Barrie. When the trunk arrives from England, we can really make it like home. Oh look - we can see the mountains from our kitchen window."

"A couple of weeks, and the trunk will be here."

"And Petros has found me a new washing machine in place of the old one." I observed, "he's a good man."

"Whether it works is another matter. Tea now or later? " asked Barrie, knowing full well that first ritual of arriving anywhere after a journey.

From somewhere deep inside, I said goodbye to England - for a little while. My spirit reached out to this Mountain Kingdom. Home was now Leribe. Barrie and I were together.

I took the silk ballet shoes out of my bag and walked around the new house, looking for the right place to hang them.

"What are those for?" he questioned, as I untangled the silk ribbons which held the shoes. My fingers shook as I did so.

"Wings for Abigail's feet. They're going to live here- on our wall. One day they might fly. Lizzie made me promise.

Chapter 8

A Basotho Maid

If I live to be a hundred I'll never tire of waking early in Lesotho. The morning greeted us with a rose pink sunrise. There is a freshness about dawn in Africa which is immeasurably invigorating. I couldn't wait to see the garden and tore out to find the roses in bud and trailing vines busting into leaf and there in the corner next to the fence our rampant strawberries. They looked divine and and the sprays of little green fruits looked so healthy and promised masses of delightful meals in the days to follow. Purple irises glowed iridescent in the patch beside the verandah and eucalyptus smelled heavenly after last night's rain.

Most of all I loved my two weeping willows which hung in lime green feathery strands outside my kitchen door. Brilliant sunlight through their leaves brought constantly moving patterns onto my window and ripples of light touched the wall like slithers of rainbow glass.

The restlessness which I had felt in London left me like a flight of birds and the intoxicating mountain air brought with it a freshness of mind, a feeling of unbridled vitality. Our new life together could start for real. The love affair was not only between Barrie and I, but between me and Lesotho.

Standing underneath the willow, I gave my tears to the new grass and made a promise not to mourn for my family and friends, but celebrate them. My September diary would be filled with new experiences so that one day they should know how we lived. The Maluti mountains and the stories of the ancient Bushmen would take my pen and write for me. The transformation of our lives from England to Africa still had not sunk in. We owed a debt of gratitude to the company who had brought us here.

This Spring would last until October. Then the summer rains would begin. The rondavel in the corner of my garden with its round thatched roof was a possible studio for me and soon it would be swooning with honeysuckle, roses and the glorious flaming red cana flowers which were errupting in profusion all round the house.

My watch said 10.00am South Africa time. One hour ahead of Greenwich. In London, the chestnut leaves would be falling in St James' Park and the kids would be collecting conkers ready to take to school for the autumn term. The copper beeches would be aflame and John Betjeman's 'church mouse' would be nibbling the edges of the wheat on countless congregational windowsills of the shires. I looked across to the mountains for the first time since leaving England.

Though mellow thoughts of an English autumn invaded me momentarily, I climbed out of the 'long discarded cassocks' and leapt unceremoniously into a pair of cool shorts and went to prepare breakfast. Barrie had left early for work. 'Might as well eat outside' I thought. The dappled sun between the vines cast shafts of golden light onto the tablecloth The fresh pineapples and guavas bought from the market looked most inviting; the air smelled fresh and the coffee was good .

My verandah was shared with the small lizard-like creatures which darted along the edges of the concrete stairs to the garden. The shiny green *gekkos*, like miniature dinosaurs, darted to and fro between the trailing leaves of the honeysuckle around the back porch. Like rubber, they glued themselves to the house wall and blinked.

The arrival of Noi, from the house opposite, accompanied by a smiling Basotho lady, wearing a bright apron and scarf, distracted me for a moment.

"This is Betty. She want a job " sang my friend Noi, who always got straight to the point. "She come and clean your house. Very good. She clean my house well and always she comes - never has day off .You must give her food for lunch."

That was my first introduction to Betty. She was one of the local Basotho ladies who was employed as a maid on the camp. It seemed that all the village ladies wanted to be employed and there were several already working on our camp, as nannies or housekeepers. Betty would like to work for me and she spoke English quite well. I agreed to pay her the going rate and she promised to come two mornings a week.

It was the beginning of a beautiful friendship. Betty was the mother of three children and was pregnant with baby number four. She lived in Leribe village, where she had a one-roomed wooden house with a tin roof . She shared a water tap with a neighbour and grew mealie and cabbages in her garden.

Betty had to pay a landlord ten rands a week to live in one room. (equivalent to one pound sterling). Her four year old daughter Margaret lived with her, but the older children were looked after by her mother in another village. Next to her house, tethered to a nearby fence was a cow and a baby calf which provided them with milk.

Betty's estranged husband lived in Leribe with his parents, and was not part of her life in the financial sense, the supportive or the emotional sense. Betty provided for her children with the help of her mother, while her job as a maid on the camp during the week, provided her with enough money for food, for herself and Margaret.

Her man, seemingly, got drunk daily, didn't know how to hold down a job, but knew how to make babies. Sometimes when he arrived late at night to try and make yet another baby with Betty, she would call for help and the neighbours would help her to throw him out.

"He sleep with de cabbages 'M'e – all day he sleep with de cabbages. He no good man. He only drink de devil water- too much. Never bring money. Never speak to de children."

"Why can't you leave Betty, move away ?" I asked, saddened by her plight.

"He not like, he want me stay because he father of my children. He make big nuisance if I leave. His parents give him money for joala, so expect me to work for food for family."

"Are you married to this man Betty?"

"Not married, 'M'e – but all children have his name.That is what the tradition is in Lesotho. He want that I live near him. I have no passport 'M'e. I must stay."

Even though she would like to move away to another village, she knew he would not approve. She must continue living near him and continue to receive physical abuse.

Betty worked every day on our camp, walking the two kilometres from her house, sometimes with Margaret at her heels. Noi and I employed her full time, sharing the days between us. She breakfasted and lunched with us, then at the weekends, we filled a box of food, for her to take to her mother's. We were only allowed to pay her the same amount of money as the other maids - otherwise it would cause trouble between them. The answer was to give her clothes for the children, when we could.

Betty wanted to be able to write in English so that she could better herself. During the day in between her duties, we sat at the dining room table and Betty started her lessons.

She had been to school in Lesotho and reached Standard Eight, which was a fairly basic level of language. Then she had to leave school because her father was out of work.

In exchange, she taught me to say some useful seSotho words and phrases. In their language, there is a kind of 'click' which you do with your tongue inside your mouth. Although I tried, I could not make this sound and Betty laughed hysterically at my efforts. She could not understand why I was unable to make the 'click'. Some of their words are pretty unpronounceable especially when a word begins with two consonants - as in '*ngoaneso*' which means my sister/brother, or '*tsamaea*' - meaning, to travel. Remembering to say, '*Hlatsoa liphahlo*' was a big effort on my part, when asking Betty to do the laundry. When it came to washing the dishes, a new pact was agreed - in English.

A kitchen tap with instant hot water was an enigma to Betty. She had only ever washed up in cold water. First she would run all the dirty dishes in cold water. Then wash them a second time in cold water and leave them to drain. There is no word for 'Fairy Liquid' in seSotho. However, once she discovered soap in a bottle, it could all disappear in one squirt and there would be enough lather to scrub the car park. Betty's whole dishwashing process took the best part of half an hour. She would come away from the sink soaked to the skin and say, "I water the dishes 'M'e, in the hot bath."

SeSotho had no written characters until the first French missionaries translated their religious writings and hymns into the native language in the 19th century. The Basotho people began speaking English little by little after many years of British government until eventually English was taught in the missionary schools. Today, Lesotho has two official languages, seSotho and English.

Betty was a Mosotho and she began telling me about the role of the women in her village, about their traditions and their culture. She told me how the people in her village are very poor and they live as best they can, with little or no money, growing their own food and making clay pots, which they sometimes sell. The crops are completely in the hands of the women, as many men are away working in the mines. The women are also responsible for fetching water – perhaps carrying it from quite a distance - grinding the mealie and raising the children.

"There is no employment in our country" she said flatly, "our people are poor. We want send our children to school. The government says we must pay school fees - we have no money. Many people not send children to school. People are having much troubles."

"I am glad to have the work for you Betty. For me it is the first time I have a maid. We will pay you well. Next time you come I have some spare clothes – perhaps you would take them to your mother?" This meant that Betty could say she had given them away. She was very proud.

"Yes 'M'e. I would like. Many ladies like to work in this camp and I have to be careful because some people have jealousies of me. They say I am different."

Once initial courtesies were over, and basic boundaries established, Betty and I found in each other, a mutual respect, which later on, flowed naturally into a bond of friendship.

With each new day, as the sun rose over our mountain, my understanding of Africa went further and I knew without a shadow of a doubt, that this was where I wanted to be. Inevitably, because our ex-pat lifestyle was privileged, we were somewhat protected from things outside, but I was determined to find out more about the lives of the Basotho people.

Some days Betty took me to the market in Leribe and helped to translate, interpreting my amateur attempts at seSotho. We had fun buying vegetables from the pavement stalls, and bartering with stallholders. Their coins, which are called *Moloti* are a different currency from South African Rands. I loved the noise and clatter of the street and soon learnt to shout. In Leribe everyone shouts – and everyone smiles.

In the big supermarkets, there was a counter near the door where people had to leave their bags. I was staggered when someone suggested I left my handbag in a cubicle. This practice was to try and eliminate shoplifting. My handbag would probably never be seen again if I abandoned it on the way in, so we settled for buying from the stalls outside.

Betty was a perfect companion and it really helped having her with me. Prices would double if you were a white customer and you didn't know the language. Here and there, men peeing in the street, would turn away, to offer a modicum of decency, if you chanced to look in their direction. It seemed they chose any place to relieve themselves. 'At least the men are not exhibitionists' I thought. The building of public lavatories is an unknown concept in Lesotho.

Now if parking in England means queuing for a space in a multi-storey car park and dealing with a broken Pay and Display machine, it is simple compared to the navigational skills needed to park a small Volkswagon Fox in Leribe High Street.

First you must aim for your moorings in good time, manoevering your position in between the herd of goats in front and three mobilized wheelbarrows behind, packed with carcasses of meat and sacks of mealie, whose drivers cannot possibly see where they are going. If you sight ten paces of dry land somewhere conveniently near were you want to park, you must put hand on horn and indicate left (although indicators are not in general use) and, with the sun in your eyes, try to avoid the open drain on your left and the crowds of people on your right. The middle of the road seems to be a combination of motor traffic, wheelbarrows and pedestrians, plus small herds of goats heading for the market. Rights of way are anyone's guess.

My only radar was Betty, who would let me know if we had circumnavigated the crater on the left, or the back end of the truck in front, whose owner had suddenly appeared, waving his arms at me to move away from his cooking pot. He was roasting his mealie by the side of the road. The man's voice could be heard at thirty paces. All street eyes were upon me, as though I were trying to park a fully rigged ship. At that moment, with the hot sun blistering the steering wheel and the market place music playing at stadium decibels, I longed to see a sign which said 'Pay and Display' and would have given the earth to see a white uniformed traffic warden quietly licking his pencil!

This naval exercise complete, Betty and I hurriedly disembarked. By the time I had locked the car doors and wound up the windows, a plethora of white teeth had assembled on both sides of the car.

"Lumelang," I yelled, as this was the only word I felt confident enough to use. This obviously pleased them. The result was a grin which spread like sunshine through the crowd. All were intent on having a good view of a white lady with a purse in her hand.

'Look confident and smile', I thought to myself. It's quite disconcerting the first time you see a street of black faces bearing down on you. Betty flexed her pregnant stomach muscles and led the way.

We set a course straight to Altaf's Supermarket. It wasn't so much the empty shelves which surprised me, as the poor quality goods which were on sale inside. Jars of un-named vinegar stood in pride of place on the first stand, alongside packets of poorest quality biscuits and unlabelled bottles of unidentifiable sauces, and some very old looking tins of beef. The shelves themselves were made of wooden slats, most of them empty. There was an abundance of paraffin, firelighters and charcoal, boxes of soap, some cheap plastic cutlery and a small selection of hair products, including Brylcream and a few jars of Ponds cold cream - my mother's answer to anything from adolescent blackheads to housemaid's knee. There was an anxious pause while I tried to find something I actually wanted.

The smiling assistant who wore a pair of badly scorched trousers, was loitering at the back of the shop. A white lady with money to spend was obviously a rare sight. Immediately he changed his lounging position to one of sentry duty outside the King's Palace.

"Madam – I 'ave de non-drip candles, soap and pegs. Here is a Surf for washing clothes (cold water washing powder, great if you want to wash your clothes in a stream). I have paraffin – do you want? "

He hoped that my purse would empty in his shop. I was sufficiently aware that the shortage of goods related to the shortage of spending and again felt that uneasy feeling in the pit of my stomach.

"Two packets of Joko tea bags please." I said apologetically. They were unparalleled in my kitchen cupboard as the 'God of Tea.' There were no butter shortcakes for Barrie, nor even a decent jar of jam.

The boy looked pleased anyway. As we left the shop, he came running after me.

"Madam Madam!" he shouted, holding out a tin of Reckitts Blue. It is uncertain if you could find it in England, even if you tried.

Taking Betty home in my little car most afternoons, was another kind of education. Nothing in my life could have prepared me for the poverty in which these people lived. The road up to the top end of her village was a mud track- dusty and dry in the summer time but which turned into a bog during the rainy season. Fences made out of anything from bamboo sticks to bits of old engines, lengths of corrugated sheeting or pieces of wire strung together, made their own territorial boundaries between the houses.

As Betty's pregnancy advanced and her skirts grew tighter, I would make the almost daily trek up the rutted and bouncy track, pitting my wits against great boulders and uneven rocky channels, enough to reduce my silver Volkswagon Fox to a pile of metal pieces. Bouncing past the yellow sunflower groves and the leggy stalks of giant thistles, white lilac and massed blue pom-pom heads of the agapanthus, my tyres skidded and skimmed the puddles. The hard baked earth was also right of way to bleating goats and meandering cows whose haunches were so bony it was hard to think of them as remotely related to the word 'dairy'. It was not the place to practise having a puncture, but if I did, help would have been at hand.

Hoards of small children, with skimpy dresses and bare feet would run after my car and shout "Hello! Hello!" following me in clouds of afternoon dust or pelting rain. No matter what the weather, the smiles and waves never abated. Women carrying babies on their backs and containers of water on their heads, always looked pleased to see me. Sometimes along the track, they would be bending forwards in the act of first wrapping blanket around baby, then standing upright and tying the knot around their waists to secure the position of the sleeping child. It was all a delight to me.

"Lumela 'M'e, U phela joang" I called, ("Hello lady, how are you?") and their broad smiles would answer me. I saw in their eyes - friendship and an irresistible curiosity.

Betty introduced me to her neighbours and the children danced for me under the peach trees. A plastic chair was brought from the house, plonked down on the ground and I was handed a cup of drinking water straight from a nearby tap. One day I had with me a small jar of nail varnish and put some on the fingers of one of the children. They absolutely loved it and kept asking if I would bring it again.

It would be about the time of day the children came home from school and the colours of different uniforms bunched along the tracks leading through the township. Gangly adolescents balancing their school books, would make their way through a thick patch of maize and disappear inside a tin shack, out of keeping with a smart school gymslip.

Waving goodbye to Betty, I would freewheel almost all the way back to the taxi terminal at the bottom of the hill. Young boys with wheelbarrows careered along beside me at top speed, racing one another to the tap, while fetching water for the families' evening meal. In this village, a Volkswagon car was not a common sight - I would have been less noticeable in a battered old truck. Some trudged along carrying heavy kerosene cans, batteries or gas cylinders for use in their homes– not an easy task if you lived on the top of a hill. This was a neighbourhood of ordinary families going about their daily business, doing the job of surviving.

They lived on cabbages, spinach and mealie pap and would no more think of going to the shop to buy a loaf of bread than flying to the moon. There were no electricity cables. There was no running water. Toilets were those little tin shacks at the bottom of the gardens where plumbing services were connected to the earth. Having recently left behind the beautiful tree-lined avenues of Kent and Surrey, with their town planning laws, wide pavements and well sprinklered lawns, it was like living on a different planet. Animosity or resentment, were never present, nor had I any reason to feel threatened. In all my journeys, I never saw a white face or an unfriendly one.

Poverty at this level has to be the fault of national governments. Migrants migrate and squatters squat. They have to survive and they have to live somewhere. It wasn't clear to me yet why so many people lived below the bread line in Lesotho. But poverty had no reflection on their dignity or self respect.

To live without jobs, transport, light, sanitation and water means you have to fight to stay alive. Resourcefulness isn't born- it's developed from necessity. Its easy to criticize when everything you have is offered on a plate. Housing conditions in Betty's village may have been deplorable, yet somehow these families were bringing up their children without the privilege of free government education, and passing on the few skills they could. Without their own levels of resourcefulness, they wouldn't survive at all.

On our camp, other wives were not at all sure about my journeys into the black community. I was warned to be careful - even by Betty herself. Racial awareness was something I had never had to think about before. I was even told by one of our ladies, "you should not give lifts to black women – even if they are pregnant."

Unwise or unwordly, my beliefs were directed only at the sympathetic level of Betty's swollen legs. After cleaning two houses in one day, she would obviously feel very tired and I had four wheels and an engine. So I continued my afternoon trips to her village and categorically ignored their advice. I was prepared to accept that in the midst of such diverse cultures, there was bound to be violence. It would have been my misfortune to be at the receiving end and perhaps I was lucky. To me it seemed that people were prepared to criticise the symptoms and not the cause. If there is a nasty smell – one only has to recognise the cause and the smell can be eradicated.

One hot afternoon I asked Betty when her baby would be born? She made periodic visits to the hospital in Leribe to see the medical nurse, she didn't seem very clear about her expected date of delivery.

"In five moons or six ," she would say, "the nurse she say April or May or June – one of those anyway."

Her size increased enormously before the Christmas holiday and as she waddled through her bed making and floor sweeping, it seemed possible that her baby would arrive very soon. One afternoon, while talking with Betty, I asked her again, "Betty do you have a date when your baby will come?"

"No 'M'e," she replied, " but I would like if you will choose my child an English name. Not common!" she said strongly, "it must be not common!"

I was delighted to be asked to choose the name of a Basotho infant who was not yet born and might well be born in our house.

After that, whenever she squeezed herself into the front seat of my car, on our journey up to her house, we would talk of English names. The children here are given a seSotho name and when the child is baptised, at two or three months old, an English name. It is one of choice, not a translation of their seSotho name.

Betty went through the lists of Thomases and Edwards and Williams and onto the more unusual ones of Anthonys and Tobys and Christophers, but none seemed to have the right ring to it. It was an on-going game of ours for several months, in between the hot Spring days and the afternoon thunderstorms.

On one occasion she invited me to look inside her tiny house. It had only one room. A single bed dominated the space, crammed beside a small table, a primus stove for cooking and a flat iron in pride of place on a stand. Several half burned candles perched in precarious places and clothes in bundles lay around the floor. She had an old wooden cupboard for her crockery and bowls of different sizes for carrying water from the tap in a neighbour's garden. There was no sink or toilet. She was pleased to be able to have a door on her house, as some houses didn't have doors and were an open invitation to thieves. As it was, Betty's warped wooden door wouldn't deter any determined and lightfooted burglar.

This predicament worried me continuously. How on earth would my maid have the space to accommodate another baby?

"The baby will sleep with me and Margaret. Francina and my boy will still stay with my mother in Maputsoe. I will still be able to do the work 'M'e."

Betty's nightmare was not having a job at all.

"I will bring baby with me to my work. It Okay 'M'e. In Lesotho it is tradition for women to do this. Many Grandmothers bring up grandchildren."

This was Lesotho and not England and there was no National Health Service, pre-natal classes or Family Credit to help the likes of Betty.

How many more babies must her little bed must accommodate, before she was through her childbearing days and how many more fights she must engage in with her 'husband' before he withdrew his beery advances and got kicked into the cabbages?

Those first few months of living in Lesotho were quite traumatic. Sometimes when awakening early to another day of radiant sunshine and clear skies, the shock of coming to Lesotho shook me awake. My world had gone topsy turvy. I would not be able to think clearly for a few minutes, between sleep and reality. Somewhere amid thoughts of our home in Kent where Barrie and I had begun our new life together, the terraces of summer roses and lavender beds at Chartwell and the yellow harvest of the Weald - an aeroplane was flying. Then in a bright light, the lovely auburn curls of my grandaughter danced before my eyes and I saw her smile as we walked through the park. I tried to reach out and touch a small hand that moved and it woke me.

The journey of a lifetime had brought me here to this Mountain Kingdom, where the heat prevails and crinkles up the soil and the people pray for rain. The answer seemed to lie in some poignant words written by Grace Nichols, who came from Guyana. She wrote,

.............I am here......with all my lives
strung out like beads.......before me
.....charting my own futures / a woman
holding my beads in my hand.

I would not change places with any woman now. Like an adventurer on an unknown sea, my life had taken on a richness never encountered before and even the unbearable pain at parting with Abigail, was beginning to lift. The tears had been shed and my longing to follow this quiet man, who had brought me to Africa and healed my heartbreaks, brought with it a great contentment. It was time to learn new values. Women in Lesotho contribute very little to political life – their work is in the family and the homestead. Mine would be the same. Although the punishing tasks of agriculture did not face me, nor were we dependent on cows for our income – one thing was certain. I could not overrule the chief.

On first hearing the stories from engineers and tunnellers of how the new road up to Katse had been built, it was obvious that we had missed out on an exciting part of the Project.

After many years of study and international debate, the main principle of the Lesotho Highlands Water Project was born. The Treaty, signed by the Republic of South Africa and Lesotho in 1986, instigated the scheme which would mean the headwaters of the great Orange River was to be dammed high in the Maluti Mountains where it rises as the Senqu River. Through a series of five vast reservoirs, and a network of more than 200 kilometres of tunnels, water would be diverted from their natural rivers and delivered into South Africa.

The scheme was initiated to ensure adequate supplies of water and hydroelectricity to the industrial and commercial heartland of South Africa, once dependent on areas which were much drier, with much less rainfall. It includes the construction of two dams at Katse and Muela and an underground power station.

Implementation of this ambitious project depended first on a road being built up into the highlands to enable work to begin - an engineering feat in itself. The road only went as far as Pitseng in those days, petering out into mountain tracks between villages. A further 100 kilometres of asphalt and bitumen road had to be built from Pitseng to gain access to Katse, crossing mountain passes and deep valleys. The first charts were done by engineers in helicopters to mark out the rocky and dangerous levels which the new road would have to take. Katse is almost 4,000 metres above sea level and provided a great challenge to construction engineers and road builders.

Since that time, the combined efforts of client bodies, consulting engineers, contractors, funding agents and suppliers of machinery and equipment have succeeded in the enormous task of bringing the scheme to its present stage of completion. Together with thousands of South Africans and local Basotho, the international communities have been able to operate a long chain of working schedules.

First there had been the drilling and the excavating. In 1991 construction began. By July 1992, all five of the tunnel boring machines, destined to complete the 82km of tunneling required on Phase 1A of the scheme, had been been assembled on site. These giant moles are capable of carving 5 meter tunnels through mountain rock.

The building of Katse Dam has been the subject of a succession of comprehensive studies for more than a decade. The impact on the agricultural and grazing land of Lesotho was at the forefront of negotiations and an organisation called the EAP (Environmental Action Plan) was drawn up to ensure adequate compensation to the people directly affected by the project, as well as preparing for a scheme which would be of optimum benefit to the country as a whole. Relocated families have been provided with new homes in neighbouring villages as well as being paid long term compensation. It has been the greatest environmental change that Lesotho will ever have to face.

The men would talk for hours in the bar on the camp, when they had chance to escape their baking-hot underground caverns. Conversations were puctuated with comments about TBM's, geological strata, precast concrete segmental linings and how a man can turn a mining miracle into a disaster by misjudging a bolt by a fraction. We met some of the men involved in the blasting operations- huge beefy men, South Africans, Germans, French and Italians, whose lives revolved around the choking dust and noise from the rock drilling and explosions.

There were thirty nationalities represented in the tunnelling contract. At times the construction work was held up whilst Basotho village folk decided that one of their ancestors was buried at the site chosen for one of the tunnel portals. Locals with shovels would appear on the hillside to dig up the remains of their forefathers before their resting place became part of a working platform. As a mark of respect, the contractors gave them time to remove the bones of their ancestors and this might take anything from a few hours to a few days.

By December 1996, Phase 1A of the thirty year master plan was realised.

Three hundred millions years ago, dinosaurs roamed this land. Lesotho is a rich source of fossils found in the sedimentary rocks. A whole range of pre-historic creatures, whose abundant fossil remains and footprints can be found, now make Lesotho a prime target of scientists interested in the evolution of life on earth. Dinosaurs and many other early forms of life disappeared millions of years ago. Mountains were thrown up violently by explosions deep inside the earth. The natural processes of erosion and weather created a table top plateau. Peaceful hills, beautiful valleys and spectacular waterfalls, now characterize this country, sometimes called the 'Roof of Africa'.

Man entered into this unspoiled paradise of temperate climate and indigenous trees, only recently in terms of antiquity, and their descendants are known as the San Bushmen. These early inhabitants of Lesotho, who were nomadic hunter gatherers, left thousands of rock paintings as evidence of their long occupation. Many of these are full of symbolic messages.

The Natural Heritage Organisation made a fully documented report in the areas of the Maluti Mountains to ensure the protection and preservation of the many Bushman paintings and evidence of dinosaur fossils, found in the rocks and caves. The scope of their work was enormous, particularly in the areas affected by the tunnels so that these important works of art from the early civilizations, should be preserved for future generations. This postage sized kingdom is probably one of the most valuable scientific and historic countries on the map of Africa.

Chapter 9

Life by the side of the road.

Correctly speaking, the people we lived among were called Southern seSotho, (locally known as 'Sotho'). At precisely 1,700 metres high, we were known as the lowlands. Lesotho, with its high mountain ranges, has the highest 'lowest'point of any country in the world. Our camp was near the western border which is formed by the Caledon River. Around us were massive sandstone flat-topped mountains, featuring layers of orange and yellow where a cliff face appeared. The deep river beds and wild open vistas of the plateau (known as the *lowveld*) are awesome and beautiful.

In past wars with the Boers, the Basotho lost a great deal of their territory. They had previously owned much good farming land west of the Caledon River, now known as the Free State. Because that land was ceded to the Boers, many people were forced back East of the Caledon River and settled in towns like Butha-Buthe, Leribe and the capital Maseru. The population growth gradually forced people to move further up the river valleys and deeper into the mountains. With the pressure mounting, King Moshoeshoe 1 appealed to the British for protection and in 1868, the country became a Protectorate of Great Britain and under the new agreement, the present day boundaries were established. Maseru is Lesotho's capital. It was the first administrative post occupied by the British in 1869 and has grown slowly since then. Now it is a flourishing town with a National University and many fine buildings.

Although political independence came in 1966, ties with Britain have been maintained, throughout the harshest era of apartheid rule in South Africa.This fact alone, prevented real economic progress in Lesotho.Today, it is a changing society, combining western influences with its old traditional practices. The population is assessed at around 2 million.

I was fortunate enough to have my own car and most weeks travelled into Ficksburg, which was our nearest town for shopping and this meant crossing the border into the Free State. It was like no other shopping expedition I had ever experienced. The journey there, of about thirty five minutes, was far more of a highlight than the destination.

Sometimes other ladies would travel with me, but quite often I went alone. The list of essentials was long. The hot midday sun meant that it was impossible to go anywhere without a hat, so I bought a grass hat bought from the ladies at the mission. Then there was that essential bottle of iced water in a cool box in case of dehydration, a sun block factor thirty for my face and arms, and a pair of good sunglasses.

Allowing for police road blocks, floods, ox cart pile-ups, storms, border strikes and diamond miners queues, one never knew how long a journey was going to take. If I got bitten by something nasty on the way, I could be scratching for hours, so an essential insect bite spray, in addition to my cream for peeling noses was always in my bag. I regularly forgot to put in the ice-box to hold the fresh food and Betty would run after me and shout,

" 'M'e, 'M'e, you forget de snow-bag!" Without this, my butter and cheese would melt and any fresh vegetables would be sure to die on the way home.

If you were to mention, 'umbrella' to an Englishman, he would immediately think of rain. It is not the same in Lesotho. Umbrellas are used to keep you cool while walking along the roadside or across the mountain in a burning heat. One of the prettiest sights is to see a group of black ladies beside the main road, or climbing the hillsides, carrying sky blue or pastel pink umbrellas. You might see a field of maize growing green and healthy in straight rows along a pasture, and bobbing about in the middle, like sails in a harbour, a dozen or more umbrellas.

Most of the women wear something to cover their heads, whether from tradition or climate I wasn't sure. Bright sunny days are always associated with the sight of these tall slender African girls wearing their wrap- around dresses, with multi coloured headgear, carrying umbrellas and fluttering along the skyline like butterflies.

Rainy shopping days are also fun. Plastic anoraks are a must, with tie-on hood, as the rain is always accompanied by typhoon-like winds, which snatch at your skirt and your sunglasses and guarantee to change your hairstyle into a mutilated haystack. Strong boots are essential if your car stops in a waterhole, and it's a good idea to carry an old carpet and a few bricks in the boot of your car, for when the road you are travelling on has turned into a quagmire and your wheels get stuck in a rut. There are no roadside telephone boxes between towns, no Highway Patrol, or standby free telephone links to the equivalent of the R.A.C. or the A.A.; no petrol stations, or any other kind of highway service.

The local garage was cheap and efficient. I made the mistake of going to buy petrol without earplugs. Our garage owner had discovered that electrical device which ampifies sound to pop concert decibels. After placing my petrol order with the guy at the pump who was dancing in time to the music and didn't understand English, I admit to loitering with intent. The needle on the petrol guage was linked to a well established practice of respectable cheating.

Then I had to pay the attendant *inside* the garage, which involved edging through a tide of banana sellers, ladies with oranges and papayas, children selling bracelets, and local walkabouts with greasy trousers. The rubber legged petrol attendant would beam and wait for a tip.

At first I was not very accomplished in the art of saying 'no'. Saying 'yes' to one person meant dealing with others clamouring to sell. There was a special kind of walk which meant 'no, and I learned to shake my head and turn a deaf ear after my first experience of arriving home with too many bananas and not enough petrol.

Signposts are few in Lesotho and you need to know your route well. The edges of the roads are marked with intermittent white strips of paint - sometimes. These are easily visible in the daytime, but far from visible during darkness when people are walking along the side of the road in dark clothes - without smiling. Travelling at night on mountain roads you should allow for a variety of hazards. Both animals and humans cross main roads at night - often slowly, always unlit and not terribly sober. The only signal you can hope for is a pair of eyes or a set of teeth and if you're lucky, enough time to apply your brakes.

The Basotho don't just walk along the edge of a busy tarmac road, they sometimes go to sleep on it. On one of my journeys I passed a man asleep on the roadside, with his feet well over the white line. It was unbearably hot and the tar road was almost at melting point. There were some insulting exchanges from passing traffic but the man (or it may have been a corpse) didn't move. On my return journey he was still there and still had two feet.

Because my intention was to cross the border, my passport was essential. Many times during those first few months, we both forgot our passports and had to turn back. The other compulsory document was a long term Border Pass, complete with a correct six monthly renewable date stamped on it. Without the correct date one could easily become an illegal immigrant, while going to collect the groceries.

Just before you reach the Caledon Bridge, the road narrows and there are parked cars, stacked like sardines on both sides. All border traffic grinds to a halt to get through the business of the passports. Stalls selling Basotho hats and *knobkerries*, shout their trade from all sides and mealies are roasting within inches of your number plate.

A two rand piece was essential to pay the border official, which was a fixed fee allowing people to drive across the Caledon Bridge. I would dash from car seat to window to pay, hoping my vehicle wasn't commandeered with uninvited travellers while my back was turned. Lifts for ladies were allowed and I met a beautiful young woman one day who was late for work. She was crying because she had left a sick child at home while she hurried to her job in a furniture store in Ficksburg. Her English was good, her tears genuine. After that we arranged to meet on the same day every week when I travelled into Ficksburg. Her name was Grace and we became friends.

Taxis queued up behind, trying to turn round because they were not allowed to carry their passengers into South Africa. Foot passengers alighted and built Bailey bridges of baggage around the tyres of your vehicle. There was no turning circle. A double row of potholes indicated where you could turn a vehicle round. Once lodged between two high-sided vehicles with a smoking paraffin stove inches from your bumper, and a wailing wall of street sellers, patience at the border was vital .

This was the megga business centre of Lesotho. It's where deals were struck, money changed hands and respectable thieves thrived. Pipe-smoking yokels mingled with the crowds and the air was scented with something like stewed vegetables and leaf mould. One morning, split sacks of ground sorghum fell off a lorry and caused a golden opportunity for a street argument. A lone pig arrived to have a nibble.

Now the Gospel according to the Basotho border guards is why do things quick when you can do them slow. Just when you think you are going to get through without a halt, the truck in front which is carrying too many passengers has to be inspected, fully inspected and take-off-everything-down-to-the-wheel-bearing inspected. As a mark of good will, you wait. Horn pressers don't get across quickly – in fact they may well be relegated to the back of the queue for questioning. It doesn't do to cock a snook at authority, it is far better to smile, wait and melt. It seemed a good time to do my yoga exercises. Buttocks, chin and facial muscles all improved.

The passengers in the truck in front, sit down on the ground for a smoke, meanwhile the queue lengthens. It could take up to twenty minutes for passports to be inspected and floorboards taken up. Every bag, every haversack, every mealie bin has to be dissected. Meanwhile, the game is to try and interpret whether it is an official 'go slow' strike- which happens frequently, or simply normal procedure at normal speed- which could increase activity marginally - with a bit more good will.

Some mornings, groups of miners sat on the ground at the border post waiting for the big trucks to come and pick them up to take them to the diamond mines or the gold mines in South Africa. They would be leaving for many months, perhaps even years, to work away from their families.Gathered in groups of thirty or forty, carrying their few belongings, the men would board the vehicles and leave rather sadly Generations of migrant labour has been essential for the Basotho economy to survive. Nowadays the word 'Retrenchment' keeps cropping up. There is talk that the gold mines will stop the employment of thousands of Basotho workers. This fact alone could precipitate a new kind of poverty.

On the outskirts of Leribe on the main Maseru road, I was often stopped at a road block by the Military Police.This meant possession of an International Driving Licence, at all times. On any road in Lesotho, you can be stopped and held waiting in a queue for several minutes, for your Driver's Licence to be inspected. Tyres, brakes and lights must be seen to be in working order and your road licence date checked. If one of these things is found failing, an apology is expected and if the policeman in charge is having a bad day, you can be fined on the spot or receive a piece of paper to say you must appear in court on a certain date.

Police road blocks can happen on any road at any time. And you may find that the policeman who stops you has big pockets. On one of my early journeys, as I pulled up at the red 'Stop' sign along with a queue of bakkies and trucks. The Police Officer it seemed, was checking everyone's papers. He called me over.

"Please give your Driving Licence."

"Yes - here it is," I muttered nervously.

He strolled away to the patrol car and showed it to another Officer. I knew it was in order. It was a written document, translated into ten different languages, signed, sealed and signatured by the Royal Automobile Club of Great Britain, with a current photograph of me on the back page, allowing me to drive in any country in the world. The seconds ticked by. Meticulously, he scoured every page and scrutinized the Seal of the Secretary of State for Transport on the front cover. I decided to play my teacher role if I had to – it had worked before. Then the officer broke into a huge grin and said,

"I can't read any of it. Drive on 'M'e! "

Life by the side of the road, in Lesotho, has it's compensations. Like a perennial peptic ulcer, it has its good days. The wonderful open landscape which is principally grassland, with its donkeys and its baby donkeys sheltering under the early green willows; the sprinkling of yellow buttercups across the meadows, are enough to overcome the obstacles. There is only ever one road to any place.You don't need to consider which way to go.You don't need a digital radio news bulletin to inform you of traffic jams ahead or rush hour road blocks.The world of contra flows and diversions and road rage does not belong here.The only stampede of epidemic proportions will be animals.

The single lane of traffic on the road to Ficksburg usually travels about 30 mph and the ox-carts about 3 mph. Wayward cows usually cross diagonally at about 2 mph followed by a small boy with a stick and half a pair of shorts and castrated bulls in pairs generally are not far behind. Ox-carts carrying mealie, love to meander gently down the middle of the road, especially when getting close to the brow of a hill and when meeting one of these coming the opposite way, one has to allow a grass verge and a half to pass safely by. Unaccompanied donkeys crossing the road are also fairly common.

When ox-carts gather speed as they are driven at an angle of ninety degrees to the road, it is better to let them have unlimited carriageway as the driver has an unreliable breaking system. The hydraulics of ox-powered streering plus a Basotho driver, trying to halt a cart plus its load is an impossible equation.

One morning, I stopped to let the loaded cart which was accelerating downhill towards the main road pass directly in front of me. As it drew level with the tarmac, there was a great creaking of harness as rim of wheel hit gravel and bovine rump shuddered into a slide. The boy up in front holding the reins shot straight over the top of the animals and landed in the road. In a trice he had rolled over in the dust a couple of times, readjusted his cap and climbed back up onto his seat. Thinking he must have at least two broken arms and a ruptured spleen, I leapt out of my car but he was back up on the cart, his sights already set on his homeward route and with a great poke of his stick on the backside of the offside ox, the whole charabang clattered into first gear and disappeared over the ridge.

There are no organised road systems, traffic lights or planned villages. Homesteads arrive and spread over hillside or valley. Sometimes they are built in the lea of an overhang of rock or out in the open by a stream There are no town planning laws, only rules about land, controlled by the chief. And to build a house here you have to be black. No white man is allowed to own land in Lesotho. Neither King Moshoeshoe nor his successor, ever allowed white settlers to obtain leases to the lands they occupied.Today, there are still no white landowners in Lesotho.

Basotho families are often large, and their houses small, which evokes that rare phenomenon of spending most of life out of doors.When the woman is doing her sweeping, children and menfolk have to go outside. Food is either prepared in a separate dwelling because of a smoking fire, or in the doorway of a hut, so the kitchenalia is placed upon the ground outside in full view of the neighbours. A few houses have a courtyard in front (known as *lelapa)* to provide a little privacy. A landscaped garden in Lesotho means an unfenced cabbage patch blessed by the wind, the sun and the stars.

The families who sleep inside the house at night, are outside their homes in the day. Young ones look after the animals, women are busy bringing in water or preparing food. Leaning against a rock or sitting amongst the hens and chewing their tobacco, the old folks watch and dream their lives away. It is a familiar sight to see public meetings or gathering taking place out in the open, with an audience of herdboys and a bunch of goats.

Where lots of homes are built together, myriads of mud paths run between the houses and a few crudely erected barbed wire fences, though mostly their pieces of land are divided by patches of crops. The dwellings snuggle between mimosa and peach or simply overgrown clumps of cactus. Somewhere, hidden amongst the cows and carts, you will spot the litle earth closet, made from corrugated tin with a chimney poking from the top; the status symbol of a well ordered family dwelling.

Imagine England without walls. Take away the bricks, the ornate pillars and the slate tiles and one could inspect the uninspectable - that is the only way I can describe what I saw. Like the eye of a camera with an extraordinary lens, I saw into their lives as a privileged witness.

In Lesotho, families squabble or celebrate, men drink joala and fight, people mourn their dead – in abundance and in full view of the world. Whether feasting or fighting, the Basotho lives his life at the mercy of lashing rains, winds as barbaric as any eastern desert storm, or relentless blue skies - not behind a front door and a brick built façade.

Between each cluster of houses an expanse of wild open *veld* weaves a rhythm into the landscape like a natural breathing space. A variety of settlement patterns studied by archeologists, indicated that early Basotho tribes would choose to build their homesteads overlooking river valleys where materials were close at hand, within reach of a source of clean water and adequate grazing for their animals. Cultivation may take place some distance away where the soil was more fertile. A house that is sheltered from the fierce winds and the heat of the sun is also preferred.

Nowadays new dwellings are built closer to the tarmac road because people value modern transport facilities, such as they are.The road is like a magnet. The passing of traffic and transportation brings with it a new excitement. A traveller has a purpose – he is going somewhere. By observing life by the side of the road, it was possible to discover the lifestyle, the patterns of the people and the jigsaw into which their lives fitted.

Attractive bold patterns which decorate the outside walls of the houses, embroider the hillsides with colour. These are called *litema* and often represent furrows in the earth, or circles – to the African a symbol of life, cycles of the seasons and fertility. Some designs follow zigzag lines representing opposite poles, which might pull a human being in different directions. Respect for their culture seems to confront the traveller in every direction

One morning a group of ladies were having their hair done by the roadside. It was too good an opportunity to miss. An open air beauty salon caused me to put my brakes on and stop. Basotho ladies love fashionable hairstyles and can do the most intricate plaiting and beading. The children ran to my car and looked me up and down as I walked towards their salon. I was breaking all the rules that white ladies should not stop by the roadside, or speak to strangers.

With much hand waving and laughter, I discovered it costs ten rands for a black lady and twenty rands for a white lady. Pointing to my hair, they told me mine was 'difficult to style' but they would try, and they may have to use different scissors. Auburn hair is quite unusual to see in Lesotho, and they all stared at me hard. The young woman who was having her hair washed in a bucket of water, looked up at me through dripping locks of hair.

"*Na u bua seSotho?* " (do you speak seSotho) one of them said.

" *Lenyesemane* " I answered, telling them that I was English . "*Lebitso la hau u mang?* " (what is your name) directing my question to the girl holding the scissors.

" Selina," she answered.

With a magnificent profile and her hair piled high on top of her head, she turned to address me in a friendly manner. She indicated that I should sit down on the only seat – a box of oranges. I stopped to watch and wait. They combed, twisted and tied with nimble fingers, smeared the hair with a kind of gel and tied beads around the ends of the hair so that it fell over the shoulders like a string of shells. A tribe of children gathered to watch .

"*Haeno ke kae?*" (where do you live?) I was able to point and tell them I lived in Hlotse and my name was Annette.

My turn finally came. Perhaps it wouldn't suit me after all. I might end up like an *Ipi Ntombi* look- alike with a frizzed up fringe and plaits. Far from being fashionable, it would look silly. Basically, I panicked. Thanking Selina, I said my goodbyes and left the mountain salon amid plenty of smiles and curious children .

"*Salang hantle*," (remain well and goodbye) I said, afraid that they might be offended.

"Tsamaea hantle 'M'e " (Go well lady) replied Selina, handing me a gift. In my hand was a small wooden comb.

Schools are usually situated about a kilometre off the road. Between tarmac and places of learning, lines of children crocodile their way along rocky paths. Their uniforms contrast with the earth and the sky, not buildings and streets. Satchels and books are balanced on heads. Feet are bare. These children have the gift of space around them which must be euphoric. Kids being kids with their alarming energy, they chase from one side of the wide track to the other, without stopping to consider the possibility of danger from traffic. They might hit a cow pat or a sheep turd. Like bouncing balls, groups of energetic youngsters run and chase in exhilarated pursuit of a playmate; deep tracks in the dust show where skipping toes have been.

In Lesotho, boy - girl relationships are the same as in any country in the world; the same confrontations and whispered flirtations. The girl looks at the ground and the boy stands a distance apart and searches the sky for the answer to her question. If the young man is succesful in his amorous attentions and the girl likes his body smell, he may find, when the girl has moved away, the word 'yes' written in the dust with her toe.

I began to understand a fraction about survival, after seeing several times, the sight of a child carrying a child on it's back. The older child would be carrying the smaller one - probably a six year old carrying a two year old infant. Perhaps they were going for water, perhaps to find food, but my heart always missed a beat whenever I saw a little girl in bare feet running along the track, carrying another child.

One icy cold morning by the bus stop outside our camp, two small children stood in one coat. Each had an arm of its own, but they were joined together with buttons running down the middle of the garment. And as I waved at them, two arms from two identical children waved back, whilst the one body stood facing the road. Within the space of two villages, you could detect the poorest children, having nothing to wear but an old sack or a plain cut down dress; sad little figures in pathetic poses. They would stand by the road and rub their stomachs at passing cars.

Riverside washing days in Lesotho were fascinating. Where the river bends, the flat yellow rocks open into a wide bay, where the children play and the cows water and the herd boys sit or splash near their drinking animals. These areas, often quite near to the road, offer ideal washing facilities.

The ladies go with their buckets and big washing bowls, often the old zinc bath tubs with their packets of Surf or Omo, (Double Action - to remove even the heaviest stains) bend their backs and wash the whole families' clothes in the stream. Aching backs do not seem to appear in the vocabulary of the Basotho women. They stoop with their feet in the river, rubbing clothes and huge woollen blankets against the smooth rocks, for hours. Then they wring out the clothes, pile them into bowls - this time original weight plus water- lift them onto their heads and climb back up the hillside. It takes three or four women to wring out a blanket, which is hung outside on the nearest barbed wire fence or bush along the roadside, to be dried in the sun.

I felt guilty every time I pressed the 'Start' button on my own 'Auto Maid' electric washing machine after that first experience of seeing a washing day in Lesotho. I will never again see a packet of Omo without thinking of these super powered ladies with tin tubs and bare shoulders, up to their knees in the stream.

During that spring and summer, I began to love my journeys where life seemed to happen out on the mountains. No journey was ever wasted. There were no barriers due to language or colour or race. I became a bi-linguist in body language and colloquial Basotho. Communication comes first from the eyes. Making the first move with a smile never failed to get a positive response or greeting. I learnt their humour and their attitudes. I learnt how to shout. Looking a person in the eye with a shake of a hand and giving a greeting wasn't enough .You had to shout. People everywhere shook my hand off and gave forth a torrent of seSotho which perfectly described a hearty slap on the back. I couldn't help but compare it favourably to the English stiff upper lip.

After a few weeks of driving this road to Ficksburg, I felt entitled to know about my surroundings. I asked questions to the taxi drivers.

"Who are the men in red uniforms who are breaking the stones at the side of the road, just outside our camp?"

"They are the prisoners supervised by a Prison Guard, who come to work for the government. They are breaking the stones to be used in building houses," answered Patrick, one of our drivers.

And I soon learnt what' *Joala*' meant.

"What does it mean when you see a tall tree branch on someone's property flying a white poythene bag on the end?"

"The white bag on a stick means somebody is making the *Joala* and if you see a yellow bag it is made from pineapples, and the green means that it is very strong brew - enough to make a statue fall down!"

Despite being illegal to sell your own brew, flags still flew in many places.

Many of the men in this country go to work in the gold or the diamond mines in South Africa.There is little employment here and there are few jobs open to the men except those in retail trades, labouring, road building or latterly taxi-driving. A minority of families own a small tractor and with this, the single handed farmer can offer to plough his neighbour's field for payment. But there many hundreds of men who say goodbye to their families and travel into South Africa to the mines. Wages are low, but outgoings very small and they work long hours down the mine and over a period can accumulate some money to take back to their wives and families at home.

Every sizeable town has a recruiting office and men can be signed on and get work in the gold and diamond mines in the provinces of Natal, the Free State and the Transvaal. The number of men who work outside Lesotho at any given time is impossible to calculate but it has been estimated at sixty or seventy per cent. Migrant workers on a contract usually sign up for six months at a time.When their contracts expire, they return home, laden with gifts for the family or enough money to buy a new plough or mend the roof.

Nowadays, there is another frightening statistic which carries with it a different message. That of Aids.The alarming prediction by the NAPCP states that the movement of men from Lesotho to South Africa is associated with the high risk of infection amongst migrants.

Such a potential risk would have grave consequences to the economic development of their country. Southern Africa is quoted as being the worst affected region in a world wide epidemic of Aids, it is interesting to note that in Lesotho there is a national organisation which plays a leading role in the formation of policies to control and monitor these trends. Though in a country where children are a high percentage of its labour force, it is difficult to see that the condom campaign will succeed .

Traditionally, large families are preferred, and those behavioural changes needed to significantly halt the spread of Aids are impossible to achieve while tradition and culture are the opposing force. Aids education is simply not enough here, existing programmes overlook poor literacy and educational levels. Efforts to promote the use of condoms are still being met with resistance and there is general distrust that these messages come from white men's countries. Changes in sexual behaviour will not come about until the average male does not want to make babies and in Lesotho, that day is a long way off.

Not all men who leave Lesotho work in the mines. There are those who find work on farms or sheep ranches; some in the larger cities such as Durban and Johannesburg. They sometimes become quite prosperous by working in restaurants and other retail trades.With so many men out of the country, the women are left to do a great deal of the daily work in raising their own crops and livestock.

As the children grow older, they have to take on the jobs around the house and the yard to help their mothers. Children from seven or eight have to do the sweeping, polish the pans, iron with a flat iron, or look after the cows and put them into the *kraal* for the night. Young boys are often given the job of taking the maize to the mill, ready for grinding. They hire a working donkey for two Rands a day and walk several long journeys between home and mill carrying heavy sacks.

Each homestead farms a piece of land and is responsible for feeding themselves. In the mountain regions, the almost barren treeless land causes severe problems of soil erosion. Fields have been over- planted and pastures overgrazed, until the quality of crops has become poorer. Farmers do not like to leave land fallow, for fear of running out of food, with the result that the soil is never allowed to regain its strength.

It is fascinating to watch the sights around the mills, the donkeys standing around the yard; the children playing, the women gossiping. What do these women know about fashion and style and 'power dressing'. Here the working girl's wardrobe is the first piece of cloth which is at the top of the pile in the morning which is washed and clean. She puts a coloured scarf around her hair and if she is carrying a baby, wears another blanket on top.

One morning, travelling the road a few kilometres from our village, a friend and I stopped to talk to the people waiting at the mill and try out our few words of seSotho. A handsome young man sitting up on the seat of his cart wanted to show off his well fed oxen and turned the cart round so that we could admire, then beamed and doffed his hat. These diesel free beasts of burden with their sleek shiny coats glistening with sweat, are still employed by farmers for all the daylight hours on every day of the year.They are amazing animals of great strength and fortitude and standing next to one, within two horn distance, is like standing next to a J.C.B. with its engine on full revs.

Venturing a little further, we went inside the mill to watch how the machines worked and how the maize was ground up into mealie meal. The man on top of the machine was covered in fine white powder and jumped down from his seat to show us how it worked. At first, the people waiting were rather suspicious of us, but after we greeted them in seSotho and assured them we were not jumping the queue, they all wanted to talk to us and be in 'the photograph', except one young woman who wouldn't join in the fun, because she had not washed herself and did not want to be seen unwashed on camera.

Again came the questions, "do you eat mealie in England? Do you take your sacks to the mill on a donkey? How many oxen do you have to take in the harvest?"

Such questions always left me reeling. How would they begin to understand our kind of society? The Basothos live close to the earth. Their relationships are between the sun and the rain and their traditions. Clothes are threadbare hand-me-downs and homes, shelters from the cold. Their business is simply caring about their families and each other.Possessions are cooking pots and blankets. They love their country and they are proud. Poverty does not alienate, it does not brush aside the weak, it embraces with joy the simple act and the small pleasure. I wondered how in England, I had failed to appreciate my many privileges.

As each boy in the family reaches the age of eight or nine, sometimes even younger, he will have to learn from his older brothers how to look after his animals. In Lesotho, all land is common land and every herd has the right to go foraging for the best grazing. It is up to the boy in charge to lead them to the most fertile pastures, and keep them away from crops. It is estimated that there are over 30,000 herd boys in Lesotho and they often travel away from their homes for several days and nights, just taking a small amount of maize meal with them, the rest of the time living on what they find to eat out in the mountains. Their lives can be dangerous and very lonely. During these months or even years, the herd boy cannot go to school and does not have the opportunity to learn. The countryside is his book and the weather his guide. Hopefully, another brother will come along in time, and then it will be his turn to have lessons in school.

A favourite game played by herd boys out on the hills, is *morabaraba*, played with 12 black and 12 white stones, which represent cattle .They often carve a 25 hole board out of solid rock and become so engrossed in the game that they allow their own cattle to stray into growing crops.

One day, a young boy about nine years old, wearing an old blanket and an ancient pair of boots, rode a donkey along the track beside our house. He was carrying what looked like a petrol drum with strings attached to a long shaft of wood coming out of the drum. I was on one of my walks up to Leribe village with a friend.

"The boy make himself a musical instrument called a *mamokhorong* " she explained, "and when he is up on the mountains with his animals, he will make his own music."

The 'strings' were made out of pieces of wire and fashioned a bit like a bow and he had a smaller bow to strike the main string which reverberated into the petrol drum and made a sound. He and his donkey came nearer. The boy smiled at me, and the moment was precious.

In Basotho children there exists a pattern of natural acceptance. You never hear a baby cry or a small child whine for some attention. Girls of seven and eight know how to go and fetch water from the spring for their mothers, without being asked. They carry the water home on their head. This is one of the first things that girls learn from their mothers.Younger female members of the family are expected to work alongside their mother and help with washing days in the river. They take a bag to gather firewood or dung for the fuel. Often they carry younger brothers or sisters on their backs and even take the responsibility of feeding them. They have to learn all the household chores at an early age, as a mother may well spent part of her time out in the fields. Leisure time is unknown in Lesotho. Telling the time, is looking at the sun and playtimes are running round the yard with a friendly goat and a piece of twine from a mealie sack.

If there are several children together, they play a game called '*cheko*' which is similar to our game of 'hopscotch' but without a piece of slate to slide along the ground. They seem to hop on one foot and count.

One day, I was enchanted by a little girl on our camp who came with her mother, to the canteen. She was about four years old and had been given a present of a *popi,* (a doll) which had on its back, a baby doll, resembling the life of a Mosotho mother. The child playing in the sun carried the doll, wrapped in a blanket on her own back as she would one day carry her own child.

Young girls often help their mothers at the roadside stalls and sell apples or bananas. If it is hot, you see them building a shelter from anything they can find; branches or grasses; even cardboard boxes or discarded polythene bags, anything which will give some shade from the blinding sun.

On days when a new floor is laid in the hut, the little ones go out and collect cow dung from the fields and bring it up to the yard, then watch whilst the adults mix it with water and clay from the river, into the mixture which they call '*liso*' When the mixture is ready, the women will dive in it up to their elbows and with their bare hands, daub it onto the floor until the surface becomes smooth. It will then be left to be baked hard by the sun. In a few days time the girls make a kind of polish, of paraffin and wax which is then smeared over the new floors. This can be polished it until it gleams. The finished floor looks durable and ends up the colour of the clay, and can now be covered with more layers of the polish mixture, until it resembles John Lewis heavy duty lino - fit for a heavy duty family to play on.

Each time I set out on a journey, during those first few months, I felt dizzy with new challenges. It was as if the whole rhythm of my life had shifted. New images and new attitudes began to change me.The initial shock of being in a country without streets or buildings or pavements, had subsided. Instead, only endless blue skies and long green distances, watching the maize grow from seed to cob, to shoulder high harvest were what really mattered. Realising all too well what 'Africa time 'meant, I had already moved down a gear. 'Soon' could mean anything between one day and one week, and it was clear to me that 'tomorrow' was a metaphor for 'in three or four days time, maybe later.'

Late in the afternoon, as the skies turned to pink and purple, herd boys on their donkeys, laden with mealie sacks, rode leisurely back to their home fields. If I stood on tiptoe and watched from the top of our verandah, I could see the women carrying their water pots - often a group of them together, dressed.in soft colours, gliding slowly, elegantly, along the valley bottom into the setting sun. The sight always took my breath away.

It was Spring in Lesotho, the cactus was coming into bud and soon the great shoots of the aloe plant would start to make telegraph poles in the sky. Counting the weeks before Christmas in my diary I thought how I would *not* miss the 'Only 39 Shopping days to go' notices and the yearly round of tinsel and queues at the till. This year was totally different to any in my life. My November birthday had been celebrated in strawberries instead of dead rockets. After years of teaching in primary school, I rejoiced in the fact that Guy Fawkes and wet bonfires were non existent in Lesotho.The passing of Halloween was honoured instead with a charcoal braai on the verandah with our friends. The fillets of beef bought at Leribe market, grilled to medium rare then washed down with a bottle or two of Drosty-Hof Claret Select Vintage 92 from the vineyards of the Southern Cape, made a memorable celebration.

Chapter 10

The New South Africa.

Like all countries, South Africa has a set procedure for employment. I had applied for a post of part-time teacher in Ficksburg at a high profile primary school. It was a school with an excellent academic reputation in the town and both black and white pupils attended.

Afrikaans is the language used by white South Africans whose origins are mainly Dutch. It is a phonetic language and words are generally pronounced as they are spelled, rather gutterally and with the rolled 'r' of the Germanic languages. There is a distinct difference in the pronounciation of vowel sounds. As in all South African schools, the children speak in two languages, English and Afrikaans. But when English is spoken by an Afrikaner, it sounds very different to our ear. The Board was pleased to receive an application from an English English teacher.

My interest in the post was purely for the experience of teaching in a South African school, however my hopes were dashed when I was turned down. My skin was the wrong colour. As things turned out, any pecuniary rewards would have been minor, compared to the rich rewards of an experience which came from an entirely unexpected source.

It was in October that I met Janet Barrett. She was the headmistress of a nursery school called 'Kindi' in Ficksburg; a charismatic lady, whose love of life eminated from her face, like the sun. She loved her school and the school loved her. It was roses all the way - from the minute you entered the building and saw Janet with her children, whether they were white or black, coloured, European or Oriental. Janet had that quality which doesn't come often in life - that of making each and every person she meets, feel special.

She asked if I would like to help out at Kindi one day a week. On my first morning, Janet introduced me as the Thursday teacher and much to my surprise, I was greeted by twenty children aged between the ages of five and six, who said 'Good morning and welcome' in thirteen different languages.

"*Ciao, Bonjour, ...Lumela,...Ola.*" Their softly whispered salutations delighted me. Indeed I felt very special.

Kindi was the first school in Ficksburg to open its doors to non-white families after the new government was formed in 1994. Here in this room was the first generation of the new South Africa; English, South African, Indian, Chinese, Basotho, Jordanian, Portuguese, Spanish, Austrian, Danish, Zulu, Dutch and German.

As each child stood one by one and spoke their natural language, I felt the tears prick my eyes. Ambassadors of this age would grow up believing their friends may be black or white, clearly not a problem between the walls of this classroom.

I struggled to remember names like Orefela, Sybrand, Mpho and Mvula. There was Mohammed and Fatima, Annika and Martinette, Hesme, Leticia and Afzaal - my mind was in a whirl and my memory had gone into geriatric mode. How I wished there had been a few Johns and Sarahs and Williams to make me feel at home. Once you have forgotten a child's name you are doomed. Once they have told you their name, they expect it to be imprinted on your forehead.

During my first morning, I was assigned to play 'Match Up' with Ricardo who was Portuguese and Sunny who was Chinese. It was one of those card games where you have to look at a mixed assortment of pictures and match the tool with the correct person. When Ricardo matched the wheelbarrow with the gardener, all was well but when Sunny matched up the hatchet with the musician - war broke out between the Portuguese and the Chinese and a black pencil mark was left imprinted on somebody's forearm. Tears ensued. As the peacemaker, I had to find the right words to resolve the matter which isn't easy when you can't speak either language and all you can muster is a few words in English. All was forgiven when Ricardo went off to rehearse being Joseph with a beautiful little Mosotho girl called Orefela, who was playing the part of Mary. In her hand she carried a little black doll, who was playing the part of Jesus.

In South Africa, nursery children start at four years old until they are rising seven, when they move to primary level. The children are taught social interaction, language development, motor skills, music, how to listen, how to obey instructions, politeness and good manners. At Kindi level, children are not taught to read or write.

Creativity is encouraged in all kinds of craftwork, from the usual cutting and sticking techniques in which young children revel, to inventing and playing games; first learning what the rules are and being able to follow them. This applies to both indoor and outdoor games or sports. Safety awareness is a high priority.

They learn how to express themselves through drama and music and demonstrate an amazing ability to communicate with other children from other cultures. Written symbols are left until the child has explored his social environment, come to grips with a range of energetic physical outdoor activities and learnt something about getting on with his peers.

The child's own language is sacrosanct. The teacher speaks to the children in either English and Afrikaans. Printed material is in dual language, so that the children see both sets of words on things such as calendars, notices, or letters to parents. The library contains a selection of books reflecting their needs, in the two versions. Staff switch from English to Afrikaans fluently and most of them speak a little seSotho as well.

Even though some children arrive at Kindi with only their home tongue, by the time they have attended for a couple of terms or less, they are understanding and speaking English quite well and after a year or so are quite fluent. Charmingly, they chatter to each other while they are working, trying to make themselves understood, helped by use of hands and eyes. As new children arrive, older ones teach them how to queue in an orderly manner for their lunch and take turns to go first. No one is allowed to push and table manners are corrected when necessary.

Living in an English climate, you forget what it is like to see children play in the sun. Springtime here means bright bright sunshine, especially during the mornings and early afternoon. Their playground is a paradise of climbing bars, swings, trampolines, tree houses and other physically exhausting equipment in addition to sand-pit and water pool. The sounds of them playing are fresh and vibrant and full of energy. Black legs and white legs go flying past and when it comes to swinging from the highest bars or the toughest jumps, the six year old champions go undefeated, yet I observed some of the gentlest assistance to the younger children from some of the older pupils. My dear friend Ricardo, who could out-manoeuvre, out-match and out-play the whole school, could also display an amazing degree of kindness to the tiniest tot who couldn't quite manage to get his knee up to the first step on the swing. These kind of sensitivities were par for the course at Kindi. It was a pleasure to see the results of Janet's special kind of caring.

At breaktimes the teachers sit at the table out in the garden, in the shade of the trees, enjoying both the coffee and weather. It isn't so much a staff room as a staff garden. All visitors are made welcome.

One morning, a beautiful Mosotho child, ran up to me with an urgent request. His skin was the colour of dark molasses.

"Ke kopa ho ea ntloaneng?"

For a moment I hesitated. Looking into his eyes, seeing the worried look and the way he hopped from one foot to the other, his words could only mean, "Please may I go to the toilet?"

Every Thursday morning I would arrive at Kindi, to the sound of children's voices singing, 'Mary had a Baby' and *'Daar ver in n' Kribe'*, accompanied by chime bars and African drums. Nursery school nativity is a beautiful experience anyway, and I was privileged to watch rehersals. On stage were Spanish shepherds, three kings who had travelled from Jordan, India and Kwa Zulu Natal and a multi-cultural band of angels, from Germany, Denmark and England.

Being part of a school on the approach to Christmas in South Africa was a memorable experience. I was a newcomer, yet Janet and her staff generously shared the joy of their Christmas as if I were a member of their full time team.

The musical performances were truly international. Gold awards should be given to all teachers of nursery school children, who can inspire four and five year olds to present this age old story of the birth of Jesus. When dressing gowns become Eastern robes and tea towels become turbans, it is time for adults to take stock of their lives and find Christmas again in their heart. To witness these delightful scenes, in a country such as South Africa, where children of every creed and colour can sing together, is a revealing illustration of how nations can behave towards one another.

Watching their Christmas preparations brought on my first taste of homesickness since leaving England. One morning in early December - my fingers glittering with silver paint, I was helping to prepare decorations in the big hall. I had just glued my thirty fourth party hat, when the tears started to fall. On the stage a little band of angels were trying on their wings. The school caretaker, balanced on top of a ladder was fixing candles and a tray of fairy cakes had just arrived in time for the final rehearsal. From one of the classrooms I could hear 'Away in a Manger' being sung in Afrikaans. My fingers trembled and the tears came splashing into the glue. Through my mind sprang the generations of countless shepherds I had costumed; all the Josephs and Marys I had pushed onto the stage. That feeling, that mixture of nostalgia and maternal pride, known only to mothers of Christmas shepherds and angels, swept over me.

Spellbound, I watched the final performance of the Christmas concert, the following day; atmosphere tense, hall bursting at the seams. We were hundreds in number, but one in heart. Squashed like sardines - parents, grannies and nannies held their breath. Ex teachers, ex pupils, not to mention cooks, cleaners and large aproned maids, waited expectantly for the play to begin. The Christmas tree glittered and the room was filled with hip- swinging calypso music. Looking around, we constituted a grand assembly of United Nations.

If you have never been off-stage at a childrens' concert you have never lived. It's the moment when the hero not only forgets his lines but also discovers he has left his crown at home. The queen's train predictably becomes detached from her dress, every staple in christendom magically springs open and there are never enough safety pins left to pin the dragon back onto his tail. The adrenalin is enough to send a rocket to Mars.

At this point, about twenty six year olds jumped onto the stage dressed in red and white and let rip with their rousing song.

"Hello, Good Morning, South Africa!"

Little blonde heads jumped and jived amongst brunettes and curly black topknots - it was a riot of colour and race. They pounded the stage with impossible energy. Jamaican Rhumba music competed with Spanish castanets, Dutch clog dances with African tribal displays.Turbaned bare-chested mystics brought a touch of Eastern promise.

These were the stars of tomorrow. I have witnessed worse performances in the footlights of the professional London stage. Despite its mistakes and its mishaps, when the odd crown fell off and the yellow polka dot bikini didn't quite fit, the audience shouted for more.

Somewhere in the middle of the performance, an excited procession started to assemble. In South Africa, when a six year old graduates to 'big school', he dons black gown, mortar board - tassels and all - and is presented with a certificate to mark the passing out of one school to another. Pupils lined up waiting their turn to receive scrolls and shake hands. This charming ceremony of black gowned mini-graduates, would not have disgraced the portals of an English University.

A fitting end to the concert, was a fully costumed version of the Nativity. Every child in Kindi took part. An Austrian Joseph called Stephan and a Dutch Mary called Leticia, blessed with a baby doll called Jesus, sat underneath a star-clad evergreen tree, surrounded by angels in tinsel wings and shepherds in white sheets. Five year old Mpho, the little Zulu boy in the front row, held me rivetted. Earnestly he sang the words which he knew off by heart. The magic of Christmas shone from his face.

Then 'Away in a Manger' sung softly in two languages, to an audience of probably twenty different nationalities, left everyone searching for a handkerchief. At the final curtain, there was not a dry eye in the house.

I drove back to Lesotho in calypso mode, singing from my car window to the passing sheep. The mountains smiled in the sun. The sky was a heavenly blue.

"Long time ago in Bethlehem, the Holy Bible says...."

The sheep were not impressed.

Chapter 11

Late developers.

November had been a busy month. In addition to helping out at Kindi, I had started giving English lessons to the ladies at Butha-Buthe camp once a week and set up an afternoon class to teach English as a foreign language. It was great fun and maybe even a little learning took place on those Monday afternoons, when we all got together - French and English, Venezualan and Thai. We borrowed an empty room on the camp, a blackboard and some tables and got ourselves organised. Everyone was very keen to start.

Perhaps mature students isn't the right expression - late developers may have been more appropriate. Anyhow we were a motley crew. Willing to share our knowledge, we were prepared to throw our joint talents in the melting pot and let our aspirations run amok.

Collectively my students boasted the *B.E.P.C.(Brevet d' études Premier Cycle)*, the *Baccalaureate,* a diploma in Midwifery and a specialist degree in French Literature. Not only were they academically and medically qualified, they were a formidable and street wise lot.

Well acquainted with the precise location of the nearest good hairdresser, the cheapest *Salon de Beauté* to Butha-Buthe camp, and an intimate knowledge of the surgery opening hours of the best gynecological clinic, my pupils excelled in their usefulness. They ran unlimited and up-to-date information on Air France timetables, current rates of exchange and the latest political scandals to a breath. These well travelled wives of well travelled engineers gave unbargained-for benefits to my classes. Between them, there was nothing they didn't know about French cuisine, South American tango dancing and the 'Ladies' of the Oriental nightclubs in Bangkok.

At 2.00pm on Mondays, House 45 on Butha-Buthe camp became a university of international humour, rivalled only by the rather wicked glances of two Basotho guards listening through the window, in the off-duty guard hut next door.

We numbered ten ladies in all. Entering into the spirit of English grammar with great enthusiasm, their efforts at writing letters progressed to more than just the date and the weather, in no time. There were respectable sorties into plurals of English nouns, comprehension and word games. Talents were honest and varied. When one lady said she had wanted to learn to write in English and had been trying for thirty years, it didn't matter. We were all ages, all aspiring language students and from all kinds of backgrounds.

Tentatively, we ventured into the realms of English figures of speech, origins of words and metaphors.We argued about direct translations to the French, we reminded ourselves how many of us could remember our junior Latin and then threw back our heads and laughed over how someone could be 'rooted to the spot' without being a flower. At the mere mention of food, the French - who were obsessive about things related to '*le palate*' - went off into hysterical chatter, and in order to restore peace I almost had to climb on a chair and shout.

One dear lady, who was wildly excited about teaching French cuisine to the Basotho cooks in the camp kitchen, wanted to write a bistro menu '*en Anglais*'. Suddenly, gastronomic possibilities in the canteen, took on a revolutionary format and it was agreed that present menu standards might rise to impossible heights. Bowls of indiscriminate mashed potato might be replaced by *soufflés d'aspèrges* and ' *le poulet tarragon avec les herbes Provençales'* following my pupil's innovative ideas. It was obvious that the digestion of the resident engineers would improve *immediatement!*

"I must educate the Lesotho taste buds, " she stated convincingly. "Do the company not realize that the dam will not be finished without a little temptation in the diet - my poor `usband.... his stomach `as been neglected."

Translation from French into English always invited extreme contradiction. There were a few die-hards who worried over literal meanings, but it was a sure fire way of getting everyone talking and joining in the discussion - usually sending us miles off track and resulting in somebody going to put the kettle on to make tea. I changed my programme to include more work and less chat. Yet our efforts were always creditable and gave rise to valuable progress .

Common and neuter gender nouns were bound to result in complete confusion to the French, and total abandonment by Noi, my Thai pupil, who had no idea what a gender was. I was at a loss to explain in her language, so hit upon the idea of pointing to a picture of a man, a women, a dog and a kennel. Seriously, she nodded. It was a few days later that she called me over to her house, pointed to her black wolfhound sitting beside her and asked me the question, "Hercule - is he a common or a neuter?"

The following week we tackled the complicated subject of English prepositions; the difference in meaning, of 'fall off , fall out, fall into, fall for and fall over'. It was daunting for my hard working pupils and they obviously needed much assistance and looked completely baffled. My attempts at explanation in words proved unsuccessful so I took to '*les gestes theatraux* '. I demonstrated falling off a chair, falling out with my neighbour, falling into a swimming pool and falling in love with *l' amoureux imaginaire, à la Romeo* et *Juliette*. So far so good. I hesitated. They had all understood.

"And lastly," I said brightly, "there was a party at the bar and a man fell over because he had too much booze- e*h bien*?" The Fench ladies laughed hysterically and couldn't stop. I was mortified. Perhaps they thought it was a reflection on my social habits and I tried again ."If you drink too much booze, you might fall over."

At this, they shrieked even louder. Bravely, one of my pupils said, "Do you know what is the meaning of *booze* in French?"

I shook my head.

"The meaning of *bouse* to French people is the cow shit!"

"Mon Dieu, I see I have fallen into the soup!"

A couple of weeks after the classes began, I found a new pupil. Her name was Liliane and she was the mother of four children and the wife of one of the senior engineers. She arrived in Leribe in time to join our lessons and her enthusiasm for the classes redoubled my efforts to lift my pupils out of the Elementary and into the Inter-mediate level of our language course. A fluent linguist, Liliane had travelled widely and had lived in several different countries. Her spoken English was *par excellence*, but she still strived to improve.

There could hardly have been two ladies thrown together, who enjoyed more, the same interests, the same fascination for life in Lesotho and the same ridiculous sense of humour. We discovered parallel lines in our lives, matching tastes in music and books. We both admired the same artists and had a love of classical paintings. On our weekly journeys to Butha-Buthe, we discussed everything from English literature to French painting and often South African politics. The two of us seemed to click into gear with each other and soon became good friends. We felt as though we had known each other for ever.

Passing through Levis Nek, our journey would be interspersed with notorious taxi drivers who imagined they were driving on a speedway track. They would come up behind us and commandeer the entire road, weaving in and out of sheep and pedestrians, leaving us in no doubt why the edges of the road was littered with smashed vehicles. The double white lines down the centre of the road failed to stop them. Antiquated vehicles with exhaust fumes like a travelling bonfire, took turns to pass us going uphill. Illegal emissions of black oil fumes, belched from underneath their vehicles. Over loaded taxis leaned outwards against the camber of the road and swung dangerously in front of us. Incredibly, we never witnessed an accident.

Butha-Buthe itself, was a seething tangle of pedestrians and animals, stalls and roadside kiosks. There, the taxis would hum around the stopping points like bees, overtake or double park, carelessly overstepping the edges of the road. Shouting for passengers was standard practice and prices were sharp, so the cheapest taxi fare would be the one with all the passengers hanging onto the side. There were no organised transport companies and it was up to the individual driver to tout for business.

Single decker buses pulled up alongside the cafes and filled up with passengers inside and mountains of cabbages up on the top deck. At the rear of each bus, a ladder reaches to the roof. Passengers have to heave luggage up on top, before taking a seat inside. Buses with roof gardens of vegetables, boxes of bananas and huge green pumpkins, were common. Live chickens clucked amid rolls of bedding and swaying suitcases, as the vehicles set off to Joel's Drift or Muela - villages high in the mountains. Raucous laughter and plenty of shouting went on, as ladies climbed up the ladders to place their possessions aloft. The women were strong and hauled up heavy packages while the men sat on the ground and watched.

Zig-zagging our way through the taxis and the odd stray goat, we could not help being amused at the names on the shops; 'Willie's Wonderful Photos' a tin shack painted with large pictures on its roof . 'Rock and Roll Driving School', a name to set the nerves a-jangling. Carts pulled by stringy horses clopped along beside us carrying large ladies, with large bags, who used this taxi service for one rand a trot, and you had to be quick witted to develop a sense of when the cart in front was going to turn. Drivers didn't indicate, and the shafts of a cart would slip and creak, so when I braked hard to avoid a horse, Liliane, with her head out of the window, shouted, "Mon Dieu, attention, attention !" We often wondered if we would make it through the mêlée.

Monday afternoons became the highlight of our week.There was the day that one solitary chicken strolled across the road and threw all the traffic into 'emergency stop', while it clucked its way diagonally from the taxi rank to the shops.The poor creature was sworn at in several languages. The truth about why 'le coq' crossed the road, carried the subject into an international joke amongst my pupils.

At two o'clock.sharp, my students arrived with their books. The company of the other ladies was always entertaining and there would invariably be a few camp stories thrown in. Like the time all the television channels went off. No one on the camp could understand why their sets would not work and it was getting towards one of the big international Rugby finals - a high spot in the lives of most of the tunnelers. Everything was checked out and several irrate phone calls made by the management to Lesotho Telecom It eventually transpired that one of the workers on the camp, a soccer fan, had gone out and sliced through one of the main cables to the satellite dish in a fit of pique. He had been in an argument with one of his colleagues, and his temper had reached boiling point. A big row ensued and the man suddenly disappeared off the camp. I never heard the end of the story or if the T.V network was restored in time for the big game, but it was the sort of story that engulfed the whole camp.

Every week, after my lessons in House 45, my day would finish with a private lesson to a young French student who was a graduate in English and wanted to keep her studies going while she stayed for a few months in Lesotho. What a pleasure it was to discuss classical English poetry and and literature with Alexandra. She had studied Dickens and Shakespeare and Austin. Re-living my passion for poetry and discussing the merits of Kipling and Browning and Rossetti for one hour a week, meant that I was able to raise my head above the parapet and create my own ideal world. It was a privilege to be part of a stimulating literary discourse with such a bright student.

Ficksburg Library became one of my favourite haunts, and although many of their shelves contained out-dated books, I began to search out information on South African history. A young Afrikaner librarian apologized for the half empty shelves. I quickly developed an appetite to learn about my country. Slowly, as I pieced together the bits of my early learning, the terrible truths of this vast and savage continent came alive to me again.

The story of South Africa is one of racial clashes, violence and bitterness. From the cruel days of slavery, through the decades of tribal warfare between conflicting civilisations, the years of the Boer War against Britain, through the struggle for supremacy, it has been seen by the world as a place without its rightful destiny. The policy of apartheid divided its people. In the last decade, the policy of reconcilation has sown the seeds of tolerance and forgiveness. Nelson Mandela is the statesman whose personal struggle has triumphed over one of the most difficult conflicts of the twentieth century.

In the eyes of the world, South Africa is inevitably viewed through black and white images. It is also a beautiful country with breathtaking landscapes, a warm climate and a wealth of natural resources, including both diamond mines and gold deposits. After centuries of violence, in a country where it was almost impossible for a black man to be part of a humane society, equality replaces prejudice, hope succeeds oppression.

Almost forty four million people living here represent four basic cultural groups.The blacks, who number over thirty million, from several different tribes whose traditions date back centuries. The whites, who are mainly Dutch, British, French, German and Portuguese descent, total six million. The remainder of the population consists of nearly four million coloureds and more than one million Asians. The majority of these are of Indian descent. Many came from India to work on the large sugar plantations of the Natal.

There are also large communities of Greeks, many of whom have become South African citizens. And thousands of Italian soldiers captured during the second World War, were sent to South Africa and have now opted to remain.There are about 40,000 Germans now in South Africa who have contributed much to cultural and technical services and the Jews, who have settled in some of the larger cities- Johannesburg, Cape Town and Durban. Their contribution to the economic and cultural life of South Africa has been considerable. Approximately 12,000 Chinese reside around Johannesburg and the Free State, controlling most of the shops and restaurants. They continue to play an important role in South African society.

With the end of apartheid, descendants of British and Dutch, the black Africans, Asians, and the other small minority groups, now yearn for an honourable freedom. The future of South Africa depends on how the four population groups can live together. The true test of their devotion is just beginning.

Housing is one of the major problems. During apartheid, most of the blacks were forced to live in separate rural areas known as 'Homelands', unless they had permission to live in 'townships'. Eighty per cent of the population were made to live in thirteen per cent of the land. Since 1994, people are moving away from these areas and are trying to go back to their old lands, to search for jobs. Many young people are moving to the townships, such as Soweto, to look for work. But jobs are in very short supply in South Africa and new arrivals often end up as 'squatters' living on the edge of the city, in self-made shacks.Three quarters of black townspeople live without running water, proper sanitation or electricity.

It is hoped that by the year 2020, eighty per cent of the black population will be living in cities. It is a high ideal. The new government has allocated money that is to be used to upgrade life in the township, to replace the squalid conditions that existed under apartheid. Urban black communities still live around South Africa's major cities, in homes generally made of corrugated iron and wooden planks. You see them outside every town in the Free State. Mile upon mile of small shacks with tin roofs, a natural breeding ground for discontent.

Slowly life is changing. In addition to English and Afrikaans, there are nine more African languages now legally recognised by the South African government. Official documents are still written in English and Afrikaans, but attempts are being made to incorporate more black languages, especially in schools and the media. Whereas, in the past, English and Afrikaans were compulsory in schools, now pupils are taught English, and one of the other ten languages dominant in their area. A number of books and magazines are already published in Xhosa and Zulu. These changes are vital steps forward.

Since my arrival at Kindi, I had begun to realize that within my classroom, there was the grass roots of an important new generation. Already this small provincial town was trying to establish itself under the flag of the new South Africa.

The comparative numbers of blacks and whites who can read and write in South Africa, tells its own story. The whole educational curriculum is being revised. Black people have the same rights as white people for the first time in three hundred years. This small school in Ficksburg, where children integrate at the ages of five and six, perhaps will have a lasting effect on their own lives. Entrepreneurs like Janet, will be instrumental in making those first steps towards a better society. Fresh out from England, living in Lesotho and travelling regularly into South Africa, I saw the struggle between blacks and whites with my own eyes. My struggle was in learning to understand.

Chapter 12

Does Queen Elizabeth have any Sheep?

We began to explore further into South Africa in our off duty time. The Golden Gate Highland National Park was not far away and we spent our weekends climbing some of the well known peaks. On Barrie's 60th birthday we climbed to the top of the Sentinel, to take in the spectacular views. It was a hot climb. The only shade was beneath the overhang of several rocky ledges, which lured climbers to stand underneath the spray of cool water which dripped like a shower of diamonds from the cracks above. Long tailed birds darted to their nests hidden under the eaves and small green tufts of alpine flowers tumbled from the liquid walls. From the top of the Sentinel, we looked down over fabulous open landscape and sandstone ravines stretching into an ocean of blue sky.

The Golden Gate cliffs are characterised by their sandwich appearance of purple, terracotta and ochre stripes, topped with butter coloured sandstone summits.From the top you can stand and survey the vast plains of grassland, bleached by the sun. It was challenging enough for the mediochre walker like me, the grass long and springy, with the occasional vertical rope ladder to clamber up. We watched the baboons jumping and rolling down the rippling grassy banks on the opposite hillside, their shiny brown heads bobbing up like corks in a choppy sea. In the hope of seeing a black eagle or a bearded vulture - those rare species which are occasionally sighted diving from the top of the peaks, we searched the skies with binoculars. There are various kinds of antelope hiding in the corrugated landscape; the black wildebeest, mountain reedbuck, eland and blesbok, which have been re-introduced in recent years.

Over the centuries, wind rain and sun have carved these cliffs into bizarre formations. In the late afternoon, they seemed to glow with a special essence of soft golden light, soothing to look at, imposing and fearless.

On Sundays, Liliane and I went climbing in the caves, while our menfolk went horseriding in the reserve at Bokpoort, in Golden Gate. Barrie hadn't actually been on a horse for more than forty years when he decided to join the posse of riders which went across the game park in search of wild zebra. He returned saddle sore but went again the following week in search of blesbok and wildebeest. The horses from Bokpoort were beautiful stallions, used to rough country and river crossings, so it wasn't long before his party of riders were galloping across the plains alongside a herd of zebra and wading across a dam up to their knees.

Despite the long years in between, my other half took to the saddle with a vengeance and was willing to bear the blisters where saddle and the girth chafed his legs - in fact it did more for his morale than anything had done before. Untroubled (or so he said) by the earlier discomfort, he assured me that South African saddles were more comfortable than English saddles to ride on and that there was no better way of seeing the magnificent scenery than on a horse. He liked Mexico, a fast and excitable chestnut mount, and my apprehension turned into admiration, as week after week he kept up the same pace on the bracken covered slopes for the two hour ride, as the seven or eight younger riders who went out every day. On Monday mornings he walked stiffly down to his office with that fairly distinctive lumbago lean. On occasions like this one says not a word.

Twelve kilometres to the west of Golden Gate is the town of Clarens, remarkably attractive for its dressed stone architecture which glows from the reflected light of the Rooiberge, known as the red mountains. We came to love Clarens, with its blossom trees and broad leafy avenues and the memorabilia shops, which sell South African arts and crafts. Merle and her painter husband Enslin ran a gallery on the main street. They told us that it was the most beautiful place in the world to live. Witnessing a crimson sunset over the Malutis from their gallery window, one would not hesitate to believe them. Enslin's subtle water colours portrayed the magic of South Africa sensitively and we were full of admiration for his work.

Clarens has a fishing paradise at each end of the town; lakes set in a backcloth of pine forests- intoxicating after an hour or two of rain. Barrie and I walked the paths winding upwards through waterfall and *kloof* - a kind of high sided valley between the rocks - and pitted our wits against slippery caves and a tangle of overhead ferns. A velvet green light filtered through wet matted undergrowth – the air soundless except for dripping water. A heady smell of soaked pine needles filled our nostrils.

Clarens is named after a Swiss town, where Paul Kruger ended his days after leading a campaign against the Basotho forces in 1865. Kruger became President of the South African Republic and when he found that he was on the losing side against the British in the second Anglo-Boer war, fled to Swizerland to live out his days in Clarens. In the main boulevard, around President Square, the low slung corrugated iron roofs and wooden decks of the verandahs give the town a relaxed atmosphere which tones well with the live music from the street cafes.

It was there we first met Eric, the proprietor of the Guinea Feather Restaurant, who piped us through the door with the lilt of his Scottish bagpipes, to the tune of 'Scotland the Brave' then proceeded to cook us a delicious meal of trout from the local reservoir. Eric was about forty five going on nineteen -a photographer, turned chef, turned raconteur- size and personality as generous as the gates of Edinburgh Castle. We often dined there, if not always for the food, for one of Eric's stories. His bagpipes hung on the wall beside the piano, waiting for invitations to perform. It became one of our favourite resting places, especially after a gruelling hike in Golden Gate.

One Sunday after a ride and a testing climb, and later waiting for the horses to come in, we had a visit from a rather smelly goat which playfully attached itself to Liliane for most of the afternoon. When finally our party descended on the Guinea Feather for a good meal and a round of Scottish bagpipes with Eric, the smell came with us. We hardly fancied eating with this persistant stink of stale goat wafting up from our table and no one wanted to sit next to Liliane. With a wink and a nod, Eric moved us discreetly to the end of the dining room where we wouldn't be an embarrassment to other diners. Seating Liliane next to the open window, he dished up the most delicious tandori smoked chicken cooked in a deep clay pot, accompanied by lashings of cold beer.

His seasonal menus include guinea fowl, porcupine pie, crocodile stew, ostrich fillet, blesbok and warthog. And his fresh pizzas cooked in the old wall oven could be a banquet or a disaster - depending on what he threw on top. The local trout was his speciality, dressed with all the trimmings of a gourmet kitchen. After the meal, Eric usually livened things up with his customary jokes and bagpipes - he played them rather well. Whether you requested a special meal or a special tune- you came out feeling you had had a good evening. And his malt whisky was a wonderful nightcap

We both loved the African climate. Spring was rolling into Summer and our days were constantly sunny and hot. The temperature always fell at night, but as the stars turned milky pale and the early mists rose on the slopes, another beautiful morning came to meet us. We regularly breakfasted outside and wrote our letters home, listening to the camp waking up and the taxis pulling into the yard through a thick hedge of a million roses. Green gekkos slithered on the steps to the garden and basked in the early sun. My studio at the back of the house was the perfect place for messing about with brushes and paint. In the following weeks, my complexion turned from pink to brown and my freckles spread like weeds.

There was a good feeling on the camp and our lives were full and busy. My days at Kindi and English classes at Butha-Buthe came round with great speed. The rats in our roof became noisier and smellier and Petros spent several days up a ladder trying to coax them out or poison them. Part of the plan seemed to be watching the flies under the eaves around the house. He would stand still with arms folded and stare at the roof. It kept him happy for hours.

"I put in de bad medicine, 'M'e. In three days de rats will be dead. Now I must watch to see where flies are going. Dis will tell me where are many dead rats."

Events took an even more sinister turn. The numbers of four legged creatures increased. By degrees, the scuffles got louder and Petros resorted to standing on the roof to listen. As Director of Infestations, Petros was the king, but he always managed to extend the job into double time, while he thoughtfully deliberated. On this occasion Petros sank into a deep gloom. Eventually, the medicine worked and our down pipes became very smelly. Betty shouted at him to do something and became angry in case we thought the problem was of her making, and while she curried favour with Petros because he owned a car, she gave him a good ear bashing over the appearance of dead rats in the drain pipe.

The dreaded mosquitoes were becoming a nuisance, mainly to me. My red blotches were unparalleled. We tried to combat the nightly infiltration, by filling the house with the pungent smell of 'Doom' when we retired for the night. At first we made the mistake of lighting the mosquito coils just before going to bed and placing them in the kitchen. The next morning revealed that all winged creatures had secretly migrated to our bedroom and I was evenly covered in swollen red bumps where they had taken up their positions in rows up my legs.

Neither rats nor mosquitoes spoiled our happiness. We never felt healthier. During evenings and weekends, we swam in the pool or walked up the mountains and exercised Hercule, exploring the villages (*metse)* around our camp. We discovered the friendliness of the Basotho families who lived nearby. We must have been an unusual sight - two white people out walking with a dog on a lead. Nobody in Lesotho walks for pleasure and no dog is ever on a lead. The Basotho dogs are either with a herd boy, or scavenging across the fields, lean and hungry. We certainly got some strange looks, but having realized we were no threat to them and our dog was not going to eat their sheep, we were invited to walk through their mealie patch, past their homesteads and up the steep rocky paths around the camp. The village children would come around and talk to us and show us the best way to go. Hercule liked to nip the odd sheep if he got the chance, or roll in the muck, but we kept him under close supervision.

One Sunday, we set off with Hercule leading the way, and hadn't gone far before a couple of village children raced after us, appearing from somewhere in between the cluster of cows and tetherered donkeys.

"Hey Mister, where you go?" they shouted behind us. Before long other kids came running and soon we had collected some ten or fifteen children. They were like a pack of mountain goats, without a pair of shoes between them.

We had set out carrying a small picnic, intent on spending the day climbing to the top of 'our mountain' the one which greeted us every morning. It was quite small by Lesotho standards, maybe an hour's climb. The children, all jabbering away in their own language, led us up the grassy slopes and dry stony paths, sometimes going far ahead of us and calling out where we should walk. Hercule pulled at the leash and thrashed his way through the long grass.

It was hot. Hercule's strap was chafing my hand. My legs itched with insect bites. Here and there, patches of wild flowers draped prettily over rocky ledges. Slowly we picked our way along deep gullies and sharp rocks, walking through the tall willowy grasses which were shiny and pink in the sun. Locals use this kind of mountain grass to weave and plait into many kinds of baskets and mats.

Far below, the houses on our camp looked like matchboxes. The road to Pitseng curved like a snake between the hills.

"Look there's the stone cross, we're almost at the top." Barrie pointed an arm upwards.

"And guess who's got there first."

Standing by the ancient monument, the children waited for us to catch up.Out of breath, we flopped down onto the ground, with Hercule, still reined in and quietly observing the newcomers.

England seemed so far away; our traditions, our sort of Christmas – the shopping, the stress of buying presents and managing money – like a catalogue of distant images. Sitting on the rocky summit, surrounded by these beautiful black children, dressed in not much more than rags, it was hard to think of city life in London. If the kids had stood in a line, there would have been a child from every age, between five and fifteen. We tried asking their names and some of them were eager to talk. They laughed at our attempts to pronounce their Basotho names.

"Where you come from?" they asked.

"England," I said, addressing one of the older girls.

"I know about your Queen. She is the Queen Elizabeth. Does she have any sheep?

"How many sheep does she have?" asked another.

"No, in England it's not like Lesotho. The Queen lives in a big house called a palace."

"Does she have sheep in her palace?"

We gave the children our picnic.They shared it out between themselves with good grace. I asked them if they would sing for us - suggesting one of their Christmas songs. One of the older girls called Heleyn, with her hand round a hard boiled egg and a sandwich, started humming the tune to 'Mary's Boy Child ' very softly and others quickly joined in. Every child sang, even down to the smallest. With bare feet and shaved heads and hardly a shred to their name, they sang their song of Christmas; first in English, then in seSotho. Their young voices which fell easily into harmony, were beautiful and confident. Almost without realizing, they swayed to the rhythm - rows of little black toes beating time on the rocks. Each one smiled at us. This was their song and they were telling it to us for the first time.

We were both misty eyed. This was the other side of the Equator. Yet in exchange for our picnic, a few weeks away from Christmas, we were listening to one of the tunes we had known since childhood, sung specially for us in another language. Even the smallest child, who was hiding behind her sister's skirt, came closer and joined in the moment, crestfallen because the older ones had eaten everything. We offered her sweeties instead and she dared to thrust out one very small sticky palm. She resembled a cherub carved into the rock.

It was a steep climb down the mountain and one of the older boys became my personal guide and helped me over the most difficult parts. He was wearing an old overcoat six sizes too big for him and he told me his name was Kaizi and he was twelve years old. When we got to the lower slopes he wanted to show me his house and introduce me to his mother, so we followed him towards one of the rondavels situated inside a wire perimeter next to a small patch of planted beans. Kaizi disappeared inside one of them for a few moments. Suddenly four or five more children peeped round the doorway and Kaizi's mother, dressed in an old red frock with a white shawl around her shoulders, appeared and smiled. She beckoned us inside the hut and rather hesitantly, we stepped through the doorway. This was the first time we had seen inside a real Basotho dwelling.

The hut was only one room- crowded with a double bed , a table, a large cooking pan and pieces of unidentifiable furniture - pots and spoons littered the floor. It was unbelievable. They had neither water, nor electricity. Several tiny tots and a baby were lying on the bed which was covered in a dark coloured blanket. It was airless and dark because there were no windows .We were suddenly faced with the raw reality of poverty and as we looked around, I was filled with incredible sadness. Kaizi took his mother's side and stood proudly by her. He was the eldest son and it was his job to look after the family. Barrie was still holding onto Hercule's lead. The dog growled restlessly. One of the girls who had been on the walk with us, it turned out, was the older sister of Kaizi. Her name was Annacleda.

"Perhaps Annacleda and Kaizi and Heleyn wish to come for lessons at the camp?" I spoke slowly with hand signals, knowing I was not being understood. Heleyn brightly stepped in and explained in seSotho, to Kaizi's mother. The lady nodded her head and smiled a toothless smile. It was agreed that all three would come the following week at five o'clock on a Thursday afternoon.

We left the hut in a crowd, having gathered even more children than before - most of the village it seemed, who loved this very strange happening on a quiet Sunday afternoon. Hercule, aware that he had a large audience, was confused and started to bark. The children leapt backwards and jabbered loudly. This only made him worse. It was time to go.

As they followed us back along the homeward stretch, one angelic little girl aged about four, who was dressed in a lovely white cardigan, came and put her hand into mine and just smiled as she walked beside me. Others were shy and wouldn't approach us but followed closely on Kaizi's heels. There was no doubt he was the hero of the hour and he grew in stature visibly. He suddenly filled his long brown overcoat, puffed out his chest and strutted ahead of the pack, grinning from ear to ear.

At the bottom of the mountain, we left them all waving goodbye; a row of little brown feet kicking up the dust; a row of white eyes staring into the sun. Kaizi stood head shoulders above everyone, his long overcoat reaching to the ground. I saw Heleyn standing a bit apart from the others and knew that I must keep my promise.

Chapter 13

A Festival of Cherries.

The Sheckletons were English friends of ours, who had become South Africans by virtue of living there for twenty seven years. They were the kind of people you felt as though you had known for a lifetime even though you had only just met. They kept good beer, good company and a good bar. In South Africa the word 'pub' falls flat on its face when you mention it. There are bottle stores, there are hotels, restaurants and clubs - but no public houses. So Judi and Ian opened their own bar - in their own house. No money changes hands and it's legal.

The institution is the man himself. Ian is the Mr Rent-a-truck of the Free State.

He will organise a double sided telescopic tunnel boring machine, with two sets of thrusts and ten pairs of shove rams at the top of a mountain, or install a tertiary crushing plant at the entrance to a tunnel - you've only got to ask. He calculates everything in pints of beer and fork lift trucks. If he hasn't got transport, he will carry it up by himself- on the right day. Shouting is his forte. Ian is full of fortitude, guts and good humour and must hold the world record for personal effort with disastrous results.

His reputation as a 'good bloke' had already reached us, before our paths crossed in the rear bar of Ficksburg Golf Club. We met him one Sunday, perched on his bar stool and facing three or four empty glasses. He doesn't play - he supports. His drinking partner was still standing - Lt. Col. Bob Smith, ex naval helicopter pilot, V.I.P., Fellow of the Royal Aeronautical Society and wine taster extraordinaire. They had spent the afternoon 'supporting' the golf tournament.

Col. Smith made a polite bow, kissed me formerly on the hand, and slipped into a well known operatic chorus, sung with a strong Scottish accent. It was a nostalgic moment. We became instant friends. I always had a weakness for being kissed on the hand.

Ian, chirpy and red faced, slid down from the bar stool and embraced us both heartily. He was a stocky man with a rare sense of fun. So far, we had met very few English speakers and fell easily into conversation.

"Well, don't we just need some Yorkshire folk in Ficksburg" he beamed. "Welcome to this God forsaken place. What will you have to drink?"

By the end of the tournament, both supporters were rather marinated. We offered them a lift home, as Col Smith's Rolls Royce was parked in the road outside- facing the wrong way. It was a happy discovery for them.

You don't often see a Rolls Royce in the Free State. Bob was the very proud owner of a 1980 Silver Spirit with a Royal pedigree. This queen of cars was presented to him on his retirement by his company. The famous, the titled, the high ranking military and senior government officials had travelled in it. In the nature of his profession, Bob has been privy to many dark and delicate secrets. He was always the master of discretion, the chauffeur without ears. As a mark of respect, he continues to drive it today wearing the same white gloves and with the same privileged air, as he used to escort his honoured guests.

Having found its way to Ficksburg, one of its duties was to transport these two gentleman to their weekly meetings of the Grand Lodge of Masons, to which they both belonged. Ian had recently finished his year as Grand Master. On formal occasions, they drove sedately to their Masonic functions in the Rolls. Ian, broad chested and dashing in his ceromonial attire; Bob, the epitome of protocol and correctness which came naturally to him after his days as a military test pilot.

One afternoon he took Barrie and I for a ride, wearing his white gloves. It was my first ever experience of sitting in a Rolls Royce. Being driven through the streets of Ficksburg, on a maiden voyage of soft leather and elegant arm rests, the trip was a memorable delight.

Bob, having once been the most senior helicopter pilot in the British Army, is unable to resist telling the most amazing stories of air rescues, both true and fascinating. Part of his career was managing a fleet of helicopters engaged in whale spotting on Antarctic expeditions. His voice would run on with his strong Scottish brogue and we loved his warm generous character. No gathering was complete without one of his legendary whaling escapades. Now well over seventy, Bob's memory was still on 'red alert' most of the time. These days the Rolls was parked unceremoniously in the shade outside in the yard, polished, cherished, graciously retired from duty - gleaming like a galleon and watched over like a Royal Princess.

Most Friday evenings, if Barrie and I could get through the Lesotho border without incident, we would call in at Judi's comfortable bar, (the Shekleton Shebeen) for a relaxing drink. An hour or so of listening to Bob's helicopter stories, or one of Ian's disastrous accidents would make us crease with laughter. Whatever had been stressful or difficult that week was forgotten.

Ian's blow by blow account of how his truck had broken down in the desert, a hundred miles from the nearest town usually included a policeman, a naked woman or a manhole cover. He feels a moral obligation to exaggerate. He also knows every road in the Free State and his wheels have covered hundreds of thousands of miles in the interests of his business. Nevertheless disaster always seemed to dog him.

"I have always tried to avoid doing anything heroic," he mutters, "my luck always runs out in the end."

His wife would just shake her head and pour him another pint of beer. She knew his unconsious inaccuracies were a foil for his own personal disappointments.

In his early days in South Africa, Ian had tried his hand at being a chicken farmer, but abandoned this when his twenty six coops of ready-to-lay hens turned out to be cockerels. After that he tried keeping horses. This worked well for some months until one day, his yard hand tied his horse to a water pump outside. The horse took fright and ran away, taking with it the external pipework, the bathroom wall, the bath with taps, and the toilet, on which Ian was sitting at the time. His house wall demolished, the plumbing gone - not to mention his trousers - Ian retired gracefully to his office to continue writing his accounts. They moved to another town and opened a fish and chip shop. He appeared not to notice the trail of disasters behind him.

Judi is the cornerstone of their business. An emigrant to South Africa in 1971, she arrived with her new husband, having no idea what her future would be. She survived homelessness, unemployment, and racial riots. This remarkable lady raised a family in South Africa, lived through the painful apartheid years, upped sticks and moved house umpteen times, and survived a horrific mugging. Amazingly she stayed married to Ian. She attributes her stoic tranquillity to her unhappy childhood days in Stoke -on-Trent and says that her move to South Africa was the best thing she ever did.

It was on one of our Friday evenings with them in Ficksburg that we were introduced to Priscilla. She is an old friend of Ian and Judi's and has a colourful reputation which arrives before her. When Priscilla enters a room, everything else is shelved. After meeting her you're never the same person. She is a class act all of her own. She doesn't cause ripples, she causes tidal waves.

There is no rational explanation for the effect that Priscilla has upon you. She is both potter and painter, drinks tequilla and ice like we drink cups of tea, and collects antiques. Her arrival at a gathering never goes unnoticed. Everyone in the bar lit up when she arrived, Bob saluted her and Ian poured himself a large whisky.

With one hand round an enormous glass of ice cubes, the other holding a cigarette, and playing to her audience, Priscilla launched into the saga of her current acquisition from the auction in Jo'burg - a most unusual chandelier made from a Boertrekkers cart wheel. It was so big it wouldn't fit anywhere in her house. Instinctively, you all become the auctioneer with Priscilla the bidder. She is a natural storyteller.

Surrounding her face, masses of dark hair winds and plaits itself around combs, scarves, ribbons and dingle dangles; her strong character intensified by heavy jewellery jangling around her neck. Priscilla is one of those quick witted people whose personality is rigged like a fuse - light the touch paper and then duck. She could throw comments as quick as horse manure on Derby Day and dismantle a male ego like a pile of dominoes. She has the timing of a professional entertainer.

Priscilla spends her life either throwing pots or driving round the auction houses buying up bits of unusual junk. In between - she paints. Once, with an impetuous wave at Lot 133, she bid for a Rolls Royce without seeing it. The auctioneer accepted her bid and she acquired it. She owned it jointly with two other ladies, for three years and they took it in turns to drive it. The adventures she recounts mostly involve *robots* or policemen.

Priscilla is the mother of three lovely boys who adore her and the wife of an exceedingly patient husband who spoils her. Together with their two great danes and an assortment of other dogs - which Priscilla has rescued from one source or another, they share a beautiful old house in Ficksburg and another in Johannesburg. She hurtles from one home to the other, driving an old truck which she calls Betsie, juggling school sports days, clay pots and half finished paintings.

November in Ficksburg is 'Cherry Festival' time and Priscilla was in the throes of making pots to sell at the town fair. Ficksburg is famous for its cherries and every year there is a festival in which the whole town takes part. This year was no exception. A whole week of festivities were being planned. From tours to cherry farms, cycle races, golf tournaments, The Great Cherry Fun Run, camel racing, and of course the showground itself. The town was hopping with big beefy Afrikaners driving cattle trucks, parachute teams and drum majorettes. On every corner there was a wine tasting stall or a beer tent. It was not long before I joined in the preparations and began my pottery lessons with Priscilla.

We spent many happy days slopping about with clay and getting filthy dirty, in her workshop in Fontein Street, which was an old converted chapel - or rather half converted, into a pottery. We called them our 'clay days'.

The chapel roof leaked and it was full of rats and spiders and bags of concrete. There was a huge sink and a table where she did her work and stacked the dozens of pieces of work, in varying stages of distress. Some would be waiting for the first firing, or waiting to be glazed; others already fired and cracked, a few mishaps; each one well designed and unique to Priscilla. Her great danes wandered in and out and knocked the odd piece onto the floor with one swipe of a huge long tail.

I soon learned about slips, glazes and kiln temperatures and my early efforts at making pots were most rewarding. My pieces of art were quite ordinary, but Priscilla's were characteriscally her own. She designed the most unusual clay houses, and would very cleverly add a lion looking out of the window or a giraffe with its neck stuck in the chimney. Everything about Priscilla had to have a practical joke in it. Her sense of humour triumphed over everything.

We talked nonstop and found in each other a kindred spirit. We shared our auctioneering stories and when she dicovered I had been in the antiques trade for several years, a lasting harmony settled in and our friendship was cast in stone. Priscilla told me how she left America twenty five years ago and came to settle in Kenya. She loved Africa so much she never went home. She married her Italian husband there, her three boys were born there and as young men, they all have a high regard for the African bush. The family lived in Kenya for many years and Priscilla herself has developed a deep interest in animals.

Vividly, she described elephant in their natural environment, giraffe drinking at sunset in the water pool and hearing the roar of lions at night. Suddenly I caught the magic in Priscilla's voice.

"If you listen, you can hear the grasses whispering around a water hole. And after you've waited for a long time…and the hippo comes to the surface, its unbelievable." She paused to pull on a cigarette while remembering the moment. "Just before it gets dark" she whispered, "you can hear so many movements around you."

Already I was transported into the animal darkness and the moon shadows. In the telling of a story, mystery and intrigue became mixed with reality. No longer was Africa pure fantasy. Excitement for 'the bush' had never really hit me – until now.

Priscilla and her husband had brought up their boys 'safari style', travelled widely in east Africa; their family holidays had been riding camels in the Kalahari Desert and sleeping under the stars. Our one week cycle rides in the Norfolk marshes felt lamentably tame.

At two in the afternoon, we paused for a break, left our chapel potting table and went inside the large family kitchen .The sun was very hot and you couldn't walk across the yard without a hat. Priscilla wore a wide brimmed straw hat covered in clay droppings. Eventually we managed to finish several works of art, in readiness for the Cherry Festival stall.

Priscilla's house was full of her half finished drawings and paintings. Even her animals followed the line of the riduculous. She would paint laughing frogs and upside down elephants. One of her most ridiculous was a water colour painting of a pickled pig. The brushwork was so clever, you could tell it was a pig in a spice jar even though it was all curled up. Frogs in pyjamas lined the bathroom shelf and beautiful doe eyed owls, sat scrunched up on the top of the kitchen cupboard. On the table by the phone there were hippos in skirts and stripy zebras in spotted frocks Every bit of paper in the house seemed to be a half finished masterpiece. Here was a wonderful talent and not an ounce of commercial sophistication. Her crazy snails and smiling oysters would be an asset to the boring menus of famous restaurants and her leap -frogging cats would jump from nursery wallpaper, but Priscilla's commercial inclination is nil.

We had such fun on those sunny afternoons in the old chapel. Whoever turned up was another new face to me and often the yard would be full of bakkies and people shouting.Tamu would bark and Esther would run and fetch more ice cubes.

Esther worked as the family maid and was quite used to emptying sinks full of clay and jugs of slip. She had worked for this crazy household for more than five years and loved Priscilla's boys as if they were her own family. It was a hard life in the township of Meqheleng, outside Ficksburg. Esther had no husband but was well looked after by Priscilla and Guido. She had a secret liking for the drinks cabinet and the levels of gin invariably dropped when Master and Mistress went away.

There was also a garden boy called Johann, who was a bit lazy and used to spend most of his time leaning on the chapel wall, but he had the most beautiful smile and grew wonderful cabbages. When Priscilla's truck arrived in the yard after her four- hour long haul from Johannesburg, he always came rushing to open the big gate but somehow his speed of movement wasn't very convincing. We nicknamed him the 'Idle Apprentice.' Priscilla suspected that he spent most of his time laying horizontal and smoking *dagga* instead of attending to his duties, when the family were absent.

The Ficksburg Cherry Festival always ended on a note of solidarity on the last day of the festivities with a beauty competition and a grand banquet which was a real tuxedo style occasion. Modelling is one of the most popular and serious careers of young girls in South Africa. It promised to be a lively evening. Guido and Priscilla, Barrie and I, and our mutual friend Bob Smith, decided that the whole affair was a matter of national importance. The girl who won tonight's Miss Cherry Queen title could go forward into the Miss South Africa Competition and if she was lucky enough to be the winner, had the opportunity to enter for the Miss World title.

The show was run on exactly the same lines as the Miss World Competition. First the parade of about twelve lovely ladies with long legs and gorgeous shapes , described by the compere as a collection of eye catching contestants and requested that everyone stay awake and concentrate on a few vital statistics. He then proceeded to read the names of last year's winners, while everyone seated at our table concentrated hard on the vital statistics of number two, number eight and number ten.

Guido said bravely, "Well they are much better than last year's lot." Priscilla agreed and ordered another gin. The banquet had been delicious, Bob was feeling very pleased with life after his fourth glass of wine and greeted every next bathing costume with sounds of rapture while Barrie was concentrating hard on the silver bra strap of number ten, which had slipped a notch.

Each girl now had to present herself in evening wear. Gold satin bodices and diaphonous gowns paraded onto the stage, some girls chose to be black and satiny and slinky, while others chose to be more elegant and regal and looked beautifully poised. One girl, who had a wonderful peaches and cream complexion and a 'double d' bosom began to emerge as a bit too countrified and her broader beam and shoulders made her fit more into the mould of a rather voluptuous dairy maid than a graceful Miss Cherry Queen. Her walk was more of a bounce but her undisguised flirtations with the farmers sitting at the back of the hall was received with loud foot stamping and applause.

The dusky maiden from Natal chose classical couture and her manicured fingernails and flawless hairstyle set a wave of dignity around her chic hemline. She was smooth and sophisticated right down to the buckles on her shoes. Next the leggy blond girl with the ravishing smile and the precocious pout swung onto the stage with her hair swinging like the girl on the Bristows Lanolin Shampoo packet. She looked sensational in her evening dress of white chiffon, and raised the temperature in the hall above boiling point.

Bob was red in the face, Barrie and Guido were placing bets on who would be the winner and Priscilla and I were busy discussing diets and aerobic classes. Next came that moment when the compere does the 'one to one' diction test.

Every contestant is asked three questions: what her ambition is, who would be her ideal man and what she likes doing in her leisure time. The host moved closer to the microphone and the first lady. The compere repeated the three questions. Lady number one said that she wanted to fly on Concorde with Nelson Mandela and loved to grow roses in her spare time. The vivacious dairy maid gave an unrestrained preference for drinking South African wine in her favourite restaurant, sitting opposite the captain of the Springbok Rugby side. Her ambition was more what she didn't say than what she did say and she leapt unashamedly down the catwalk towards the marauding farmers.

The girls bravely gave voice to their ambitions with fragmented whispers or coquettish charm, while the host demonstrated how to thrust a roving microphone into their faces, whilest peering into their cleavages. It was getting towards the end of the contest and he was wondering which of the girls was going to romp home with the prize. Last year's Cherry Queen was sitting at the front of the audience awaiting her turn to go up and present the crown, as is the tradition. Patiently we listened to all the contestants. More waiters than usual slid near to the spotlights and there was a spate of heavy breathing when the beautiful black girl from Johannesburg said she like dancing topless under the stars and her ambition was to play a part in a movie. She left the stage amid thunderous applause.

Now it was time for the judges to complete their marking and choose the three short listed finalists. Barrie and Guido had both agreed on the dusky maiden from Natal. Without a doubt. Bob voted for number two, number nine and numbers four, five and six. Priscilla and I elected the blond one with the long legs and the smile. Everyone in the hall held their breath. It was the moment everyone had been waiting for.

The waiters stopped clinking their glasses and stood still. First the 3rd runner up was chosen. Then the two finalists stood together at one side of the stage, wringing their hands and hoping their mascara wasn't running down their faces with the heat.

"Ladies and Gentlemen. The winner of tonight's Miss Cherry Queen is - Miss Julie Gruywagen from Bethlehem."

It wasn't the dairy maid and it wasn't the dusky maiden. The chosen number eight emerged into the spotlight, suddenly looking one hundred times prettier, more glamorous and more natural than any of the others. She didn't look anorexic, she didn't look as though she would wake up in the mornings looking like the 'bag lady' - she looked young and attractive and as though her looks would remain with her through another forty years.

There was an overwhelming applause from the audience followed by the touching ceremony of the last year's Miss Cherry Queen placing the crown on the new Queen's head. She looked radiant, dabbed her eyes while her crown slipped- all according to tradition.

There was a good feeling in Ficksburg that evening; the Cherry Festival was over for another year and a new Cherry Queen was on her way to meet the new President of South Africa.

Chapter 14

Umhlanga

It was Petros who first told me about the coastal resorts near Durban, 'the big sea' where sharks and hippos swim.

"On the first day of every new year, the blacks go there to dip themseves in the water. All over Africa it is the custom for people to take a day's holiday and go to their nearest sea. I go there with my family every year." I liked the sound Umhlanga. And I wanted to see the sea.

Umhlanga - pronounced *Umshlanga* - is a Zulu name, meaning, 'Place of the Reeds.' Umhlanga Rocks is a beautiful coastal town in Kwa Zulu Natal on the East Coast of Africa, overlooking the Indian Ocean. The resort is dominated by a tall lighthouse, that has no keeper. Kwa Zulu means 'place of the people of the Heavens'.

It was very exciting preparing for our first long journey out of Lesotho. We were not very roadwise. I fondly imagined that every Zulu was a big black man with a headdress of ostrich feathers and a spear, preparing for war. The image needed to be rationalised. In fact the Zulu people believe that their daily lives are guided by ancestral spirits. They still place great store on physical courage and are deemed to be a peaceful and respectful society, with many talents.

According to Zulu custom, the arch-ancestor of their tribe can be traced back to *Unkulunkulu* - 'the great great one' and their paradise is believed to be in the bowels of the earth, the place where their ancestral spirits still exist. They are the largest black nation in South Africa. Little is known about their pre- history because no written language has evolved prior to their first contact with whites in the 1820's.

A Zulu man can have as many wives as he can afford. His homestead is arranged in a circular group of beehive-like huts, with his first wife on the left hand side of his and the second wife on the right hand side. Senior wives are treated respectfully and each wife knows what her obligations and rights are. Each woman has her own plot of land to tend. She rears the children and maintains the house. In addition, she helps to cultivate the crops. Her husband requires her to provide him with a good supply of sorghum beans that she makes into a kind of a beer called *umqombothi*, an essential part of his diet.

In the evenings, the families sit around their fires talking and teaching their children the many arts of warrior tradition and bushlore. Zulu women are very talented in the art of weaving and pottery. These are leisurely affairs between families and the offspring are expected to value good manners and a respect for their elders, above all.

Their lives are conducted with dignity. Ceremonial festivities are proudly maintained. With this in the forefront of my mind, I tried to put away my childish fears and fantasies of Zulu warriors and embarked on this trip with a solemn countenance. Bravely, I clung to the idea of Yorkshire girl in Zulu country, ready to sacrifice my uncertain notions, determined to know the truth.

The day dawned with heavenly blue skies with just a breath of wind to cool the air and the promise of a long hot day ahead. Our journey should take about seven hours through the Drakensburg Mountains and eastwards towards the coast. We began in the early morning with hazy mist clinging to the landscape in golden strands. Looking far into the distance, the cattle were standing full square and still, like geometric blocks that a child might place on his paper when he first learns to draw. Small homesteads spun past; stretches of green veld contrasted with the glassy pools of watering places. Where the willows drooped, nests of the little yellow weaver birds dangled prettily in the sun like threads of cotton.

Our car thundered along hundreds of miles of hot tarmac roads, through rolling hills and mountainous terrain towards the land of the Zulu people. For the very first time, we witnessed the vastness of this country where the sun beats down mercilessly in the dry heat of the midday. Mirages appear before you on the melting road. For several hours, we swept through a parched landscape of acacia trees, thorn bushes and great wide savannas.

On the wide sweeping highways leading towards Durban, we stared in delight at our first ever glimpses of jacaranda trees; luminous purple branches, melting into blossoms of indigo. They were majestic and breathtaking. Flashes of orange cana flowers came now and then through the green foliage of suburban hedgerows. Miles of agapanthus grew along the edges of the road, like a pale blue river.

Unfamiliar names - Ntabamhlope, Pietermaritzburg and Mpumalanga were written on road signs as we swept through toll routes and tunnels cut through the rock. We marvelled at the achievements of the Italian road builders who had made travelling through South Africa so much easier than it was in the early pioneering days of the ox waggon. With the establishment of the Durban international airport, road building has become an important industry.

Umhlanga, situated beside the warm waters of the Indian Ocean is now a place of coastal beauty which offers peaceful forest and lagoon, for people who want to enjoy the world's great eco-tourism destinations. The region of St Lucia estuary contains three huge lakes, where the last of South Africa's wild elephant still roam; where coral reef and marine life run alongside the Mkuze reed and sedge swamps. The area is listed as one of UNESCO's World Heritage sites. Sodwana Bay, higher up the coast, east of Mkuze, is a bird watcher's paradise as over 330 species of birds have been recorded and the Ozabeni forest, which runs all the way down to Lake St Lucia, has become a magical place for walkers using the protected hiking trails.

Stopping for a break on the long hot drive under the shade of a great jacaranda, we gazed upwards into the bright blossoms, unable to believe in the glorious purpleness. We bought golden papaya fruit from the children who were selling their fruit from roadside stalls.

They stared at us with big round eyes and said, "*ngiyabonga bawa*" meaning 'thank you father' a respectful term for an older man. They had gaudy clothes and gentle manners. These moments were so special to me. I was curious to know about them and see into their world. How did they see us? White men in the twentieth century had hunted their wild animals in plenty. South African landscapes, however beautiful, are memorials to apartheid – and this was 1996, only two years after South Africa's world changed. And we were not their countrymen, but their past oppressors. They smiled and gave us fruit.

On either side of us were lush green sugar cane fields, which grow well in this part of South Africa, where the rainfall is high and the soil is good.

Today I discovered something unique about this country. You can be travelling on a deserted stretch of road, that leads in a dead straight line for maybe ten miles ahead with not a building in sight, not a fencepost nor a roof top to be seen - and you will come across a man or a woman walking purposefully, with no other human being in sight. You have to wonder where they are going on foot, alone, down this far-reaching road in front.

Up on the skyline, scattered between the distant rocks, rows of small round huts blend into the backdrop of the mountains. Then comes that strange experience - the feeling of being watched. There may be hundreds of pairs of eyes watching your moving vehicle, hidden eyes that see and wonder about you. That afternoon, on an empty stretch of our journey, a Zulu woman with her two babies, were sitting as still as a stone in the dust by the side of the road. She must have walked from some invisible place which I could not see. From the burnt grassy plains behind her to the clefts in the rocks beyond her, there was no dwelling place.

It was at this time that I began to understand something about the hotness, the magnitude, the breathing pulse of Southern Africa; its vast land that is savannah, plateau or valley - protea, acacia or thorn - the land where bitter battles have been fought.

The major battlefields (*slagveld*) lie in the northwestern part of the KwaZulu Natal, where the Boers first entered Zulu territory and inflicted a severe defeat on the Zulus at the Battle of Blood River in 1838. Their victory was seen as the fulfillment of God's side of the bargain and the Boers thought it gave them a divine right to 'civilise' the country. Their interpretation of the Old Testament they took as a mandate to conquer everything in their path, as they trekked northwards.

In the Anglo-Zulu war of 1879, Zulu tribes were again beaten back from what was the home of their ancestors. A great many were killed when poison arrows and tribal spears defended their homelands against British machine guns, marking the end of an independent Zulu nation.

Some say King Shaka was the 'African Napoleon', some say the stories about him were wildly romantisized. Both myth and legend abound here and it is not for me to attempt a historical makeover, but the feeling that we passed close to where terrible wars had taken place was a moving experience to the inexperienced traveller. The wide skies enveloped us. The beauty of the landscapes, the massive gorges and waterfalls, attached a certain mistique to our maiden journey into Natal.

It started to rain. In England we would say it was a shower. In Africa there are no showers- just heavenly swamps. The skies were black and leaden and the water bounced off the road like a steaming torrent. The ditches by the side of the road filled up while we watched and the windows of the car were a river. The windscreen wipers went on strike and the car aquaplaned uncontrollably down the middle of the road like a raft with a life of its own. Just as suddenly, the rain stopped. The sun came out and played rainbows on the bonnet of the car and the bright clouds sailed high above us and sparkled. The monster-sized cactus leaves along the edges of the fields, became huge shiny plates of light, reflecting the sun between their prickly squat shapes. We opened the windows of the car and breathed air that tasted like wine.

"Another first," said Barrie, looking a little more relaxed. "Not far now, we should be there quite soon. Can you see the monkeys by the side of the road?"

As we approached a scatter of tiny grey monkeys ran to and fro as though they were expecting us. We slowed down to watch them play among the trees and saw their velvet coats, eyes as black as coal. There must have been thirty or more, bobbing about between grass and tree, hiding yet not hidden, like children in a game of hide and seek. These were the vervet monkeys.

By 4.30pm we had travelled more than five hundred miles and arrived hot and tired at our destination. We both remarked how crazy it seemed to come all this way, which in

England would have compared with driving to the North of Scotland for a weekend. But as our car slowed down to halt alongside a river bed, just as we were approaching Umhlanga and we read the words 'SLOW HIPPOS CROSSING' on a sign, we realised that the stories of Loch Ness were going to sound tame by comparison.

The cool interior of the Oyster Box Hotel was heavenly. It was to be our home for three days. On the ground floor, the elegant marble staircase was arrestingly gracious, and the huge pots of flowers tumbling from ledges and windowsills gave the rooms a perfumed and heady fragrance. It had a colonial atmosphere, where uniformed Indian-looking waiters moved quietly carrying trays of drinks. People were already dressing for dinner and the light chatter around us told us that there were quite a lot of English guests.

The tiny coloured birds in huge cages, the highly polished mahogany furniture and the sparkle of crystal chandeliers enchanted me. Swathes of African flowers were everywhere and the verandahs were hung with purple bougainvillaea. And there was the unmistakable perfume of frangipani.

Then we saw the sea; the sparkling silver sea which went on and on for ever. Terraces of frondy palms and peach coloured camelias grew down towards the endless white stretch of sand. In front of us, the famous Umhlanga Lighthouse looked out to sea. The light on the the water glistened with a brilliant light. It was breathtaking.

"So this is the Indian Ocean," I breathed. "Come on Barrie, let's go down the steps and put our toes in the water – now before we go to our room."

The hotel porter who was assigned to help us find our room, appeared with a key and on seeing our direction, came over to speak to us.

"Sir, Madam, please - you must not go near the water at this time of the evening. There are many sharks. It is better to wait until tomorrow morning. Then you can swim inside the area of the net."

We exchanged glances.

"Beats Cleethorpes on a bad day," Barrie decided, unable to contain his excitement at the prospect of swimming in a shark net. "Tomorrow, after breakfast - a swim in the Indian Ocean."

"Don't forget to take a bottle of sea water home for Betty, she'll never forgive you for coming to the sea and not taking water back for her to drink."

In Lesotho, women drink sea water because they believe it will help them to be cleansed inwardly. Traditional seSotho beliefs claim that sea water is the catalyst to producing many healthy children and most childbearing women like to keep the Gods happy.

We were up early the next morning, the Oyster Box breakfast was a mere banquet, and we couldn't wait to go down the terraces onto the beach. It was very hot. I decided it was going to be a painting day for me. The beach was wide and under –populated. The black families sharing our hotel, were not the same in colour as our Basotho friends at home. They were what South Africa calls its Coloureds; people of mixed race, with brown handsome faces and wearing western style clothes, many of whom were more Indian than anything else. They were well attired and well educated. We guessed they were families of successful businesses or professional people enjoying their leisure time by the sea, but it did not escape our notice that they kept a polite distance from the whites. In retrospect, we realized it was a legacy from the days when white and coloured could not share the same beach. Suddenly we understood the nuances of segregation and for a moment, felt their injustices and their pain.

I sat on the rocks, covered in sunblock thirty and a very wide hat, sloshing my brushes in aquamarine and cerelean blue, feet burning in the sand, while Barrie eagerly approached the thirty yard safety area for his first dip in the Indian Ocean - inside a shark net.

While wrestling with the dark and light tones of rock and sea, thoughts were of my own childhood seaside places after the war, and walking the promenades of Bridlington and Scarborough with my two sisters; choosing sticks of rock with writing all through the middle and picking crab claws from a paper bag while sitting next to my father, who would be casting his line from the harbour wall. It would be evening time, when the seagulls came screaming and wheeling round the fishing boats and the men pulled their day's catch onto the quayside.

The three of us with our long chestnut coloured hair, (Yorkshire landladies never failed to comment) scrambled up the narrow steps of the 'Bridlington Queen' or the 'Yorkshire Belle' for an evening cruise round the bay, with a red sky above us and the smell of seaweed in the air. I remembered the donkey rides and sand castles and ice-creams that dripped; my father with his trousers rolled up round his knees, wading into the sea for water to wash the sand from between our toes.

Two brothers were born after that. Those mountains of fishpaste sandwiches multiplied by five – precious memories of family beach picnics. That and getting squashed into the back seat of my Grandfather's car and singing war songs - which my mother loved to sing, until we all tumbled to sleep. I had been a restless energetic child, always looking for adventure, wandering off and getting lost. My father used to say that I chased too many rainbows. Mother soothed me – always brushing my hair and mending my plaits. My lost ribbons drove her demented.

Suddenly I felt too hot, threw my brushes into a bag and dived up the terrace into the shade. Barrie arrived back from his swim, quite disappointed that no shark had even nibbled his toes. He said everyone had swum with sideways glances, almost anticipating that there would be one that got through the hole. Unfortunately, neither of us had taken enough care with the African sun and during the evening meal, somewhere between the oysters and the turtle soup, we began to feel sick.

We spent the night covered in white cream and red blotches, listening to the sound of the sea, and painfully avoiding each other in bed. We woke stiff limbed and itching, and felt very stupid. The hotel staff were kind and I went down to breakfast wrapped like an Egyptian Mummy, in a white cotton sheet. It would have to be a quiet day in the nature reserve with the vervet monkeys or nothing.

As luck would have it, after a gentle but painful walk in the late afternoon under the cool canopy of the forest, we came face to face with a crowd of Zulus in ceremonial dress. My first glimpse of a Zulu warrior.

The men were wearing white feathery shinguards, which rippled when they walked and carried an assortment of drums adorned with tails and swatches of animal hair. The tallest of the group had a long spear and a shield that was highly decorated. My painful arms stopped hurting for a moment and I wanted to cry with excitement. In my delight, I almost let out one of my famous Yorkshire 'Eeeeks' but just managed to control it in time.

The ladies wore lots of strange garments, heavily decorated around their heads and necks. Some of them were carrying handwoven baskets hanging with ilala palm fronds and long grasses. As they walked along, the shells around their ankles jangled and shook. I knew that beads are an important means of communication and have different meanings. Zulu girls sometimes make beaded necklets for their boyfriends which are regarded as love-letters. The colour of the beads is very important. White is for purity, red for anger or pain, and blue for faithfulness.

Most of the men had shaven heads, except for a beaded tail at the back. Their profiles were statuesque - foreheads and noses architecturally chiselled. What struck me most was the colour of their skin. It was so black - a kind of dusky charcoal black - not shiny black like the Basothos.

We stood still to let them pass and their white skirts swished around their coppery limbs. They looked friendly and smiled at us. They had just been somewhere to perform a traditional Zulu festival and their muscular figures danced proudly along the edge of the path away from us - in measured agile steps. They seemed out of place walking along a pavement.

"Oh it's made my day! Real live Zulus," I exploded, "don't they look fantastic!" I want to rush home and read all about King Shaka, and the Battle of Blood River. We were thrilled by the sight of the dancing warriors.

"I wonder if they performed the Reed Dance."

Perhaps now, after seeing them in the flesh, strolling peacefully beside us, in leather thonged shoes and garments of animal skins, I could dispel my lifelong fears of this distinctive nation. They had proved to be a welcome contrast from the Zulus of my avid cinema-going childhood.

The next morning, while exploring our surroundings, we followed the reed beds of a narrow inland waterway and came upon the white sandy beaches of a beautiful bay. A pale blue haze hung over the horizon and the waves were edged with lacy foam lapping ever inwards. The ocean sparkled and drew us. There was no other being in sight. We were alone with the sweeping birds and the soft white sand.

It was our last day before going home to Lesotho. As we walked, the endless surging rhythm of waves coming together and parting, seemed like voices pulling us, together and then apart. The sun was high and the breeze from the sea was like a whispering song around our faces.

"One day we'll come back here" I said quietly. "I feel we belong - it's got a strange kind of feeling…Barrie, do you remember Lizzie's dream?"

I don't know what made it come to mind at that moment. Before we left England, Lizzie reminded me that many months ago she had dreamt about Barrie and I with our arms around each other, walking slowly along a white sandy beach in the bright sun - away from her.

"This is the place she described……but then in the dream there was a thatched umbrella, you know like those in hot countries."

"What do you mean?"

"She knew I was going to Africa, even before I knew myself."

"How could she?"

"I don't know. She just did."

A sudden longing to see my children and Abigail - a child who would probably never be able to walk on a beach like other children, nor feel the sand in her toes. In that moment, I felt a deep aching pain. I was gripped by the fear of separation and the love for my new life. Barrie turned his head and looked straight into my eyes.

"Honey, are you beginning to regret it?"

"It's the sea - it always stirs my soul."

Trying hard to control the aerodynamics in my head, I knew that only the swooping birds saw my tears as I screwed up my eyes against the bright blue day.

Like beachcombers, we picked up shells and driftwood until we reached a point along the coast where Barrie decided to take to the waves, sharks or no sharks. A little way off, sitting on the rocks, I looked out to sea and watched him while he cooled in the delicious water. It gave me time to collect my thoughts. Calmness turned to peace and I enjoyed watching the foamy white clouds scudding across the sky like mare's tails, as I collected pink shells from the sand into the hem of my skirt.

Soon it would be Christmas and my granddaughter and I would play endless games with shells from a South African sea and she would listen to them tinkling in her hand.

We left Umhlanga that afternoon after sharing a picnic with a little Zulu boy who arrived out of nowhere and stood by the boot of the car looking very shy and hungry. He accepted our sandwiches, fruitcake and bottles of Coke, afterwards making a little sign of thanks by touching his stomach and making a bow. He was the colour of ebony and his eyes were as dark as the raisins in the cake.

As we left the forest track which lined the beach, the picture of a hippo appeared on a wooden notice stuck in the sand.

'Do not place yourself between the Hippos and the water' – a thought tempting enough to hasten our return, if only to watch the evening parade of bottoms bumbling towards the sea. Further along a poster nailed to a tree read, 'Natal Parks Board. Night Turtle Tours in December and January.'

This part of the coast has much to enjoy. The nesting sites of Loggerheads and Leatherbacks are part of the ecological story of this area and a glimpse of baby turtles making a dash to the sea must be a sight worth seeing. There are breeding grounds of pelicans, storks and fish eagles. It has to be remembered however, that it is a malarial area and there are plenty of mosquitos -and crocodiles.

Setting out for home, we chose a different route. Taking the Drakensberg direction we ran into a powerful storm. The purple sky was magnificently lit with lightning as the switchback road curved in and out of the mountains. Every few seconds the blackness was cut into silver ribbons and we could see the peaks in front and behind. Thunder boomed and echoed from every side. For two hours, an avalanche of rain continued to lash, and the road was a shiny wet lake of reflection, like shattered glass. At times, the window wipers gave up and we stopped and simply watched the powerful melodrama. You could feel the electricity in the atmosphere. The black night was eternally lit with spasms of light and the dragon's teeth spat with rage. There was a savagery here never known to us before.

We were not used to travelling in these conditions at night and undoubtably rash to chose the Little Switzerland route. At any time of the year storms can arrive - and you have to have your wits about you.

The awesome Drakensberg, translated means ' dragon mountains' and tonight there was a wicked glint in the eye of the dragon. This rapid weather change is typical of this part of South Africa. Raw out from England, we still had much to learn.

Chapter 15

Midsummer Christmas.

It was getting close to Christmas. In Lesotho it was almost midsummer, the season of high temperatures and heavy afternoon rains. The spectacular storms that lit the whole of our valley came almost daily. I used to stand at the window on November afternoons and feel the thunder boom across the mountains wondering if the roof would cave in or if the whole house would be swept down into the Caledon River and be carried away in a steaming torrent.

The shafts of lightning glowed like the veins of a cabbage leaf across the purple sky and lit the peaks for an instant. Qoqolosing, the volcanic mountain, pointed a magenta finger at the angry clouds. The din of thunder crashed around the house and rolled away into the distance. The lashing rain made our eucalyptus trees bend and sway, tearing at their delicate leaves. Willow fronds thrashed like palms in a hurricane. Hercule crawled underneath the house next door, where he could hide until the storm abated.

On the dirt road which surrounded our camp, rivers of mud shifted and flowed like lava lines, criss-crossing the road and leaving sunken hollows where trucks seized up and cows sank down to their knees in deep clay drifts. I found it a great challenge driving into Leribe, sliding around in my car between the mud holes and the newly exposed lumps of rock that hadn't been there the previous day. My vehicle was forever up to its gunnels in mud. Basotho ponies picked their way along the tracks bearing riders wrapped in blankets. Not many discomforts can be worse than riding a horse wearing a soggy blanket.

The shifting ground made it impossible to reach the camp the same way twice and on several occasions, passers-by helped me to push the car out of a waterhole and I arrived home splattered in yellow clay. After ruining several pairs of shoes, I began to think differently about wearing anything on my feet and got into the habit of driving barefoot. We became used to being at the mercy of the weather. Without cancellations, devastations and the appearance of overnight water channels, life would be dull.

Barrie spent a long time each evening muttering over his storm beaten vegetables, pleading with his spindly plants to produce normal sized courgettes and beetroot. He loved growing vegetables, had missed the Lesotho bean planting season by a few weeks and opted for these instead. The courgettes had flowered, but their stalks were thin and leggy. The beetroot looked even less promising and the spinach positively anaemic.

Thabo, who weeded and planted all the camp gardens, assured us that they would grow. Thabo was into trenches. He spent his days moving slowly and methodically amongst the roses and the aloe plants, pulling up weeds and putting on the bad medicine to stop the bad insects from eating the good flowers. He tried to assure us that fat vegetables would spring out of our little patch of garden.

Thabo's limited vocabulary was a mixture of wrong verb tenses and good intentions. He was a very hard worker and everyone on the camp liked him, from Sophie in the canteen who gave him extra sandwiches at lunchtime, to the project director himself.. Thabo was the most popular gardener with the happiest smile. He was the father of five strapping sons, each of whom he brought to my door to ask the same question.

"Madame, please give him de good English words, so that he can speak when I am coming to my house," all of which was impossible since they lived far away on top of a mountain.I gave him an English school dictionary to take home. He seemed to think they could learn a new language by magic- no studying.

Thabo took up a constant vigil in our strawberry patch.Whenever I looked out of the window, he was either digging a trench or watching one fill up. Other gardeners would have long since given up. But Thabo held our courgettes in the highest esteem and just when we thought that our Ratatouille supper was never to take place, there was a knock at the door and Thabo, breathless and triumphant, holding one very lean courgette in two hands, beamed with grand excitement:

"Madame, I am coming to carry de big vegetable to Mr Glenn. Yesterday, I will make another trench!"

Every evening, after the heavy rains, the sky opened up into the most beautiful and dramatic cloud formations. Often there were brilliant rainbows. Looking from our house, the entire arch of colour reached across our valley and over our mountain; vibrant and breathtaking. It looked as if the rainbow had planted itself at the end of our garden - it was almost touchable. Then, just before sunset, the skies would turn a strawberry pink. The wide vistas of flaming red and orange dazzled the eye as the sun dropped behind the mountains. Scoops of ice-cream clouds topped with purple souffles, errupted into the fading light. Twilight lasted about fifteen minutes and it began to get dark about six thirty.

Night came on suddenly. Bushes and trees in the garden quickly turned into shadows; their silhouettes outlined against the inky blue light. The little pink and grey laughing doves who lived in our garden, flew to the overhead telephone wires and sitting there in the half light, made a strand of dark pearls between the poles.

I often went into the garden and watched this spectacle, transfixed by the sheer magic overhead. It was about the time Barrie came home from his work. If there was enough daylight, we would take Hercule for a short walk along the road outside the camp to enjoy the last rays of the sun, pounding through the long grass as the dog panted and pulled at the leash. Across the low meadow, the landscape was a deep yellow, the colour of grasses and earth together stretching into the purple distance.

Local people waved and said goodnight as they passed us on the way home from their day's work.

'*Tsamaea hantle Ntate, Tsamaea hantle 'M'e'.*

If it was too late and the light had gone, we would just walk together in the night garden and watch the stars come up. I have never known stars catch my emotions as they did so now.They shone like jewels.

The night skies were luminously bright. If you looked up into the deep blue of the night sky across the vastness, you felt as if you were floating. At full moon, the heavens were bathed in light .The roses on the verandah were lit with silver where moonlight fell on the petals. The ground shone with eerie paleness and where Hercule stood, a ghostly tail waved sadly, as he waited for his evening walk. The laughing doves turned into cultured pearls on a silver string.

As the sun went down, the air became cooler. We linked arms and walked in the darkness.

"Look honey can you see the Southern Cross? They're the four brightest stars which form a cross," Barrie would say in my ear, pointing out the different constellations. "It always shines much brighter than the others, have you noticed ?"

"I can see the Milky Way - its so clear."

We craned our necks and stared into the heavens. In Africa the moon hangs in an arc quite differently from the Northern Hemisphere. Instead of the new moon showing its crescent as we know it at the side of the arc, it lies underneath, hanging in the sky like a cradle. And the man in the moon seeems to be standing on his head. It was strange to us at first.

Our evening walk was the time for talking and going over the happenings of the day. Barrie was working on plans for the hydro-electric power station at Muela Dam, the second part of the construction for the Highlands Water Scheme. It was all so new to me and I hadn't a clue what a tailrace tunnel was, or an upstream surge chamber. Muela Dam was a double curvature arch structure, 55 metres high, which had to be ready for impounding by November 96. Work on the power station had started in May 1995, with the drill and blast excavation of the access tunnel to the underground power house caverns.

Muela Dam, immediately downstream of the power station tailrace, controls the water coming through the transfer tunnel system from Katse Dam, higher up in the mountains, for delivery into South Africa. At 45 kilometres long, the transfer tunnel is believed to be one of the longest headrace tunnels in the world. Barrie's job entailed the programme for the construction of Muela power station, located 300 metres underground, and measuring 100 metres long and 30 metres high, carved out of solid rock. With the power house completed and the dam in operation, Lesotho would be able to derive all the electricity it needed from Muela Power Station, instead of being dependent on South Africa for its energy.

When he arrived home from a day on site - tired, hot and covered in white dust-telling me about inflows, outflows, overspills and by-pass chambers, our pre-dinner stroll became a new interest for me. I knew nothing about the 'muck and bullets' of tunnelling, nor the daunting logistics of powering such a project, so my contribution here was nil. My role was to keep the store cupboards full and balance my life with his. It was the first time in adulthood that I had been without children or chores - and life was brimming with new experiences.

As the bats flew around the one light outside the house and the noisy *circadas* screamed in the grass, almost drowning conversation, we would go inside, batten down the insect screens on the windows and start to cook our evening meal. I admit to dreaming about English pork pies and would have killed for a jar of Branston pickle to go with it, yet even this dream faded, as I waded into a bowl of fresh mangoes with a pair of copulating preying mantis sitting on the top.

Evenings of television and newspapers were replaced by listening to long forgotten music, reading and writing letters. Courier correspondence from friends at home was blissfully received and answered, and to my astonishment I discovered that my children could write.

Our Sundays were special because it was Barrie's day off. One Sunday we travelled out to Hoekfontein Game Ranch, just outside Ficksburg, which boasts accommodation for visitors as well as game viewing drives in Gerhard's jeep- with the hope of zebra spotting and hippo viewing by the lake. This was our first trip out entirely alone, where we turned off the beaten track and realized how big Africa was. When a sign from the main road points to a place and you can't see it, you know that you are in for a long ride.

Ten kilometres down the driveway, and only a flock of guinea fowls to be seen; we wondered if we were lost.

Their brochure intrigued me. 'No servants allowed, no pets or dogs allowed, no motor bikes allowed.'. But they do have camping and the advantage of the 'Lapa' which is a central open *braai* area - which we would call an outdoor barbecue- with a bar and a camp fire, where you can spend the evening eating, cooking and making new friends. Could this be achieved without a servant?

It was a quiet Sunday and the flies were the loudest thing around. The walks around the ranch were magnificent. We climbed to the top of the viewing platform only to learn that hippos sleep incognito on Sunday afternoons and not a single ripple stirred the pond. Feeling a bit let down, we stood quietly appraising a magnificent elephant skull sitting on the hot patio near the reception area and suddenly a very loud wheezing throaty sound came from round the corner. Very skilfully, two giant turtles locked in sexual combat whizzed across the lawn. It was of some significance that the female turtle was able to run, while the amorous male turtle, locked on behind and wheezing with obvious glee, gripped her round her shell-like waist - while still running. All this on two legs. As we turned to see what the commotion was, they shot past us again - still at roller skate pace - and exploded in the middle of the lawn. Then both got up and plodded resolutely in opposite directions.

Sadly it destroyed two of my childhood myths: firstly that a turtle is unable to run and secondly, that a turtle on its back cannot turn over by itself.

Weekdays were fulfilling and I was extremely happy with my new routine: a journey to Butha-Buthe camp on Mondays to teach my class of ladies, travelling over the border to Ficksburg to teach at the nursery school on Thursdays and going to Bethlehem to do my weekly shop on Fridays. One of the drivers would take us in the kombi - the Lesotho equivalent of a mini-bus. Then there were my afternoon classes with the girls from the mountain and swimming in the evening before the sun went down.

On Tuesdays and Wednesdays Heleyn would turn up with Annacleda and her brother Kaizi, if they could get past the duty guards at the gate. The guards soon began to know them and let them come across to our house for their lessons. They walked a long way from their schools and always arrived hungry and thirsty. Heleyn, looking quite smart in her Mount Royal school uniform, Annacleda in anything she could find and Kaizi in an old pair of shorts and torn shirt, looking like a rag bag. We transformed him with a pair of Barrie's too big trainers and a 'has-been' M&S t-shirt.

"De shoes are for my feet." he exclaimed looking down at his feet as if they didn't belong to his legs. It was obvious he had never possessed any before. " I run to home with my shoes - my mother she is very happy," he beamed.

Once inside the house, Heleyn would make a dash for the sink, turn on the taps, squeeze the life out of the Fairy liquid bottle and do all my washing-up. I used to save it for her. She liked to fill the bowl with steaming hot water from the tap and stand up to her elbows in it. Annacleda would stare for ages in the bathroom mirror and look at all the bottles of shampoo and hair mousse, moisture creams and perfume, She loved to touch all the jars and containers and I'm sure she thought English ladies had strange habits, as she would pick up first one and then the other and ask, "what is it?" many times over.

It was hard to visualise the kind of home life they had, living up on the mountain in their tiny houses, as part of a large family, with minimal amenities. Yet they seemed so carefree and good humoured. Kaizi, with his beautiful eyes and mouthful of black teeth, would make funny faces in my long mirror in the lounge and then stare solemnly at himself as though he couldn't believe it was his own face he was looking at. Then he would gaze up at me and smile again. I would think of English dentists and what they would have done to save his precious teeth.

On those sunny afternoons with the children, we would make cakes. The girls took turns at mixing the ingredients or heating up a saucepan on the electric cooker; they discussed temperatures and baking tins and what kind of food they liked. They told me how their mothers made yeast bread without an oven, cooking the dough on an open fire. A kitchen to them meant a kerosene stove with a few metal bowls.

Once a week, at my dining room table, we would do some writing, in English. The kids had very limited vocabulary. In Lesotho, every child has to study agriculture as one of their subjects and often the children would tell me how important it was to know about cultivation and the rearing of animals. I learnt how sorghum beans are harvested and used to make porridge, which the women of the village prepare to give to the mother of a newborn baby. Raising cattle is an essential part of their lives and as their chief source of protein is from the milk, maintaining healthy cows is seen as very important. The fields are cultivated by the women, the task of sowing and weeding and finally the harvesting of the sorghum and maize are mainly the job of the women.

Sangoma witch doctors still use their age old medicine practices in some villages. We wrote about things in their lives, like dust storms and lightning strikes; about the *mofifi*, the twig of an evergreen shrub which they use to ward off lightning and the term *motsoetse*, which means a mother and a new born child. It was all so fascinating, I often felt like the pupil, not the teacher.

The girls told me stories of the 'Sangoma', who was also called the 'traditional healer' who would be called upon to forecast droughts or epidemics or avert a disaster. They elaborated on this story by telling me about a girl they knew who went to the mountains to see a Sangoma and never came back.

"It is de will of God," said Heleyn firmly, looking straight at me with her brown eyes full of tears.

"Yes, it is de will of God that she go to the mountain and not come back," agreed Annacleda, nodding furiously.

They were both fascinated and horrified. This explanation was something I heard time and time again in Lesotho, when something happened which was beyond a person's understanding. It is still a belief in some families that the ancestors or departed ones could afflict the living descendants for violating the customs of the society. In addition some believe that the ancestors can choose certain individuals to be their channels for communication, by means of dreams or visions. To disobey one of your ancestors might bring misfortune on an individual.

"The girl she still speaks to her grandmother." Heleyn went on. " My friend now lives as a spirit in the mountains. If we want to talk to her we can go and see de old grandmother.".

Annacleda, with wide eyes, added solomnly, "I have spoken to my friend who is a spirit. She says that she is very heppy, but she will never come back."

The relationship between the living and the dead is very important to the Basotho. Traditionalists still believe in a continuing involvement between ancestors and those who survive and that the well- being of the living is the ultimate concern of the ancestors. In return for ancestral blessings upon them, they must conduct themselves in a way likely to retain their favours. To disregard the ancestors is believed only to bring about misfortune to one's family, community, animals and crops.

Therefore the elders of each family are responsible for the behaviour, both socially and morally, of the young generation who should abide by the philosophies of the community. Great importance is placed on parental respect and obedience, bravery and courage to defend the well- being of the family. In all their feasts and festivals the embodiment of the successful community stems from the belief in ancestral spirits. The ritual killing of a goat or a sheep is performed in thanksgiving for good fortune to the 'living dead' or to solemnise an important family occasion.

In Lesotho the Sangoma is sometimes known as the 'doctor priest' and is quite often a woman. Highly informed about herbal medicine, they have a remarkable ability to cure illnesses, although their practice of divining bones is strange to the westerner. Religion and healing are closely interrelated and the Sangoma's task is to preserve and pass on their traditions. When someone has been to see a Sangoma, or Diviner, the advice which is given is taken and acted upon without hesitation.

In addition to treating individual illnesses, the Sangoma is called upon to serve as advisor and protector. Dreams can be analysed and interpreted and healing can take place whether the illness is merely an infection in the body or there is a state of imbalance owing to a family misfortune. For the Basotho - all misfortune is illness. They do not regard a human being as being neatly divided into the physical and the non- physical and the healer has the multi -purpose of caring for the whole psyche.

Before colonisation by whites in the 17th century, there was a common belief in a female deity in heaven, who once created everything. The indigenous tribes believed that their ancestors would pass messages to the living through a sign or a vision concerning such matters as rain or fertility. People on earth could contact her through the 'living dead' and at times of a feast, when an animal was slaughtered, the ancestors would be offered a portion, as well as each member of the family. Their beliefs, even today, are characterised by holistic thinking - symbolized by the circle. For this reason, the African huts are round and people sit in a circle at their gatherings.

One afternoon I plucked up the courage to ask my pupils if they would teach me how to carry a bucket of water on my head. Every day Heleyn and Annacleda fetched water from the spring before they went off to school. I could hardly spend my time in Lesotho without learning a few cultural techniques - and how would I face my students in Croydon again if I couldn't show them the traditional art of the Basotho womenfolk?

We began with a cardboard box and progressed to a bucket full of water. Out came my camera and they took pictures of me in various stages of balancing and wobbling. 'Perhaps there is some magic trick to this,' I thought. 'Perhaps they put something onto their heads first.' In some countries this was true, but not in Lesotho. One of the girls picked up my briefcase, placed it squarely on her head and walked up and down the room, proud to show off her skill. The others grabbed anything they could and did the same. Whatever they placed on top of their heads stayed on. They could even hold a conversation with me, bend down, alter their stance, turn round and the object still held on.

I tried with books – it worked for a few seconds, but of course the kids were eager to go for gold and see me with the bucket of water. Kaizi went to fill up the bowl. They followed me into the garden.

"First you must pick it up and place it on your head" instructed Heleyn in a fit of giggles. It was easier said than done. The feeling of a weight on my head was not one I was used to. Then when you do manage to place it aloft, there is that terrible moment when you must let go.

"Take your hands away and stand straight" shouted Annacleda. "Let go! Let go!" they yelled. By this time we were all laughing so much, there wasn't a hope that my burden would stay in place. Instinctively everyone jumped out of the way when the water flew in all directions.

Kaizi was most amused and sat with his chin on his hands grinning like a cheshire cat. They treated me with good humour, sermonizing and pleading as if they couldn't believe anyone could not balance a bowl of water. I felt like an elderly crusader with a slightly crushed ego.

Afternoons like this were precious. I learned far more from the children than they learned from me. I shared with them the few books brought from England, but what use was the English curriculum when their main pre-occupation was how to survive from one week to the next?

"Do girls of thirteen have babies?" they asked me one day as they came running in from school. Annacleda offered, "one of my friends says she will be having a baby, but she's only thirteen."

I didn't know what to make of that one, so carefully answered, "well….. sometimes," and left it at that.

"And do the people in England eat mealie pap every day? And who looks after the cows?"

"In England, only farmers have cows and they are kept inside a fence, in their own fields. They are only allowed to eat the farmer's own grass, not anyone else's grass." Both girls looked mystified. It was going to be a day of many explanations. Neither did it go down well when I explained about people who owned a rabbit (kept inside a cage) or a cat (who lived in a house) - but who didn't have any cattle or sheep.

If an animal is ever killed on the road, the herd boy is in serious trouble. He takes to the hills and runs away. When he comes back, that is if he returns, he is severely *sjamboked* by his father or whoever is the owner of the beast - or both. Losing any animal is a case for serious punishment.

An accident happened one day a short distance away from our camp. During the morning a cow was hit by a car and died by the roadside. The herd boy was seen running away before anyone could catch him. Later that day, locals arrived to take off their share of the rump and soon little bonfires were burning and the smell of roast beef rose in the afternoon air. There was no squabbling. Everyone in the village was welcome. There is no point in keeping a dead beast in a village without electricity. The carcass soon disappeared, the smoke fires crackled. The offal, which the Basothos love, was taken away and cooked. A roadside party erupted and dancing went on most of the night.

It was said of their ancestors the San Bushmen, the smallest of people who inhabited this land for many centuries, that they could fill their stomachs at one time with enough food to last them days or weeks. The Basothos love to gorge food - on the basis that it may be a lean day tomorrow.

This brings me to the 'African bottom'. Some of the Basotho women have the loveliest of feminine attributes - a shape which many men admire- rounded buttocks on which you could place a cup and saucer. Perfect for carrying babies.The life of the Bushman hunter depended on food and water. These people, before all else, were nomadic hunters.They kept no animals, did not cultivate the land and grew no food. Their lives depended on harvesting the *veld* for fruit and berries and hunting animals for meat. Nature provided the Bushman with a way of keeping a valuable reserve in his body for those days of starvation by giving him the bottom, which extended visibly in a good hunting season, rather like the hump of the camel. Laurens Van Der Post in his book about the vanished people of the Kalahari wrote:

'this loose plastic skin was 'a wise dispensation of Almighty Providence' to enable the Bushman to eat more food at one feasting than any man in the history of mankind had ever eaten before.'

Perhaps a legacy of the Bushman is the broad African beam.

As the weeks went by other pupils joined my afternoon classes. The ladies from our staff kitchen discovered that English was being taught on the camp and asked if they could come and learn. Valerie, one of the cooks, a large lady with a backside that took up two chairs, and Lydia a fifteen year old who spoke no English, asked if they could attend. Trailing along behind was a tiny child called Rose, whom Lydia looked after. Rose was her sister's child and Lydia her nursemaid. Rose was three years old, as mischievous as any other, but the first time she came to the house she sat on a stool, quietly sucking her thumb, never taking her eyes from Lydia's face.

Valerie, always wreathed in smiles, brought her own book to write in and happily copied anything down on paper, but could not read .Gradually she picked up more phrases and soon learned to say the things she wanted. She did not allow herself to speak to the others in seSotho, and made herself speak in English for the whole hour. But she never learned to read. In the seSotho language, words are generally spelt phonetically, but this did not help Valerie. She was unable to make any attempt at reading a 'cat' or a 'mat' sentence and it was obvious that English to her was like Chinese to me. When it came to the reading part of our lesson, Valerie would get up and boil a kettle of water and make strong tea for all of us. And while she was about it she would mop the floor and wash the windows. It was meant as a gesture of gratitude.

They left the house carrying much laughter into the garden with them as they went, Kaizi's pocket full of apples and the girls taking English newspapers to read. The game was to look for Princess Diana pictures – they thought she was 'very beautiful lady' - then troop off down the road back to their village, carrying all books and bags on their heads. Sometimes I drove them part of the way home to the nearest path where they climbed upwards. What they loved most was to be seen to disembark from a white lady's car. Heleyn once asked if she could be driven the whole way to her house, so that her grandmother would see her emerge. She lived on a very steep incline a good distance from the road, more suited to a pony than an engine.

The girls and Kaizi gave me personal challenges, hours of fun and entertainment, and what was far more important, an understanding of the way they lived, which I would not have learnt by staying within the confines of the camp. Most of the camp activities did not interest me, although I did enjoy a painting class which took place at Butha-Buthe with an inspiring teacher called Sue. I have her to thank for introducing me to Ray Nestor, one of the most talented water colour artists ever to paint in South Africa. When I first saw his paintings of African animals in the wild, my love affair with this vivid continent began.

The Basotho people are warm, generous and full of vitality. They are also in great need of affection. Historically they are a very young nation. They have a natural inquisitiveness about the country which protected them in times past; they are aware that England, once a large Empire, had a hand in shaping their independence. The children from the Malutis grow up with the knowlege that on the other side of the world there is a country called England which is full of white people, has a Queen called Elizabeth and is somehow connected with them. These children of the eighties recognise that when their backs were against the wall, Great Britain came to their rescue. That affiliation is still apparent.They are taught at school that England is a country which still knows them and cares, though it is from a different perspective than ours – and a reminder to us that this balance has gone a little haywire.They long to discover, to fit together the pieces of jigsaw which make up their history and help them internalise their identity.

Education had always been left to missionary schools set up by the different churches, especially the Roman Catholic denominational centres. During the 1980's the government began to take more responsibility to educate its children. Church based teacher training colleges were amalgamated into one large government institution on a national level. The National Teacher Training College placed more emphasis on teaching agriculture and commercial subjects. Technical Colleges were set up, including the one in Leribe.The Ministry of Education emphasised the need for every child to receive training in practical subjects as well as academic subjects.

In reality there are thousands of drop-outs who never have the chance to learn. The parents have to pay fees for their children to attend school and many families are too poor. Animals are integral to their way of life so many children are engaged in these tasks and looking after younger siblings. The lack of adequately trained teachers has led to overcrowded classrooms. A shortage of equipment accounts for poor quality teaching.The absence of so many men who work in the mines for years means that most young boys have herd duties for years, which accounts for the fact that the majority of pupils are girls. One of the advantages of the new schools is a mix of religious backgrounds, which has produced a better tolerance and understanding. In Lesotho, teachers' salaries are so low, that anyone with an ounce of motivation, moves to South Africa, where salaries are much more realistic.

In the cases of the children I knew, poverty was a way of life. Heleyn was one of the lucky ones because she went to Mount Royal, the Roman Catholic School and her parents were able to pay the fees, but she often went without food. She was not allowed to take part in the sports events because she had no shoes. She was an excellent sprinter, but denied a place in the team. Annacleda and Kaizi went to school more on a casual basis, when their family had a little money, with months of absenteeism in between. They have no concept of the way we live. There are few books about England in their schools and only on a rare chance would they meet or speak with an English person. Our meeting on the mountain before Christmas had been fortuitous and we were all gaining something from our new friendships.

I felt privileged. I enjoyed the company of the local kids, although noticing with growing concern, how the Afrikaners on the camp resented me teaching them. I nursed my unpopularity for a time, then, in order to demonstrate the fact that we have entered the twentieth century, decided to settle for supporting my pupils.

Never having suffered this kind of indignation before, it felt unjust and undeserved. Beyond a shadow of doubt, it was based on the legacy of apartheid. Throw in a few relevant differences between the white settlers and British imperialism and it was enough to re-open old wounds.

In future years, it may come to pass that such hatred between Afrikaners and blacks will diminish. As for myself, I had no preconception of such a dilemma other than to appreciate cultures of every race I came into contact with. In my enthusiasm to settle into the camp, I had already begun to help Afrikaner children with their language lessons, but overnight their attendance dropped to nil.

There is need of healing, forgiveness and reconciliation, but I as a visitor to their country had no right to interfere. I was in their eyes a double enemy, having ancestors who took part in the Boer War one hundred years ago, which explained in some part, why I felt such a cool breeze. This alienation felt like a remnant of historical grievance best buried and forgotten. The main issue was that the Basotho children did nothing to deserve my rejection and it was questionable whether they would have understood my reasons. I continued to teach.

It seemed natural for Lesotho to become a monarchy, following the example of the British monarchy for more than a century. In some ways, Basutoland was better prepared for Independence than were many other African states.

In 1965, Basutoland suffered the worst drought for thirty years. The fight for political power in the months before the elections was so bitter that Britain sent troops to keep the peace. Chief Jonathan, heading the National Party, came to London for a second round of talks with the British Government.

The British were convinced that Chief Jonathan's government was strong enough to represent the Basotho fairly and approved the new Constitution. They may be poor, but the people of Lesotho are extremely self reliant and proud of their ability to remain a black nation politically, independent of white controlled governments. For the first time, women were allowed to vote in the 1965 elections. The women's vote was thought to be decisive as many males worked out of the country in South Africa.

The Election lasted two days. More than ninety per cent of the people went to the polls, many of whom could not read. Each party was identified on the ballot paper by a symbol. National Party were represented by the picture of a cow, the Congress Party by a knobkerrie, the Freedom Party by an elephant and the Labour Party by an open hand. The BNP won by a narrow majority. The Pre–independence Constitution declared that the leader of the winning party in the National Assembly would become Prime Minister.

The actual transition to Independence did not cause a disruptive crisis. There was no question of blacks suddenly being faced with running a country which whites had controlled completely. On the night of October 3rd, 1966, the British flag was lowered for the last time in Basutoland. The next morning, the Kingdom of Lesotho was born. Thousands of people watched the official ceremonies in Maseru. Queen Elizabeth was represented by the Duchess of Kent. Moshoeshoe II became the nation's first King and Chief Jonathan its first Prime Minister.

Post independence, Lesotho still upholds some of its old traditions. In addition to a seSotho name, every child is baptised with an English name. As they grow up, children are encouraged to sing and dance. Their schools, although poor in the academic sense, have an attractive institution of music. Musical activities play an important role in domestic and social life and singing is an integral part of their lives. Many schools have talented choirs which perform religious and choral music and no village celebration is complete without a show of traditional songs and dances. Sometimes it will be for the rain or the harvest or even to bring contentment to grazing cattle. The Basotho people love to express themselves with songs about their work, their games, initiation ceremonies or to celebrate a new birth.

A bride on her wedding day is involved in a long and complex series of customs and festivities involving music.On the wedding day, the cattle which the bridegroom is giving to the bride's family nowadays called *Lobola*, is driven from the man's village to his bride's village. After the animals have been inspected to see that they are in good health in accordance with arrangements made beforehand, the bride's father produces the *tlhabiso* - the beast which is to be slaughtered for the wedding feast. This is an important moment in the ceremony. Then the celebrations truly begin and both sets of relatives wearing traditionally decorative clothes, perform wedding dance accompanied by songs. The wedding feast can go on for twenty four hours or more and is usually followed by a second feast in the bridegroom's village, at which the bride's relatives are entertained. After this the guests attend a marriage blessing in the church.

A bride on her wedding day must never smile. To do so would be regarded as showing gladness that she is leaving her parents and is disrespectful. Usually the bride returns for a few days to her own village to prepare her trousseau of clothes and domestic utensils. Relatives then accompany her to the house provided by her father-in-law, where she will live with her new husband. After she becomes a wife, she must wear her skirts below the knee and use a new name, given by her father-in-law, in anticipation of her first-born.

In the situation that a boy wants to marry and his parents disapprove, he will wait until he can enter his girl's house and snatch her away from her family. This is mainly because he cannot afford his *Lobola*. Some couples elope like this but are never able to return to the girl's family as man and wife, unless they go to see a priest and ask for forgiveness. This brings retribution down on the head of the husband and he will have to suffer a long period of punishment before he can be accepted wholly into his wife's family. It is seen as unsocial behaviour of the worst kind.

Betty came to work for us on Tuesdays and Thursdays. She walked from her home, after taking Margaret to be looked after by a young nursemaid and arrived about ten o'clock in time for breakfast. She had worked on the camp since the project began in 1991 and valued her job highly. Now that she was pregnant again, she still wanted to carry on working. She was sensible enough to attend the clinic at Leribe hospital to make sure that her health was all right and on those days she would sit for a whole day in a long hot queue and come out with a headache and a card with a stamp on it. I hesitate to call them anti-natal clinics because the mothers were not informed about anything to do with the birth of their babies. Betty seemed very anxious about this and used to ask me the most surprising questions.

"How will my baby come out? Will my baby come by itself? Will the nurses shout at me?" Betty already had three children and it was to my amazement that she seemed to know so little about the actual birth. She was obviously confused and worried about the forthcoming event. I took her to see Liliane, who was a qualified midwife. Betty explained that the nurses in the hospital had shouted at her for crying out in pain and she did not understand why they treated her in this way, but she wanted to know what it was they wanted her to do. She gave us a graphic description of an angry nurse standing over a woman in labour. The memories of her previous births were already causing her distress and she had absolutely no understanding of would happen to her body.

Liliane was horrified. She told Betty that she would make many explanations during the coming months and help her to understand the things she had not been told. Both Liliane and I were appalled that such a thing could happen and could only guess at the psychological condition of other patients if they had understood as little as Betty.

After several 'talkie talkie' sessions between the two of them, Betty declared, " 'M'e, I am heppy now. I am not frightened of going into the hospital when de time comes."

She still didn't know how many moons to go before the baby would arrive and Liliane guessed it would perhaps be late April or early May. We could only wait and see.

If Betty was anxious about the baby in her life she was draconian when it came to the hoovering. Heedless of chairs and tables, she tore into the vacuum cleaning routine like a charging rhino. Her over enthusiastic polishing we didn't mind until we discovered that the brass had been worn down to the base metal on our wall lamps. She went through Brasso like tubs of ice-cream. She knew that white people liked shiny polished surfaces and in her determination to please me she rubbed hard on the dining room table until it shone like glass, no matter what there was lying on it.

It was clear that Betty couldn't appreciate our interest in paperwork. Why should she? Letters are not delivered to the little tin houses in a township, nor does life revolve around electricity bills, car insurance, income tax or bank statements. Lesotho has no printing industry, newspapers, printed handouts or postmen. Anyone who wants to receive letters has to have a Post Office box with a key and pick up their mail personally.

With great enthusiasm, Betty cleared the dining room table in one, reduced all our bits of paper to a single pile - not essentially in date order - and put it away tidily in some hidden place. What she tidied up on Thursdays, usually stayed hidden until the following week.

We had a large lounge and a long wide hallway with five doors off, which were the two bathrooms and three bedrooms.Once Betty was harnessed to the vacuum cleaner, conversation was impossible for twenty minutes, while furniture legs crashed and door bottoms pleaded for mercy.

Hell bent on cleaning every speck of dust from every inch of floor, she commandeered her way down the hallway as in pitched battle with the enemy. If I dared to stick my neck out of the room where I had been quietly typing a letter, the hoover would fly past me with Betty at the helm, intrepid and unshakable, as if on course for a championship medal.

One morning, prepared for this onslaught, I locked myself in the bathroom with Frank Sinatra and Billie Holliday. It was the planned day for the hair rinse and for sitting on the bath covered only in a polythene bag and a towel. I heard the hoover go on and carefully poured the two little bottles together. The instruction leaflet read, 'Always use immediately after mixing.' Poised with the towel round my shoulders, I heard the hoover go off. There was an ominous silence. Then I heard Betty shout,

"'M'e, 'M'e, de snake has jumped into de vacuum cleaner!"

I was out in the hallway in an instant, wrapped only in a pair of shorts and a towel, shouting to Betty,

"Don't move, I'll go and get Petros!"

I ran down the dirt road yelling for Petros, who wasn't far away. He very quickly caught the panic in my voice and ran towards the house.

"What is de matter, 'M'e? Is it an accident?"

Inside the house, Betty had retreated into the bedroom and shouted something to Petros in seSotho, which I couldn't understand, while he picked up the cylinder carefully and we both peered into the bag of matted fluff.

"Betty says there is a snake inside this thing," I said quickly, unsure of what to do next. Petros took a small stick from the garden and then approached the open end of the cleaner. Then he broke into a huge grin, with his white teeth showing perfectly against his black skin, as he pulled something shrivelled and brown out of the tangled mass of hair and muck.

It was Barrie's best silk tie.

The rest of my day was spent in trying to reshape and wash the only bit of Christian Dior we had brought with us from London to the point where Barrie wouldn't notice, while the bottle of natural bright auburn fizzed into nothingness and Sinatra sang to himself in the bathroom.

Betty carried on undaunted. She finished tidying our paperwork into a neat pile, retired to the garden to hose down the verandah table, then tied the unwilling Hercule to the washing line and hosed him down too, collected her wages and left. That evening, there was a slight blip in domestic harmony as Barrie tried to find his half completed letter to the Inland Revenue, which by then had been filed between the re-direction correspondence from British Telecom and the letters from the bank. While he stomped around trying to guess which room it was in, I breathed a sigh of relief he wasn't going out in a suit.

With the house so often full of students and Betty, I would welcome the days when the kombi arrived at 8.00am to take the ladies to shop for groceries in Bethlehem. There were no supplies on the camp and we had to buy our food in bulk. Sam was in charge of driving the ladies safely there and back through the border post to buy our stocks of food

It was already quite hot, when we set off and it would get much hotter throughout the day. It was 96 kilometres to Bethlehem. Sam counted the ladies and the cool boxes aboard and we bumped off down the road with sunglasses and hats, bottles of water and very long lists.

On one particular trip to Bethlehem, we were three ladies: Noi, Liliane and myself. This meant that we numbered four different nationalities, speaking possibly 12 languages between us. Sam spoke seSotho, Zulu, Afrikaans and English; Noi, Thai and English, and Liliane, some six or seven languages, but predominantly French. That left me - with only one language. It was fruitless to try to remember my schoolgirl French, so as usual we chatted away in English which was very feeble of me.

The road to the border meandered through the scattered villages and we passed through a police road block about 2 kilometres from home.The military police were always in smart uniforms and hats, but they must have been sweltering out on the road under the hot sun, for hour after hour. There was never a problem with our vehicles as the company always looked after them, but there were always tired, rusty looking cars, with bent bumpers and ravaged bodywork, pulled up by the side of the road. Many owners could not afford to make repairs; they would drive their vehicles until they dropped apart and then push the lifeless carcasses into the nearest donga and leave them to rot down into the soil. Next season's rains would drag them further into the ditch and in a couple of years, they would disappear from the landscape altogether. No road in Lesotho is complete without the skeletons of old vehicles showing through the vegetation like rusty teeth.

My favourite part of the journey was a few kilometres west of Butha-Buthe, where the mountains were shaped like a huge canyon, with high rocky caverns and stretches of evergreen forests below. The exposed parts of the rock, where the soil had eroded away with many years of rain, shone in the sun like gun metal and from a distance looked like a series of waterfalls. From the road there was a marvellous panoramic view of the whole amphitheatre and you could imagine how, millions of years ago, it was a dinosaurs' playground. Fossil footprints occur in many places in Lesotho and many kinds of tracks have been found dating back to the Triassic period. Sam told us that this was one of the few places in the world where dinosaur fossils have been found in abundance.

Today the mealie crop looked a healthy dark green. Now waist high, it would provide the main food for the people next harvest. Rows of women worked with rakes and hoes to weed between the lines, their colourful scarves scattered like confetti across the green landscape. As we passed through one village, sitting by the side of the road was a group of girls, with white clay smeared on their faces.They wore beaded tunics and were decorated with bracelets on their ankles and upper arms. They held forked sticks in their hands. Next to them sat the *Sangoma,* who was obviously in charge. She was highly decorated with beads and a kind of headdress.

"Those are the girls who are going to the Initiation School, known in Lesotho as *Bale.*" Sam spoke softly, as though relating something special. "They will leave their villages soon to go and live in a special house up on the mountain, where they'll receive traditional education for about four or five weeks and learn what is expected of them in womanhood. You'll see them next year when they come back and they'll dress in cow hide skirts and cover their bodies in ochre. When they graduate they will be called '*litsoejane*' "

Traditional education is a closely guarded secret and seSotho law imposes a fine of one head of cattle on anyone who reveals initiation secrets. In addition, there are severe penalties for anyone who tries to approach these schools while they are in progress. After they have been to Initiation School, the girls get married soon afterwards, often about the age of fifteen or sixteen.

It seemed strange to be setting out on a shopping expedition and to learn so much about the historical and traditional life of Lesotho. Sam was well informed and knew his country well. He always let us stop and take photographs along the way. I loved travelling this road to Bethlehem.

On the South African side of the border, the verge was lined with stalls, people squatting behind piles of fruit, mothers sitting on blankets feeding their babies, small fires smoking between the stalls, and a never ending sea of bananas. This was where the local people came to sell and gossip.Their only shade was a few strips of polythene slung between sticks of wood and the odd plastic sheet tied to the fence.

By the time we arrived in Bethlehem, it was just after 9.00am. The big broad streets were busy with traffic, mostly cars and a few open trucks and jeeps. Sam drove slowly through the *robots*, their name for traffic lights, and headed first to the dental practice. I had my first appointment with a South African dentist that day.

It was a relief to go indoors to an air-conditioned room, after being in the hot vehicle, into the cool clean interior of the patients waiting area. The receptionists looked like fashion models straight from the catwalks of Paris. Groomed to perfection, their movements were stiff and they used the keyboard as though they had jam on their fingers.

"I have come for my appointment." I said, in English - with a smile. I felt a cold draught on my neck. Miss Star Wars answered in Afrikaans through a glass screen.

"Wat is u naam?" My face tingled with embarrassment as I had to ask her to repeat the sentence. My first brush with something I could not quite understand.

"Kom sit asseblief." She instantly wrote me off and without so much as a glance banished me to the corner of the scrubbed waiting room. I listened for my name to be called, while other clients were received in clipped tones, " *Goeiemore, Mevrou. Hoe gaan dit met u?"*

"Uitstekend."

I tried to pretend I wasn't there. Something to do with the psychology of rejection. Once in the dentist's chair, with my mouth open, looking at the pristine white gloss ceiling, I was a prisoner of hygiene and cleanliness. The smell of disinfectant jammed itself up my nostrils. In perfect English, the dentist asked me what the problem was and then proceeded to speak rapidly in Afrikaans to his lady assistant in her white cardboard coat, two inches away from my ear, while ramming a tuning fork into my upper palate. Perhaps they were discussing what was on television last night. Or they might have been planning a romantic assignation. The fact was that they were excluding me from vital denture information. I didn't learn anything about my aching tooth. It was excruciating enough having a gloved hand holding my jaws apart, without having to listen to another language and not being able to understand a word. It was more than rudeness - a sure test of anyone's patience. Relieved to find myself ejected swiftly into the horizontal knee lock position, packet of dental floss in one hand, appointment card in the other, I tried to accept the notion of social integration with good grace.

At reception, the cardboard smile wished me, *"Goeiemiddag, Mevrou."*

For whatever reason, the tone was noticeably unfriendly. There were some crosscurrents here which were baffling. Later I discovered their bills were astronomical.

Back in the kombi with Sam and the girls, the next stop was the Pick 'n Pay arcade, which sold just about everything. This was the hi-tech centre of the town where a seething throng of ladies drove their trolleys; the metropolis of supermarkets and the best value in town. After living out in the mountains on a camp, it was shopping heaven. Here we found fashionble clothes in the Woolworth store, a good pharmacy, safari suits and hunting hats in the equivalent of an English camping shop, presents from Africa to send home, a high class jeweller, a hairdresser, an optician and the Pick 'n Pay food store itself. A cinema lived on the upper deck and for ten rands you could choose from two movie theatres and have a meal afterwards at the restaurant.

The supermarket was smart and clean, the staff friendly and helpful. Once one was used to the different brands, shopping was fun. Labelling was in two languages. It was fascinating to try the different vegetables, the sweet potatoes and many kinds of pumpkins. Rows of huge dark green bulbous heads of uglies, covered in wart-like bumps, stared at us from the high shelves and yellow pear shaped things which tasted like parsnips beckoned the curious shopper like me. Asparagus came in armfuls and beetroot in huge dangling stalks. Eveything which was pulled from the ground came with a barrowload of muck clinging to it; gritty giant lettuces and cabbages as big as footballs: mangoes-large, pink and very cheap, sold in boxes of ten; papayas the colour of honey in mountainous heaps from floor to ceiling. The luscious smell of pineapples, full flavoured and ripe, seduced my nostrils and I bought seven - one for every day of the week.

As it was Friday, we had missed the cheeseboat. Had it been a Thursday we may have been lucky. If by some slim chance, a carton of brie had been left behind by the cheese-eaters of Bethlehem on a delivery day, it might be there hiding underneath the pile of *biltong* - the Afrikaners' choice delicacy, of which they never tire. Biltong is meat - which has been hung for a long time, dried and smoked until unrecognisable as either edible or tasty. It comes in wiggly brown strips and is sold by the mountain.

South Africans eat biltong when they are drinking, driving, camping in the bush, shouting for their favourite team or having a pee. They are weaned on biltong from babyhood - like tobacco it is ritualistic and addictive. Its tasteless texture is known to have kept whole armies from starvation in the trenches and is regarded as the equivalent of English bully beef without a tin. There would be a major slump in South Africa if biltong eaters stopped chewing it, though an increase in cheese production might help to stabilize the economy.

The first time I shopped at Pick 'n Pay, I asked at the counter for stilton cheese. The blank stare of the girl gave me the answer I did not wish to know. With dread, I knew that it meant no stilton until I reached the Northern hemisphere, at the very least. Neither was there a chance of creamy camembert or delicate dolcelate to round off a good meal. I hadn't bargained on feeling so many withdrawal symptoms for bog standard cheddar mousetrap and the tasty thought of wensleydale was simply a pipedream. Cheese to an Afrikaner is the equivalent of garlic to an Englishman. To a Frenchman, the South African cheese counter may well be the cause of his nervous breakdown.

On the meat counter, lay giant coils of rust coloured sausages, (*boerewors*), huge pieces of beef, and burgers of every shape and size. Chilled meat came in enormous chunks or thick slices, ready to throw on the braai. There was nothing small about a South African appetite for meat. In the interests of national pride, they remain a doggedly non–vegetarian race. The charcoal braai is their most popular way of eating. Beef and pork are consumed in enormous quantities indicated by the rows of deep freezers enough to fill a football stadium. No cheese.

The shelves were full of maize flour products and dried beans of every imaginable variety. These were the ingredients which the black families bought. The ladies piled their trolleys high with Jungle Oats, cereals and large family- sized packets of maize products, placing their stocks of soap, candles and mothballs on top. They purchased pumpkins and groundnuts, bottles of cooking oil, sometimes rice and sometimes eggs, never luxury food. Living without electricity means a different kind of shopping list, limited choices and walking quickly past the frozen food section. A chicken with feathers on would be far more attractive.

After a satisfactory tour round the South African wine section, I hit a tricky problem. No wine was allowed into Lesotho without import duty. I trollied off to find Liliane to ask her what I should do, as my shopping list included two white and two red. A 60th celebration loomed and the cellar at the Glenns was empty.

"Don't worry about one or two bottles of wine, we'll hide them in the boot underneath the food. The duty guard probably won't look. If we get caught, the bottles will be confiscated and the guards will throw a party."

All this made shopping much more of an adventure than a trip to the labyrinth of concrete car parks in Bromley or dealing with broken ticket machines and cowboy clamping. Carparks were free but you were expected to pay a few coins to the touts who offered to 'look after your car' while you went inside.

Travelling ninety six kilometres through the mountains in the baking hot sun, hiding four bottles of Stellenbosch and two dozen eggs under the seat and getting through the border without being searched or hi-jacked, was a tempting challenge. Not only that, Sam had a good day out with the ladies and a free lunch, we had a running commentary on the landscape and a headbanging afternoon of Radio Africa.

If this was to be my weekly shopping trip, I could face life without stilton and Barrie would have to change his habit of a lifetime and eat Weetabix instead of Shredded Wheat, as there was none to be had anywhere. I might even try him with biltong for breakfast. If we could get through the border without being searched, the bottles from the Cape vineyards should be more than enough to compensate. My toothache had almost disappeared.

Chapter 16

Priscilla and the Buffalo

One afternoon in Leribe our phone rang. That was most unusual. Our phone line had been down for about three weeks. It was a pleasant surprise to hear Priscilla's lively American drawl.

"Now come on you two Yorkshire guys, when are you going to come with me into the bush, the real thing I mean. Not your glossy hotel by the sea. Yea, I know you liked swimming with the sharks in Durban - but there's more to South Africa than a canned beach party!"

I told her about our trip to Umhlanga. Apart from us both peeling off layers of skin from head to toe afterwards, Umhlanga had been a fabulous experience, but Priscilla was right. We had not seen so much as a hair of a hippo.

"Come on you two, get with the real Africa now! Camp out in the bush and listen to the lions roar at night. It'll be hot - you'll soon get used to the mozzies! Stand up to your knees in rhino shit and you will know what excitement is! Now go tell Barrie to buy a pair of binoculars and a bush hat!"

She stopped mid-track and laughed uproariously at the thought of us all standing up to our knees in dungheaps.

"I'll go book us in at Hluhluwe - you pronounce that 'Shushlooie', it's a Zulu word. It is the sister camp to Umfolozi Reserve, 280 kilometres North of Durban. It's one of South Africa's oldest game reserves - famous for its herds of black and white rhino. In the park they have the 'big six', you might see them all."

I stalled a little.

"Will we be on foot ?"

The thought of being in close proximity to a wild animal really unnerved me. My idea of game viewing was through the bars of a cage at London Zoo. My feelings of discomfort were enough to send me searching for my last valium pill .To Priscilla, camping out in the bush was an affaire of the heart. She would sooner spend three weeks in the bush with the elephants, than be turned to a crisp on a sunny beach in Hawaii. Her American soul had become an African spirit. She had bombarded us with tales of bush camps, nature trails and wildlife encounters, both in Kenya and in South Africa. Her experiences in the Umfolozi Reserves in Northern Zululand were many and varied and her stories of hyenas coming down to drink at the river and stealing the Sunday roast were nothing short of a filmscript.

Seduced by the idea of seeing real animals in the wild, we agreed to spend our last few days holiday at the Hluhluwe Reserve with Priscilla and one of her sons, before flying home to England for Christmas.

Priscilla's phone call was followed by one of her crazy letters containing a strategic route map to St Lucia estuary, a visitor's information sheet and a long list of things to bring. The sheet was scrawled with ridiculous pictures of paragliding lions and a buffalo in Biggles glasses.

'Pack as if you are going to scout camp. Bring everything except the sink. We will be sleeping in rondavels, very cheap - plates, pillows and a fridge provided, but extremely basic.You'll have a mattress, but bring your own towels. No running water, no plumbing, no toilet. Bring plenty of insect repellent, flea powder, gallons of sun cream, water bottles, ice packs and a barrel of ice cubes for the journey - and don't forget the peejamas. You need as many ice boxes as you can find, one for food, the others for ice.'

Bring a potty and a torch if you don't like the idea of bumping into baby zebra on the trek to the ablution block in the middle of the night. That's all really, apart from hats, sunglasses and long socks to stop the ticks from biting your ankles.' Finally, she signed it with a dancing elephant brushing his teeth and on the back of the envelope, a swarm of mosquitoes blowing kisses.

Our Doctor advised that as we were only going for a few days, malaria tablets were unnecessary in this part of South Africa and risks too low to worry about. As long as we drank bottled water and used sensible insect bite precautions, there should be no problem.

We left on the morning of 30th November, Lizzie's twenty third birthday. What would any daughter have thought of her mother going off into the bush for the weekend carrying 'Predators of the Wild', (bedtime reading) in one hand and a large can of 'Peaceful Sleep' in the other. Wearing his Baden Powell hat, khaki shorts and a pair of designer sunglasses, Barrie was already on safari. He whistled as he loaded the boot of the car with ice boxes and we waved goodbye to the guards on duty at the camp gate. Would attempts be made to search for missing engineers, come next Tuesday morning and we were still not back?

Priscilla's written instructions were quite accurate - apart from her timing. The journey should take six hours. It took us nine and a half. We were the ultimate dignified English couple, used to Constable country, cycle tracks and tea shop routes, now flirting with the subtropical jungle and the African bush. The scale of our adventure in our minds compared with the crusades of King Shaka himself.

The first eight hours of our journey were uneventful. We had embarked upon this prestigious venture almost impetuously, armed to the teeth with tick powder and spare toilet rolls, but unwisely ignorant of the all-in wrestling techniques of the black rhino, should we chance to come across one in our path. The rhino is extremely shortsighted and you must always stay down-wind of him to avoid an attack, but how did you know what was down and what was up when it came to meeting one in the bush?

We took the Bethlehem-Harrismith route and then headed east into Kwa Zulu Natal, passing through Glencoe and Dundee (named after an early settler from Scotland), and on past the historic battle sites. Terrible clashes between Boers and Zulus over land and freedom, power struggles between Boers and British, makes this part of South Africa notably fascinating. This journey offered me an opportunity to piece together my understanding of South Africa with a little more definition, now that I had witnessed the battle fields where English soldiers ranked among the war dead, in this far graveyard.

The scenery was breathtaking; long straight roads and steep sided valleys - so far down you couldn't see the bottom. Hillsides rich and green, open thornveld and distant crags, showed South Africa at the height of it's most beautiful season. Between acacia and thorn, we caught glimpses of brilliant coloured birds. Flowering cana, flamed red and ochre. Wild ostriches appeared near the road grazing in grey feathery groups and in the hot afternoon, a group of baboons played by a gushing stream. In mountain grassland, patches of red hot pokers shone a deep orange, where hawks fluttered high above the ground, searching for one single movement below.

About 40 kilometres before we reached Hluhluwe Camp, our instructions read 'take the dirt road off the Magudu road- this is a short cut to main road -it should save you about one hour' In South Africa, there are thousands of miles of good dirt roads that are indicated on the map by white lines and are well used by motorists and often cut hours off a long tarmac route.

At that time in the late afternoon, the Monet skies were a mixture of deep aquamarine and purple. The flat tops of the acacia trees were almost in silhouette, unyielding and resolute, their short branches locking into position to prevent the sunlight hitting the ground beneath. No image of Africa is complete without these thorny characters; their shade dark and undiminished beneath the thickness of their thatch.

The air was still and heavy and we were both feeling tired. As we took to the dirt road, the open panoramic views of the mountains changed almost at once into a narrow avenue of tightly woven thorn bushes. Once inside the forest, the trees seemed to arch closer together and grew much taller, searching for the light. Splinters of sunlight shafted down here and there between the trees, but soon disappeared altogether as we became surrounded with thick forest gloom. It seemed as if we were being sucked into mile after mile of dark green undergrowth, like an endless green nave.

Depressing thought – it could be one of Priscilla's jokes. It was twenty minutes since we had turned onto this road and not a single signpost indicated where the track led. As we drove deeper into the dejected darkness, we began to wonder if we had missed a road. A strange cloistered ride without a familiar landmark, there was nothing but fluttering birds which burst from the forest and flew up in front of us - and the dusty track ahead. The absence of sound made us nervous.

Barrie increased the speed of the car and now we were hurtling along, bumping on the gritty surface, trying not to worry about a breakdown or whether the R.A.C. Recovery Service would be able to find us. Neither of us voiced our thoughts. We had come too far to turn back. The silence strangled us. My stomach felt knotted and sick with tension.

Twenty five minutes after we had started out on the dirt road, a barely readable sign, saying '35 kms' appeared out of the darkness.This was the distance we had travelled on our 'short cut.' Quite an experience for two rather naive *uitlanders* with nine hours on the clock. We still had a lot to learn about Africa.

We drove onto the verge and stopped, to recover our composure. Barrie looked at his watch.

"Five o'clock. We have about one hour to find the entrance to Hluhluwe Camp and Priscilla before it gets dark. Lets go."

Thirty minutes later, we were driving into the Reception Lodge at Hluhluwe and slid to a halt on the gravel drive. A ranger in a dark green uniform smiled welcome and offered to book us in. It was bliss to get out of the car and stretch our legs. Barrie disappeared inside the gatehouse to show papers and a few minutes passed while I began to read the blurb on the information sheet we had brought with us. My eyes fixed on the warning at the top. 'Please note that all wild animals are potentially dangerous and that there are no fences surrounding any of the camps except Hilltop. Visitors are advised not to walk around after dark and should this be absolutely necessary visitors should make use of a torch.'

'Amazing device, the torch' I thought to myself, not over impressed with the idea of elephant and torch meeting in the dark. I happened to look up at that moment and, as if from nowhere, a young Zulu girl stepped in front of the car, clutching a loaf of bread in a plastic wrapper. She stood and looked at me. Dressed in a turquoise blue dress with the same coloured beads around her neck, she appeared so petite and so pretty. I was spellbound. Somehow I expected her to be carrying a spear or a dead pig- even an earthenware pot would have seemed more normal. Having a polite regard for proper social greetings - this delicate meeting left me completely speechless. Standing face to face with a smiling Zulu child for the first time in my life drew on all my discretionary reserves. I bent forward.

"What is your name?" I asked softly, and held out my hand. She took hold of my fingers gently and then very quietly, almost in a whisper, she spoke in perfect English, "my name is Sinquina."

"Sinquina, do you mind if I take a picture of you?"

I was seized with such excitement for the moment and knew if I didn't have a photograph I would not have believed it had happened. Sinquina stood by the car, her shaven sculptured head very still, in front of the camera. Taking some sweets from the car I gave them to her. She waved goodbye, the sliced loaf still securely tucked under her arm.

I had no time to reflect on my charming encounter before Barrie reappeared with full passes for us to enter the reserve and a note from Priscilla addressed to us, written in her large flowery hand.

'Hi you two - Where the hell have you been? Just pouring my first gin and tonic. Hurry up and find Rondavel 64 - it's 2.30pm. Love Priscilla'.

As we passed underneath the barrier, the ranger in khaki with a gun on his shoulder, leaned over and addressed us clearly.

"Keep your windows up and don't get out of your car."

Our excitement level soared. 96,000 hectares and we were on hectare number one. We felt that thrilling moment that penetrates your whole being; the uncertainty of not knowing what we would see next. Nervously, we drove into the setting sun.

It's when you see your very first zebra that you believe. Not more than ten yards away from us, silently grazing - a harem of zebra; a stallion, mares, foals - with dainty hoofs and swishing tails. As they nuzzled the undergrowth, quite unaware that we were close, several baby springbok arrived to stare; tiny brown creatures with stripey white marks on their behinds. Leggy statues, they held still for a blink of a moment – as if awaiting the conductor with his baton, then leapt on puppet strings into the trees and were gone.

Tears sprang to my eyes. Suddenly, I loved Africa even more. Animals only ever seen in the pages of childhood picture books truly existed. The mystique of the bush had become a reality. I was aware of a strange quality -an intensity, a smell that couldn't be defined – or could it have been the heat coming from the earth.

Look Nettie, something in the trees!" Barrie pointed at something up on the higher ground. He had experienced the same rush of blood to the head.

Several buffalo, perhaps ten in number, each carrying a hundredweight of heavy curled horn, stood engraved in the twilight beside the great rock. They trod like noble warriors on the prowl. I gazed transfixed by their sheer size and weight; each one of them a figure of stone, rising out of the burnt dry bracken that broke around them. It was beginning to grow dark and we still had a long way to go.

Game reserves have miles of roads leading through the bush, and as long as you are in a vehicle, you are probably quite safe, though to be complacent would be a mistake in any rule book. We headed off in the direction of Hilltop Camp.The trees stood in sillouette; creepers twisted and gnarled, hung from rocky places forming a canopy over our heads. Everything was waiting for nightfall.

Neither of us spoke during our journey, with the sun going down in the wilderness and many hidden eyes watching. We held hands tightly. My heartbeat hurtled into overdrive. How could I ever recapture this moment when I was back in England? I longed to store away the vital element so that it belonged in my memory forever.

Hilltop Reception loomed up in lights - a romantic oasis with verandah and palms, men in khaki shorts and long socks and delightful black girls in smart hats. I was quite relieved to hear a telephone bell. A sign on the ramp said, 'Electric fence around the compound'. It was heartwarming to a Yorkshire girl with nerves like jelly.

We drove very slowly round all the dimly lit rondavels - shapes well known by now. Groups of people appeared out of the dusk, preparing food on their fires, arranging chairs and bottles of wine in readiness for evening suppers. Wood-smoke filled the air - delicious on a fine tropical evening. Cicadas had started their nightly shrieking and sounds of bull frogs belched from dark ponds.

At number 63, there was a long table set with chairs, white china plates arranged beautifully, wine glasses prepared, and in the middle, an elegant silver candleabra with candles lit. The stars were out and the whole sky twinkled. Priscilla, wearing a large bush hat, was sitting by the fire smoking a cigarette.

Destinations nine and a half hours from home, make for grand arrivals and our reception was rowdy and affectionate. We had survived bush, storm and wild animals and arrived in time for supper. Michael and his young friend Shaun, a level headed boy of about seventeen, were thoroughly enjoying outdoor cooking and when the meal followed a while later, ate like starving gladiators.

Our spirits rose up out of the fire, the bottles of wine, the candles and the tales of our travels. Pricilla's drink was toppling with ice, in a glass the size of a goldfish bowl. Our adventures grew tipsy with pink champagne and I told how a Zulu girl had stood naked in the path of our car on the road to Mkuze and almost caused an accident - to Barrie's glasses. Our meal was animated and hilarious, punctuated by Michael turning another steak on the braai, and moths the size of bats hitting the white linen tablecloth.

We were lit up by the excitement of tomorrow. Should we go hippo watching or do a game drive to Nqabatheki viewing site or embark on a guided walk with a foot ranger?

"What shall we do first?" I asked after the meal was over. Barrie wasn't listening. He was already inside Number 63 trying to find the light switch - there wasn't one.

"Where's the toilet?" he shouted from inside a pitch black hut.

"There isn't one," called Priscilla, "It's about thirty yards away in a building that looks like a toilet. Mind the dung beetles!" She blew out the candles and rapidly threw all the washing up into an empty bowl, while I went in search of my torchless man in the dark, treading carefully across the grass and feeling winged beetles catch my hair.

We slept our first night in the bush like two dead men. We heard no lions that night. Nor the in-house zebra who grazed in the moonlight on the grass outside our door. Complete exhaustion saved us from unpleasant encounters with surrounding cockroaches, zebra spoor and creepy crawlies. The ablution block, when we did find it, was purposeful and clean, as long as you didn't mind stepping over a few flat leathery beetles on the concrete floors in your sandals. Sinks and loos were quite adequate and the luxury of a shower felt immoral in the bush.

By eight o'clock the following morning, Priscilla, was up cooking bush breakfast. wearing a baggy shirt and Michael's giant sized boots. I looked out of our stable door and smelled bacon frying. Last night's dinner party looked like a dead bonfire. Shaun and Michael pitched up looking lively, sporting designer stubble, baseball caps and shades on strings round their necks, announcing they were going on a bush drive there and then. Priscilla, marshalling Weetabix packets onto the table, alongside empty champagne bottles, poured herself a large glass of orange juice and sat down on a chair to enjoy the first cigarette of the day.

"Michael, be careful with that truck. I don't want you coming back with paw marks on the bonnet. Just drive carefully."

The day was bright and warm. Waking up in the bush was a whole new craft. Surrounded by terrain of bright green foliage our hut of reed and thatch looked primitive enough. 'Chez Nous' was basic and comfortable with an electric kettle the only luxury. My jet lagged Englishman was still asleep as the two youngsters set out in the truck to find hippo breakfasting in a swamp. Priscilla and I had a quick stock-take of ice cubes, food and tick powder as we prepared for a day of game viewing and bush walks. I went to wake Barrie, to find our hut filled with huge insects, like floating seaweed on bicycles.They pedalled past my head and I flung them aside irritably then realized they were coming at me in swarms, through open windows. Me and mating hornets didn't like each other much.

"Get out! Get out!" I shrieked, ducking and diving with a rolled-up newspaper in my hand. All offending winged creatures just floated upwards into the thatch and sat waiting for another chance to get into gear, buzzing and gyrating in insect heaven.

From the sleeping quarters, an unshaven face peered out.

"For heavens's sake, they're only hornets. Nettie they live here."

After an open air breakfast, a vicious cold shower and the return of two adolescent bush rangers who had seen one warthog doing not very much, we gathered all cohorts into the truck ready for action. Priscilla was in the front with emergency supplies of canned drinks, ice cubes, sandwiches, mosquito spray, first aid, spare shoes, water bottles and hats; on the seat were maps, books on hippo watching, binoculars and gin. She never went anywhere without this huge basket of 'spares'. Her big bush hat spoke volumes about her character and her frequent laughter was most infectious.

The rest of the platoon were rolling around in the back of the truck, covered in sunblock and trying to hold binoculars while hanging on to the sides. What we thought was 11.30am soon became 12.30pm. Only mad dogs and Englishmen think they will see a mid-day elephant going for a stroll. We did see lots of zebra, impala and springbok, but no swimming hippo or slinking leopard. The truck lurched and rolled along the baked mud sides of the river bed as we took in the crocodile pool and the hippo hacienda at Nzimane Loop.

We were all extremely hot. All other sensible creatures had surrendered to the coolness at the bottom of the lake. However, it was our first experience in the bush and had been enough to whet our appetites. This afternoon we were ready to tackle a guided bush walk with an experienced ranger. I was prepared to be a territorial foot soldier and demonstrate coventional female fortitude, provided we could have a gallon of water to drink between now and then. Priscilla laughed and took out a huge water barrel from under the seat.

"It's okay to drink" she said, "it's only three parts gin."

"Let's go back to base camp and the hornet's nest, then get ready," said Barrie jokingly, " we can book a walk for three o'clock. and that should be the time of day to see more animals. We'll have time for a cup of tea before we leave."

"Tea!! What's the matter, are you ill?"

The bush hat tilted back and our host rammed the gears of the truck into reverse. We turned and skirted the southern edge of Mbhombe Forest, en route to Hilltop. Michael and Shaun bucked and reared about having to go on the walk with us, in adolescent fury, but conceded the point when Priscilla said they could drive the truck as far as the compound where we would meet up with the ranger. Michael regained his composure and we put him in charge of tick powder and First Aid.

Hluhluwe Reserve is home to 84 mammal species and 350 varieties of bird. Apart from Hilltop, none of the other rest camps are fenced off, so by deduction, we would be sure to see some of the wildlife as animals wandered freely through the jungly forest.

At the appointed hour, our regiment assembled. Barrie with socks tucked into trousers, strong walking boots, binoculars and iron rations in ruck-sack, with Swiss army knife in zipped pocket. I was the nearest thing to the sun cream advert, with the addition of anti-mosquito spray on all exposed parts, dark glasses and large straw hat. Priscilla had a good store of ice-cubes hidden about her person, wore her familiar bush hat and binoculars around her neck and looked ready for anything. Everyone in our *Corps d'Elite* completed the tick powder routine, as we were told these insects can bite you through your clothing and can bury themselves into your skin.

"And they sure don't mind which bit they bite," laughed Priscilla, walking away in a haze of 'Doom'.

We drove to the middle of a large clearing where we were to meet the bush ranger, the spearhead of the party, who would guide us on foot, through the Tarzan country of upper Hluhluwe Reserve, which in the nineteenth century, had been the private hunting preserve of King Shaka, the Zulu King. I was now on overload of excitement, fear and dyspepsia. Barrie had that 'be prepared' look and was seen stuffing ever more Mars Bars into his pack.

There were a few more people in our party - a honeymoon couple holding hands and Michael and Shaun pretending not to be enjoying themselves, with no extra provisions. The sun was very high and I felt a trickle of perspiration running down the back of my cotton shirt. A jeep drew up alongside. A tall ranger climbed down and surveyed his party of prospective bushwalkers. He had a knife in a sheath on his belt, a gun, in repose, slung onto the back of his hunky shoulder and a look of complete disinterest on his face.

We mobilized ourselves into a kind of amateur infantry patrol, with honeymooners wrapped around each other like toffee paper and Priscilla abreast of the squad, excited at the prospect of our forthcoming sortie into the bundu.

"These people have never been on a bushwalk before," she said, in loud American.

Silence. The ranger did not appear to be moved by this statement. Priscilla glared and repeated herself. Still no reply. He obviously was saving himself for when important instructions arose.

We set off in a line behind him. Barrie, at his purposeful pioneer pace looking resolute and calm, khaki socks tucked well in. My footsteps were close behind the Zulu Warrior along the narrow track and Priscilla walked a little way behind, taking the first sip of iced water from a flask, obviously irritated at his blank refusal to answer her. It would have been useful to learn which animals we were likely to see and a few hints on how to act when downwind of a white rhino, but nothing was said about that. Here I was, straight from the green hills of Croydon, and expected to be able to deal with a hungry lion or a charging rhino without even an induction course. The honeymoon couple were no longer holding hands and were looking quite worried. Michael and Shaun, meandered quite far behind, like puppies on a picnic.

The track lead upwards, out into open terrain, over rocks and boulders and through occasional prickly thorn, with dagger sized needles. We noticed some rather large paw prints. Heaps of dung were scattered like dead footballs along the track. They had to belong to something big. The ranger didn't stop to explain.

We were all extremely hot and my legs started to prickle and itch. All this at good parade ground pace following the silent ranger. He was quite far ahead of our party now - gun nonchalantly thrown across his shoulders; just a green beret and a determined figure heading off into the distance. No interesting feature or heap of dung was going to induce him to speak to us. There were many things we wanted to ask. The heat was fierce and my head felt somewhat disconnected with reality. Nevertheless, morale was good and everyone was enjoying the topography.

There was a long gap between myself, the honeymoon couple and the two youngsters. Barrie was at the rear behind Priscilla. She had brought ice cubes to drink, pour down the front of her frock and cool her face. She looked very hot and flushed. The temperature was nearly ninety.

The Zulu warrior came to a halt and stood with his back to us at the top of a ridge, while the rest of our party climbed thirstily to join him. Reaching for our water bottles the whole party flopped down onto the parched ground. We had been walking for almost two hours. No one had told us what to do if we did meet one of the big six featured in the brochure and it occured to me that we were in quite a vulnerable situation.

The view down below us was stunning. Hluhluwe River wound like a snake through the reserve, brilliant in the late afternoon sun. We were so high up and the air was still. Insects buzzed constantly around our heads. Unanimously we agreed that the ranger was most unco-operative. Perhaps he was having some sort of personal crisis. When asked politely if he would mind a memorable photograph being taken of him in his smart uniform, he answered by turning his back.

Priscilla almost exploded.

"Excuse me – but why are you ignoring us?"

She pressed him for more informative instruction about our walk. He answered by waving his arm and motioning us to move on down the steep incline towards the river. There was clearly a problem. The grass was longer now and my knees itched from an insect that had crawled inside my trousers - a tsete fly or a hungry mosquito? Keeping close behind the ranger again, I was quite sure that if a marauding elephant emerged from the bush, it would run over him before me. Not even my hormone replacement therapy could save me now.

Suddenly he stopped dead in his tracks and beckoned vigorously to us all to stand still. Priscilla grabbed my arm and pulled me back. Below us was a large water hole, surrounded by reeds and down a short slope in front were two enormous rhino. They were standing in shallow murky water with short tails flicking - their huge horns held in profile; their creased wrinkly skin hanging like rolls of wet wallpaper around their clay baked jaws. Their shortsightedness made them blink their eyes in our direction, but they didn't focus directly on us. Both my feet were suddenly buried in wet cement.

In a split second, the ranger had become a commando force all of his own. He silently picked up a stick from the undergrowth and, moving extremely slowly, he began to scrape it along the ground so that the rhino could hear. Number one rhino started to climb the bank. He turned his dinosaur head in our direction. The ranger waved his hand behind him which left us in no doubt what we were required to do next - keep absolutely still.

I wasn't prepared for the scale of the beast but then I had never been so close to one in my whole life. The first rhino looked like a prehistoric monster with the smallest eyes; the second, obviously the female, was not quite as big, but splashing in water not more than a few feet away, she was big enough to combat a legion of dithering ladies.

Somebody squeezed my hand. I was standing behind Barrie who was behind Priscilla, who was behind Michael, who was behind a tree. I shut my eyes and soared into autopanic. My nerves had gone haywire and someone had padlocked my knees together. The nearest tree had thorns like carving knives and was about four feet high.

The ranger moved his stick again and made some kind of noise that the rhino heard He moved his great head in our direction. Two steps forward and he was out of the water and coming towards us. I leaned backwards onto the feet of the honeymoon couple who were plainly planning some kind of suicide pact. Two heads were inside one anorak, their arms wrapped tightly around one another. With a moan, the male half dropped to the ground and as he got to his feet, a pair of sunglasses stuck firmly to the seat of his pants.

There was a long silence. All eyes were on the ranger. If the rhino had charged at that moment not one of us would have been able to move. After a tense pause which seemed endless, loud bellowing snorts were heard in front and there was the ranger with arms raised in the air, chasing two fat rhino backsides in the direction of the bushes at the other end of the pool. Our hero of the advance guard, for the first time in two hours, shouting colloquial Zulu after retreating rhino, with hand on gun, was in complete contrast to his previous silence. Perhaps he was the chief of a monastic Zulu style organisation which dealt in animal communication skills only. People with real blood in their veins were obviously beyond the pail.

My adrenalin levels still riding on four cylinders, I decided in that moment, I would stick to scenic sketching in one of England's leafy lanes as my hobby. But for a swig of Priscilla's gin laced with water flask and a few ice cubes stuffed down my bosom, I might have passed out. Barrie, Michael and Shaun celebrated in Mars bars and we once more set off following the ranger. Priscilla's face was alive with anticipation and she was triumphant that we had shared this exciting confrontation.

"Wasn't that just wonderful! You realise he couldn't see us clearly. He knew there was something nearby, but he wasn't too sure. The ranger was right to do what he did."

In an instant, she had forgiven him.

Ahead were thick bushes and the ground had become swampy. Trees were enveloped in canopies of jungly-looking ropes and twisted grasses. There was far more variety of vegetation.

"I don't think we're far from the road now," volunteered Barrie.

We were still travelling downhill .The ranger was hidden from sight under the matted slimy ferns and dangling roots. Priscilla began to look uncomfortably hot and was not making such good progress. Michael was helping her to navigate the obstacles; the bucaneering adolescent now a considerate offspring and as they crawled underneath saplings and over boggy ground, Michael the man, was plainly visible.

Huge frondy trees waved around us and the monkey tails of the branches dripped greenly with moisture. Barrie whispered 'crocodiles' in my ear as our host cocked his gun and dived into a buzzing hive of forest. Obediently we followed. We had to thrash forward, ducking and diving under the low branches, beating the mosquitoes away from our heads. The heat from the ground rose to my nostrils like hot fat and my shirt stuck to my back with sweat. Everyone seemed to be struggling with the sucking mud. Negotiating fallen trees made our way difficult. The last part of the route was like some military commando assault course.

"One of his short cuts, I suppose," I said with optimism, though my insides were feeling thoroughly miserable. "I wonder why he's cocked his gun?"

"His last meeting with a crocodile I expect," piped up Michael who was just behind me. Our whole party were following him, with blind faith and ignorance, without advice or instruction. The two youngsters, having the most energy left, crashed down overhead jungle for us and beat a good path, avoiding the worst of the swampy ground. To our great relief, we felt tarmac under our feet.

It was some minutes before I could get my lower lumbar number three vertebrae to connect to my brain. We emerged stooping, onto one of the roads running through the reserve. Relief from the whole regiment was unanimous; the end of a strenuous and exciting bushwalk - but not quite the final episode.

The honeymooners appeared from the undergrowth like unhinged territorial foot soldiers. Without a word, they stumbled weakly up the final incline after the disappearing ranger, who was already half way up the hill. He had not even stopped to bid us goodbye. All I remember of him was the back of his bull neck and the barrel of a rifle on his shoulder.

Priscilla, the dedicated hands-on walker of numerous bush trails, sat down in the middle of the road and flatly refused to budge. She was extremely hot and suffering from exhaustion and nothing was going to induce further movement. Her hair had fallen around her face and her cheeks were red. The binoculars swung from her neck on a leather strap. Her camera was beside her.

"Michael, go get the truck!" She threw the keys at him. I sat down on the road and offered to stay until the others returned to pick us up.

"You go with Michael and the others, I'll stay with Priscilla," offered Barrie, noble and polite to the end.

We were still in the bush - but now totally abandoned by Mr Zulu warrior who couldn't wait to get home. Any one of us could have been left in the swamp and he would have been none the wiser. His monastic vow of silence was uncompromising.

Michael, Shaun and I walked on, leaving Barrie and Priscilla sitting opposite each other in the middle of the road. In the five minutes it took us to go and fetch the truck, there was an incident on the bridge by Hluhluwe River which went something like this.

"Priscilla, don't look now, but there's a buffalo coming towards us. He's about twenty yards away."

"Aah Barrie, don't give me that crap!"

"Priscilla, I tell you, there's a buffalo and he's coming very close. Turn around slowly and have a look!"

"Don't try and frighten me Barrie, I know you're kidding!"

Beshaken and bedraggled, she turned her head slowly. There indeed stood a huge buffalo, a tank of an animal by all accounts, with wide curly horns; hooves pawing the ground as he put his head down. He was standing four square, with a thirst like a crew of navvies in a dry dock. And he could smell the river.

"I think we're in his path, look out!"

"The tree over there, go for the tree - jeepers he's big! No not the river, there might be crocodiles!"

Priscilla, exhausted though she was, scrambled to her feet, boots scraping the road and in doing so, snatched at her camera which was still sitting on the tarmac. The animal must have seen a wild gesticulation he did not understand. It alerted him and for a moment he lifted his giant dustbin head and stood with nostrils wide, heavy hooves planted forward in readiness. In their panic, the two must have startled the buffalo so much that he thought better of an argument between a wild American woman and a polite Englishman in a Baden Powell hat, with a Swiss army knife in his pocket. In a couple of seconds, without sound or trace, the buffalo had pulled off into the bush as quickly as he had emerged, leaving not a footprint or a tell-tale mark that he had even been present. That left two rather foolish figures, clinging to verdant forest tree trunks, like turtles left stranded by the tide.

Michael, up at the clearing put the truck into gear and more or less rolled down to the bridge to pick them up, expecting them still to be there. At the bridge by the river, two jibbering individuals climbed aboard and started to laugh hysterically before a sensible word was spoken by of either of them. Priscilla's bush hat had fallen off. Barrie was quite pale.

At the crest of the hill, we stopped to witness the going down of the sun in the crimson sky. We wanted to share this moment and watch the pools of purple light fade along the riverbank. As we gloried in the African sunset, standing altogether with the river far below, neither Priscilla nor Barrie could tell the story of the buffalo without disintegrating into loud laughter, of course more from relief than anything.

"Do you know they can lick you to death – even if you're up a tree?"

"I don't believe you," answered Shaun who hadn't spoken a word until now.

"Ya, through the soles of your feet! Barrie have you got goosepimples at what might have happened?" questioned our host.

At that moment, neither of us felt it was something we wanted to repeat there and then. Two dramatic escapades were enough for one day. My rhino knees had not quite stopped shaking.

Heading back towards Hilltop, the sky was indigo with pale stars flickering like fireflies. We looked forward to another evening of mosquitoes, tame zebras, a good fire, some wholesome food and a few good buffalo stories.

Chapter 17

Brave Faces.

At Christmas we exchanged the rainbows of the Mountain Kingdom for rural snow bound England. It was a masterpiece of engineering to flee the delectable climate of Lesotho in a searing hot four hour taxi ride to Johannesburg and arrive eleven hours later at London Heathrow, wearing enough clothes to stop the frostbite seeping through our veins. Long-johns and thermals meant we couldn't show anybody our brown knees. I put my sunglasses away and donned a woolly hat.

Mid-tarmac I wept a little for the golden early morning of the mountain outside my window in Leribe. The grey mist of London tasted on my tongue and blanketted the concrete airport buildings. The cold weather ate through my bones. At Staines we stopped for petrol and expected to hear banana music and see fruit sellers sitting around the forecourt.

Northbound on the M25 I would have given anything to see an ox-cart or a donkey. Instead we followed a thread of red cones and tortuous contraflow systems until well underneath the Thames and it was clear life had changed when three lanes of traffic zigzagged alongside.The tribal gangs of roadbuilders had won their battle for more diesel fumes per square mile.

What made everything worthwhile was the quiet Christmas madrigals on radio three and the thought that soon I would see Abigail's smile. A warm gathering of families in an English country farmhouse, would unwind the knot of guilt in my heart. While I had been soaking up early African rock art and legendary tales of nomadic hunter gatherers in Basutoland, my daughter had been mother to the daily needs of a paraplegic child. It was our longest ever separation, this past three months and I couldn't wait to see them.

Since Abigail's first brain scan at less than a year old, we have known that she has microcephaly. Her condition will never change. Her quality of life involves the sheer dedication of others. Inside her there is a personality that shines out of her eyes. Her smile is like sunshine. And she gathers people who love her. Meanwhile, my daughter's own life is suspended in a vacuum of time.

Being home for Christmas was wonderful. Our hired whitewashed farm cottage with central heating made up for leaving a South African summer and while we hosted dozens of guests and played Christmas carols, the snow fell on the fields outside. Both our families visited and relationships flowered. Midnight Mass in our village church was a candlelit embrace of old friends. Mincepies and spiced hot punch had never tasted so good and our walks along Hertfordshire country lanes were beautiful in the snow. Barrie and I were extremely happy. One evening with my sister and some friends we plugged in the electric piano and sang till morning. Struck by the feeling of Christmas, we littered the tiny room with song sheets, emptied the South African bottleof port, followed by the last bottle of Uncle Harry's home made parsnip wine.

We always sang at Christmas, especially Barrie. About 4.00am, in the belief that if you sing it wrong, sing it loud, he gave us three highly untuneful verses of 'The Spaniard who blighted my life' and then collapsed in his chair, asleep.The pantomine fairy who rented the cottage next door was probably sorry she hadn't signed him up. Through the thin wall we could hear her cough.

Everything we did revolved around our families for three whole weeks. Abigail sat at our table and shared our meals. She would hear a car draw up outside and look towards the door, then say a quiet " hello whoisit" followed by a kissing sound. If she heard her name mentioned she blew more kisses. New voices entering the room were quickly recognised and immediately the trust began. She has a wonderful listening memory even though she may not be able to see clearly across a room. Behind those piercing blue eyes, there is a personality full of humour.

She has grown so tall and now her long legs are difficult to manoeuvre. Normally a child will cling round a mother's body and hold on - Abigail has no cling. She cannot hold or grip with her arms and hands and so you are holding a straight stiff body with no bend at the waist. Her muscles are locked on tight and she slithers from your arms without warning. Most men find it difficult to hold her. My quiet son James, sitting with her on the floor amongst the torn christmas paper, not speaking - just stroking her hair - seemed to have an empathy with Abigail which needed no words.

She may never be able to tell us what she wants, or what she likes; when she is ill we may not realize her pain; if she is frightened of the dark she cannot tell us. She only eats when someone feeds her. In her world there are no choices.

My daughter is the strongest person I know. When we said goodbye and returned to the mountains of Lesotho, her words almost destroyed me.

"It's your time now Mum - you and Barrie. Abigail and I will be fine. There are lots of people to help and I know you're at the end of a phone. We've got school to help us now don't forget - we have so many friends. I promise to write every week. Hope to see you in April."

I glanced once more at the pink shells lying on the chair in Abigail's bedroom. Lizzie wasn't one to waste words, especially not on melancholia and neither of us cried during the last round of hugs. For most of S.A.Flight 233, seated on the flight deck, I sat in a big handkerchief, sniffed into my book, then penned a letter to my daughter telling her she was very brave, ready to post in Johannesburg.

High summer in Lesotho extends from November until the end of January. The stunning mountainous terrain was ready to welcome us back and the tall blooms of the aloes sprang towards the sky. The mealie fields looked lush and green.With an average of 300 days of sunshine a year, we were sure of a warm welcome and were not disappointed. Along the road to Butha-Buthe, on the banks of the river, families were sitting on the flat rocks or splashing in the river and the kids by the roadside waved to us - naked to the waist- some holding out their hands for cans of coke. The empty cans are used by the young boys to make toy cars. First they find a piece of wire and then fashion it into a car shape with a long handle so they can push it along. Then wheels are added, made from empty coke cans, or sometimes shoe polish tins, and the lads find great sport in pushing their tin- wheeled cars along the main road, to race one another.

Sam was at the wheel as we drove through the usual chickens and goats hovering around the market place at Butha-Buthe. As we passed the trading stores we saw again the red baked earth and the women's colourful skirts as they swished along beside the stalls, carrying their bundles. A flotilla of bright umbrellas danced along the road and the street music sent vibrations through the windows of the kombi.

When you first arrive from Europe, it usually takes two or three days until your lungs become acclimatised to the altitude. Our village was 1,700 metres high. The result is an attack of breathlessness. We both noticed the effect on us when we arrived back in Leribe.

On that first January morning after our return, I took my usual walk alongside the meadow by the road to Pitseng. The morning dew was infinitely sharp and fragrant, like walking in Scottish heather after the rain. I inhaled the pungent juicy smell of the earth and in it, there was great joy. Walking alone, I needed to clear my mind of worries and rationalise my thoughts on leaving my loved ones, remembering our reunions which were to be my strength for the next few months. Our mountain looked across the valley at me and smiled in the sun. The sky was plain and still. I allowed the gentle breeze to heal my wounds like stitches of silk. In the corner of my mind, like a quiet lullaby, was the face of a little girl with blue eyes.

Later that morning, Betty arrived looking very pregnant now, with four year old Margaret and Francina, her eldest daughter who was home for the school holidays. We greeted each other warmly. The postcards of London buses, Buckingham Palace and pictures of the Queen were a great success. It was strange looking at them myself, here in such different circumstances.

Betty and I ate our lunch together on the stoep while the children sprayed each other with water from my hose and ran naked round the garden. Soon Annacleda arrived with Kaizi, who was dressed in a smart jersey, shorts and some shoes- looking remarkably grown up, and they had news to tell. Their mother had taken a job as a cook at the local Agricultural College and they had moved from the house on the mountain onto the college grounds.

"Kaizi you are growing as tall as your sister" I said, observing quite a change in him since early December. His legs were like sticks, but he was noticeably growing.

"Yes, now I have eaten the chicken from my mother," he replied, " and I like the chicken." I turned to Annacleda and asked her if they had good meals because of her mother's new job and she nodded.

"My mother cooks the food for the students. And if the food is left, we can take some."

This was a good piece of news and knew it would make a difference to their lives. Annacleda though, still in her wrap-around untidy dress and bare feet, said she would go and tell Heleyn that I had come back from England. We took down the world map, so they could see England and follow our journey to Lesotho. Kaizi sat on the floor, thumb firmly placed upon London, looking deadly serious.

"Where is the river?" he asked firmly.

"Which river Kaizi?"

"The river where your cows drink."

There was my next lesson. I promised to let them look again at the big map, when they came the following day and sent them off to the camp gates with squashed English mince pies in their pockets.

My New Year resolutions came round regularly like the number fifty four bus. This year was like all the others. Lose a stone in weight by Easter and start yesterday. Liliane and I found an old aerobics video and organised our daily keep fit routine at eight o'clock after the men had left for work. Her maid Agnes went into profound shock when arriving to find her daily routine disrupted by choruses of loud music and two energetic ladies rolling around the living room floor. Our swinging hip routine sent vibrations through the walls and our twenty two -each- side buttock reducing exercises nearly melted the nylon carpet. When we bravely went to get something more suitable to wear, we found that moths had eaten through my cotton leotard and Liliane's shorts. We both fell about - 'killed of laughing' as the French would say, at the sight of our moth-eaten garments. I now realized the significance of those boxes of camphor smelling things issued by L.H.P.C. strategically placed in every wardrobe in the house.

Undaunted, we continued our efforts until we could reach our toes without bending our knees. Ham strings were stretched on dining room chairs whilest Agnes flitted from one room to another trying to be invisible. Basotho ladies do not recognise 'keep fit' routines. When Agnes switched the washing machine on we were forced to come to a halt. Liliane's washing machine was the noisiest motorised gadget in Leribe and performed like a bucking bronco with vibrations terrible enough to cause an earthquake.

These invigorating hourly routines every January morning and our long late afternoon swims in the pool gave our post Christmas spare inches a nudge in the right direction and our fitness improved. We even went so far as borrowing hand weights from one of the French boys on the camp and raised a few eyebrows by exercising in the garden. Our daily walks up to Hlotse airstrip and back, helped to stop the cellulite from increasing. It was on one of these walks that we met Esther.

Esther was nineteen, still at school and studying hard for her exams. We met in the low meadow as we jumped the boggy ditches and lost our way and she directed us to safer ground. She asked me if I would teach her some English when she knew that I taught pupils at home. I replied with an invitation to come and join the others when they came for lessons.

Esther was a different kettle of fish to the other kids. She had ambition. The following day, she arrived at the camp and Thabo brought her to my door.

"Madame, a lady she is coming with a book."

Esther's English was very poor but somehow we exchanged words and managed to understand one another. Her school books showed that she was a good hard worker, but her language difficulties were holding her back. She said that her English teacher had left the school and that no teacher had taken her place. Her parents and siblings could not speak English and her friends at school only spoke seSotho. I asked if she knew anyone who could speak English near her home and she said her father's friend was a policeman and he knew how to speak English. She promised she would ask him for help. I told her she must practise - otherwise her skills would not improve. She wanted me to give her work to do and in a couple of days was back with it completed. Esther's keenness to learn was admirable and I thought perhaps I could help her. Her mind was like a sponge and she didn't need twice telling about anything. Each of our meetings begun like this.

"My Mother she says thank you. I like to learn."

"Would you like something to drink Esther?"

"No. I like to learn."

And she did learn. The genuine progress made week by week was astonishing. From not having more than a few words, Esther quickly began to understand more and speak in sentences- although slowly at first. She knew a good deal about diseases and medicine, about life in other African countries and told me she would like to be a doctor one day. She never broke an appointment and even though she lived quite far away from us, always arrived exactly on time. Her manners were impeccable and she always thanked me when she left. Esther was quite happy to do all the work she was given and more. I never saw in her a wasted gesture or effort. She was a delightful student and through the summer we became good friends. When eventually she accepted an English cup of tea, she found she liked the taste and we sat outside in the garden and talked of her life.

Esther did not want any babies. Other girls she knew already had children and she did not envy them. In Lesotho, a girl's marriage means she collects 'Lobola' from her bridegroom's family. This could mean several cows for the girl's family and meant an increase in their wealth, the number of cattle agreed upon before the marriage. Sometimes a horse can be given instead of two head of cattle, or sheep may be offered at the rate of ten sheep per head of cattle.These days money may also be substituted for cattle. Lobola is for compensation to the father for losing his daughter, who probably works hard within the family.

Married life did not appeal to Esther. She knew lots of girls whose husbands had gone off to work in the mines and never returned. Families in which the husband has been missing for many years are not uncommon and the abandoned wife can only survive with the help of her parents.

We talked of planned families and birth control. Esther told me she had heard that in some countries, girls could swallow a kind of medicine which stopped them from having babies. Her information was sketchy but fairly accurate. She told me that the men would get angry if their wives ate that medicine, which was difficult to find, but some girls knew where to go. Sometimes they might be beaten and badly treated by their husband, or in some cases, even turned out of their home.

Esther was the product of twentieth century thinking in her country. She knew that if she became a doctor she could help people, especially the women, about whom she cared a great deal. Her opinion of men was that they were irresponsible, fickle and untrustworthy. Esther had other plans

"I will work hard, to pass all my exams and then go to a college where I shall qualify as a doctor of medicine. I will travel around the world."

"Some men do not care about the health of their women. They want lots of children because it means more workers."

She understood about Aids. "Many people in our country will die of this disease."

Her wide knowledge, self motivation and determination were enough to put in her in line for success. Her lack of English was the only thing which was holding her back. Esther thought it was God who made it right for us to meet.

When you live in a country where the culture is totally different, it tests your understanding to the limit, especially when there are so many strong social and religious traditions, some of which go back hundreds of years. Most African parents regard education as extremely important but cannot always send their children to school. Esther was lucky to be only nineteen when in her final year at School. She had only missed two years of education in her life.

I came to realize just how hard it is for some parents to send their children to school when, during the following week, I was invited to go and teach in Tlotlisong High School over the border in Ficksburg. Some time before, I had been introduced to the headmaster of this School and he sent a message to say that his school would welcome a white teacher to go in on a part- time basis to teach English to their Standard 10- the equivalent of our old fifth form. There were no white children at the school and my class would be forty students.

I accepted on the condition that I was not paid and therefore could chose my own hours. The classes with my French ladies at Butha- Buthe were still running, my French university graduate, the nursery school in Ficksburg and the Leribe children all took up my time. Not to mention my dedication to my fitness regime which took presidence over my time in the mornings.

The Headmaster, Solomon Malebo and I liked each other from day one. He was a charismatic man, goodlooking and tall, with the presence of a Shakespearian actor and made me a good welcome. By then I had learnt the special handshake of the African people and he laughed handsomely as we shook hands. He invited me into his staffroom and introduced me to the other members of staff.

Tlotlisong High School has more than three hundred pupils, with a staff of about eight teachers and a secretary called Selina who typed all official school documents on her manual typewriter. There was one cupboard for school notepaper which was kept padlocked. Selina's small desk was positioned at the door of the Headmaster's room and she was first in the firing line when there was trouble. She was about four feet ten and very pretty. There was one luxury. A wall telephone with an outside line, which was on constant ring.

Solomon has that energy which is both infectious and indestructable. Nothing defeats him. He is utterly devoted to his school. The atmosphere was alive with industriousness and bustle. The staff greeted me enthusiastically and assured me of their support. Around me English, Zulu, Afrikans and seSotho voices were engaged in morning chatter. The kids came to talk to me and crowded around to ask which class I would be teaching. I didn't even notice the colour of their skin.

The school had been squatting in run-down premises in the town, while awaiting new accommodation which was in the process of being built. A political saga surrounded these issues of which I knew very little. The classrooms were shabby beyond belief. Howeve, they did have desks.

My first mistake was to ask what time the classes finished for coffee break and my second, to ask where the toilets were. No one knew what a coffee break was and they didn't have any coffee. In answer to the second question, I was handed a key and given instructions to walk to the end of the school building and told not to forget to lock the door from the inside. I wasn't sure where exactly the teacher meant, but found my way by the smell.

Solomon had asked me to introduce the subject of 'Careers' and talk to them of life in England and jobs. Lesson notes seemed in short supply. It was nine thirty. The timetable read that after one lesson, someone would come to relieve me. Not knowing what one lesson meant in terms of time, I walked into 10A classroom where forty pairs of eyes looked at me. Everyone stood politely. Solomon introduced me and then left the room. A large hole in the back wall of the classroom room and several broken windows held my attention. Someone brought me a chair but my knees would not let me sit down.

Chapter 18

The Choir.

"*Lumelang,*" I said nervously, "I hope we shall have a good lesson."

Standing before a sea of black faces will be indelibly imprinted in my memory. It was an experience for which no one could have prepared me. Clean white shirts, pressed skirts and trousers, identical in dark blue; the unspoken thoughts of forty adult students - all waiting. I felt hundreds of eyes were upon me. There was nothing in my educational training which related to this moment. Nothing in Plowden that provided a course in spontaneous teaching in a black country, with pupils from a post-apartheid black township, in a squatter school, in a town run by whites.

They sat on their chairs quietly, with hardly a murmur and waited for me to begin.

In theory, it was an ordinary situation of teacher and students, but the formula was unique. Excited to be given this opportunity to have direct contact with the kids from Tlotlisong High, I ploughed in.

They had cheerfulness and eagerness.They were full of humour, hope and compassion. There were other moments so sad, that I could not believe I was hearing them. A harrowing expression flitted across the face of a twenty five year old boy who, two years ago, had seen his grandmother murdered before his eyes. Soon, he told me, he would have to go into a court to face the attacker. Joseph, another bright energetic boy has to look after his sick mother in a hovel, which is just a mud shelter, and find someone to stay with her while he comes to school. His eyes filled with tears as he spoke. Joseph was desperate to learn English and wanted to write to me when I returned to England. Every day, he thinks his mother might die before he reaches home. Then there was Klaus, the leader of a group of gospel singers who sang in the church every Sunday, and longed to be able to play hymns on a real piano. He lived for music and could talk of nothing else.

There was dear dependable Jacob, who was twenty eight; the sort of student every teacher would die for; intelligent, sensitive, thoughtful and gentle. I came to know Jacob quite well in the time I was associated with the school. His determination to lift himself out of the mire of his childhood and bring in money for his brothers and sisters whom he had fought hard for, was truly amazing. Jacob spent all his spare time in the town library teaching himself Afrikaans because he knew it would increase his chances of getting a job, with three languages to his credit. He told me of his hope to become a security officer. He knew only seSotho and English and this was not enough not secure him a job anywhere else in South Africa. Jacob was a realist, a peacemaker and a born diplomat.

My pupils ranged from seventeen to twenty eight years. Everyone was in school uniform. Most of them looked too old to be in a classroom and many were too tall for the chairs. A conglomoration of protruding legs stuck out into the aisles.

It is common for children to miss years of schooling in their primary years and then return to it. There are many reasons for this. A boy may miss a year, if it is his turn to look after the family's cows, while his brother goes to school. The day may come when a younger sibling is old enough to be herd boy and the older boy can return to his education. If there are no male siblings, a boy may have to wait until he is eleven or twelve before he starts his education.

A girl might have to look after her younger siblings, or an elderly relative. Sickness and poverty are powerful ingredients. Family circumstances and a share of domestic chores can be in conflict with education and in any case, girls do not often begin school until the age of seven. Displacement from village to village means educational disruption; even when the family does settle in one town, places in school are difficult to obtain.

The resulting practice is that no pupil can move through the system until he has passed the exam for a particular year. It could take a child two, three or even four years at one level before he qualifies for the next. Consequently, the classes are known by Standards and the range of the students within any Standard, can span several years.

Thousands of children never go to school at all and end up illiterate and unemployable.

Most of the students in Standard 10A were residents of the sprawling squatter camp at Meqheleng, on the hillside overlooking Ficksburg, a kind of shanty town with a hopeless unemployment problem. No white people live there. It spreads across the skyline, some distance from Ficksburg, like a membranous sea of corrugated tin rooftops. Craters of refuse and garbage abominate the outskirts, picked over by the dogs. There is no money for services and the householders do what they can to survive. A few of the houses have electricity, many live with candle power. Water is available through communal standpipes and garbage is a huge problem.

The new government has made promises but as yet nothing has changed. Every morning the people who live in Meqheleng, walk down into the tree lined avenues of suburban South Africa, past the large gardens of residential properties of the whites. Many are employed as maids, garden boys, and childrens' nannies and work hard for their host families. Several families we knew spoke highly of their 'dailies' without whom they would not cope – the loyalty between them obvious. It was a common sight to see a black lady nursemaiding a white baby or collecting children from school for her 'Madam'. South African women make good surrogate mothers.

A high percentage of the men from Meqheleng worked in the gold and diamond mines in South Africa and lived away from their families for months at a time. Residents of Meqheleng did not own land or grow their own food like the homesteads in Lesotho. Money must be earned by working and there is no Government Benefit system. Hundreds of families are housed in small houses and shacks, built in long rows with little space between, in the hope that they can find employment in the nearby towns. It is obvious there are not enough jobs to support the black population - the system breaks down and criminality follows. Ficksburg is a typical South African town with a typically post-apartheid carbuncle waiting to burst.

Ficksburg is home to both blacks and whites. Along the streets some of the black women have stalls on the pavement, others work in the supermarkets and cafes scattered around the town Many work as shop assistants in larger stores owned by whites. On the main street, there are several large banks, a Post Office, one or two large furniture stores, clothes shops, a good stationers and other busy traders. You can find most daily commmodities, food is cheap, and decent wages can be earned. Ficksburg boasts two or three hotels, a public library and a Town Hall. Second-hand car traders and videoshops are flourishing and a Kentucky Fried Chicken Restaurant has recently found its way into Ficksburg. There are couple of bakeries which generate a lot of trade and an excellent wine shop.

Emerging from the supermarket with your trolley, you are met by hoards of young boys from Meqheleng who want to earn money by pushing your trolley across the car park, help you to unload and take the trolley back. The first time this happened to me, I found it a bit frightening. White ladies in cars are good prospective tippers and much pushing and shoving takes place amongs the lads. Occasionally fights break out.

After several trips to Pick 'n Pay car park, I learnt a few of the children's names and would ask them, with my poor seSotho, which school they went to or where they lived. They always pointed to the squatter camp up on top of the hill. Then I found them helpful, polite and eager to engage in conversation.

I fully understood their need to make a dime, but what I didn't understand were the drivers who shooed them away like flies and wouldn't part with their small change. I felt desperately sorry for the kids and admired their savvy. One or two became my 'regulars' and would wait for me until the shopping was finished, then give me that special service with that special smile. This went on for months and they prided themselves in having a customer who knew them, which made them feel special. No item of food ever went missing. When the key to my car disappeared I feared the worst, but a thin little waif called Samson had seen me drop it and came running towards me. He had a special lunch that day of 'Tucky fries' sitting crosslegged on the pavement, chewing ferociously. After that Samson and I had a special thing going and he would always be the first one to see me enter the carpark and come dashing to the window.

The pupils in my class today, had younger brothers who worked the carparks. Their mothers were the ladies who passed me on the streets early in the morning in candy floss pink overalls on their way to work in the big houses. Their fathers were away working in the mines. At home, they had no space of their own to study in, nor light to read by. Elderly relatives shared their cramped accomodation and the food on the table, was probably stolen from the stacked shelves of the town supermarkets.

My students spoke hopefully of change in their lives. They wanted things to be better. Most of them lived with poverty and squalor, lack of food, overcrowding, problems of space and the inevitable violence bound up with these things. Prostitution was a word they were familiar with. Abortion was the thing you didn't talk about openly. Murder was accepted as the norm.

They all had a genuine desire to learn and wanted to have better lives than their parents.They wanted to study and pass their Matriculation exams this year. And they were desperate for knowledge. Solomon had told me of their great need for books. Books are so few in this school, that eight or ten students have to share one reader. The ones I saw were old, out of date, dirty and torn. Classrooms were bare of necessities such as writing materials and paper.

A major liberating force for these young people was their hope that the new South African Government would open up new opportunities for them and their families.

Without exception, they were immersed in their country's politics and had controversial opinions which fitted over them like a second skin. Steeped in tradition, outlawed by virtue of their colour, they were graduates of a corrupt society that was struggling to discover itself.

The New Constitution, approved in May 1996 is one of the most progressive constitutions in the world. The major issue for these black South Africans is the outlawing of discrimination, on the grounds of race, ethnic or social origin. It is hard to imagine living in a country where the majority cannot enjoy free speech and free movement and where it is a criminal offence to protest. Freedom for the blacks in South Africa has waited too long. Hope has to begin somewhere.

They knew more about survival than all my past generations of English pupils put together. Their parents voted in the 1994 elections which changed the century. 'Reconciliation' is a word with which they are becoming familiar and Mandela their greatest hero.

They stared at me, searching for a hint of humour which might lift their spirits. The boys asked me about how things worked in England. They asked how old students must be to get a Matric; if English students have lots of books and how many young people have the chance to go to Universities. They asked what kind of houses we lived in and if everyone goes to school - and who looked after the cows -and in all of their questions, they talked as if it were a completely male dominated society. There were two distinct groups in this room - male and the female. The girls hardly featured at times. They seemed to withdraw from this agenda. I deliberately set our course of conversation towards equal opportunities in employment. They had never heard that phrase.

The girls sat up and listened. Their minds were full of babies and domesticity and weeding crops. They had all learnt how to do cooking and washing, from their mothers or sell fruit in the town from a pavement stall. Bearing in mind the status quo is having no electricity or kitchen tap, their duties cannot be under estimated. One rather sullen looking girl took her nose out of her her lunchbox and glared.

"Miss have you got any cows?"

"No, I'm afraid not Elizabeth."

Her estimation of me went down and she spent the rest of the lesson asleep, with her head on the desk. Several girls wanted to work as a housekeeper for a white family and saw this as a position for life, one or two had ambitions to become nurses or child carers, but the words 'studies' or 'further education' were noticeably absent from the conversation. Several of them were mothers already.

"Is abortion legal in your country?" asked Sylvie, a twenty seven year old, who retreated into silence and hung her head the minute she had asked the question. I promised to have a talk with her after the class as many of the girls' faces showed interest. It wouldn't be wise to embark on this subject right now. Her pertinent question had stopped the flow of conversation and all the females, without exception, were acutely interested in my reply.

These youngsters had a better understanding of their place in society than their parents. There was Charlotte, Elizabeth and Agnes; Rachael, Rose and Esther - all lovely young girls who had grown up to accept that it was the men who made all the decisions. How diminished was their own self worth. Their eyes held that light of disbelief and when we spoke of women role models, they drifted into contrition and compromise. And yet they were intrigued. It was as if their minds had taken that first step into the unthinkable.

I tried to tell them that they had a voice.

"Share your ideas, exchange your views, someone might listen." I saw a blankness in their eyes. "There might even be a leader amongst your group. You are the future generation - your opinions count. If they are reasonable and fair, they will stand the test of time."

The boys wanted to voice their hopelesness at the level of street violence and criminality. They spoke of pressures beyond my comprehension. Some had seen members of their families attacked in the streets, also rape, gang fights, houses broken into, and yet they had a built-in survival kit. I was spared the details.

" Many people drink alcohol Miss," voiced Jacob, his eyes showing dark shadows, his shoulders hunched. "There is too much violence…drinking makes people fight often, even every day." His face showed true contempt at the mention of alcohol abuse. "The police do nothing…." His voice trailed off as he sat down.

Despite the horrors of living in Meqheleng, they spoke of their ambitions. Some of the boys wanted to become shoemakers, carpenters, own a shop or drive a taxi. One wanted to be a politician and change the world. A few wanted to become teachers or policemen. One young man said he liked clocks and could mend any clock you could give him. Another lad came to tell me he had organised a debating society, where people could go to talk and argue about any family or social issue. He wanted to be a social worker. Only one or two expressed a preference to travel away and work in the diamond mines or the gold mines. Klaus wanted to have his own choir.

They had dreams – dreams that in their lifetime things might change. Ideas rose from them like bobbing corks and yet, in their hearts they were already defeated. I felt honoured that I was part of that hope within. Woefully unprepared, they knew that in their future, choice was an empty word. I couldn't even guess at the quality of their lives. I tried to imagine what they had seen and felt, but could not.

They would not let me go. At twelve thirty, another teacher came to tell me it was almost the end of school. The kids wanted to go on talking. They asked when I was coming back. They wanted to know where I lived. And they wanted to sing for me - a totally unexpected surprise. Their elated cries drowned everything else as I was shown into the school hall, escorted by Solomon and Elizabeth, a very beautiful young woman, who was their music teacher. An excited crowd followed, knowing that there was a treat in the offing.

Inside the big hall, dozens of pieces of broken furniture lay around the floor, it was an uninviting space. Desks, chairs and tables were heaped around the walls and there was precious little order. And yet, some fifty or so pupils stood attentively in a horseshoe formation facing the stage, waiting for their conductor - faces glowing and ready. The others who had come to watch, climbed up onto the broken desks and tables and sat quietly.

Solomon initiated the proceedings, stepping in front of the choir and speaking first in seSotho and then in English.

"Our visitor from England would like to hear your good singing. Please give her a sample of our music culture and so she will take back to England with her, memories of our fine African songs."

One of the most thrilling moments I have ever had, was the moment I sat in front of Tlotlisong School Choir and they sang - just for me. I had never heard trained African voices. Elizabeth drew up her arm. There was complete concentration.

Voices vibrated around my ears; rich and deep. The magnificent quality of sound melted my soul. My spine tingled. There was no accompaniment.

Harmony seemed to be so natural as to be effortless - as though they needed no lead or direction. Melodic and penetrating, the sound enveloped me. As Elizabeth conducted three songs, I could only think that at home in England, music lovers would be ecstatic to hear this quality of massed voices. The musicianship and the dignity of this group was heartwarming.

Then they danced side by side in time with the beat, putting actions to the meaning of the words. Rippling shoulders and feet moved in a tight dance sequence. Eyes shone.

Repeated chords pulsated, tones of bass voices leading and then, soft melodies of the final song faded away gently, like the dying of a flower, cut at the root. As the song ended the choir bowed their heads and were still.

There was utter silence. It was hard to speak. Solomon pulled me into the centre stage. I was actually shaking. With difficulty, the right words came. How could I tell them that I had never before heard such a beautiful sound. Then in a moment of spontaneity, I promised that I would do all in my power to arrange for them to come and sing for us in Lesotho at some time in the future. Somehow, I would make this event happen. Elizabeth and I shook hands and I thanked them for their wonderful recital.

"How do you get them to sing like this?" I faltered, "how do these kids get to this standard of musical ability?"

"They are born singing," she answered, "I hardly have to teach them anything. They can harmonise naturally, it comes from the heart. I just introduce new songs. Music is part of our culture."

Solomon congratulated her and she knew he was pleased. Music gave the school status and was an important part of their curriculum. They had no piano or other musical instrument, no tape recorders, no recording equipment whatsoever, no television or radio. With her new assistant music trainee, whose name was Miriam, Elizabeth had indeed brought them to competitive standard and Tlotlisong had, for the second time, entered a national competition.

Here was a most uncommon talent. The school was so poor - yet hidden amongst the debris of their environment, was a unique musical genius. And the world would never know. The kids at Tlotlisong High had never seen black dots on sheets of paper or heard recorded music. Their ability to sing must indeed come from the heart. I was stunned by the morning's experience and by their courage and humility.

Solomon came to say goodbye. He squeezed my hand and thanked me for coming. I would not rest until I had accomplished my wish to bring their music to our families at L.H.P.C. Plans were already forming in my mind . Somehow there would be a way.

"It will be a dream come true," he smiled widely and went back to his desk.

I drove out of the school courtyard in the blazing sun, with a crowd of 10A kids and choral singers, hanging onto my car as far as the gate and dancing along the verge.

"When are you coming back 'M'e?" they called from every direction.

Watching them in my rear view mirror, they looked as though they had not a care in the world. I heard their laughter. I saw their blue uniforms disappearing in the direction of Meqheleng.

Tlotlisong was certainly not a land of wandering Oxford scholars and fountains of Latin prose but you could see they were artists of expression and had a love of beautiful things. They were intelligent people, robbed of their place in society by the colour of their skin, but not poor in terms of their spirit. The sound of their voices will stay with me as an enduring treasure in life's memories. I salute them.

Chapter 19

Katse Dam.

The following morning after my visit to Tlotlisong High School, my attempts to organise a concert at Butha-Buthe camp began.

Several people told me that it would be impossible. Neighbours and colleagues, helpful and well intentioned though they were, thought it would not be practicable because the choir would have to cross the South African border into Lesotho and the children would require passports. The price of a passport was fifty rands and every person would need one. But I had grown weary of faint hearted and irresolute ditherers. I have met them many times in my life. The idea of bringing English children, French children and South African children together in music became my passionate wish.

Strictly speaking, a mere engineer's wife may not be too welcome in the Company's offices,where a hydro-electric power station was underway. Screwing up my courage I made my request known to the management. Within the sound of ringing telephones and wall-to-wall secretaries, the Administration Manager agreed that L.H.P.C. would greatly appreciate a musical event like this and the concert could go ahead. A high ranking rubber-stamp from the senior Frenchman was all that was needed.

"Why don't you use the English School Hall at Butha -Buthe – it's the largest space we've got. Invite the French School children as well – it's an excellent idea."

"What about transport for Tlotlisong Choir – can you give me a bus?"

"That can be a arranged- I'll have a word with the Transport Manager. Let's give them supper after the show, why not?"

I was delighted.

"*Merci beaucoup,* Monsieur. I'll arrange a meeting at the school tomorrow, and thanks for your blessing. We'll give you an evening to remember!"

This was the easy part. The following day, I travelled to Butha-Buthe, alone in my car, head bursting with plans, after arranging a meeting with Nia Hughes, the headmistress of the English School.

Our meeting was cordial and resolute. Nia's commitment to the event and enthusiasm for bringing together the three choirs, could not have pleased me more.

"Why don't we set up a donation scheme- put the money towards musical instruments for the Tlotlisong kids." responded Nia enthusiastically. She thought the whole idea educationally sound and remarked it would be good for the children from both camp schools to see what an African choir could do.

The English school consisted of children under fourteen, whose parents were connected in some way with the Highlands Water Scheme, whether engineer, doctor, teacher or contractor. Some of the pupils were great travellers and had been educated in schools in many different parts of the world. They brought a global talent into this small establishment, and were a joy to teach - their music lessons a treat for any ear, and directed by an amazing blind pianist. There were about fifty children altogether. Thrilled at the prospect of a visiting South African choir, we swapped ideas, chose a few songs, while the concert sparked into life.

"What about the French School – can they sing?"

"Bi*en sur,*" came the reply.

"That should add a little *scintillement* to the occasion. A lot of the Missions were started by the French, that's another reason for inviting them now. It's only the problem of passports. We'll resolve it I'm sure."

"It will be good for the men here to see what their children can do!"

It was late afternoon when Nia and I said goodbye. Exhilarated at the prospect of organising a joint musical venture, we vowed to make it a success. My journey back to Leribe should take me about thirty five minutes. The skies to the west of Butha-Buthe were streaked with pink and the market place hummed as usual with dusty traffic. I turned right towards Leribe.

The road wound through Levis Nek. I climbed higher and could see the rugged landscape, criss-crossed by dongas and lush green grass.The hillsides glistened warmly as they did at that time of day. People carrying home their water cans passed by on worn tracks by the side of the road and the ladies selling oranges looked fat and full of laughter.

I was intrigued by the young females near one of the village water taps as they gathered in small groups. Bare legs danced through tattered dresses, strong young arms sailed like windmills. Their faces were lit up. Water jars and babies were set on the ground for a moment, broad hips swung, hands clapped. When work is finished and before they prepare their evening meal, the women like to tell the world they are glad. Dancing is mandatory for the Basotho people, as though part of the ten commandments and the statute book.

With no daily newspapers, these are times for gossiping and consultation; the water tap a council chamber for the mother of parliaments, the senate, the legal assembly and the synod. Being news carrier or confidante, the women go their separate ways, and take away their collection of trivia to spread among the menfolk and other relatives.

As I neared the Subeng River, suddenly and without warning, the acceleration on my car faded out and no amount of foot pressing would restore power to the engine. I came to a halt on the rocky shoulder about 3 kilometres from Leribe on a long open stretch of tarmac.

The predicament I had dreaded most! To break down in your car when you are carrying passengers is one thing, but to be marooned alone in Lesotho is quite another. Remembering that it would be better if I took charge of the situation and didn't sit inside my vehicle and look helpless, I emerged from the driver's seat, trying not to look too terrified. An old man with a cart pulled by two oxen rumbled past and some children came to sit a little way off and stare. Across the road, was a square stone house with a tin roof. A young woman with a child in her arms smiled. She beckoned me over. Handing me a cup of water, we greeted one another but our exchanges meant nothing to either of us. The western clouds were beginning to turn late afternoon pink.

A few low buildings straggled the roadside, otherwise the landscape was bare. Towards the top of the mountains on the other side, a few houses showed on the skyline with lighted fires. People were starting to prepare their evening meals. A steep dirt track led upwards from the road, lonely and uninviting. Not a vehicle in sight in either direction.

It was almost five o clock and would be dark by six thirty. I didn't relish the idea of being alone on the unpredictable road for too long. After five minutes or so, I could just make out a white car, coming towards me from the direction of Butha-Buthe. On the open stretch it was travelling very fast.

'I hope to God it's one of the company cars' I thought, as it came nearer. At this distance I couldn't tell if it had a white driver, but there was no chance I would let it go past. Using a white t-shirt, my arm flagged like one of those stewards at an international race meeting. The car skidded to a halt on the gravel and a familiar voice shouted,

"*Mon Dieu*, it is you Annette! I will go and fetch Barrie. Stay in your car!"

It was one of the senior staff from the camp on his way to Leribe. The dust clouds followed his wheels up the steep slope ahead. It meant at least half an hour would pass before help arrived. Anxiety returned and as there was no point in wandering up and down the road, the driver's seat offered the only comfort. It was hot inside the vehicle and a huge buzzing insect had managed to get locked in with me.

Turning to look in my mirror, I saw two men walking towards me on the empty road . My heart sank. Instinctively I wound up my window. They were an oddly contrasting pair. One man was tall with a beard and looked a bit uncertain of himself, but the younger man came nearer. He leaned down to the window and spoke.

"Do you need help, 'M'e? We saw your car from a distance.We may be able to assist you."

He had a handsome face and was clean shaven and looked about twenty four years old. He had a lovely fresh smile and his seSotho/ English was admirable. Faintly nervous himself, he moved nearer to the front of the car and passed a hand over his forehead as if trying to think what to do next. His manner was gentle and respectful. I decided in a moment that he was not intent on hurting me. Aware that I had done very little to appreciate his interest in me, I wound my window down a little.

"You speak very good English! Where do you live ? What is the name of your village?" I asked, deciding to invest in conversation with this young man. We both relaxed.

He waved his arm in the direction of the mountain.

"My father is the priest of St John's Church in Ha Simone. It is where you are now. He is Reverend Stephen Makibi and my name is Walter Makibi. Our house is over there beside the church. You cannot see it from the road. I was going to the shop over there when I saw your car had stopped for a long time."

By this time I was enjoying myself . The boy's friendliness was genuine and I wished that I could say something useful in seSotho.

"I am waiting for someone from L.H.P.C. to come and bring help." I said, indicating to the stranger that someone knew where I was.

"Do you live at L.H.P.C. camp?" asked Walter. "I was working on Muela Dam before the strike of last year. Now I'm out of work. Please would you ask them for a job for me. I am a good worker. Now I am worried about my family because I am bringing no money." Walter's face looked solemn and he indicated with his hand on his heart, how much he wanted to work again ."I will stay with you until the truck comes," he offered. "You will be safe in our village. But please will you come back?"

He spoke with precision and some degree of eloquence. Warily, I began to trust him. The man with him had not spoken a word.

"Please write me your name and I'll show it to someone at Leribe camp. There might be a chance of some work. Why did you finish?"

"During the strike last year, everyone was sacked and there was a lot of trouble around here. I was sent to my cousin's house in Welkom.When I came back there were no more jobs. I definitely want to find one."

Walter did not hold back from the truth about the strike – indeed almost 2,000 men had been sacked in all, when at the height of the trouble, the main core of the troublemakers had held the company to ransome with violent attacks on individual staff. Afterwards, most of the workers were re-instated, good men who wanted to have jobs and earn wages - but only after personal assurances that they were not part of the violence.

Walter stood beside me until help arrived and we waved each other farewell – me clutching the piece of paper on which he had written his name.

Barrie was shocked when he was told that I was stranded outside Leribe and came straight out to find me in his car. It was almost dark as we left the roadside at Ha Simone.

"Who was that man? You could have been robbed or worse!" he said more from worry than anger. "This road is no place to be after dark."

"If in doubt – talk," I said with satisfaction when we were safely back inside the camp. Barrie, accustomed to my methods of wriggling out of a difficult situation, warned me not to be so impetuous and fussed over my explanations. The face of that boy and the proud eyes remained so clearly in my mind. He had not asked me for money, nor put me in his debt by any gesture or fault. There was something about him that was worthy and loyal. I kept the piece of paper in my pocket. There would be a better time.

Early the very next morning, with Betty as my interpreter, I retraced my journey along the road to Ha Simone, carrying with me, a box of groceries and some clothes in a bag. I shared my secret with no one. It was a perfect sky; blue and cloudless.

As we came near to the place where my car had stopped the previous afternoon, I recognised the tin roof of the shop and next door to it, a fenced off area where men were doing welding machine work, putting together those tin toilets, with a chimney on top, that is a feature of the landscape in every part of Lesotho. At the bus stop, a taxi drew up and spilled out passengers carrying large cabbages, a few children, and several unseen clucking chickens. The emergent bodies didn't seem to equate to the size of the vehicle. A hen squawked as it was stuffed inside a jersey. Bosom and brown feathers disappeared along the path towards the river.

I stopped the car and waited. The box of groceries firmly balanced on her head, Betty strode purposefully across the dusty yard. She was to ask that the parcel be handed to Reverend Makibi and his family at St John's Church by the river. In minutes she came out smiling .

"I gave him ten Rands 'M'e" she said with a grin. "De man, he gave a good promise. He knows very well de village Priest. I shout loud to everyone my message. See that it is not get stolen 'M'e."

I wondered if my mission would work. Free food to a hungry Basotho is like gold. All I had to rely on was the word of the shop owner. I might never know if Reverend Makibi would learn of my appreciation for the goodwill and honesty of his son. Walter's chivalry was a credit to his family and went against much of what I had previously been told of my countrymen. Despite the unpleasant rumours that surfaced on the undercover camp gossip line, I could not bring myself to believe that Lesotho was as dangerous as people made out.

Betty was very pleased with herself. She sat in the front seat of the car as we drove back, and patted her broad belly. Today's conversation centered upon the fact that we had not yet chosen a name for her baby. She had been glad to assist in the secret visit to

Walter's village and knew that we shared a closer friendship than most of the maids on the camp did with their host families. She accepted her difficult life with grim determination and was always pleasant and smiling. We had shared many funny moments when things went slightly wrong or we misunderstood one another.

Betty's favourite word was 'Okay'. In answer to any question, Betty would say, "Okay 'M'e" sometimes once, sometimes four or five times in a row. When a person says 'Okay' it usually means that the request has been understood. But Basotho girls do not always understand the language well. Betty used to go away and think about what she had been asked to do - and instead of asking me to explain, she would do what she *thought* I wanted her to do. On one occasion I asked her if she would make sure she put a black plastic bag in the dustbin before she threw out the rubbish.

"Okay 'M'e" answered Betty. There my responsibility ended - I thought.

Every Mosotho thinks it quite mad to use a dustbin in any case. Goodness knows what they would make of a Croydon Council wheelie-bin. Betty did the thing she was asked. She neatly folded up a black plastic bag and placed it in the bin before she threw the rubbish on top. I soon discovered to my horror, that waste food in a hot climate means a bluebottle convention in minutes and a milling throng of ants from every orifice within ten yards. When an unpleasant odour crept into the air outside the back door and a whole army of ants marched in columns from the bin up the wooden steps to the kitchen, our misunderstanding was discovered.

Immediately with another string of 'Okays' and much good natured laughter the matter was put right. She redeemed herself by subsequently tying up almost everything in a plastic bag - even plastic bags.

We were still engaged in selecting from the English 'not common' boys names for her baby. Betty liked to have several names to ponder over while she worked and today it was Thomas, Nathaniel, Oliver, Jeremy and Adam. She was convinced her baby was going to be a boy. I wrote the names on a piece of paper so she could keep referring to them. She would then practice the names as she did the ironing and for the whole of one morning, I would hear, "Thomas- thump, Thomas - thump" in strict timing with the bangs on the ironing table until she had finally got the sound of the name to her satisfaction. Then another name would be lifted up and played with and ironed into the shirts .

My morning was interrupted by a bevy of French ladies from Butha-Buthe arriving to discuss the prospect of a trip up to Katze Dam the following weekend. The weather being so fine in January, a few families had proposed that we should take a day trip to see the reservoir which was now almost full. As part of the Highlands Water Scheme, it was time we made the two and a half hour trek up into the mountains.

There was such excitement in getting ready. Between talks of travel sickness pills and expected bouts of vertigo, we prepared gallons of cool drinks and sun protection, climbing gear, sweaters and cameras. It was extremely hot as our convoy of three cars drove upwards towards Pitseng on the steep incline, past the villages of Khanyane and Mahobong on that Sunday in late January.

The new asphalt bitumen road is a feat of engineering in itself and took almost seven years to build. It is the equivalent of a journey of 240kms there and back, winding a slow climbing route through hairpin bends, up and over the Mafika Lisui Pass at 3,090 metres high. The road rises steeply, clinging to the mountainside, and the spectacular view of Lefikeng Pass where mountain waterfalls cascade through the ravines, is breathtaking.

A special lunch had been prepared for us at Ha Lejone camp, as guests of the L.H.P.C. camp manager, an hour's drive up the mountain. Ice cold drinks greeted our arrival and we spent a pleasant hour dining beside the water pool with a heavenly view of the Malibamat'so Valley spread before us. One day, when the construction of the dam is finally completed, this village will be situated on the banks of the new lake. All along the valley, white markers indicate where the water level will come to, once the reservoir is full.

The tarred road winds up into more hairpins, and crosses the river by way of Malibamat'so Bridge. This is the Northern access route to Katse and the bridge, an astonishing engineering achievement, crosses the river with a 465 metres span. After this, the road climbs up over another series of hills to the Matsoku Valley until it reaches Katse at 4,000 metres. The dangers the engineers must have faced in building this first road up to the top of the mountain are unimaginable. The initial inspection had to be done by helicopters. Surveyor plus theodolite on the end of a rope, invites a bizarre spectacle.

Many Basotho families were going to church, dressed in their spiritual best , emerging from high slopes and over sandstone rocks. Ministers in purple cloaks, black flowing robes and strange shaped hats dotted the landscape.This is a land without walls. Smartly dressed men and women with their offspring in bright church day outfits, bobbed up and down through fields of maize. Fashion came in candy floss dresses gathered up with purple bows; boys in pink shirts with choking collars, flotillas of umbrellas embracing each family, shading them from the sun.

They spread in large circles around the doors of their mission churches, gathering together like a flock of sparrows, ready to clap and sing their chants and rhythms on the open hillside. The French missionaries had been the first people to bring Christianity to Lesotho to begin their centres of worship and education. The Mountain King, Moshoeshoe 1 wanted his people to be taught Christian principles and in 1833 welcomed the first missionaries from Paris. Many small communities have flourished from those days and perhaps what we were witnessing today had sprung from those early Evangelists.

One family was moving house across from one side of the valley to the other. Balanced on their heads was a household of furniture. Father carried the wooden table, mother the mattress and each of five children a chair or a wooden bench. The youngest carried a clay pot. They walked in crocodile fashion across the road in front of us - very intent on keeping on the heels of the one in front. From far off, we could see a kind of segmented beetle, slowly crawling upwards, the tail as tiny as one clay pot.

During the journey one of the children in our party felt unwell from the zigzagging nature of the ride and we stopped so that she could walk and get some fresh air. Immediately we were surrounded by village folk all wagging their heads and pointing, almost enclosing our little group so that we found confusion rather than a little solitude. Out of the jabbering crowd stepped a man in a suit who looked as if he had just disembarked from the ten thirty train to Waterloo. He could have been the sub-editor of the South London News on the way to his city desk.

"How old is the child?" he said smartly, in English, to which no one in our party answered. "I can help you perhaps. I am a village medical doctor. I can give you some medicine, to make the child well."

By this time, there was an interested crowd gathering, appearing as if from nowhere.We declined his offer, very politely, so as not to offend, but having sudden thoughts of witch doctors and ancestral spirits. The art of the medicine man still exists in these remote villages. Sangomas are still held in high esteem by many people. The practice of herbal medicine and throwing bones to determine the health of a sick child, is still used. To continue our journey seemed the best thing.

At Katse, the homesteads were humming with life; ox carts in the fields, herdsmen tending cattle and angora goats - the special breed found in Lesotho. The people we saw looked bold hearted and vivacious, as though they had been joined at the hip with the land they were born on, refusing to be spirited away onto other mountain tops. They had lived here for generations, existing through the harsh winters, with only their foodstocks of mealie and sorghum. We saw herdboys, some as young as eight or nine, wrapped only in tattered blankets with their working donkeys and dogs that went with them up to the mountain pastures; busy women with their cooking pots and clean swept yards.

How must the villagers have felt, when the first trucks rode up the pass, carrying their huge load of tunnel boring equipment, rotadump cars, and shotcrete conveyor units, ready to turn their back yards into a historical water scheme working site?

Rivers which have flowed through these mountains for millenia have now been diverted through concrete tunnels, excavated by powerful machines called TBM's - giant cutting and rock-splitting animals which eat into the hardest dolerite dyke with steel teeth. Ventilation systems designed to force fresh air to each rock face as the machines bite and gnaw their way through the basalt lava, spell out the extent of man's progress through the earth.

The mountains at night used to be lit by the homestead fires. Now the daylight hours of the Basotho herdsman has been extended to a pre-determined twenty four hour power circuit that lights up the entire construction area. This must have been a strange phenomenon to both shepherd and sheep. It is said that the whole chicken population during the first few months refused to lay.

Enormous drilling machines and cranes moved in, mobile houses were brought up the mountain for the workers and a whole organisation of dramatic proportions swallowed up their mealie fields.

In the space of a few years their beautiful land has become a reservoir. A wide sweep of curved concrete wall of immense proportions, rises 185 metres into the sky.

The entire project will take thirty years to complete – expected by the year 2020. The first phase, located on the Malibamat'so River north of Thaba Tseka, has been the subject of years of international discussion, mostly because of the size of the project and its ecological effect on the remote villages of Lesotho. Katse Dam is one of the largest and most intricate construction projects anywhere in the world. In real terms the Kingdom of Lesotho has been affected by an infrastructure of dramatic proportions. Environmental protection is of the highest priority and the companies involved in the project have pledged to safeguard the standards of living of individuals and communities.

Jobs have been created. The spin-off for Lesotho is self sufficiency in terms of power.The financial benefits are that Lesotho will receive 25 million rands a year for the next fifty years, in revenue. Meanwhile, it is considered to be the ninth poorest country in the world.

As for South Africa, the water is urgently required to supplement the existing supply in the Vaal Basin catchment area, the country's commercial and industrial heartland, south of Johannesburg. From Katse, 200 kilometres of underground tunnels will take the water through the layers of rock, downstream to Muela Dam, now in its final stages of constuction, and from there to the South African border. Eventually the delivery network out of Lesotho will join the Ashe River near Bethlehem. From there millions of tons of water will flow into the Vaal Dam, where it will be used for South Africa's rapidly growing conurbations in Greater Johannesburg and Pretoria.

The price of this whole venture culminates in Lesotho's own supply of electricity, which will end its dependence on South Africa. Little wonder that in these parts, water is known as 'white gold'.

We stood on the top of the hill overlooking Katse Dam in complete awe. It is spectacular. It is monumental. Surrounded by high mountains, in the heat of the sun and the glare of the sky, the dam curves in a great arch; a living national monument.

Katse is a great tribute to twentieth century engineering - yet will it impoverish even further, the little arable land available in Lesotho - or will it bring the kind of wealth which improves the quality of life to these primitive tribes? In years to come it will be a good fishing ground, and people will bring boats to sail. Perhaps fish will feature in the diet of the Basotho people, and their menfolk become fishermen instead of farmers. A new leisure industry is possible for the first time, which will bring employment. Babies will be born within the boundaries of modern technology and their education will reflect great changes in Basotho traditions.

Whatever happens in the future, the people of Lesotho will know that white men featured in the history of their country and that Katse Dam ranks among the highest in the world, certainly the highest in Africa.

Our journey was almost at an end. Now came the fast downward helter skelter ride, through cobweb mists and fleeting glimpses of wild flowers. It was chilly enough to wear a winter sweater as the sun sank down like a red ball and shadows enveloped each cliff face, one by one. We seemed to plummet from day into night and back again, almost freewheeling down and down, the car almost turning in pirouettes, through the hairpin bends.Cactus stood black against the pink light. Pale waterfalls fell from the sky.

Drowsiness and headaches affected old and young alike. Two hours later we reached Leribe; our driver only just awake....

For the whole of the next day, I wanted to hide my head under a blanket in a darkened room and talk to no one. I felt my dizzy brain whirling round and round, like a circus of cotton wool. Apparently this effect is a predictable conclusion of a Katse climb. One of my Basotho friends offered me a donkey for my next trip.

Chapter 20

Walter and the Dinosaur.

In January, Mrs Petros had a baby. It was a Monday morning, I was at home and Petros came running across the garden, arms waving, to tell me something very important.

" 'M'e, I have some news. My wife has given me a baby daughter. She was born on Saturday - she arrived too soon - but my wife, she is now Okay."

His smile told me everything.

"Come in and tell me about it Petros. I want to hear about your baby daughter."

"Yes 'M'e, her pains came quick quick. She did not know de baby would come on this day. But she shouted me to go and find a truck to take her to de hospital. So I went to look for de driver, but he was not at home. My wife she yell loud - Petros hurry !"

"So what did you do Petros? Is your house a long way from the hospital?" I asked impatiently '

"Yes 'M'e, it is too far far away. But I have another friend who has a truck, and I went running to his house. He was gone away. Then I ran back to tell my wife there was a problem. Then when I reach my house, a lady came out of my house and she tell me, Petros, your child is born already, you do not need to find a truck!"

At this, he paused for breath, as tears ran down his face, and he showed me with his hands how tiny the baby was. Then he added, "she is named Thabiseng and she is very healthy."

"Petros, you must be very proud today. Please tell your wife I am very glad that you have a baby girl. And when can I come and see her? "I handed him a hot steaming mug of tea - it seemed the only thing to do. He beamed at me .

"I will tell my wife that you will come to see the baby. She will be so pleased to speak to you. But our house is very small 'M'e, it is not like your house. I will show you where it is."

"Fine, Petros, we will make a plan. I would like to bring something to your new baby girl, as a gift. You must show me where to go."

I was fascinated to have the opportunity to talk to a Mosotho woman, who had just given birth without doctor or medical aid. The cutting of the umbilical cord was probably done using a piece of glass; the birth would be accompanied by singing from the other women and the baby delivered by one of her neighbours. The placenta would be given to the cows and the baby washed in water from the well. Thoughts of sterilized maternity wards in England flashed through my mind. A Mosotho mother could not begin to understand the idea of powdered milk and clinically hygenic plastic bottles. Mrs Petros would be lucky if she lived close to a source of clean water.

Usually two reeds are placed over the doorway of the hut to warn others that there is a *motsoetse*, that is a mother with a new born child inside and no male visitors other than the husband are allowed to enter. Other village women assist at the motsoetse by fetching water and cooking food and they make a kind of thin porridge called *lesheleshele*, which is made from ground sorghum and water. This is a necessary part of the healing for the newly delivered mother.

Only when the child emerges from the womb will it be given a name. The Basotho often give their children names which indicate the circumstances of the birth, such as *Tseleng*, which means born on the roadside, *Paseka*, born at Easter or *Malehola*, a name given to a girl at weeding time. The name *Tseliso*, means 'consolation' and is often given to a baby boy when the previous child has died and the name, *Puseletso*, meaning 'compensation' is given to a girl when the previous child has died. If a child should die during confinement, it will be placed inside a clay pot and buried in or near the house.

When a Mosotho is born, the news is broken to the father by pouring water over him – if it is a girl, or beating him with sticks - if it is a boy. On the occasion of the firstborn, a young woman has to go and live in the village of her parents, where her mother and sisters look after her until the baby is born. Some of the older women of the village come and tell her grizzly stories of childbirth, just to remind her of her duty to deliver a healthy child.

As the time for confinement approaches a special place is prepared known as a 'birth-house' where the girl will live with her new child, alone, for eight weeks, feeding her baby on breastmilk. Soon after birth the mother makes small incisions on the child's wrists, forehead, neck and chest. A special paste made from herbs is smeared onto the skin to help the child's growth and survival.

After remaining inside the house for two months, the mother is allowed out with her child and the baby is rolled on the ground, if possible during a shower of rain. When this has been done the relatives believe that the child's future is going to be happy, secure and free from disease.

Even though the father may live a great distance away, his friends will go and find him to perform the ritual of beating him with sticks or pouring water over him. If he is in church, they will find him and throw great bowls of water over him in celebration of his newborn daughter. He has a right to feel very proud though he has not even seen his new child.

In most cases the whole village celebrate the birth of a healthy child, even a beast may be killed and roast on a spit and everyone comes to enjoy the feast. Songs are sung to the ancesters in thanksgiving of a new life. Then the birth-house has to be cleansed. The cleansing process can take several days, when it is the duty of the grandmother to inspect the work to her satisfaction. Afterwards the young mother prepares to leave, carrying her newborn baby on her back.

In the old days the journey on foot could take several days, now she would normally take a taxi if she has any money, to return to her husband, who will be there to greet her – that is if he hasn't gone to find another wife. Tradition allows a man to have more than one wife, but he must support each wife in the same way, educate all the children of his extended family and pay the same money to each wife. In practice, a man cannot easily afford the luxury of two wives, yet having learned from my friend Dentle in Fouriesburg, it is still possible.

Petros only had one wife and he loved her. She was his reason for living. He spoke of her with great pride and felt a strong duty to protect his family- now two girls and a boy. He was well educated, worked hard at his job on the camp and felt fervently that it was his duty to serve the Lord. He belonged to the Church of the Seventh Day Adventists. When he wasn't on duty, he would be driving miles to their Mother Church in South Africa. To be invited to meet Mrs Petros and the new baby was quite a special privilege. He was worried that I might not like his house because it was small but was so proud of his new child, that this point was overlooked for the time being.

Through most of the month of January it was a joy to have a strawberry patch. Fruit came on in clusters, day after day. The berries could be green in the morning and red by evening. The sweetness of their taste was different to English strawberries. Spinach was also proving easy to grow and the crop of courgettes was modest, hoed and watched over lovingly by Thabo. Betty delighted in taking strawberries home for her family and one morning brought Margaret to help. I gave them a large bowl.

"Betty would you and Margaret like to pick some strawberries for Mrs Petros?"

In the afternoon, I was due to go and teach the French ladies at Butha-Buthe and was preparing to leave. Margaret, bowl in hand, came to sit on the stoep and appeared not to look too well. Her skin colour didn't look right.

"Betty, I think Margaret isn't well. Her eyes look very sleepy and she is a little paler than usual."

On further inspection, we discovered that her skin was starting to show tiny spots on her chest and arms. We laid her on a blanket and she slept, curled up, covered in a white towel on the bedroom carpet for the rest of the day while Betty did her work. I went in to see her before leaving the house and she looked very peaceful. I gave Betty ten rands to take her to the hospital. That is the minimum fee to see a doctor. I left soon afterwards.

After the class, Liliane and I were driving home towards Leribe Camp where the road goes through Ha Simone, engrossed in conversation, when we heard a loud piercing whistle, sometimes used by the herd boys to call in their dogs. It made me glance back through my rear view mirror. A fair way behind, I saw Walter running up behind us along the tarmac. Leaning my head out of the window I pulled to a standstill on the gravel shoulder as he raced towards us. The sun was in my eyes and I had been concentrating on the road ahead. He was out of breath when he reached the car.

"Please wait 'M'e....my father .. he wants to meet you... he wants to thank you for the food. He asked me to tell you that it was appreciated. I have been waiting for you for several days. I knew your car would come along this road at some time."

The implications of this question meant driving off the main road - something which I had been forbidden to do. White ladies should not go wandering into villages without a known guide. Common sense and caution surfaced in my mind, but seldom had I held back from a desire to embark on an adventure, more than at this moment. Walter's solemn face bend down towards the level of my window. He was quite a tall young man, slim and rangy and by Basotho standards, well shaven and attractive. He had a beautiful voice and his words were spoken easily and confidently.

"Down at the Subeng River, we have the dinosaur footprints. We would like to show you that they once lived in our village. The rocks are written in a book. Many people come to see them. Please say you will come. I will first take you to meet my father."

I looked across at Liliane. Like me, she could not resist such a request and she too recognised that Walter had spoken very politely and we could see that his offer was genuine.

"Dinosaur footprints !" we both said at the same time.

"Walter please tell your father that we will come, but not today. It is too late in the day and we are expected home at a certain time. We must leave now. But we'll come again in two more days. Both of us will come. I will drive to the bus stop on the other side. At two in the afternoon. Thank you for waiting – we'll see you again in two days time. Please tell your mother I look forward to meeting her."

As we drove off towards our destination, we were both absolutely certain beyond a doubt, that we would go back to Ha Simone to meet Walter and his family. Nothing would prevent us from accepting this afternoon's invitation. Our excitement level was uncontrollable and to keep it a secret for two days required a supreme effort. We both knew it would not be appreciated in other quarters.

The following morning, a strange lady came to the camp gate to ask for me and the guard came over with a note addressed to 'Mis Clen' to say that Margaret had 'an attack of the chick poxes', which meant that I had a free day. A short time later, Barrie rang from the main office to say that there would be a truck going to Bethlehem about lunchtime and the driver could take a couple more passengers. Liliane and I were mid flight doing our morning excercise routine with Cindy Crawford, bent in not the prettiest of contortions, when the call came through.

Without more ado we abandoned our thigh reducing ham string pulls, changed leotards for shorts and shirts then ran down to the office to catch the truck. Sam was the driver and promised to take us into Bethlehem, which meant we could go shopping for a present for Mrs Petros's new baby. It was extremely hot in the kombi and the sun shimmered on the road ahead like pools of water. The sky was the colour of cornflowers in England on a summer's day.

Baby donkeys were dotted over the landscape or gathered in small groups by the mill. They were still too young to carry sacks of mealie but their time would come later on in the year when harvest came round. Their biscuit coloured coats were still shiny and healthy and they sauntered along behind their mothers like a cavalcade of skinny desert mules. The leading herd boys agonised on how to cope with skidding legs on a tarmac road and did their best to control the unstable animals.

On the way out of Leribe we passed a group of perhaps ten or twelve young men, running along the main road in a pack, wearing red shorts and blowing loud whistles, waving their arms like a triumphant football team. Everyone they passed stopped to stare.

"Sam, why are these men running on the road, blowing whistles?" we both wanted to know.

"These are the *Makoloane* - they're graduates of the Initiation School," he explained. "In addition to formal education, there is the traditional education in Lesotho, which some boys attend, if their parents wish them to go through the ceremony of circumcision. There is a place called the *Mophato*, situated far away in the mountains, where boys can go for several weeks,where the elders prepare them for manhood," offered Sam hesitantly. "These boys are returning from that school and they're coming mainly to collect money. They are very proud of their position in society and they come to tell everyone that they have graduated. Somewhere along this road, they will stop running and perform special songs. If you also stop to listen, you are obliged to give them money."

We learnt that the young men return to their villages and try to find themselves a wife. Until he is married, a young man is regarded as a minor and his father, or his nearest male relative is responsible for his conduct. The whole affair seems to be shrouded in some sort of mystery. Sam, who always answered our questions explicitly, was clearly guarded about the subject and there was a trace of something unusual in his voice.

We passed through the border at Caledonsport without incident and entered South Africa. A river of yellow flowers billowed along each bank. Armies of sunflowers - bent and swaying like shards of topaz, winked with a million eyes. It was so bright, we had to shield our faces from the glare. These seeds are mainly part of South Africa's exports. Farmers are offered subsidies for a good crop. Sam said that this year looked set to outweigh previous good years.

At the junction with the Fouriesburg Road, where the usual cluster of people were sitting on the ground waiting for a lift, a dead horse lay in the grass just off the hard shoulder. It was on it's back with its legs stuck out stiffly. We couldn't see its neck or head, just the great bloated body, stiff with rigormortis. Craning our necks to look, Sam said quietly, "the horse was here yesterday, when I passed, in the afternoon."

We both gasped. The potential health risk of a decomposed body of an animal, the size of a horse, left to rot in the heat of the sun made us feel quite sick.

"It will probably still be here next week."

The first time I had seen the corpse of a dog left flattened on the road, I had felt anger and outrage. It is a common sight here. Carcasses are abandoned on the roads and left to the ravens, the rats and the weather. Dogs are not regarded as pets and are left to scavenge for food. People are so poor they find it hard to obtain enough food for themselves. Dogs are regarded as working animals and as such, are left to forage at night, often travelling across country. Unwittingly they run across a road in the dark and cause many an accident.

There is no organisation which takes care of animals killed or mutilated on roads, no vetinary services, no treatment centres - the process of nature itself is the only effective service in animal welfare in this part of the world. The scene at the roadside stayed in our minds a long while.

Thanks to Sam our journey was worthwhile and we brought back our gift for Thabiseng from a clothes store in Bethlehem belonging to a friendly Afrikans lady; a papoose made of patchwork cloth, soft enough to lay any baby in - and a woven blanket. These would please Mrs Petros enormously, we were sure.

Our journey home was along the same bit of road and it was a painful exercise to view once more, the lifeless body of the horse, half hidden in the long grass. We learnt, many days later, that the unfortunate animal ran out into the road and was hit by a car driven by an elderly couple travelling home from Bethlehem at night. Both driver and passenger had been killed.

Approximately 3 kilometres from our camp, we drove past the spot where we had met Walter the day before and where tomorrow, we would come back to see dinosaur footprints in the river. We related to Sam what had taken place and he assured us that there were indeed pre-historic remains at Ha Simone and that we would be quite safe to go and see Reverend Makibi at the Church of St John. He was well known in this district and all that Walter had said appeared to be correct. He was known by the chief and had a respected family name.

In my diary the following day I wrote, ' Walter and a dinosaur! Drunk on excitement!' After filling a box with groceries and leaving messages for our menfolk saying where we had gone, Liliane and I drove towards Ha Simone in time to meet Walter at two o'clock, having decided that if he didn't appear, we would return straight home. This was going to be a milestone in our lives - whatever happened.

From the top of the hill, we could see the tall figure of Walter waiting patiently by the bus stop. When we drew up beside him it was plain that he had dressed especially smart for the occasion, and was very pleased to see us. Although there was a look of under-nourishment about him, he had that sinewy shape which was trim and muscular, and his clothes fitted him well. His welcoming smile was all the greeting we needed .

"Walter, this is my friend Liliane," I said, opening the rear door of the car, "I hope we're on time. Jump in and show us the way to your house. We're looking forward to meeting your family - you must tell us all their names. We've brought you some food."

Walter sat in the back seat and directed me along a stony track which went alongside the tin toilet factory, past the shop where Betty had taken the first box of food. Everyone inside the fence waved and the small children came running to see the car, with their black toes kicking up the dust.

"Turn to the right and follow the track down towards the river. On the right you will pass our mealie field. It is our good crop for this year. Ahead you will see the beautiful mountains where we live. Every day they greet us."

"Walter were you born in this village?"

"Yes I was born in the very house which I will show you today. It is still the same house where all my brothers and sisiters were born. Now you can see the road leads down to the river, where we will go later this afternoon. But you must first turn to the right. You will see the track is very bumpy, but take it and you will see our little church ahead of you."

Turning right meant having to leave the main track to go across a shallow inlet where the ground was boggy and full of boulders and stones, then the ground rose and fell steeply in muddy channels. We were all being jerked from side to side in our seats and I wondered if my car springs would hold. It was like driving across the moon. Walter apologised for the state of the road and said in the rainy season, the way was always difficult. Daring to glance sideways I could see the deep ravine that was the river below us, the valley rising away, the dark green of good crops.

There is a white wall which circles St John's church, built by the boys in the family to give a feeling of security within. It is made from boulders and clay from the earth and painted with whitewash which they make themselves. As you approach the entrance to their homestead peach trees are dotted here and there, and a small square hut with a tin roof, to the left side. A skinny lad with a shaved head, of about six years old, sat on top of the wall and waved. He was wearing the remains of a pair of old shorts and carried a stick.

Walter explained to us that he was the child of the sick woman who lived in the hut. The family had come to their church to be healed. Through the open gateway, the edges of the path paved with whitewashed boulders, we came into a square yard of hard baked earth, with enough space to park four or five cars. This looked onto a single storey stone house with blue painted door and windows, fronted with a kind of terra-cotta stone stoep - polished and gleaming in the sun. A perfect place to sit and look across the mountains to watch the sun go down. On the other side of the yard, which was clean and twig-brushed, were two more stone houses - without proper doors and windows; their flat tin roofs laden with stones. An ox waggon was standing to one side and a pile of logs lay cut and ready under the peach tree, next to their fence. Up beyond the house was a kraal, which I learnt later was used to shelter the newly born calves.

In the middle of the yard stood Rose and Stephen Makibi.They were wearing the blue and white uniform of St John's Church. Today was their midweek day of family worship. My pulse raced as we walked towards each other.

"Nettie, I would like you to meet my father, Stephen."

Stephen Makibi, stood with outstretched hand.

"And this is my mother, Rose. She has been dying to meet you."

We shook hands with the special Basotho handshake.

"A very special day for us." said Rose. In our moment of shaking hands I felt she almost curtsied.

"Liliane, please come and meet my parents," said Walter, gathering confidence.

"Bonjour Madame, Monsieur. Comment ça va?"

Rose and Stephen - delighted at being addressed in French, smiled broadly and welcomed us both with sincere generosity. Rose just melted my heart. She had a kind face and dark eyes that never stopped dancing. She spoke softly and her manner was of that rare breed of women, born to be a mother. Stephen obviously adored her. Here was a woman who was loved.

Walter's father shook my hand with both his. A patriarchal portly figure, his delightful humour, which was bursting from inside him, made us feel glad that we had made this journey. He thanked me heartily for sending the food.

"No Stephen, I should thank you. For the kindness of your son. You should be proud of the way he acted towards me when I needed help in your village. I will always be grateful to him. I could have been badly treated or robbed - instead we have been invited into your home. Walter is a true friend."

We were invited to go inside the house out of the glaring heat, to sit down at their table and talk. They had nothing to offer us but water from their spring. They apologised that there was no food to place on the table.

We went through Rose's big kitchen which was furnished with cupboards and some kind of a stove. There was a flat iron like the one which Betty had, standing on a table and a deep plastic barrel with a lid, filled with fresh water. Liliane and I were hesitant about drinking but they assured us it was fresh from the spring. It tasted good but was lukewarm. There were some stairs up to another level into their main room. A fine big table too big for the roomspace stood in the middle, polished like glass. There were several arm chairs, a sofa and what had once been a bow-fronted cabinet, now faded and without its glass doors, in which sat Rose's pride and joy - two best cups and saucers. The walls were painted white and the floor was rosy with some kind of polish Everything they owned was stacked neatly round the room and reflected order and cleanliness. Not one item looked new, but all were cherished.

On the table, one very old hand sewing machine. Rose's sewing lay beside it. Emily, Walters's nineteen year old sister, was occupied with her school books at one end of the room and stood to greet us. Like her mother, she had soft features and gentle way of speaking.

"Emily, I hope we're not intruding - your father asked Walter to meet us on the road. Your brother came to my rescue last week when I broke down in your village." Emily smiled and sat down next to me. We took to each other instantly and there was a bond. She was was a friendly girl, with an easy manner like both her parents.

Walter stood at one end of the table - glowing. He and Liliane were deep in conversation about his church and she spoke English for Walter had no French. The whole family spoke so clearly and confidently in English, it seemed as if it was their first language.

I shall never forget that first afternoon. We all talked at once. Our first conversations with the Makibis were spiralling into friendships so quickly that it felt as though destiny had brought us here. Liliane and I were the first white people ever to enter their home and sit with them at their table. Instead of feeling like strangers, we felt like returned travellers.

Rose was charming; she could not thank us enough for coming. Stephen wanted to tell much about the church.They had built it with their own hands many years before. The full name of their church is St John's of the Apostolic Faith Mission which is linked to an established church in South Africa.The mother church is in Durban. Both Stephen and Rose are ordained priests. They call their little church a branch line.

St John's Church is a Christian church which sprang from the English Anglican Church, originally called the Church of Lesotho. Our Bible is their Bible,translated into seSotho, on which basis their belief in Christianity is sustained. They hold the same Christian principles as our Anglican church and alongside they have a Healing Ministry which embraces needy people from outside the church to come and seek help. People travel long distances to come here - and Rose feeds them. They stay until they are ready to leave.

"I would like to show you inside our church today " said Stephen eagerly, " but unfortunately there are some services going on. The people are still there - you will hear the singing if you stand in the yard. You must come soon, on another day, and I will show you how we do in our church. It will be such an honour to show you inside."

In a natural gesture he raised his hand and very quietly he and Rose together spoke a prayer in seSotho - a blessing on our visit to St John's. I remember the shaft of sunshine showing deep red on the polished table top as I looked down and bent my head. I knew I was standing on the threshold of something very special. The serenity of the moment took me by surprise. Then someone else came into the room.

Justice, their second son, a good looking boy of eighteen had arrived home from school and came in to shake hands with us. He had the same kind eyes as his mother.

"Are you the lady who sent us the food? I am glad to see you. My mother was very happy on that day.You are welcome."

The tone of voice was mellow for his age. His greeting was warm and he looked across to Walter with approval.

Presently, Liliane and I walked down to the river, surrounded by the family. Walter's youngest sister, Bernice, had arrived home from school. She was nine years old and extremely shy, but she skipped along behind us with a host of other children who had sprung from nowhere. The only missing brother was Petros, the fifteen year old.

"Petros is with his beloved cows. You won't see him, he will be out on the fields somewhere. He comes straight home and takes them out to graze. He hates talking to us. Petros is the quiet one of the family. He would rather have a conversation with his cows!" exclaimed Walter with a fondness in his voice. "You will maybe see him next time. You will come again won't you. There is so much I can show you of Lesotho."

We were cool by the river. The children sat on wide flat stones where the ladies came to wash their clothes. A ford straddled the river at one point which the ox carts used. The opposite bank was steep and it was hard to imagine how a cart laden with crops could be pulled up.

"You will see them at harvest time. The oxen are very strong and the young boys know how to handle them."

It was the most natural thing in the world to think we should be there at harvest time - it was spoken as though, from now on, this was to be our home.

"Come on, I will show you where the dinosaur footprints are on the rocks" said Walter proudly. "You will see many of them here, they are well known all round the world. Somewhere there is a book….with important information.The dinosaurs are walking up our river bank just like you and I - one of them has taken twenty steps."

Because it had rained that day, the fossilized imprints stood out sharply and the shapes were clearly visible.

"C'est impossible, Mon Dieu," gasped my friend standing beside me.

"Incredible!" I echoed. "to see actual evidence left by creatures who lived three hundred million years ago" I looked into Walter's face. He seemed surprised by our pleasure.

"From a time when dinosaurs were the only inhabitants of our planet." added Stephen. "Many people come to this spot on the Subeng River; geologists, students of geography and history – tourists from lots of different countries….sometimes they stand and look for a long time."

It was impossible to quantify such strange and rare imprints in terms of the twentieth century. They belonged to a quadruped bigger in scale than anything we had ever seen. Walter pointed to two very different sets of prints.

One was a huge griffin-like claw and the other, a giant sized padded paw with five toes, deeply imprinted in the rock, spaced at intervals and continuing alongside the water's edge. Liliane and I looked at each other, "now - we will have to come back."

No longer strangers to this place, we agreed to make another visit to take photographs the following week. Apart from Lesotho and a few adjoining areas of South Africa, the only other parts of the world, where with comparable remains of the Upper Triassic period appear, are China and Brazil. Fossil footprints in Lesotho sometimes occured in stream beds, or on the sloping sides of boulders which have tumbled down the hillsides, or even on the roof of a cave.

Standing by the river with the Makibis, joined by half a dozen inquisitive children, with the pink sky overhead, I felt drawn to this lovely spot. Shielding my eyes from the sun, seeing the mountains on every side, I suddenly felt immensely calm. There was something quite magic here. Slowly it dawned on me that the reason for my journey from England was to meet Walter and his family at Ha Simone. A state of complete contentment came over me. I can only describe it as a feeling of homecoming.

"You live in a beautiful place Stephen."

"Yes, we are blessed with a beautiful country Nettie. We would like to show it to you. It is very different to England eh ?"

"I'd like to tell you about England" I promised, " perhaps one day I'll bring some pictures?"

A few thin cows strolled towards us led by a young boy in a pair of old rubber boots and some shorts that had seen better days. He carried a stick, for prodding the sauntering animals. We were right in their path. There was a familiar pleasure about their slow movements, solemn and fateful – the river belonged to them too.

"Walter, we must say goodbye now. But next week we'll come back – to take photographs of your dinosaur footprints. In England, they will never believe it."

He took my arm and we walked back up the steep slope towards the house. On the skyline we could see Petros with his cows coming in from the fields. It was five o'clock. As we passed the church, a flurry of ladies with babies sauntered across the open yard and the acrid smoke from a bonfire raised up behind one of the little huts.

"My mother is boiling water ready to cook the evening meal. And there is another family who are staying here, in one of the little houses. The man is very sick and has been attending the church services."

"Who are they?" I enquired.

"They have come from another village because the father is sick. My mother will give them food for a few days. They are staying in one of the spare huts for a while."

I noticed a sack had been pushed into the open window of one of the buildings and walking towards us, a man in a blue blanket, wrapped inside it as though he wanted to hide himself from the world. Slowly he came towards us. His eyes were hollow with sadness. Cradled in the folds of his blanket, his hand held an empty bowl.

"The man is suffering from bilharzia." Walter spoke softly so that the man would not hear. "It is a disease caused by a parasite which burrows into the soles of your feet. You can catch this in a river or a stream. This man cannot work any more."

Hardly able to stay upright - more corpse than alive, the slow figure shuffled across the yard. The depth of his misery showed in every faltering step.

Rose came to say goodbye. Bernice was hanging onto her skirt. Liliane and I thanked her for their warm hospitality. We walked together over to the car and handed her the box of food which had been carefully stored in the boot. Bernice took the box inside. Rose made the sign of the cross on herself and then whispered, "*kea leboha 'M'e.*"

"Sala hantle," I answered and she inclined her head slightly. "Please tell Emily, I'd like to help her with her lessons. If she'd like to come and join the other girls ...next time I come."

"So there will be a next time...."

We drove out of the yard with Rose shading her eyes from the sun and watching until we were out of sight. Stephen stood in the doorway and waved with both arms. Walter came with us down the track as far as the road. His eyes were full of happiness. When we came to bid farewell he put his strong hands on the steering wheel, over mine. Still reeling from the things we had witnessed that afternoon, my brain was full of new thoughts. It would be some time before I could grasp the the differences, the contrasting values in our lives. Questions were spilling out of me, but I didn't voice them. Walter spoke at last.

"Nettie, I am so glad you broke down in my village. Come soon again. You and Liliane will be safe in our village - everyone will know your Silver Fox has been to the Makibi's house. No one will harm you. You will always be welcome here."

Chapter 21

Proposals

In Lesotho, it is common practice to build yourself a house in lots of small stages. First you go and see the chief. Every village has one.

If, like me, you would expect to see a chief looking somewhat different from the rest of the human race you would find him in dress, like any ordinary citizen and following the same life patterns as anyone else. The only difference would be that he has to be available to any resident of his village who comes to ask for help. He must be psychologist, adviser, doctor and teacher all rolled into one and responsible to the King for his actions.

Normally a chief will inherit the title from his father or other senior male member of his family and by tradition, he is chosen because he is fairminded and wise. A chief is expected to help and advise people, no matter what their age, tribe or religion . He will discuss with you, pray for you, throw bones for you or confront your worst fears - but whatever the chief decides for you - must be carried out to the last letter. And nothing may change it. He is both judge and jury in his community and you must not displease him. Like every kind of society, the system is open to corruption. Offers of money, cattle and alcohol all play their part, but in essence the village is run by the wishes of the chief and most people still respect this.

One of his duties is to allocate and control the land in his area and make sure that it is truly representative of each family unit. Land in Lesotho is vested absolutely in the Basotho nation.The King, as Head of State, traditionally allocates the land to his chiefs, who in turn lease it to Basotho families.A few years ago, it was the custom for the chief to grant a field to a couple on the occasion of their marriage, but in recent years, with the growth of population and stricter control on land, this is no longer the case.

There is no rule of thumb over the size or the shape of your house, the type of roof or environmental design regulations- the only regulation is that it must be weather- proof enough for the variable climate and big enough for your family to live in. There are no bye-laws insisted upon by a buildings inspector or planning officer, no estate agents' fees or surveyors' reports to contend with. As long as your doorway faces the view of the mountain you most like to look at and your relationships with your nearest neighbour half a field away are in tune, you may build whatever type of house and have as many animals on your land as you wish.

Petros had been building his new house for three years. First he obtained the permission of the chief and the blessing of the priest. Then he dug the foundations and bought his first truckful of concrete blocks. Soon after this he ran out of money. The house stood for a while and the cows nibbled the grass inside the walls. The following spring he bought his second truck load of blocks. The walls went a little higher, but the roof was still a pipe dream. Lesotho is sprinkled with half finished dwellings like this. It sometimes takes a man ten years to be able to finish his house. When the rains come and the grasses grow high, the walls of a house almost disappear into the landscape - and sometimes vanish altogether if a thief brings his wheelbarrow in the night and removes his neighbours' walls to build his own.

When his wife had her baby, Petros wanted to finish the roof, so that his child should be brought up in their new house. But this was not possible, even though Petros had a good job, he was not able to afford any more bricks. He often spoke about his dream of putting a roof on his house. Petros had been at our house that day pointing out to me that our willow trees had some kind of disease which made the leaves go curly and the branches look dried up and twisted.

" 'M'e, I am bringing you a tree doctor, because your beautiful willow tree has been eaten by de little green worm. He is eating all de leaves."

Quite a lot of willows across the countryside were looking a bit wasted and unhealthy. Barrie and I had already commented on it, while travelling through Golden Gate Reserve. Those in our garden had that same disease-ridden appearance. Perhaps there was a pestilence over the land this year.

Petros took his postion as Director of Infestations very seriously. "I will bring a tree doctor to look at it soon," he announced. "We must kill de little green worm."

An arrangement had been planned for myself and Liliane to go and visit his wife and the new baby on the following Saturday. Petros arrived early that morning, to tell us how the road leading to his house had been washed away because of the rains and it was not safe to drive there.This meant that it would not be safe to leave my car at a distance away from the house and walk. It is not wise to leave a vehicle unattended in Lesotho for any length of time.

When he had done with assessing the damage to the willow tree, I handed Petros the parcel wrapped in pink paper, containing the baby papoose for Thabiseng with a letter to Mrs Petros . He was most happy about this and thanked me many times. I promised that we should go another day to visit his wife when the rains had gone. Then he turned and quite out of the blue, asked me a stunning question.

"I was wondering 'M'e, when Mr Glenn gets his pay, could you buy me a tractor?"

I winced. The look on Petros's face was both serious and angelic. Lurking at the back of my mind was the memory of that day when his friend had turned up with a diamond to sell.

"A tractor Petros? Why do you want us to buy you a tractor?"

The only shambling tractors in the fields around Leribe were rusty and decrepit pre-war International Harvester relics, or rather mutilated machines laid upside down in a ditch waiting for someone to get them back on the road.

"I can lend my tractor to de people to harvest mealie when it is harvest time and it can do the work of six men.That man will pay me and I will then go to another family and every day, my tractor will be working. Really, I will earn a lot of money so that I can pay for a roof on my house."

"How would this pay us back for the tractor Petros?" I asked, still intrigued by his blatant request to borrow several thousand rand for an indeterminate period. In Lesotho everything business-like was indeterminate.

"At the end of the year I will sell my tractor. I will have enough money to pay Mr Glenn back his money. And my roof will be finished."

He made it sound as easy as eating a plate of buns.

"Petros, what if the first man stole our tractor and it vanished over the mountain? Or if he caused some damage to it - or accidently drove it into a ditch - or if he didn't pay you - what then?"

Petros addressed me as if he was delivering a funeral speech.

"No. 'M'e this would not happen. I will only lend this tractor to my trusted friends. It will be quite safe and nothing will make it break down. I will make the man bring it back safely to me. Every night I will go and see if my tractor is still Okay. and collect de money. It is quite simple you see."

I felt as if I were being drawn into the teeth of a smiling alligator. After a long and involved conversation, it was obvious that Petros thought we were millionaires and the money was a simple matter of going to the bank. No amount of articulate explanation on my part would sway him otherwise. He didn't regard our lack of capital as a deterrent and could not be persuaded that his plan was open to exploitation or deceit with as many holes as a leaking sieve.

"Basotho think all English people are rich men. Not like us," ended Petros, with hopeful optimism.

We closed the subject amicably. He left me thinking hard about wealth and poverty and relative values of money. It was with caution that evening after supper, that I related the story to Barrie. With one withering look, Petros's rent-a- tractor plan hit the deck.. He was far more interested in 'de little green worm'.

That day we had received our post from England. It was such a special day when our letters arrived. We would make a pot of tea, lay out the table on the stoep with a white linen tablecloth, get out the easy chairs - then, with no disturbances of any kind, sit and devour the words of our friends and our families from home. You have no idea how much a letter from a loved one means to you, until you are parted from each other by time and distance. My letters would be read over and over again, so that I knew them off by heart. Even the most trivial detail was delightfully meaningful. If only my son realized how much he pleased me when he told me that the cat had fleas and his car had broken down yet again. Somehow it reassured me that things at home were unbearably normal and my right to remain a neurotic mother was intact.

It was on one such occasion, while seated in a comfortable chair, totally engrossed in my sister's engaging description of her most recent dalliance with a Frenchman, that a noise from the other side of the house caught my attention. There was no one around, although all my windows and doors were left open and anyone from the camp could enter and call me. The metallic scraping noise continued vaguely, then a banging noise came from inside the house- which grew louder with every passing minute.

Thabo was about somewhere because his ladder was lying on the garden. Betty was not here; she had gone home after cleaning every window in the house, and removing all the dead insects from the carpet with the vacuum cleaner. I had asked her to clean the fly screens, which were fitted to every window, as they were squiffy with bluebottle wings and those red things which used to come hurtling into the lighted kitchen at night if we left the door open. We called them Christmas beetles but they probably had a more precise entomological name. They would zoom past your ear like a corkscrew from hell, hit the wall and knock themselves clean out. Like giant ladybirds, they crunched when they fell and you didn't have to do anything except hoover them up into a bag. Betty relished this job and was spiritually uplifted when she saw that all the window sills were clean again.

She had asked Thabo if he would bring his ladder and actually remove the kitchen window screen from the outside, as it needed a few screws taking out and was too high for her to reach. It was too close to the cooker and Christmas beetles had been known to land in the stir fry.

What had started out as an irritating noise round the side of the house grew into a grinding 'thwack', followed by shouts. Laying my letter down for a moment, annoyed at being unable to continue reading the bit where the Frenchman showed my sister his true colours, I peered round the corner of the verandah - to be confronted with what can only be described as utter chaos.

Two of my eight foot wide lounge windows had been removed and were laying flat on the garden. The faces of hundreds of mutilated white marguerites stared crazily up at me through the glass. Hurrying to the other corner of the house, I met Thabo perched up a ladder, long-handled screwdriver in hand, leaning across the rose bed, intent on removing our bedroom window. One of the junior garden boys who was holding the bottom of the ladder, ran past me in the direction of the guard hut, as though chased by a pack of wild animals.

"Thabo, what the heck.... ?"

He saw my face and froze.

"Madame, Betty she say I can take out de window to clean de dead insect! She say I must do it today."

It was then that I realized, without a shadow of a doubt, that Thabo did not know his singulars from his plurals! Betty had asked him to remove one of our windows and in his basic translation he had decided that she meant all twelve. It did not occur to him to ask why. He was only doing his job.

Audibly, I drew breath. Thabo's elbow was still resting on the lower part of the window frame, preparing his next turn of the screw.

"Don't move!" I called out, as I ran along to the kitchen door. I stopped dead at the entrance to my lounge. Two large gaping holes had appeared in the wall. Every ornament, piece of paper and flower arrangement had been blown from window sill to middle of room; curtains swung from bent curtain rails like the house of horrors. My carpets were ankle deep in dead insects, which until now, had remained entombed between metal frame and fly screen - usefully filling in the cracks. Ten years worth of deceased bluebottle wings and dismembered Christmas beetles littered the floor. Betty's cleaned glass windows lay prostate on the flower beds.

Thabo's ladder miraculously and silently disappeared from its position. His blue boiler suit was seen slipping quietly behind the staff overnight accommodation block, some distance from the house. Hercule barked crustily as his territory was invaded and someone's hand tested his back gate. It was 2.30pm and the rains were expected at 5.00pm on the dot - windows or no windows. I could feel the afternoon wind starting up and watched as my precious letters blew across the garden.

A period of vague bewilderment followed. I espied Thabo with solemn countenance every afternoon, dredging the swimming pool with one of those hoses. It was his pride and joy not to let so much as a leaf enter the water. He even resented bodies swimming in it. I approached slowly with a plateful of my delicious strawberry pudding.

"Thabo, this is for you. It's Okay – you are forgiven."

His eyes lit up. He smiled his beautiful smile. "Kea leboha 'M'e."

The dredger fell from his hand.

On the road to Teyateyaneng, one morning in early February, driving out from Leribe, Liliane and I were discussing the merits of living in Lesotho. On our list of things we wanted to explore was the weaving factory on the outskirts of TY (as it was locally known) where the women made mohair rugs depicting traditional Basotho life. Visitors can watch them being made.

My friend and I were not exactly good geography students and had been told the journey would take an hour along the Maseru road. No one ever tells you in distance how far a place is, only the time it takes to get there. Tall aloes fringed the roadside villages holding their stalk arms outwards to the sun, in between splashes of golden yellow faces of the sunflowers which grew around the homesteads. The kids selling their asparagus jumped in front of the car and waved for us to stop and buy.

The landscape became more dramatic. Bathed in fairytale light the rugged sandstone peaks rising from the pale grasslands reminded me of giant Cotswold stone and the stunning views round every hairpin bend showed summer in all its glory. There were no barriers and in places the road was perilously close to the edge of a sheer drop. We found the turning off the main Maseru road, thanks to a painted sign about 100 yards away – almost a landmark in itself, pointing towards the Weaving Centre.

As we hit the muddy mountain track upwards - children legged it with us in droves, showing their exquisite white toothed smiles, waving madly. Our instructions were to just keep going until we came to the workshops. The steep track grew stonier and bumpier. After a rocky ride, we stopped underneath a glorious giant eucalyptus tree with its peeling bark, thankfully parking the Silver Fox in the shade. Wild agapanthus grew in a blue colonnade along the verge. The smell of eucalyptus was heavenly.

Scattered under the trees were groups of women, sitting on the grass, working with skeins of wool. Some of the women had babies with them or small children. They shouted for us to join them and between their babble and their singing, we sat down to admire their work. They were finishing off the rugs by handstitching. Alongside the workers, hung over a low wire fence, were dozens of golden coloured skeins of angora goats' wool - washed and combed like angels hair, ready to be woven. It shone in the sun.

"Why are you living in our country?" they asked and grew very interested as we explained that we lived at the camp for the Highlands Water Scheme and were both from the continent of Europe.

"I saw France on a map and the people, they speak with another language,"said one of them.

"Bonjour allors Mesdames" answered Liliane, which made them giggle.

"We want to come to England to see your Queen Elizabeth," said another lady turning to me, "she is keeping her people very happy, not like in Lesotho....women are working too hard here, too much people steal, not enough food."

"But you steal all the sunshine," we replied, trying to keep the conversation light.

It was warm and pleasant sitting under the trees. One lady pulled my arm and led me over to a large wooden building and introduced me to Alfonsina, the manageress in charge of the factory who was delighted to show off the work of her ladies. The door to the weaving shed was open.

Seated in front of huge tapestries, perched high on a platform, each weaver threaded cards of wool with an expert eye. Lesotho - the land of colourful people, was displayed in woven images, extravagant and rich in texture. Pungent smells of natural fibres, heat and the clatter of looms filled me with the same intoxication that I remember as a child, when taken into a Yorkshire mill or a tallow factory; that same nostalgic air of real hands doing real tasks, unchanged over the years.

Lesotho is famous for its pedigree breed of angora goats and these soft silky fibres, blended with other fibres, make a fine textured mohair wool which achieves the unique character of the rugs. The vibrant colours of the dyes used in depicting traditional scenes in the African landscape were a feast for the eye.

Suddenly and without warning, one of the ladies took out a small wooden box and began beating it with her fingers, tapping out a rhythm, at which point the others all started to sing, in a way that only African people can. One of the ladies who had been sitting high up at her loom climbed down and started to dance to the rhythm. Her excitement caught the enthusiasm of the others and in a few minutes, most of the ladies joined in and came to dance for us in the space between the looms. One girl produced a white fluffy skirt made from layers of white material stitched into a waistband, underpinned with dozens of dangling silver bottletops. The girl tied it around her waist and as she moved her hips, the skirt made a shushing sound as the medallions clicked against each other.

Alfonsina beckoned us to sit up on a high seat to watch the performance. The atmosphere was increasing in both heat and beat. Some of the women stripped to the waist, lifted up their skirts, shaking themselves in time to the drumming. Other ladies appeared dressed in the ostrich feathered skirts and shook their bottoms in a way we had never seen before. Basotho aerobics are not about amazonian fitness- but about sensual tribal movements in a striking and radiant form - the woman becomes wench, nymph, dame or bride in a dynamic display of feminine contortion of hips, buttocks and stomach wriggles. It was a feast of fertility, seduction, gentility and fun. What a contrast to the formality of the Womens' Institute syndrome which fills our village halls. I will never feel the same enthusiasm for a jar of homemade jam.

Much is spoken about the womb of the Mosotho woman, and she can be insulted more by a comment about her womb than if someone mentions her expanding waistline. The good information came from my friend Sophie- the camp's chief cook and mobile broadcasting service - who once told me about a dance which Basotho women perform when a child is being born, to stop the mother from feeling too much pain during her labour. The men are shut out of the room, told to go away, and the women perform a purely female version of a dance – the *Litolobonya* - wearing nothing but their skirts- and as Sophie described, "really, it makes de woman feel heppy again and de men must stay away until de baby comes." With a wiggle of her finger and a twinkle in her eye, she added, " but first you must lock de door !"

Festivities over, we emptied our purses into the hand of a small child who belonged to one of the weavers and followed Alfonsina across the yard where the finished rugs made a bright slash of colour under the trees. Pots of flowering cactus littered the entrance to the sale room. Not only did we buy for ourselves, but for our friends in every corner of the world. My elastic credit card was numb. We only got away when a hen wondered in through the door bringing its brood of chicks into Alfonsina's office and my pen ran out of ink.

Liliane and I fell exhausted into melting car seats, burning our legs as we did so.

"We need more petrol before we reached Leribe,"

"Lets stop at Peka."

"There have been no strikes or riots and we can buy fuel - our lucky day."

We bought oranges from the pavement stalls and a ton of healthy looking asparagus for a few Maloti, probably stolen from someone's field. The kids with their wares sat on the roadsides for several kilometres out of TY. waiting for customers. It was recognised as healthy exchange by farmers and children alike.

The sun shone like a crimson ball across the western skies as we drove home, leaving pink strands of cloud over the Caledon River. Our expedition across the mountains and back- without mishap – had been exhilarating. And boosting the Lesotho economy had been an added bonus. Only feminine logic would convince our menfolk that such expenditure was part of learning the culture of a new country. We understood perfectly how misinterpretations over spending can come about.

It was close to pay weekend. By 2.00pm the camp was virtually empty except for a skeleton staff. All the maids had gone off for a long weekend, families had driven off with their camping trailers, the canteen and bar were empty. Even Sophie's kitchen was quiet. Liliane and her family had left on a trip to explore the Karoo Desert and a few of the 'single squad' (the batchelor engineers) had gone off in search of the high life at Sun City.

Barrie and I had one last swim on the camp, before leaving for our weekend in the Drakensberg Mountains in Kwa Zulu Natal. Cathedral Peak was our destination. Our journey should take about five hours .Our main quest was to see the famous Amphitheatre plateau on the slopes of Mont-aux-Sources, situated 3,200m high in the mountains, where the Tugela River begins its life .There is a waterfall called Tugela Falls which cascades in five vertical drops into the gorge far below. It is said to be one of the highest waterfalls in the world, crashing 853 metres over the edge of the rock face. Our aim was to do some walking but mainly to share some time together after a tough month of engineering at the double, with no respite.

South Africa's earliest inhabitants, the San Bushmen, lived a simple isolated existence in the Drakensberg, possibly as early as 25,000 years ago. They were small in stature with 'peppercorn hair', yellow brown skin and wrinkled features. Their rock paintings are still to be found on the walls of caves. Strong dyes made from charcoal, ochre, blood and lime, depict their ceremonies, their hunting and their game, which abounded in great numbers.There was no alien culture to disturb the balance of their nomadic lives.

Then with the coming of the early white settlers in the 17th century, the Bushmen came under the power of the rifle. Thousands were killed in raids or simply starved when their hunting grounds were occupied.By the end of the 18th century, the conflict between the European colonists and the Bushmen intensified. The Bushmen's poisoned arrows were no match for guns.With less and less territory and depleted game, the Bushmen took to hunting and cattle raiding to stay alive. Their last known hideouts in Natal were attacked by the Voortrekkers in the 19th century, and their population almost wiped out. Unable to defend themselves, they were shot like dogs. A few moved into Lesotho where they were absorbed into the Basotho population and their descendants are called, even today 'the little people'. The few remaining Bushmen groups retreated to living in the Kalahari Desert, surviving in a land so inhospitable, beyond the reach of white men's guns.

There is still wildlife in some parts of the Drakensberg. The eland- the largest antelope can be found in the foothills of the Little Berg, while smaller antelope still graze on the lower grassy slopes. Animals that almost became extinct, have come back in increasing numbers due to careful conservation and there are frequent sightings of Cape vultures and black eagles, and the powerful jackal buzzard, who trail the skies above the open grasslands of the higher peaks.

We had arranged to stay at the Nest Hotel not far from Cathedral Peak.

"Oh look - bowling greens. Well watered ready for tomorrow's tournament," I noted as we drove up to Reception.

"With names like 'Mushroom Rock',' Pyramid' and 'Pool of the Rainbow Gorge', I'm not the least bit interested in playing bowls - what about you?"

The sandstone rock formations, the upper valleys and slopes of the Drakensberg are staggeringly beautiful. It is no wonder that climbers from every country in the world come here to explore.

"Well, Cleft Peak is a bit too strenuous for me this weekend - it's a mere 3,281 metres. What about Doreen Falls and the Tryme Trout Hatchery, that's an easy stroll along the Umlambonja River?"

"Sounds good to me."

After our first breakfast at The Nest, we took a short drive to Cathedral Peak Hotel, which looked out onto a ridge of mountains known as Cathedral Spur. One of the peaks is called the Three Puddings and next to it is Cathedral Peak itself, which is 3,004metres high. Next to it is The Bell. If you look southwards you can see Organ Pipes Pass and Ndument Dome, to the left.

In the early part of this century, these mountains were inhabited by a few intrepid farmers, and favoured by hunting parties but gradually land was bought for grazing and cattle farming became more widely known. Pine forests and lakes are wonderful combinations for any ecologist, nature lover or adventurer. The beauty of this area lives up to its name of the Royal Natal National Park.

Peak Hotel, with its balconied crimson bougainvillaea, white dahlias, blue hydrangas and pale orchids, determined its status as one of the best in the Drakensburg for scenic views. We strolled through stone archways, tropical fruit gardens of green pomegranates and lemons, palm trees, and rose pink camelias. The oldest palm, its branches a- flutter with yellow feathered heads bobbing in and out, seethed with life. Braided and plaited into its trunk, weavers' nests swung and swivelled like smooth brown coconuts, each one delicately hanging on a single twine.

The path led upwards, alongside the river. February is the month of the butterfly and the colourful wings of unusual species hovered in the air and showered us with silent landings in the long grass. Every tree every flower every plant was different to ours in England, and in the still butterfly-afternoon, the river music over the stones below in the gorge, were the only sounds to break the silence. The sun burned our shoulders. Our walk up to the falls took the best part of two hours.

Doreen Falls is a tall overhang of rock where the water comes cascading down to a clear pool below. The sparkling water forms a cave underneath the spray. In seconds Barrie was in the water, swimming towards the great torrent of falling water which looked deliciously cool, into the depths of the unlit cave beyond.

A relaxed engineer was what I really hoped for on this walk, as the previous four weeks of beavering away at the office without a break imbided a great deal of stress into our household. Barrie usually craved this degree of isolation, when he had problems on his mind- and it was with mutual consent that we agreed to tramp forest footpaths and watch dragonflies hover over lazy pools.

We were facinated by the names of the regions around the bergs - the Chessmen, the Mitre and Sleeping Beauty Valley over by the Mashai Valley; inspiring names for inspiring places. They seemed to breathe stories of witches and dragons with the same mystery and timelessness as the Scottish Highlands, which we both loved. The tranquillity of the open countryside, the spectacular views were enough to mend anyone who had been on overload.

In the evenings at the hotel, people talked about trout fishing in the Mooi River; the Sani Pass in winter after a snowfall, where the twin Hodgson Peaks form a glacier which looks like a giant's cup. The steep and tortuous Sani Pass is regarded as the highest mountain pass in Africa. It owes its existence to the San Bushmen, the first people to open up this route. Evidently, it was used by mules and packhorses from 1912, to trade with the Basutoland Government. Goods of grain, ox-hides and mohair skins hauled by mule trains, fought the steep gradients, as this was the only access route into the Kingdom of Lesotho from the east. Widened in 1949 to accommodate motor vehicles, the journey should only be attempted in a 4 x 4 Land Rover.

The weekend was peaceful, the great outdoors delighted us, and the brandy in the evenings helped the gentle flow of conversation round the table.The menu was good country food.

The dramatic bergs were all around us - Champagne Castle, Monk's Cowl, Intunja-meaning the eye of the needle; Devil's Tooth, the Spinx; names as romantic as the pyramids of Eygypt.

"Why don't you have a few days at Injasuti?" asked one of our fellow travellers. You could see the most beautiful region of all South Africa. The eNjasuthi Buttress is 3,200metres high and then the Trojan Wall, where the river tumbles into a magnificent gorge is out of this world."

Fascinated, we listened to their stories.

Since the 1930's and through the war years, great climbers have come to the Drakensberg to tackle and conquer some of these challenging peaks; French missionaries, Irishmen, Englishmen, New Zealanders; some with dubious experience, some with no experience at all - but all with formidable courage. Many died in their attempts. Some were bittten by snakes and survived. Others cheated death and succeeded in making an ascent using the most primitive methods which were extremely reckless, making it the kind of place of which brave men dreamed.

The previous June was the last time Barrie and I had talked of marriage. Then, we were still living in England, having no knowledge of South Africa or Lesotho - no idea that our lives were about to change beyond recognition. At that point in time we had plans for an April wedding blessing in an English country church.

It was our last evening at The Nest. We lingered over dinner and wine, spelling out our romantic promises to one another, saying the familiar words. In the last six months, partings and reunions had resulted in feelings of great enrichment. Emotional baggage had been dealt with. The reality was that we were in this together. Lesotho was our home for the foreseeable future and we wanted to make every minute of our lives count. There was no stopping either my adrenalin or Barrie's contract.

"Nettie, what do you say to us getting married now -in South Africa? We could keep the original date - just change the continent! We don't have any reason for waiting another year - do we?"

"None that I can think of....." I looked across the table into blue eyes that moved me beyond words. "Are you sure?"

"Yes, I'm sure… this is our time."

South Africa had arrived in our lives at the right moment and we had hopped on it like a bus.

"Yes, it's not as though we have to ask permission from our children. Come on - let's go and tell the dragon we're getting married!"

We left our table and went out through the French windows, to walk through the quiet lawns, savouring our secret. In our age group it's not traditional to get drunk and throw wild parties, but you are allowed to have a moonlight swim and an extra glass of champagne on an occasion such as this. The pool was warm and the champagne ice cold. We ran through the garden on the soft grass; laughed into a night sky spangled with a million stars. The air smelled sweet with scented flowers. Cathedral Peak shone down on us like a giant pearl.

Chapter 22

Gooseplucking.

By the time we had driven back from the Drakensberg through field upon field of sunflowers we were almost convinced it was August in England. Yellow heads nodded and black eyes winked as though in approval of our colourful plans for an African wedding. This was a February day, the sky was cloudless as we sped home, and clutches of blue necked guinea fowls flattered us with their prim footed races along the edge of the road. Kestrels hovered above the rocks while those funny cow-like beasts with humps lazed dreamily on the horizon.

It was evening as we crossed from South Africa into Lesotho and offered our passports to the Lesotho guard asleep on duty. A tall black youth in ostrich feathers with painted chest tried to talk his way through and the guard raised an eyebrow and sank back in his chair. The state of the road on the Lesotho side of the border was no credit to Maputsoe Town Council. Litter filled the sidewalks and inebriated youths lay horizontal in the garage forecourt. The end of a pay weekend was like Christmas in Woolworths.

Saving me from a happiness overdose was the fact that when we arrived back at the camp, the phones were still off. They had been down now for about three months. It is easy when you don't need to use one, but now that we were planning a wedding and bursting to tell the home contingent, the lack of telecommunication was irksome. Ficksburg in South Africa had the nearest working public phone.

Waiting for us in our postbag were letters from England and the best treat of all, a decent English newspaper, sent by my thoughtful sister-in-law. It was absolute heaven reading in our own language a few column inches of potential economic disaster, a snippet of theatreland hype and a peek at current fashion trends.

The only English newspaper we had seen since living in Lesotho was the International Express, locally known as the 'Fergie Express' (so called because it seemed she had a roving reporter strapped to her underwear.) On occasional visits to a town we might find a copy in a CNA stationers. The news was usually about three weeks old and plainly came off the late shift tabloid press, when the editorial team were on their last legs. Outdated reports of seedy sex scandals filled its inside pages. It was totally devoid of news, views or political comment. More about the the demise of the Tory Party instead of who in Westminster woke up in the wrong bedroom would have pleased us more.

Soon our wedding plans were under way. It's not easy to find a magistrate in South Africa when you live in phone-less Lesotho. Neither is communicating with the inner sanctum of the British Consulate Office in Pretoria whose phone lines were permanently engaged for days. We sought reassurance on the legalities surrounding British subjects marrying in South Africa, but after three weeks of abortive attempts at trying to contact them we gave up and went to find a magistrate in Ficksburg .

A beautiful lady by the name of Ena Swanapoel came to our rescue. Consequently, she promised to officiate at our wedding in April. Ena, as well as being a very competent magistrate, was also a singer with a famous gospel choir . She was familiar with the verses in Kahlil Gibran's book of 'The Prophet' which we asked for in our ceremony, wrote our names in a big book and asked us those kind of questions that go very deep and make the tears well in your eyes. Across the big wooden desk she spoke quietly, and made us feel that our commitment to each other was as important to her as it was to us.

Her voice was dignified, and calm. She had the eyes of Joan of Arc and the hands of a concert pianist.

The date of our wedding was fixed for 5th April - almost the same date we had originally planned to be married in England. The ceremony was to take place in Ficksburg in a beautiful garden belonging to our friends.

The following evening, we drove out to celebrate in style at the Hoogland Hotel. It was Valentine's Evening. Flushed with wedding plans and a £5 bottle of champagne, we danced the night away. There was a new Brazilian dance which was sweeping the town - known as the 'Margarena'. We were probably the last place in the world to hear about it.

Observing dancing etiquette in the ballroom, we were acutely conscious that either whites or blacks took the floor, but not both at the same time. Old taboos stuck like toffee paper. Our black guests didn't need Brazilian music to get them up on their feet. Along with the French crowd beside us, we mingle-danced, cha-cha-ed and jiggled, until that time of night when you have to sleep or die (very common for the over fifties). Preparing to leave, we noticed that the plumb faced Afrikaners who had been glued to their seats, were assembling for take-off.

A wedding on the camp always turns the excitement level up and try as we might to keep the whole thing quiet and low key, it seemed to have the opposite effect. As luck would have it, the following week Lesotho Telecom sent an engineer to mend the outside phone lines. It seemed a hopeful sign when a little man in an orange jacket arrived on camp and leaned his ladder up against one of the telegraph poles. This, after three months of no action, surely meant something. Efficiency prevailed and the engineer spent most of the day on top of the ladder basking like a lizard in the sun.

That evening staff were informed that communications were re-connected to the rest of the planet. Waves of excitement, congratulations and adrenalin satellited across the equator to our families in England. The master plan was a South African wedding ceremony in April and later in the year, a wedding blessing in Hertfordshire. And for a honeymoon, it was the Garden Route to Capetown or bust.

The following day a delivery lorry on our site backed into the newly reconnected telegraph pole.The driver not only extracted one pole, but caught up in the wires, uprooted a second and third. They fell like a row of dominoes in a tangled heap of electricity volts. The system was so badly damaged, we were disconnected from the northern hemisphere for a further three weeks. Running a major project in Lesotho was child's play beside the headache of non-functional telephone systems.

My Silver Fox turned off the main road in Ha Simone, beside the 'toilet factory' and bumped along the stones towards the Subeng River and Walter's house. It had not rained the previous day and the dyke where you cross into Makibis' field wasn't as bad as last time. Walter was chasing the cows into the yard when I arrived. It happened to be a Thursday, which was 'ladies day' at St John's Church, and Rose was conducting the service. The yard was full of ladies and children, their voices greeting one another loudly; their blue and white dresses flapping like flags as they went down the steps from Rose's back door, towards the church which stood on the lower level.

It was Stephen's day off and he welcomed me loudly into the house. He blessed my bag of goodies and told Bernice to fetch me some water from the spring. Bernice disappeared with a plastic water container. Walter joined us and managed a beaming smile across the wide living room table, as Stephen talked to me about the church and his hopes for his members who travelled long distances to come to the services, without food in their bellies or money in their pockets.

As usual, there was the smell of fresh polish in the air, unexpected in a clay house by the river.The flat iron was sitting by the stove where Rose had been ironing her church uniform. For the first time I was introduced to Petros, Walter's younger brother whose shyness was evident when he smiled his lovely smile. Petros was fifteen; an interesting young man, who escaped out to the pastures with his beloved cows because solitude suited him. He tore off down to the river now to wash his school clothes. He had few things to wear and shared a pair of shoes with another brother called Augustinus. They wore them on alternate days.

Walter was very quiet in the presence of his father.His mouth did not smile and his nervousness showed in every small expression. Leaving his poetry book on the table for me to read, he went to help Rose prepare for the service.

Stephen offered to show me round the St John's community while the ladies were still in the church. From the yard, he pointed to five flat roofed huts spaced at intervals around the church itself. One roomed dwellings, each with a step at the front, but without glass in the windows. They were built of clay and whitewashed. One had no door. The roofs were made from pieces of corrugated metal, weighted with rocks to prevent the wind from blowing them off. I longed to take look inside.

"One of these places we use for the cooking, a couple of them are where the boys sleep and the others are for when the sick people come. The people arrive, sometimes from long distances, because they have heard about St John's. We feed them.We try and solve their problems. They come to join in our prayers and we ask God to bless them and show them how to get better. Sometimes it takes a long long time. Sometimes they stay and become part of our family.

Stephen waved his hand down towards the valley.

"Our church is down by the river. We also have spring which comes down from the mountains. We use water in our services The water is blessed first with the words of our prayers from the Bible.The people drink the holy water and also use it to protect themselves from the bad spirits. Our church at St John's believe that water is the spirit of life. We believe in the power of prayer and we share in the Christian belief that Jesus Christ was the one who comes to save us."

He paused to shade his eyes from the sun. Bernice arrived and gave me a metal cup containing cold water from the spring.

"I have been a priest for fifteen years and I know that through my own experiences, God is the power and the love. One day I will tell you the story of how I came to be a priest. If you come to the end of life's road and can go no further, God will show you his love when you come to him with your prayers. Along that journey you must believe there is hope. Some of our people have lost that hope.They have lost everything. It is our duty to try and help them find their way back. Our church can show the people that we care and then they must do for themselves."

Stephen Makibi toiled wholeheartedly for the people in his community. He had a way of talking which made people want to listen.There was an inner strength in him, which shouted and laughed out loud. His Archbishop often sent for him to help at the big church in Durban because Stephen could speak fluently in Zulu and translate the Archbishop's words into seSotho for the multi-lingual congregations. He was a man of integrity and compassion.

We walked down the steps from the yard towards the simple stone church with its corrugated tin roof and bright blue doors. The St John's Community had built it with their own hands. From inside came the lovely sound of the female voices in soft repeated choruses, followed by a deep contralto voice leading into a hymn that was vaguely familiar to my ears.

"That's Emily. She has a good voice. Come- they have almost finished. We 'll go inside."

Stephen's tone surprised me. I was totally unprepared for what I saw.

Rose and her ladies were sitting on low wooden benches near the front of the church. The altar consisted of a very small square table covered in a worn white tablecloth. My eyes were drawn to the three candles that burned brightly, set in little silver tins placed on the tablecloth. The white light flickered onto the faces of the women on their knees, each offering their cup of water for a blessing.

On the plain whitewashed altar wall, hung a china plate depicting the figure of an Archbishop in crimson robes, a paper calendar and quite a handsome wooden clock. A cardboard picture of Christ crucified took pride of place in the middle. That was all. No ornate pillars, no carved wooden screen to the altar; no pulpit or eagle clad lectern; no choir stalls or pews; just a few rough wooden benches and an old table on which burned three candles. The light on the womens' faces glowed as each one came forward.

Round the doorway where we had entered, several water carriers were placed on the blue tiled floor. Stephen stood quietly at the back of the church - eyes gleaming with pride.

We waited until Rose had finished saying the final prayers. Emily looked up and saw me. She was wearing a white hat which covered her hair, like all the other ladies.

"Nettie, it's you. I didn't know that you were listening. We have been singing a song of thanksgiving for the rain."

"You have a beautiful voice, Emily. I hope to hear you sing again. In England you would be a prima donna" She laughed and was pleased with the compliment.

This was their very special place. Simplicity with velvet wings. Built with love, this tiny church had seen sadness and struggles, poverty, family tragedy – nothing here was pretentious or grandiloquent. The building was about the size of a small English barn. Wooden timbers held up a roof of corrugated tin. When the rain fell, the noise would most certainly drown any fine singing or minister's words. Several windows down each side, gave light and a barn door at the back creaked unsteadily on its one remaining hinge.

Walter was explaining about the significance of holy water in their services, when I was distracted by the shuffling figure of a man, feeling his way along one of the benches, trying to make his way to the front of the church. He looked old and very ill and was crawling from one bench to the next, almost bent double. I could not take my eyes from his face. He was smiling.

"That is Johannes," said Walter. "He is a poor man. He lives with us in one of the houses because he has no one to look after him and his blindness prevents him from working." Somehow the appearance of this thin figure drew me. I went towards him and touched his sleeve. Johannes took my hand and held it for a long time, the long bony fingers seized with involuntary shaking. He spoke softly in seSotho and swayed unsteadily on his feet. Walter, with his hand on my shoulder, translated the words of the old man.

"I have told him you come from England, Nettie. He offers you a welcome and would like to speak, but he knows no English."

Walter explained that Johannes had had an accident in the mine which caused his blindness. Now he was forty two years old. He liked to be helpful when it was possible by straightening the furniture ready for the next service, to show how much he appreciated the care of St John's. He had nowhere else to go, no family or friends; Walter's family the only light in his eyeless world.

I have never shaken hands with a blind man. His clothes were just rags but his face looked scrubbed. It was a hard thing to let go and dismiss him from my mind. Walter carefully took him to a seat and sat him down. I felt stupid and tongue tied and very close to tears. What could one say, that was any help to someone like Johannes? Rose caught me looking worried and we walked out into the sun together and then down to the river.

Slowly it was dawning on me that I was part of this family. Bernice and Emily followed, with Walter not far behind. We sat on the big flat rocks and dangled our toes in the water. A cluster of ragged children arrived from somewhere on the hillside and came to stare at this strange white lady with her feet in the river.

"We like to show you our church, so that you will know about our people," said Rose quietly. "We are a very poor country in Lesotho- we pray so much that things in our country will change - but we have many blessings. Some of the people will move on when they are well again, some will stay. We don't know when the people will come, they just arrive."

"Like Johannes, you mean? What will happen to him if he leaves here? Who will take care of him?"

"The Lord will provide us with a home for Johannes. When he is ready, he will go. He has been here for several months." Rose's eyes showed only peace and comfort and I found myself longing to believe in her. "There is a time of waiting and a time to move on. Johannes is happy."

As always, Rose had moulded her commitment to the needs of Johannes. She had given him the little house next to the church to sleep in. He ate with the family. He didn't need eyes to hear the people singing. Every morning he felt his way across the yard, down the steps and into little whitewashed church where he tidied the benches and the books. They could thank him for his part and he could feel needed.

Walking back up to the house, Emily came to take my arm.

"I wish I could be strong like my mother. She is never angry when people come to us with their troubles. I always try not to blame, but then I do. No one helps people like Johannes. They die at the side of the road when they have been hit by a car - I have seen it." At nineteen, the vigorous indignation felt like a hail of bullets in a thunderstorm.

"Emily, when will you come and join in my English classes ?" I asked. "You'd like the other girls. After the class, we can talk….about classical poets who were always angry…." I teased.

"Very soon, Nettie. My work at the school is so hard for me. I would like to improve my English - my teacher says that I should work harder – but there is no one at the school who can explain things. We do not have enough information."

"Next time you see the Silver Fox drive to Ha Simone, have your books ready."

Walter, as always, came with me to the road, where my wheels touched the tarmac. We passed Augustinus walking home from school, books under his arm, white shirt torn across his shoulder. There were taxis but this boy never asked favour from anyone. It was

6 kilometres there and back. He grinned at us and came to shake my hand through the car window, though he was very weary. He was much smaller in stature than Walter.

Augustinus is Walter's adopted brother. He had come to Ha Simone at the age of seven with his parents, who, like others before, had begged for help at St John's Church. A child had died and they were distraught. After many months, his parents went back to their home in Durban leaving Augustinus behind. By then, he was attending the local school.with Walter. Since that time Rose and Stephen have fed him and looked after him, as one of their own sons.

At nineteen years old, Augustinus is now a Makibi. He ploughs their fields, helps to build their walls, knows how to repair the roof in the windy season, looks after the cows and helps in the church services. He has the eye of an artist and the soul of a poet. His mind thirsts for knowlege and his sensitive heart bleeds for his countrymen. Passionate verse pours out of him, written on scraps of paper and locked in a tin. He is already a student of philosophy and radical change - murderous in his thoughts of the wrongs he had seen in his short life, and a vehement crusader of causes. For twelve years, Rose had been his second mother, and Walter, Justice and Petros his brothers. He and Walter are almost joined at the hip.

At night the boys sleep in the next to the end hut next to the river- it is their den, their hovel, their bedroom. There are no beds, no window, no door - only floorspace. and a collapsed wardrobe. Here, like any teenage rumpus room, there is a sharing of shirts, trousers, shoes, sheets , blankets and books. And they are glad of their space. They own nothing but what they stand up in. Augustinus and Petros take it in turns to go to school because they have one green jersey between them and the school rules are that uniform must be worn. Every night when they come home, they wash the dust from their clothes in the river, ready for the next day. Homework has to be done before the sun goes down.

"Augustinus is the clever one in our family," sighed Walter with obvious fondness. "He knows about the stars and the heavens. He knows about life in other lands. He reads every book he can get hold of. He knows about poets and painters. One day he will travel and he will leave here - but I will always be his brother."

Walter was deeply troubled because, as an eldest son, he had many responsibilities towards the rest of the family. Extremely close to his mother who supported his every ideal, Walter's father had lost respect for him, because he had no job. In Lesotho pride and respect are hard task masters. Walter badly wanted to work. He had been employed as a shutterhand at Muela Dam for two years before the big strike, when all the men were laid off. Six months later, he still had no work. Meanwhile he kept himself fit by running several miles a day across the mountains, dutifully helped his father with the business of running a church community, not least of which was attending the daily 5.00am. service. The whole family worshipped together every morning.

"My father does not get paid for being a priest. And my mother tries to feed us all - even she feeds the sick people who are living there. It is hard for her. We are waiting for the harvest which will be ready in June. Now there are some lean months. That's why my father is angry with me. "

"Can you drive Walter?"

"I have been able to drive since I was a boy. But I cannot get a licence to drive. You have to pay the bribes and the bribes are more than the Road Test. If I fail to pay them, I cannot get the necessary papers."

My mind would not take in the implications of such a situation. There must be some work for Walter somewhere.

"I will do anything as long as it is legal."

"Will you travel with me to Tlotlisong High School tomorrow? I have an appointment to go and see the Mr Malebo, the headmaster, to teach one of his classes. Your help would be useful in translating for the kids whose English is not very good. I have an idea to bring the choir to sing in Butha-Buthe soon. Mr Malebo has been trying to solve the question of passports."

"Anywhere you wish to go, Nettie, I will be pleased to be your guide. The Basotho people will treat you better if they see you have me with you. It is better for a white person to travel with a black. Then you'll be safe on the road. It is safe but......" he hesitated, " because of the language you might not be prepared."

"I'm not frightened Walter, I've been well treated by everyone in Lesotho since I came. The people here are good to me. But I understand what you are saying. Look what happened when my car broke down in Ha Simone!"

Being roadwise wasn't easy, safety was not guaranteed and there was always the possibility that people wanted to steal - but since we arrived in Lesotho, I had learnt that first you must smile, take a few steps forward, then people usually relax. Disguises are out. Pretend foreigner on holiday, important business, a hasty journey , cheating a queue and your way will be blocked. You must be conciliatory and always polite – but with a big smile.

Walter's company proved invaluable. He was as good as a rescue service. He knew all about car engines, mended my punctures and taught me the best roads. We often arrived in the yard with the car covered in mud and the whole family took it upon themselves to give it a thorough clean, fetching water up from the river in old tin cans. Petros made it gleam like a Rolls Royce. The Silver Fox became a symbol of our friendship and it almost knew its way to Ha Simone without a driver.

My housekeeping money stretched like elastic when I went shopping and my car boot was like a travelling kitchen. Barrie didn't realize he was helping to bring up a family of eight. Rose would always share everything out fairly.

Liliane and I became scavengers on our camp and begged socks, shoes, jerseys, husbands' anoraks and jackets, left-over suppers, even clothes pegs for their washing days, candles for lighting in the church, paper to write on, books - the list became longer, the more we realized that our lives were full of luxuries. We had so much, they so little. Fortunately my fridge was man enough to hold food for Betty and her children, all the Makibis and ourselves. The ladies on the camp let me raid their clothes rails for dresses and shirts, shoes and socks and no member of staff in the camp dared say to his wife that he had grown out of a jacket lest it was whipped off his back instantly.

Every trip to the Makibis after that was another adventure. From the beginning, their lives fascinated me. Emily came to Leribe for her lessons once or twice a week with Annacleda and Heleyn. She was a good student. Her understanding of English language was excellent. Bernice drew me pictures of the animals on A4 notepaper. The boys all loved to draw and paint. My hoghair brushes from England were admired and images of mountains and mud huts were placed in my car as thank you gifts.

On the bench in the yard, the boys mixed up paint in coke cans and made rainbows on large sheets of card rescued from the refuse bins at L.H.P.C. Walter sloshed poster colours on everything including the chairs in his room. His hut became a meeting place for long discussions on poetry and famous artists. He surprised me by his knowledge of Shakespeare and would stand at the top of the ridge and act out a scene of Macbeth without a fault. He could repeat famous lines of Lear and Hamlet from memory, aiming his deep rich voice at the cows across their valley while we queued for water at the spring. Augustinus read aloud his poems with great feeling and involved the others in passsionate arguments. His philosophies on freedom and wars and slavery, set in a background of humiliation and tragedy, were bent on rousing up even the most peaceful amongst them. His words cut like knives through the paper they were written on.

Petros showed me how to stake out the cows when they came in at night, tying them up with ropes below the house wall and Justice showed me how to roast mealie in a pan and make chips on a fire. Emily cooked popcorn in an old tin can and handed it round the yard in handfuls. It disappeared in seconds.There were always plenty of mouths waiting. The washing up was done from a bowl of spring water and left out on the stoep to dry.

Rose and I formed a friendship that was unsinkable. I never ceased to admire her grace and fortitude. From Rose, I leant serenity, dignity and strength. She constantly drew my admiration for the way she coped with every day problems and yet never gave in. On bright windy days, the lines of washing hung white and clean on a rope across the yard after she had carried the tin bath up the hillside from the river. She made and mended clothes, ironed white shirts for her husband to wear in church and polished the house as though it were a king's palace.They were so poor and yet their poverty was not of the spirit. My affection for the family grew deeper, as they let me share in the ups and downs of their lives.

Sometimes we sang hymns loudly sitting round the big table- they have the same tunes as ours, only the words are different. Rose had a good voice, Emily a powerful one – Walter added his deep bass tones and Stephen kept quiet. He couldn't sing at all. Walter carved me wooden treasures and Emily wrote me stories. Augustinus read his poems out loud; about liberty and truth and dying; powerful images of his own aspirations.

No one ever spoke of me going home to England. Somewhere far away there was the unspoken wish that these idyllic days would go on for ever.

Walter was my constant passenger and I grew very fond of him. He taught me so much about his country and its people. Emily, I found, was in need of female companionship. She and I shared hours of 'talkie talkie' about music and language and yet more about relationships. We became very close. Her English was superb, but she wanted to improve even more and worked unstintingly towards examinations. They had scant knowledge of England, yet both were fascinated to hear about our laws and young peoples' trends. They could not believe how, in England, young peoples' culture was so different. Walter followed English football teams and played for his team but he had no proper boots and could not play in the competitions. Liliane wrote a letter to her sons in France asking them to send a pair of boots, post haste.

In early March, when we wrote out a wedding invitation for Walter and Emily, no one on earth could have been more delighted.

"I never thought I would be a guest at a white lady's wedding," Walter said solemly when I gave him the envelope. His eyes shone. "My mother and father will be very proud." Emily stared in disbelief then gave me an enormous hug .

There was much happiness that day at Ha Simone when we drove into the yard. Stephen came and shook hands with me, but could not speak. Rose disappeared down the steps to the church .When she returned, she said that a special candle had been lit and placed on the altar table.

I used to go to Ha Simone several times a week. The young boy who had been sitting on the wall that first day, used to race up the track to meet me. He had a Basotho name which was unpronounceable. I gave him the name of Fred and from that day everyone called him Fred . He always appeared in the same tattered outfit and did not possess a pair of shoes. At five years old, he had the face of a naughty cherub. His little black feet were so hard he could run on the stones like a baby hare. His mother was out at work and his dog looked after him. When Rose dished up the mealies in the yard, Fred would join the queue. No bigger than two pennyworth of copper, Fred was the artful dodger of Ha Simone. He loved sitting in the front seat of the car when I picked him up part way to Walter's and his skinny little arms would be poking through his jersey, head just about on a level with the window. We could not exchange one word, yet he knew what I was saying almost at once and ran off to find one of the Makibis, if there was no one about.

With Walter as my co-driver, we gave all his friends a lift wherever we went. Having a car in Lesotho means that everyone thinks you offer a free taxi service. It was not unusual for me to stop and take on board four fat ladies plus luggage or a whole gang of school children going home. Once I took two ladies to catch a bus. Sandwiched between them was a bag containing a pig! I never knew if it was dead or alive! Nobody minded sitting on another's lap, babies got squashed between bosoms and blankets, children slept and passenger hymn singing was standard practice.

Picking up Walter at the taxi stop meant squeezing in a priest or two, fellas carrying kerosene or heavy battery packs, ladies with small children - two to a knee, or formidable matriarchs from the church. Two verses of a hymn meant thank you for the lift and a slap on the back meant go on a bit further.

Lebitso la hau u mang means what' is your name' in seSotho.This little phrase was infallible as a conversation piece and so began my collection of names: Angelina, Wilhemina , Blossom ,Grace, Evodia, Florence and Violet. There was a lady called 'Brightness' who was on her way to a funeral in Transkei, who insisted on giving me a piece of 'de funeral bread'. She and her packages took up the whole of the back seat. She was going to walk 'all de way' to Transkei to see her sister buried. I dropped her at the border where she and her luggage promptly climbed up onto an open truck carrying a herd of goats.

Boys' names were mostly biblical - Ishmail, Zachariah, Isaac, Moses, Elijah , Jacob , Gideon and Joshua. One of the guards on the camp was called Gabriel and another, Elliot Benedictus. Gabriel was the oldest of the guards at the camp. He liked sitting on the grass verge outside my garden to eat his lunch and those wicked old eyes of his told their own story. Toothlessly, he flirted with all the ladies as they went about their business. It was debatable whether he was capable of engaging in armed combat using the rifle on his shoulder, should the camp ever come under attack.

At Tlotlisong High School, Solomon and I were not having much luck on the subject of passports for the choir. Every week on my teaching day with Form 10A, the news was the same. Letters written to the authorities always came back with the same reply.

"These kids are so poor, "argued Solomon, "their families cannot afford fifty rands for a passport. I will write to Pretoria to President Mandela's Office. Perhaps they may be able to grant special permission. Fifty pupils in the choir and only three of them actually own a passport. We must keep trying. Our concert must go ahead."

Elizabeth and Miriam colluded with people in the town to try and raise some sponsorship and the choir was improving week by week. They sang for me several times during my teaching days and needed no encouragement to try harder. They sounded superb. Elizabeth, meanwhile, had entered them for a national competition in Johannesburg.

The company had found me a bus. It was big enough to carry sixty passengers and would be at our disposal for the journey from Tlotlisong School to Butha-Buthe English School in Lesotho, on the day of the concert. Nothing was too much trouble for the management and everything was going smoothly- apart from the passport situation.

Out of the blue, I received an invitation to go and see Janet Barrett and watch the gooseplucking at their farm.

Janet and her family lived at Boschfontein in South Africa, in a remote corner of the hills. They had several hundred hectares of farmland., bounded by the Caledon River. Peace Barrett, Janet's mother-in-law, who lived on the adjoining farm 'next door' (four miles away over a rocky mountain track) also sent an invitation to tea after the gooseplucking. Peace- who was eighty two - and I, had already met during my days at Kindi and had discovered several mutual interests, one of which was poetry. My impression of Peace Barrett was that of an educated and fascinating lady, with an eighty two year old engine and a twenty year old spark. One of South Africa's grand duchesses - if ever there was one! She left Scotland at the age of four and still remembered what it was like.

The following Saturday morning, I drove out to Boschfontein prepared for another adventure. It was quite a long way. Once through the Lesotho border, we turned off the main Fouriesburg Road, some miles north of Ficksburg, over an old disused railway line, onto a dirt road which had 'Sekonyela' painted on a sign. Sekonyela was the name of the old Basotho Chief, who first inhabited this valley. The ruined remains of an old homestead still exists somewhere on the highest plateau of the farmland. In the cliffs and caves of this valley are fascinating bushman paintings and cave art, now recorded and appreciated as proof of a much earlier existence.

On a dirt road, it is better for your tyres if you drive fast. Our driver put her food hard on the accelerator and with a choking yellow dust cloud in our wake we sped perhaps two or three miles, past wild unspoilt countryside, past the colourful conglomoration of the shambas of the black families. Prickly cactus grew in the yards and blankets spread across hedges to dry. The road wound through banks of trees and eucalyptus groves. Glimpses of early cosmos sprinkled the hedges in pastel pink and white. It was a beautiful sunny day.

Janet and a herd of dogs greeted us. With a raucous screech, a peacock flew down from a low branch and landed on the parking lot. Flurries of hens scuttled around the ancient tree which stood majestically in front of the house. While legs and feathers sorted themselves out, our party was welcomed into the house.

Boschfontein farmhouse was exceedingly handsome. A well proportioned house, built high off the ground with wooden verandahs all round, and a green sloping roof, it looked square onto a quadrangle yard. Surrounded by lovely old trees, with wrought iron crochet decorating the edges of the roof, it was stylishly colonial. The farmhouse doors opened onto a wide wooden stoep. By the kitchen entrance, a basket of kittens mewed around the grey mother cat, and the gable roof above was hung with wind chimes and tassels of trailing greenery. On the far side of the verandah stood an ancient farm carriage, as though pushing back the clock some seventy years. Facing the main house on the other side of the quadrangle was an attractive low building, once the old dairy - now used to accommodate guests.

The midday sun shone unremittingly over our heads as we followed Janet up the steps and into the house. Dogs flopped thirstily into water bowls. The rooms were filled with well loved furniture -old rocking chairs, heavy oak settles, grandfather clocks, generations of books and family china. The sound of someone playing the piano came from the next room. There was an air of normality around the old house - corners filled with tennis rackets and walking gear, fishing rods and newly muddied boots. We sat in basket chairs full of patchwork cushions and handstitched lace. Outside in the garden blue peacocks squawked from low branches and showed off their tails. The old clock in the drawing room gave a dong to end all dongs and a tall young man came to meet us.

Morgan was Janet's eldest child, home from college. He was the image of his father, Essex ; tall and confident and instantly courteous when he knew why we were there. We shook hands. The last time we had met was at the Anglican Christmas carol service in Ficksburg when Morgan had read the lesson.

Boschfontein Farmhouse dates from 1885 when a man called Morgan Harries built the house before the Boer War broke out in 1899. He moved into Leribe during the uprising, so as not to take sides as he had family and friends in both armies. Lesotho was a place of neutrality during the Boer War. His only daughter Marion and her husband, the first Charles Barrett continued to live on the farm and had three children, one of whom was called Bill, who, after fighting in the 2nd World War, had the great misfortune to be blinded while clearing an ammunition dump in Egypt.

When Bill returned to South Africa, he required personalized nursing as his various shrapnel wounds were going septic. The nurse who volunteered to do this unpleasant task was Annie Peace Gordon, a very special lady, with whom he fell in love. When Bill left hospital, he married his nurse. Together, they went to Capetown, where they learned to live with Bill's blindness, then returned to Boschfontein to raise their family, Helen, Charles and Essex . With great courage and fortitude Bill and Peace continued to farm the land. Bill's blindness did nothing to deter them from running a successful business, and he could ride a horse or plough a field as good as any able bodied man. He was tenacious and charismatic, probably inherited from his grandfather who was a missionary in the Transkei. Bill was respected by all who knew him and admired throughout South Africa. He and Peace had shared more than fifty years of fulfillment and happiness.

Essex and Janet are the fourth generation of Barretts who have lived at Boschfontein and their son Morgan, the first child to be born here. Janet came here as a young bride in 1978 and in turn brought her energetic ideas to the running of the farm. She bred rabbits, poultry, peacocks and turkeys, then bred a special kind of geese to supply down for pillows and duvets.

After lunch were invited to go and meet the geese.

"All the ladies who work at Boschfontein live on the farm. Did you pass their compound as you came up? We know all of them well. On Saturday mornings they usually come up to the house to look for work. They can all earn money- there are lots of jobs they can do around the place."

Janet walked briskly out onto the stoep. "We make our own bricks and bake them in the furnace. It is a very important job here. There are the sheep to look after, a small herd of goats and fences to build. We have some very good people and they know the farm well. Come and meet Sophie. She's her brought her baby."

At the rear of the property was a paradise of a garden, hanging with blossom and rich with flower beds. Tall tiger lilies and agapanthus grew underneath deep purple bougainvillea. Peach trees dotted the lawns full of pink fruit. Bright yellow cana massed across the house walls and roses of every colour, bloomed from every corner. By the side of an elegant stone staircase running up to the back of the house, grew a vintage member of the garden; a magnificent tree, whose branches spread wide giving heavenly shade, clusterered with dainty white blossoms.

"It is known by a wonderful name - Pride of India," claimed Janet. "It's very old - several hundred years actually Its a family friend. We love it dearly."

There were several ladies weeding. The African women have a way of digging which is a feature of their strong backs. They stoop down from the waist to the ground without bending their knees as though their arms are hanging from pivots and, with hardly a movement, seem to pull weeds from the earth effortlessly. They shuffle forwards, not standing up like we tend to do, with their noses literally on the ground. Weeding one of the flower beds was Sophie, and beside her on the ground, a tiny baby wrapped in a blanket, asleep; its small face screwed up with eyes tight shut.

The mother looked up and saw us. Janet spoke in seSotho and the girl smiled.

"Here is the latest member of the family and he comes to work with his Mum." Janet offered. "She feeds him when he wakes and he sleeps in the shade .When she's finished work, she ties him on her back."

Straight away, Sophie proudly pulled back the blanket cover and was pleased to show off her new-born child. Gently, she laid him back on the grass, under the trees.

We approached the goose shed with great excitement. Janet told us that twice a year they had a gooseplucking day. It happened every February and August.

"If we don't pluck their feathers, the birds moult anyway and the feathers get blown all over the yard. And the geese don't mind it, as long as they are held properly. We make our own eiderdowns and pillows for all the people on the farm. Come inside the barn and you can see for yourselves."

Janet led the way through several wooden buildings, hanging with farm machinery and ploughing implements, through the grain store, to where the ladies were working. Sitting beneath a cloud of dust and goosedown, about seven or eight Basotho ladies, each with a white goose under one arm, were busily 'plucking' the softest of downy feathers from underneath the outspread wings. With the sound of soft singing, the workers, in industrious mode, called out to one another, talking to each goose as they did so. With a quick movement, the ladies deftly slid a sock over eyes and beak. Arms and feathers flew, as the pulling and the plucking went on.

"This is to make sure they relax " said Janet quietly in my ear. "Look how many eiderdowns we've made today." She pointed to the box in the middle of the floor brimming with down.

All my misgivings vanished. Each goose was cradled in the arms of a lady, happily seduced by Basotho singing, eyes and beak covered by a sock, letting itself be stroked and de-plumed like a reclining patient in a beauty salon.

Once most of its downy feathers had been removed, the goose was taken to the door of the barn, its headgear removed and turned outside into the farmyard, where loud protestations were heard for a minute or two.

171

The work had already been going on for a few hours. One old lady with not a tooth in her head, resting on a pile of sacks took a small quantity of snuff from her pocket, sniffed it up her nose and gave a sneeze.

"They all take snuff you see, it is something most of them enjoy. It is quite a tradition here on the farm. Sometimes they chew the tobacco," Janet explained. "Come on, Annette, let's see how good you are with a goose. Here take hold of this one."

She led me to one of the birds which had just been brought in. A lady in a blue dress caught hold of my hand and called to me in seSotho.

"None of them speak any English, but don't worry - they would like to show you how to do it."

"What must I do?" I asked hesitantly. "I have never held a goose in my life."

The lady showed me how to kneel down and take the goose on my lap and put my left arm round its body. It felt like holding a hot water bottle. Already it had a sock over its eyes and beak so that it couldn't peck.

"Now, feel underneath with your right hand and pull firmly but gently. Hold the neck away from you - like this."

My fingers touched the softest down . I relaxed and started to enjoy this almost theraputic tactile sensation of handling a live goose. The sound effects were a kind of goose purr with the occasional soft squawk. Without a script, I resorted to my version of 'Over the sea to Skye' which seemed to please the goose and feathers came out easier than I expected. After removing enough feathers to stuff a small cushion, my bird was de-socked by one of the gang. The goose's neck was still between my fingers, with the beak pointing away from me - just in case.

"That's right, just hold him firmly by the neck – no, not like that - don't squeeze too hard," laughed Janet. The poor thing's eyes had started to bulge and the beak was silently opening and shutting. "Here, quick, bring him over to the door."

I let go.The goose let out a healthy sqawk, flapped a lot and shot out into the yard . He didn't even have time for one small nip.

Encircling a second larger goose, which was already blindfolded and fully sock-rigged, I was further instructed by the snuff-happy lady. My bird settled down to a stirring chorus of, 'O my Darling Clementine'. The feathers flew. I was really getting the hang of things. I began to feel a great fondness for this fat warm blooded creature.

"What tog rating is my goose Janet?"

"Don't know about that, but I should think he is fit for any king size bed."

Out in the yard, sneezing loudly, I realized I was covered in white feathers, from head to toe.

"Not bad for a novice," came the approval from our host.

"What a fascinating experience, not sure how much the geese enjoyed it - thanks for the introduction. Right, what's next.?"

I shouldn't have asked. It was one of Janet's route marches up to the top of their mountain, for a look back in time, at Chief Sekonyela's old abandoned homestead. On the topmost ridge his family had lived for many generations, living on the plants and natural resources of the veld. There would have been antelope and zebra then, jackals, baboons, grey rhebok and elands. Streams ran down from the mountains and their world would have been one of rituals, hunting and feasts. One of Janet's maids was old enough to remember some of the descendants of Chief Sekonyela inhabiting the mountain.

It proved to be one of the loveliest walks imaginable. From the topmost rocky plateau, we could see beyond the Caledon River and far into the distance, the blue ranges of the

Malutis. It was as if we were standing on the edge of the world. Some distance below our feet was the nest of an eagle.

Tea was served on the verandah at five thirty. We spent the last part of our day at Boschfontein sitting in comfortable chairs and stroking kittens which engagingly wrapped themselves around any spare legs. The sun was setting and the air still warm with droning honeybees and the scent of roses.

Peace told us about her beloved garden and reeled off the names of all the flowers in bloom at Christmas, When Bill was alive, she used to describe every detail of their garden, so that he knew about each tree and the colour of its blossom. She told us the story of that terrible accident fifty years before and how her husband ran his farm without ever seeing her, his children, his grandchildren or the land that he owned. He and Peace had survived their tragedy, experienced a war time romance in Braille and brought up three children to carry on farming. Boschfontein was a living legend to their dynamic energy. Now a young grandson called Morgan would carry on the name of Barretts for another generation in a very different climate.

Picking the blackjacks out of my socks afterwards, legs aching and knees itching, remembering those stunning views from Boschfontein's highest spot, I acknowledged the serious art of gooseplucking. Added to that was eagle watching. If I hadn't come to Lesotho, or taught at the Nursery school in Ficksburg, I would never have met Janet or had the good fortune to visit Boschfontein. My recent summers of growing English tomatoes and walking the Yorkshire Dales in a howling gale which had been so precious in my memory, seemed to pale into insignificance. I felt as if I had been taken by a tide and planted firmly on another shore.

As we left, the geese cackled in the barn and the peacocks flew down from the lowest branches of the peach trees. With exquisite tails of emerald green and sapphire blue they displayed their male finery, along the edge of the path in front of us. Some things will always be the same- thank God.

Chapter 23

Medicine Man.

Leribe Market is a rowdy and disorderly affair. It is strewn behind the main shopping street, linked by tortuous alleyways of potholes and puddles. Street sellers and stall holders mingle with roving pickpockets and flashy jewellery sharks - only the bold-hearted do business with them. Eye-catching scarves which every Basotho lady wears, fly from pieces of wire strung across the passageways. Smells of fried dough balls and chips linger greasily in the air. Street traffic consists of wheelbarrows, dented bicycles and bakkies held together with string and rust.

When it comes to markets, I am an addict. It can be the most squalid flea ridden heap of junk but I cannot resist investigating. Attempts at extracting me from such places is Barrie's worst nightmare. The money in my purse always leaps into someone else's pocket and we end up with something we do not need and has a hole in the bottom - or even worse - only three out of four legs arrive home.

One Saturday morning, I asked Walter and Emily if they would introduce me to this seamier side of Leribe. Not many white people go there and certainly no self respecting English lady goes there alone. When exploring a new place in Lesotho, I always had this unquestioning faith which was about one fifth caution and the remainder, a trusting calculated gamble that I would be safe. My friendship with the Makibis was a doorway to Lesotho hospitality, not usually given to visiting contract workers. Hints from our camp colleagues always advised caution when travelling abroad - and in December there was that incident when someone tried to hi-jack my car in Maputsoe when I was doing my Christmas shopping with Betty - yet my curiosity never left me. That's how I came to meet the medicine man.

About three alleyways back from the road, in Leribe market, we came across a long tin shack with beads across the doorway and a rather lugubrious pile of bones in the window. A small man beckoned us inside.

A long wooden counter ran the whole length of the shop. Walter introduced me to the owner who was engaged in a business transaction, handing over several bottles containing rather vile looking liquid, to a customer. On the floor beside me were sacks of dried up plants and seed pods, now skeletal and wizened, with heaps of what looked like dead runner beans. Along the counter, inviting bits of beaded jewellery were displayed, some rather hairy leather pouches and a selection of silver bracelets - though more suited to incantations than fashion. I could have sworn there were strings of teeth amongst the bits and pieces.

The back wall of the establishment was stacked with boxes of roots and plants; large black corm-like things resembling hyacinth bulbs, twiggy twisted roots, dried stalks and some shrivelled crackly leaves. A tray of rubbery seed heads resembled a clump of rather mutilated looking figs. Here was the ultimate collection of the grotesque to the phantasmagorical, the gnarled and the withered, the wrinkled and the putrified - all displayed like part of some theatrical re-incarnation of body parts in an Alfred Hitchcock drama. My curiosity sailed into overdrive.

"This is where you can buy a cure for any ailment or disease," Walter whispered. "The medicine man will listen to you and then he'll give you something for your problem."

Acrid smoke from a burning pipe spiralled from under the counter. A grey head appeared and and an old man leaned towards us. He wore fingerless gloves and was stirring something on a small kerosene stove, which spat.

I greeted him in seSotho. He looked from me to Walter. Beneath the smile I detected a Faginesque curiosity.

"Lumela, Ntate," I spoke quietly. "I have come to see your shop. It is interesting." Soon Emily and I were trying on necklaces and sorting through earrings made from bones and bits of wire. A box of intricately carved charms made from ivory and wood was sitting on top of a pile of black stringy stuff which smelled of terminal mildew. It looked like human hair.

The stove emitted strange and odious smells. The medicine man uttered wild incantations throwing darting glances over his half moon spectacles. With his arm raised to the heavens he chanted loudly as though expecting an apparition to come from the rafters. Then without warning he turned his bloodshot eyes on me.

"What kind of a problem do you have lady ?" he asked unnervingly.

He continued to preside over the spitting pot - giving it an occasional stir, but not taking his eyes from my face.

"No, no, I have no problem. I came because I want to learn about your medicines. "All these things in the bottles, are they natural remedies from plants and trees?" I struggled to sound calm.

"That's right. We mix together special herbs and plants and they are to cure the diseases. We can make any remedy you wish. Do you have anything to complain of ? An earache or a common cold ? "

Emily nudged me and whispered, "Nettie - tell him you are getting married soon."

"Shhh ..Emily" It was too late. Fagin had overheard.

"A wedding eh? "There was a moment's pause, while he attended to his foul mixture. His rakish grin seemed to spread across his wizened face.

"Because of your great age lady, I will give you a different medicine to a young bride. But it will have the same effect."

He then subjected me to a long jabbering lecture on what medicine I should take before my marriage as if it was the fulfilment of a long cherished dream. He shook his head and drew circles in the air above his head.

I started to shake with laughter, (or as Liliane would say - '*I was dead of laughing*') and knew that I should not offend him. He was already taking down a dried plank from one of the boxes on the shelf.

"This mixture I will give you, will make your husband very happy. You will have many children ....."

"Thank you - no!." I jumped in quickly, "Emily, tell him I don't want any of his mixture."

"I will make you some *muti*. You must drink this three times a day. It will make you feel very relaxed..... you know, like a young woman inside.You will return to full vitality. Your husband will love you even more. Take it a week before your marriage." His fingers were busy breaking up a piece of crumbly old bark and some equally elderly leaves onto a bit of reeking cloth which he then crushed between his hands. He looked up sideways, squinting with his other eye which was as bloody as a hatching egg. "Do you want many children ?"

"My children are grown up. I already have a granddaughter. No more babies please," I said with a smile, hoping the old man would get the message. "But I would like to photograph you so that I can take your picture back to England with me. I am most interested because your ways are so different to ours."

He suddenly reached across the counter and shook my hand. There was an indistict smell about him - something faintly gloomy.

"Yes, come when you wish, lady. I would like you to photograph my shop. But I tell you - doctors are no good. They know nothing. In Lesotho, we have our own traditional remedies. They still work - even today. Any problem you can tell me, I can solve. Especially for the babies! "

After that, his face did not light with any humour. He went back to the spitting dark liquid chewing on his pipe. We thanked him and returned to the bright sunlit street.

Walter guided us through the busy market, a teeming mass of stalls selling mostly fruit and local vegetables loaded onto wheelbarrows. Still very amused at my experience with the medicine man, I asked Walter if he believed in all this.

"No, not really - but many people do believe it can help them, especially the old people. In the days when my Grandmother was a young woman, plant medicine was the only thing they used. Now we mostly call those things superstitions; we must go and talk to my grandmother Nettie, she will tell you much more."

Walking around the market , we ate deliciously hot dough balls from paper bags and I had my first roasted maize cob cooked on a fire by a small boy .

Surprisingly, there was no junk to be gone through - no bookstalls or memorabilia- only basic commodities sold to everlasting reggae music. Most sellers sat on the ground - chairs were needless impedimenta. One enterprising young man was selling tables of the poorest quality wood - probably using the poorest of tools, judging by the finished product. But a can of bright blue paint can transform a rough table with splintered legs into a desirable object. They attracted a modest audience. A man bought one after much haggling - his wife stoically lifted it onto her head and carried it off.

Emily and I found ourselves in the Leribe Craft Centre, a small village industry where they made hats that were equal to anything you could find at Ascot. They cost ten rands each (approx £1 sterling), handmade from local grasses, by the ladies at the mission. They were so beautifully crafted, that I bought one to get married in. Decorated with flowers, it would sure as eggs, pass Pygmalion.

Mohair rugs and shawls of vivid colours were draped everywhere, skirts and jackets made from patchwork, ropes and belts, reeded baskets and mats all cascaded from the roof in a blaze of colour. Church vestments hung with jewels, draped themselves around the cardboard figures of a priest, displaying a blue silk robe with embroidered sleeves. It was a treasure trove.

The craft centre forms part of a sheltered workshop and employment project run by the Anglican Church. Most of the ladies who work here are disabled, crippled or deaf. Not only a hive of industry it is a place of caring and fun. People who would otherwise feel useless have small jobs to do and are paid. With spinning wheels made from bits of wire and old bicycle wheels, tin baths for mixing vegetable dyes, wooden looms and a large workshop - all manner of things are made. Everyone is busy and the workshops are lively with the singing of the women as they turn wool into cloth and cloth into garments. Village women spin rare mountain mohair in their own homes and bring the yarns to the centre to be processed. Baskets made from mountain grasses are brought in from remote villages where gnarled fingers teach young ones how to plait and weave.

Set behind the Craft Centre are the houses where the workers live. Often the ladies walk up the dirt road to shop in the market. There are no tarmac roads from here up into the town, only a wide track full of potholes - not helpful for ladies with leg callipers and a limp. At times I was shocked by their numbers with crippled limbs and often observed them walking slowly with a twisted uneasy gait. In a country such as Lesotho, orthopaedic surgeons would be hard to find. The sad facts spoke for themselves.

The area is always thronging with people. Close by is the Anglican Church probably the largest building in Leribe, presided over by Father Brown and the nuns. The Convent of the Holy Name is alongside where the nineteen Sisters of Mercy live and work. Father Brown has now retired from the Church but you wouldn't think so. He is a septuagenarian of dynamic energy who has lived in Leribe since his 'retirement' from the main church in Teyateyaneng, where he was Rector from 1975. He came to Leribe in 1978 and goes by the title of Chaplain of the Community. In his non clerical white shorts and t-shirt mode of dress, he moves faster than most men half his age.

Father Brown is English by birth, with a self taught second language - broken seSotho spoken with a slight West Country accent. I felt drawn to seek him out - there being so few English people in Leribe. When eventually we met, I realized his reputation was but a small part of this charismatic man.

From his small retirement house in the convent grounds, he has become the maker and stitcher of clerical robes, the mainstay of the Mother's Union (a very popular and influential organisation in Africa) and the Boys Brigade; mentor, philosopher and guide to everyone connected with the community; taxi driver for the sick, and the elderly. He is willing to chauffeur the odd bride to church in his car and becomes a stand-in priest when no one else is there. Baptisms are his speciality and although he doesn't know all the right words, he knows how to splash water around in the right places.

He was once known to have gone to celebrate Holy Communion at the prison, a fairly rare event. The service was conducted in the open air, with Father Brown and the Sisters inside the fence and the offenders outside. Father Brown, delivered his lines in his best seSotho and when it came to the sermon, Sister Hilda translated to the prisoners, who were most impressed with his words. Suddenly one of them asked for a blessing to which Father Brown agreed . As he did this, the rest of the inmates, all wanting to save their souls, requested the same for themselves. After the rather elaborate arrangments of segregating the prisoners from the clergy, Father Brown was taken into the compound, and ended up administering individual prayers and blessings not only to all the guards and the domestic staff, but the inmates as well.

Discussing the occasion afterwards he was heard to say, "In Lesotho, one has to be prepared for anything, you just have to go with the flow."

Some of the nuns have been in Leribe for many years. Sister Hilda from 1945. I met Sister Angelina , Sister Alphonsina, Sister Veronica and Sister Lucia the Provincial Superior and tiny Sister Maria, who has the the most twinkling eyes. When she smiles it's like the sun coming out. Most have travelled and worked in other African countries and have fascinating stories to tell. Sister Judith was the only white face among the nineteen. She came from Derbyshire and I so enjoyed meeting her. We escaped for a few quiet minutes on one occasion, to share English tea and stories of home.

One lovely hot afternoon , sitting with Sister Maria, Sister Angelina and Father Brown on the stoep, having tea and listening to their stories, I felt like an honoured guest at a royal reception. Father Brown telling how he came to Leribe to take over this religious community without knowing a word of seSotho. One of his new staff taught him to ride a horse for the first time in his life. He admits to not being a good linguist and said he learnt to ride a pony up a mountain more easily than preach a sermon in this new language, nevertheless the people said they could understand him and liked his sense of humour.

He admits that he loves the Basotho people even though they drive him to distraction and God willing, he will stay there until the end of his days. He cannot even think about a trip to England.

" I'm far too busy. And anyway I don't like the idea of all that English traffic."

He hates the new kind of hearse which has recently arrived in Leribe - a motor car heralded by a loud horn. "Have you heard the shocking noise it makes? When it's my turn, I will be happy to go and meet my Maker in a donkey and cart."

The convent itself is bordered by a handsome wide verandah covered in vines, hanging with fruit. The original root was planted by Sister Marjorie Jean when she first went there and is called a 'white crystal' vine. The saying goes in Lesotho that you must plant a vine on top of a dead horse, but it appears at the time they could only obtain a dead donkey. Now the spiralling tentacles grow in profusion all around the house, in every direction and upwards into the roof - perhaps a distant cousin of the one at Hampton Court Palace. Over the years, it has become the keeper of prayers and many secrets. Grey uniformed figures slip in and out of the rooms, like sparrows in a nest, fluttering along the corridors for prayers, seeing to the sick who come here, mending and making, bottling the fruit from the garden, meditating and chanting all inspired thoughts to heaven, while making sure that their temple fulfils its purpose to the town.

The gardens are abundant with yellow gourds, marrows, peas and colourful pumpkins; fat cabbages spread in rows and gnarled old peach trees, bright with fruit, grow among the lemons and the vegetables. Everywhere it is well tended and neat and there are nets to keep off the birds. A wonderful scent of flowers and wild garlic follow you when you walk there. Mulched and wet after a brisk shower of rain, every inch of soil is cultivated lovingly and wisely by the Sisters. I shall always remember the Convent garden as a place of dignity and peace.

Like the bees, I felt happy there. The children from St Saviours Primary School adjoining the Convent stopped and waved as they carried their school books home, curious about the white lady in a grass hat who came to be sitting there, writing quietly in the shade.

Chapter 24

Bending the Rules.

With the month of March comes the cosmos in Lesotho. It is the quite the prettiest time of the year. It is early Autumn and the approach of Easter. The flowering cosmos with its daisy like petals of pink, magenta and white, spreads in banks across the landscape. It scatters every hedgerow every valley and copse with a froth of dancing pink. As you drive across the countryside, ribbon pink strips weave along river banks and encircle the trees.

On my way into Ficksburg the road was lined with cosmos and I fell in love with it. It grew as high as the donkeys. It filled every flower container in the house. Breakfast in the garden meant three things - fresh peaches, cosmos and coffee. When the girls came for their lessons I gave them cosmos in geat bunches to take home. My tiny painting studio was covered in sketches of it. I even made Barrie stop the car on a mountain road while I took cosmos photographs from lying down.

Our house was strewn with lists of guests and crossed out lists of guests. Our wedding, which had started out being small, serious and low-key, suddenly became a big event, hilarious and extravert. Guest lists are known for causing acute stress and dilemma. For us it was no different. One evening, with great resolve, we vowed to finalize the wedding list. Gusts of wind suddenly sucked all our papers off the verandah table and threw them into the air. Hercule barked as other dogs on the mountain howled in the evening air. When it blew up for a storm, he always became restless. The gin and tonics were poured out and the meal ready to be served.

"Sixty is a wonderful age to be getting married," remarked Barrie, "let's invite them all, black white and all colours in between."

We started to count the nationalities and realized there were fifteen in all, including our friends from Leribe, Butha-Buthe, Ha Lejone, Ficksburg and Johannesburg. It read like the roll call of the International League of Nations.

"And don't forget Walter and Emily - that's sixty two bottoms on seats for the wedding itself and the reception - and about twenty more on the camp. We can't leave out all the maids and gardeners and taxi drivers - but if we invite them all to the ceremony, it'll run into hundreds - they'll all bring huge families and we'll never be able to feed them all."

"Ask them all!" was the reply. It was obviously a gin and tonic answer. There was a growl of thunder which brought the conversation to an abrupt end. We dashed inside before the rain came lashing down and the glasses were blown onto the garden. A band of steel shafted across the sky and every curtain in the house decided to fly to the moon by itself. We were in for a wild night.

"Look, if we invite everyone on the camp, it will get ridiculous." I yelled above the noise of the wind. "And we do have to consider Borrie and Elsa. It's their garden - you can't expect them to feed a stampede."

"Okay, you win Nettie. Final Decision. A knees-up for everyone on the camp the night before - wedding ceremony by invitation only."

As the hailstones pelted the roof, we ran round the house closing all the windows and for a while, all we could see was a blanket of white stones rolling in waves across the dark lawns and flattening the flowers. That night, Hercule escaped up the mountain as the storm had unnerved him so much he cleared the six foot fence. He went on the rampage with every dog for miles around and arrived back the following morning - a battle scarred wounded soldier, covered in wet cow dung and tics. The next day, he lay around the garden looking exhausted and woe-begone until Betty arrived to give him a bath. Pregnant she may be, but under her eagle eye, Hercule had to endure repeated hosepipings, de-lousings, Betty's tic removal techniques and brush scrubbings until the fur fluffed from his body like a shampooed poodle in the Kings Road. Then he was given ox-tail for tea.

On 11th March it is King Moshoeshoe's Day and a Public holiday. Our mission for the day was to drive into Bethlehem and buy a wedding ring. When we arrived at the border, there was a horribly long queue. Today, when most working people were going out of Lesotho, all passports must be stamped, every detail checked, even if they had been through ten times the previous week. I think secretly the guards were miffed because everyone was on holiday. The mood at the border was high. The drug sqad were out in force, vehicles were double searched and the queues didn't move. Suddenly a dirty pink pig waddled up to the barrier, past all the waiting vehicles, looking for something good to eat and tiptoed indolently passed the guards with their hip revolvers, the drug sqad with their shoulder rifles, and on into South Africa. The guards relaxed and waved us through.

Looking back quietly to a year ago today, to a moderate lifestyle in a London suburb, trying to cope with grey English weather, never ending viruses, too many taxes and an ailing government, we had to admit that life had changed beyond all recognition. The English have a weakness for too many rules, the Basotho from no rules at all. We had rats in the roof, no telephone system, roads that got washed away in the night and a stock exchange where goats were worth more than credit cards.

People were poor, that meant everyone; beyond that there was kindness, openness and impossible hospitality. We were immune from street violence inasmuch as we didn't go out in the street very often and we weren't careless. Add to that never ending sunshine and a wedding – and I could almost tear up my return ticket to Heathrow. In a hundred years, I would never have believed that the King of Lesotho and I could be sharing the same day for a celebration.

The transluscent white clouds produced a sky of shining blancmanges sailing across a sea of blue jelly. Everywhere the maize was ripening. It was a perfect day. The donkey kraal in Levis Nek was teeming with life, and the whole of Butha-Buthe was on holiday. It felt like any Bank Holiday in the U.K- minus traffic. Young men were out parading themselves with their knobkerries - a carved and decorated wooden stick which immediately gave them poser power. Teenage girls pretended not to flirt with them and turned away, while tattooing messages in the dust with their toes.

Funeral feasts were being prepared, and roasted oxen smoked in several compounds as we passed. Funerals are very important occasions here. Normally the family gathers and a beast is slaughtered for the mourners who come to the house of the deceased, before the body is buried. There are no mortuaries. If the family can afford it, a marquee is erected - if not, the whole gathering takes place out in the open and the whole world looks on. If you don't attend your own village funerals- it gets written in God's little notebook and when its your turn - nobody comes to yours. It is a highly principled affair. On the day of the burial, all the children in the family have their heads shaved, starting with the eldest .When the new hair grows, it represents new life. It is also a sign of respect for the dead person. Certain personal belongings are placed in the grave with the body so that they may be used in the next world, sometimes sorghum and pumpkin seeds. One month from the burial, a second ceremony takes place, to honour the person who has died and if a wife has lost her husband, a lengthy period of mourning begins.

We left the funeral fires of Lesotho behind. Bethlehem was the ideal place to find a goldsmith who would make us a wedding ring. A clever Afrikaans jeweller completed the happy deed. There is no such thing as rose gold in Bethlehem which we searched for, and Barrie's ring was to be made from new gold. My ring was my Grandmother's wedding ring which I had worn since I was twenty, with an added polish. Choosing our wedding rings in South Africa symbolised the gateway to our future and we spoke solemly about our own innermost feelings as we drove home through the afternoon downpour. The road ahead was empty.

That same evening, one of our company's vehicles was hi-jacked and the driver left stranded but unharmed, on the very same road as we had travelled. We were thankful to have reached home by nightfall. Subsequently, all the company cars were taken in and the registration number of each car painted in bold black letters on the roof. This enabled the police helicopters to spot stolen vehicles more easily from the air. Once again we were advised to travel in convoys of two or three vehicles, if night journeys were essential.

Then a journey to Blomfontein came as a surprise. Blomfontein is the provincial capital of the Free State. Its name means 'fountain of flowers'. The judicial capital of South Africa, it has a well preserved historical heritage, a famous university as well as lots of fine architecture, governmental establishments and is a city regarded as the Afrikaner dominated heartland.

It was a matter of some urgency for me to find a wedding dress. There was only a month before our special day. Blomfontein has a modern shopping centre, something I had not seen since leaving England. It seemed a good idea to combine a historical and trousseau visit the following Saturday to buy an outfit for me and a waistcoat for Barrie. The thing I wished to find more than anything else was an Edwardian parasol.

I think in the mists of time, President Brand's attempts to make this struggling frontier town into a wealthy city in the face of constant attacks by armies of Moshoeshoe warriors, will never compete with my struggle to find a wedding dress.

In Blomfontein's modern shopping precinct, after four hours of abortive attempts at trying on ponderous sequined garments embossed with peach lilies and knee high shoulder pads, or garish ivory gowns encrusted with shiny bottle tops, sharp enough to gash your wrist on, I had failed to find anything suitable.The in-waiting groom meanwhile, had read the print off the Bloemfontein Gazette in the cafe in the square and paled at the thought of being dragged before yet another manicured saleslady. Carmine nails and plastic beehive hairstyles were not his scene .

Distraught and dressless, I asked to be taken home .

"There's nothing for it," I wailed, "I shall get married in a plastic bin liner!"

We drove in silence- despair written in lights over my head.

On the outskirts of Blomfontein a country fair- cum- fleamarket had been taking place in the park. The owners were dismantling their stalls as we went by. On a hunch I suggested we take a look - a tearful one at that. A few African pots were still displayed along the pavement, one or two splashes of ethnic material hung overhead along with a few garments belonging to a dressmaker who knew a thing or two about colour. The

Afrikaner saleslady was in the process of leaving. I sniffed and looked up. There was an originality about these clothes which made me look twice. They were beautifully made, slightly bohemian, long swishy skirts in rich blues, greens, pinks and browns. A seamstress with a talented eye for style. Quickly looking along the outgoing rail of individually styled garments - I knew my search was over. In three minutes flat, without mirror or dressing room - the perfect wedding dress had jumped off the rail into my arms. Twirling and dancing on the grass, I hugged it, and shrieked with delight.

"This is it! This is the dress!"

Barrie's face was a picture of relief. Unpretentious, unglamorous, folksy -I had found a gypsy style creation made of all kinds of patchwork stitched together - combining all the colours of the cosmos. A few minutes later and the park would have been empty.

The next few weeks were difficult, complicated and stressful. Heleyn, Annacleda , Kaizi, Esther, Valerie and Emily still came for their lessons. After a tiring afternoon spent organising wedding plans in Ficksburg or some other long distance mission, I would return to find the girls sitting outside the gate of the camp waiting for me. No phones on camp meant that every time I wanted to speak to one of my wedding guests or a member of my family, it meant a journey into South Africa to use the street phones.

One squally March afternoon, I drove the half hour journey across the border to make an important call to England. It meant first buying a fifty rand phone card from a Telecom shop in Ficksburg, afterwards walking across to the main Post Office to use one of the dozen or so street phones.I tried them all in turn. Nothing worked - the card refused to connect me. Walking back to the Telecom shop, I queued again, and explained to the Afrikaans lady behind the glass screen that I could not reach England from the entire Ficksburg telephone system. She turned abruptly.

"Well- what do you expect - it's been raining," she snapped between thin lips.

"I beg your pardon?" I felt as if I had been dealt a body blow. "Is it possible then that I have a refund?"

"No lady, we can't refund your money, come back tomorrow - if its fine."

There was a slight pause while my non scientific brain tried to grapple with the entire histrionics of this woman's illogical and unreasonable explanation.

"Excuse me, am I supposed to know that the rain causes your phones to stop working? You might have informed me before I spent fifty rands on a card!"

I decided against asking to see the manager. In her eyes, the whole argument rested on the fact that I was an English woman -and my grandfather may have fought in the Boer War. The woman turned her back, the office door shut with a bang and an assistant threw a fifty rand note, unapologetically across the desk.

There was no point in crying over spilt milk. Undeterred, I decided to continue with plans to order my wedding flowers at the one flower shop in the town. My list of twelve buttonhole sprays and one red rose for the bridegroom didn't seem complicated although on the day before the wedding, someone would have to drive out to get them as the shop probably wouldn't deliver into Lesotho. Nobody delivers into Lesotho. The shopowner was busy dressing flowers for a large occasion.

"I would like to order flowers for a wedding please."

"Are they for you?"asked the woman with a pair of vicious cutters in her hand, looking me up and down with a sharp peck of her head. She spoke with a thick Afrikaans accent. Her body language spoke volumes. Her eagle eyes gave not a spark of lightness in my direction. I gave her my list written down clearly and asked first of all, if she would have the special colours I wanted - cream for the men and pink for the ladies.

She put down the cutters on the counter and folded her arms.

"One red rose, " she said, rolling her 'r's as if the words had petrified in mid air. Her hostility bit like a vice in the hot afternoon.

"Yes please, I would like it to be different from the others. That one's a bit special."

I waited patiently for a reply to my first question. Her thin nose drew itself up into a beak. She looked at me sideways.

"No lady. Impossible. I buy roses in packs of twenty.!" came the flat reply.

"I'm sorry, I thought you did flowers for all occasions, "I said, staring at the sign over the door. She turned her head away and picked up her cutters.

"And just what do you expect me to do with the other nineteen?"

The list in my hand, I fled down the steps of the shop, choking back tears of anger and reflecting on an afternoon beleaguered by historical grievances between Boer and English, more than a hundred years ago. In my mind, there was no question of what to do with the other nineteen roses - thorns or no thorns, preferably long stemmed. My rage knew no bounds.

By the time I reached St Monica's Mission and home through the late afternoon skies, I was calm again.

That evening, Barrie and I had planned an early evening drive out to Ha Simone to watch the sun go down and then machuchiana with chillies for supper. The sight of Esther with her books waiting for me on the doorstep meant we would miss the sunset - but enjoy the machuchiana. I could not turn her away - nor insist we keep strictly to an appointed time for her lesson. Lesotho isn't like that - adaptation and spontaneity are the only rules. When Barrie walked through the door that evening, I opened my mouth to tell him about our wedding flowers and promptly burst into tears. Not only for the sake of my one red rose, but for the discovery of the deep unconditional hatred that can be harboured over two lost generations.

On Friday evening at the Shekleton Shebeen, Ian greeted us loudly and playfully annnouncing that he had found me a double loader locomotive tipper truck to drive me to the wedding ceremony.

"The driver might have to stop and pick up a few tons of concrete, but you should be Okay in the cab." Ian was Barrie's best man and determined to make our wedding celebration memorable. "Would you like the use of the crane and hoist?"

Bob was there too and I felt this was the right moment to ask if he would be kind enough to give the bride away.

With a most affectionate "Och, aye the noo," in the style of a true Scotsman, he clicked his heels, saluted and kissed my hand – twice.

"Do ye think I should wear ma full morning suit with top hat, full military uniform with medals, ma full dress uniform with kilt, or white tuxedo?"

"Bob, what about white tuxedo for the marriage ceremony and full dress uniform and kilt in the evening - with medals."

"Aye - and then there'll be a uniformed chauffeur to drive ye to the ceremony - in the Rolls Royce."

We wanted it to be a real African wedding and Ian suggested flippantly that Priscilla would probably appear in one of her 'ban the bomb' outfits with a flag on a pole. At that moment Priscilla walked into the room. Eyeing her approaching figure, Barrie commented, "come to think of it, she always reminds me of an anti- nuclear demonstration!"

He ducked as she swiped his drink off the bar. Flourishing a trailing scarf Priscilla was in a warring mood that night after one of her great danes Tamu had escaped his pen and demolished her kitchen, her dining room and her bar, emptied the fridge and lined the whole house with toilet paper, while she had been at the auction. She promised to clean up in time for the wedding and with her usual penchant for hospitality offered us her house for an afternoon champagne reception after our garden ceremony. We accepted.

Our intention was to escape quietly after the wedding breakfast, drive out to Boschfontein for a restful afternoon interlude, then return for our evening reception. The grand all- nation party would probably go on until the small hours. An afternoon siesta was an important part of the day. It also meant that we could invite families with small children for the morning ceremony and extend our hospitality to other guests for the evening reception. With this in mind, we had planned a live performance by a friendly Tunisian bellydancer. This small event turned out to be the best non-kept secret of the wedding.

Our wedding night was to be spent at Boschfontein in the old dairy guesthouse. Janet had offered us the accommodation, knowing how we loved it there. We knew that she would make it very special for us. In addition, two guests from England would be joining us. Recently married themselves, we had invited them to take their own honeymoon in South Africa, with us. Anticipating the fourteen hour drive to the Peninsula, it seemed a sound idea to travel in a foursome.

During recent weeks we had searched frantically for the best place to hold a reception for our sixty guests. It appeared there were very few options open to us. Only a handful were suitable. Then, a few miles from Ficksburg we stumbled across Zevenfontein, an old sandstone farmhouse built in 1870, which was run by a lady from Birmingham called Annie. It was perfect. There was one difficulty. It was 10 km up a dirt road from the main Rosendal road and our guests would need a map. We decided, perhaps unwisely, that this would not be too much of a problem, and well worth the effort as the place had a touch of old charm and the lady was English.

The name Zevenfontein, means 'place of seven springs'. Built on a hillside, the house had an attractive stone staircase up to the main part and a wide verandah running all the way round the house. Inside, the sophisticated layout of the rooms and high ceilings were perfect for a large gathering. The house was filled with old country furniture and paintings, open fires and spacious seating arrangements. Exciting menus of home cooked fayre were offered. For Annie it was her very first wedding.

She was fascinated by our guest list which included, French, Spanish, Swiss, Mauritian, Persian, Portuguese, Venezualan, American and Thai, not forgetting Afrikaans and Basotho. Nothing was too much trouble. Annie would decorate the whole house with cosmos and prepare all the food herself. The car parking would be a field in front of the house – with a promise to tie ballons to the hedgerows for the last mile or two in case anyone got lost. The roads around Zevenfontein criss crossed for miles across open country. A map was the key to success.

Back at our house in Leribe, there was an event which took our minds entirely off the wedding. An S.O.S. from Solemon Malebo at Tlotlisong School, in Ficksburg , arrived, saying that he had drawn a blank from Pretoria and not even President Mandela's Office would give us permission to bring 50 kids across the border without passports on the evening of our concert. It was time to pull out the proverbial stops if our aim was to be achieved.

I set my mind on finding someone who could help us. Everything else was now in place for the concert to go ahead. The School Hall at Butha-Buthe had been booked and someone was going to build us a stage on the day. The transport had been arranged, the food for the singers was to be prepared and delivered, tickets were being printed and my posters were almost ready to go up. Besides the children of all three schools were rehearsing their songs and nothing on this planet would stop them from reaching performance level by 13th June. I couldn't let them down.

There was just a little matter of our wedding, a honeymoon in Capetown and a trip to England to be organised between times. My finger was hovering on the panic button. My schedule was tight enough and the birth of Betty's baby looked imminent.

The following morning, I stood quaking at the door of a most influential man. Until fairly recently, he had been the senior customs officer of Lesotho Immigration. He worked on our camp. I had never spoken to him before. I simply knocked on his door, explained my mission and asked if he would write me a letter of introduction to the chief border guard. With this man's signature I could get inside the border office myself and make my request.

Quietly he put on his coat. Then he asked if I would come with him in his bakkie. He said nothing else. I didn't even stop to tell anyone I was leaving the camp. Half an hour later, we were entering the rear door of the chief guard hut on the Lesotho side of the border. My benefactor was well over six foot tall, very broad and very black. I am five foot two. I could hardly keep in step.

We were greeted most cordially and invited to sit down. A senior lady officer asked me, "why do you want to bring a bus full of children through the border, with no passports - it is against regulations."

"Yes. I know. But it is for a few hours only. The children are very poor. They have no money to buy passports. But they have beautiful voices and we would like them to sing in our camp. European children will sing with them. They will return after a few hours."

My host and the customs officer spoke in low tones in their own language. I prayed for a positive reply. The great lady turned to me.

"You must go and get official papers from the head man at the school in Ficksburg. We need photographs, identity papers and an official letter asking permission to bring these pupils through. You must bring me a list showing the name of every person who is travelling on the bus. When this is done, I will see you again."

She stood up and left the room, leaving us to see ourselves out. We drove back to the camp in a kind of strained silence. Mr Malapo was not a man who wasted words. The business was over. As we drew up in the dusty yard of the camp, he turned and spoke.

"*Ke tla u bona hosasane.* (I will see you tomorrow), then realising I did not understand, he offered, "come tomorrow for a letter. I will sign it." I thanked him but he was not listening. He was already half way across the carpark. A few strides and he was gone.

Now all that was necessary was to obtain safe passage through the South African border and our concert could go ahead. And a letter from Solomon showing the names of the kids. This presented another set of problems as I knew no one who could advise me of how the South African passport office would react to my request. To get fifty children through two border controls would require some degree of co-operation beyween them. As far as I knew they didn't like each other much.

I flew into Ficksburg that afternoon to seek out Mr Malebo at Tlotlisong School, who was up to his neck in school problems. I managed to find Elizabeth who was rehearsing the choir and as I walked into the big hall, the kids started stamping their feet and cheering. They insisted on singing one of their songs which they were learning for the concert. There was no point in alarming them at this stage when spirits were so high.

I found Solomon at last, passed on my bit of good news and he came and shook my hands almost off.

"Annette, this is wonderful! I am delighted that the choir can go across the Lesotho border - but we still have not the permission for the South African side. The authorities in Pretoria tell me it cannot be done. I have a letter. It is against all their regulations. We must do everything we can for the kids. They have set their hearts on coming."

Wasting no time, he started to gather the information which we had been asked for and promised to have everything typed and ready by the end of the week. Staff were so keen to make a success, they beamed at me and kept shaking my hand. Evidently there had been a vote as to which teachers would be coming with the choir and the chosen few were treating it as the highlight of the year.

"Solomon," I said in a serious voice. "I have an idea. Please would you be ready to come with me as my interpreter on Friday. I will come to collect you and we will go and see what can be done at the border office - in person."

"I will be your interpreter definitely Annette! I will be ready to stop being a headmaster and become an interpreter. Yes - we will go together on Friday!"

This being the most exciting thing on my mind, I forgot to go shopping in Ficksburg on the way home and pulled up by the side of the road to buy bananas from one of the ladies on a pavement stall in Maputsoe on the Lesotho side. I locked the car and sauntered down the street past lots of stalls, feeling very pleased with life. My brain was addled from today's turn of events and my sensible self was jammed right up against my impulsive self, trying to put a brake on my galloping drama. Shades of Barrie saying, 'don't be too impetuous' rang in my ears, followed by a calm hand-on -the- shoulder speech, which usually ended with me falling headlong into a ditch before I could stop myself.

As I opened my purse to pay the woman for my bananas, I felt something being pulled from my hand and realized at that moment that I was being robbed. Immediately the thief was away from me and running hard along the roadway weaving in and out of the traffic. At the top of my lungs I yelled to anyone who would listen,

"Hey! I've been robbed!"

I must have covered a hundred yards, the thief already too far ahead. My cries fell on deaf ears. Somehow I landed in a shop doorway, with someone helping me to my feet. I surfaced to a torrent of Maputsoe shoppers who were angry on my behalf. The manager of the store who was greatly concerned for my plight, phoned for the police.

The burning question on everyone's lips was, "how much money was in the purse?" It went on being asked until I realized that a white lady's purse was much more of a talking point than a bag belonging to a Mosotho. While the shock was still registering on my shaking hands, and I tried to think where my car was, a loud siren blasted and an open backed jeep with two policemen in the back and two in the front, all carrying arms, screeched to a halt on the steps of the shop.The dust haze enveloped the whole street, pedestrians, shoppers and taxis alike. The crowd backed off. There was a lot of shouting and harsh grating voices raised in anger and the truck revved mindlessly while parked up against the plate glass shop window.

Suddenly I heard someone shout.

"He's gone to de reever! Quick!" and the great chase began. The truck backed and revved with the storm troopers holding onto the back of the vehicle - the crowd now jumping up and down with delight. It was all most impressive, but it was more for the entertainment value than a genuine desire to catch a thief. Everyone around me seemed to know who the robber was but no one wanted to tell the police. The banana lady broke her silence and said she recognised him. The shop manager produced a piece of paper and a pen but no one wanted to write down a name. The last view of the police was their jeep bouncing down a track which led to the river, in a haze of dust, with two rifled officers trying to hang on to the sides, leaving the turbulent assembly to disperse. I felt glad it wasn't the Limpopo and we had no crocodiles to contend with. I couldn't face the grisly job of identifying a dead robber's small parts. Quietly, I left the shop and drove home still shaking.

As I was advised to make a report to my local police station, the following afternoon was spent making an official statement about the robbery. In Leribe village, stands Major Bell's Tower, a remnant of the old fortifications built by the British in 1879, a humble symbol of the British Empire in days gone by. It is a relic of the Gun War of 1880. Next to it is the Police Station and at the front of the building stands the rather neglected stone statue of a European soldier, meant to symbolize Leribe's part in the Seige of Hlotse in 1880.

I walked into the grassy courtyard in front of the main office.

"I've come to report a theft."

"Why is that?" The duty officer looked at me as though I had dropped from the moon.

"Yesterday, there was an incident in Maputsoe involving a thief. I was told to come and report it to you." Without another word he gave me a seat - an old wooden box and left the room.

The larger- than- life lady officer who was sent to deal with the incident, took twenty minutes to find a piece of paper on which she attempted to write in long hand, details of the theft. Written English was not one of her favourite pastimes and over her large bosom, the pen seemed to slip from her fingers, until at length, I volunteered to write the report myself and sign it. In terms of efficiency it saved about two hours. The officer was happy to leave me filling in my own report while she went off in search of some important papers regarding a recent decapitation. Her undulating body language told me she was much more at home with murderers and rapists than petty street crime involving a pound of bananas. I got the impression she thought I was a bit naive to bother reporting it.

How efficiently she filed my documents away after observing the one broken typewriter and the rusty filing cabinets in the corner, covered in some left over straw from a farmyard, I could only guess. The table I was writing on was suffering from muddy paw prints (of what I dare not think) and the window was broken. The place was memorable by its chaos and with its quota of cells fully occupied downstairs - one had to wonder what kind of conditions the prisoners were held in.

Of course no one expected that my stolen money would be returned, but the senior policeman on duty made my jaws fall apart when he asked me if I carried a gun. I was advised that, if this was the case, I would have been within the law to shoot at the robber.

I assured him that I wouldn't know what to do with a gun if I had one and explained that no one in my country carries a firearm. With an approving smile, I was instantly elevated from yob status to peaceful citizen and left amid many handshakes and a feeling that justice had been done at least as far as the Lesotho Police were concerned. It was obvious that the known identity of the robber remained best ignored.

I was escorted off the premises by the senior police chief, who assured me that if the robber was found, he would personally see to it that I could impose my own fine on the culprit.

"You good lady citizen from England, please accept apologies and take away your dog."

Hercule, who was tied to a post in the police station yard, was busy growling at everyone who went within yards and did not endear himself to anyone.

My self-imposed deadline of the visit to the South African border control office, was to take place the following day. I tossed and turned in my sleep that night with anxious thoughts of a blank refusal by the chief. Nothing could banish my hopes for the children from Tlotlisong to come and sing in Lesotho. In the morning I dressed with care and despite the heat, wore a smart black suit with a fresh white collar and carried a handbag. If only I could manage to control my bladder long enough to see me through a long session in the guard hut, it would be all right. I collected Liliane and together we looked as though we were going to the Senior Social Workers District Conference.

We drove smartly into Ficksburg, our spirits high. In the staff room at Tlotlisong School, Solomon was waiting. He had all the official papers ready to give me. There was a list of fifty names registering every pupil in the choir who would be travelling on the bus - in duplicate. Solomon was also wearing a suit.

"When we get to the border Solomon, I have a request to make. Let me do the talking. Just keep quiet. I might need you to translate if I get into difficulties."

"Yes, Ma-am. I will be very quiet. Until you ask me to translate." His big hunky frame shook with laughter and he rolled his eyes up to heaven. "I will do my best to keep silent." Solomon parked his truck next to the passport control at the South African border office and the three of us walked up the steps to the appropriate entrance, rather nervously. I pulled up my collar and knocked loudly. A tall guard came out.

Greeting him with a big smile, I stepped forward and drew myself up to my full height. Solomon was six foot two and stood back, behind Liliane.

"We have a very special request to put to the chief. May we see him - in person? We know he is a busy man."

"Why do you want to see him? He will not see you unless you have an appointment." The guard bristled slightly.

Politely, I asked again. We got past him. We got past the next guy who stamped the passports and with a firm resolve, said that we were looking for the chief who might listen to our request because it was something of great importance. Curiosity written on every face at the sight of two white ladies inside the main office, we eventually were ushered into the inner sanctum of the main Border Control office, where we were told to wait. I dare not look at Solomon. Liliane and I exchanged glances. In this kind of establishment, one does not smile.

A serious looking officer came in and we were asked us to explain our presence. He wore a smart black uniform with lots of badges on his sleeve. It turned out to be the Chief Officer, who introduced himself as Patrick.

"I am from L.H.P.C. in Leribe," I began. "We are asking a favour for the children of Meqheleng to come and sing for the engineers who are working on the Highlands Water project. In your country, you have such wonderful singing which is better than anything we have ever heard. I am a teacher from England. My colleagues would like to raise money for their school, Tlotlisong High School. Both English and the French children will sing with the Ficksburg children - it will make a bond between us."

By this time Patrick was listening intently.

"But the children here have no passports. They have no money. We wish that they are allowed to come across the border to Butha-Buthe for a few hours only to give us their music. We will provide the transport freely. They would return the same evening. But we need your permission for this important occasion."

Liliane nodded in agreement and said that it would show that the South Africans were very kind to let us do this. The moment was tense. Patrick asked his second-in-command to fetch him some papers and without speaking, wrote something down.

"When do you want this to happen?"

"At 5.30pm. on 13th June. We would return by 11.00pm at the latest. I have the list of everyone who will be on the bus. This is Mr Malebo. He is the Headmaster of the school. He will be travelling on the bus with four members of staff and I will also travel with them."

I knew instinctively that by now, Solomon would have shut his eyes and be saying a prayer. With a supreme effort, I kept my voice low and my eyes on the ground.

Patrick finished writing and looked directly at me with a cool gaze.

"I will do this for you because you ask not for yourselves, but for the school children. We respect that you have asked in a good way. I will give you a promise that we will allow your passengers to cross into Lesotho for one evening. I will personally see that you go through. But we cannot guarantee that the Lesotho officials will allow your safe passage. Their regulations may not permit."

"I have already spoken to them and they have agreed.in principle" I took out the letter signed by Mr Malapo and he read it.

"There is one thing. If the children do not return, we shall hold you responsible." I felt like the pumpkin in the Cinderella story. Solomon, breaking his vow of silence, quietly thanked him in seSotho and Liliane and I did our best to show how grateful we were, although wanting to escape in case he changed his mind. Our papers were now in the safe hands of Patrick for his records. We had done all we could.

Using all our self control, we walked steadily past all the other guards and out towards the exit. Once out of sight and earshot of the guards, we just shrieked with excitement. Solomon's face almost split in two. He picked me up in a great bear hug and swung me round and round. We were euphoric! Our jubilant mood spilled over and we felt it was a great triumph over officialdom.

"Ladies - we did it! You spoke the right words! From now on Annette, you are in charge of all my affairs. I will always be very very quiet. It almost killed me not to smile in there. I wanted to shout for joy!"

If Solomon had been wearing a hat - it would have been thrown into the air.

"Come - we will go and celebrate at the Hoogland. We must send that guy a present."

In the cocktail bar of the Hoogland Hotel, we attracted a great deal of attention - a tall handsome Basotho hosting drinks to two white ladies, French and English - all in celebratory mood. People stared and hovered curiously near our table hoping to hear our story.

Now that the tension was over, elation descended on our small party. Against all odds, we had succeeded in extracting a gesture of willingness on all sides. No one had stood against us when it came to the point. We had asked a small favour in a polite way; a request very close to our hearts - for the sake of kids from a South African squatter camp. Many people would benefit from this truly international evening but who better to gain the most, than the young performers who would hold the stage.

"A toast to Patrick, the Prince Charming of the South African border!"

Our glasses clinked and our eyes sparkled. I had to remind myself that if this had happened few years ago, in apartheid years, our present scenario would not have taken place. Solomon and I would not have been able to drink in the same bar. Today we were celebrating a hope for the new South Africa - but the real celebration would take place in a few week's time when the kids of Meqheleng brought their voices into Lesotho.

When Liliane and I reached home that afternoon another drama was about to unfold. A short handwritten written message was waiting for me at the guard hut on the camp, announcing that Betty had been taken into Leribe Hospital as her baby was about to be born. The baby who would be given an English name of my choosing. For the second time that day, I had a reason to celebrate. The day was Good Friday and our African wedding was one week away.

Chapter 25

A Wedding and a Birth.

Eight days to go to our wedding and a mountain of plans to work through. In between the stinging storms of afternoon, the mud slides on every road outside the camp, and the erratic messages on the temperamental house phone which had sprung into life a few days ago, I finished sewing the flowers onto my hat, sent round invitations to a party in Sophie's kitchen for the staff and rushed off to Maseru to collect my wedding shoes. A quick dash into a shoe shop a few weeks previously had provided me with at least the colour and the style I wanted, as a Basotho shoemaker had promised to make me a pair exactly to my requirements. I had stood on the table in the tiny shop while he drew round my feet-bunions and all. The sketch on the piece of paper was all he required. While waiting to be measured, a farmer came in for five pairs of shoes for his children. I was expecting to see five pairs of feet come bouncing into the shop. Instead - the farmer produced five pieces of string from his back pocket and laid them carefully in front of the shoemaker. Those were the sizes of his childrens' feet.

"I will come again in two weeks," he stated . "One pair of each."

The question of the Edwardian parasol which I had set my heart on was a different matter. My idea was not to carry flowers at my wedding because the hat already looked like a Harkness rose garden. At the eleventh hour and much to my surprise, a gracious elderly lady friend in Ficksburg told me of a Lancashire lass who owned an umbrella factory in Maputsoe. She went by the name of Susan Pequino and was married to a handsome Portuguese called Jimmi. I set off to find them.

It took me three attempts of talkie talkie through wire fence and padlocks, plus three cream buns to persuade the wrinkled old Basotho guard to let me in the factory gates. Once inside, he was my best friend and took me to the main office where I found the owner. Susan Pequino was as dynamic as her name and we shot around the factory at an amazing pace, waving to the two hundred black ladies at their machines, who rolled out bales of material and stitched together hundreds of umbrellas to cope with Lesotho's climatic demand for shade.

Together, Susan and I crawled under tables, climbed up to high stacks and sorted through the 'handle room' sounding like stags in the rutting season. Within the hour, Susan had created a bride-sized parasol, sky blue spangled with gold thread, decorated with layers of pink and magenta handfrills - the nearest thing to an Edwardian parasol to be found in the Southern hemisphere.The delight of the toothless ladies who worked their machines to invent me one for my special day was as treasured a part of my wedding preparations as I might have wished for. The parasol was given to me as a gift and I departed in exceedingly high spirits accompanied by the elderly guard - whom I christened Moses, for he looked the part - to the padlocked gate and back into the mud of Maputsoe. I loved him so much by this time, I gave him my last cream bun - and almost invited him to the wedding.

The real highlight of the week was the birth of baby Oliver Majoro, weighing in at 2.6 kilograms at one o'clock on Easter Sunday morning. I had gone to the hospital to see Betty on the night of her admission, finding her on the delivery ward of Leribe hospital, which was a short distance from our camp. Betty's labour had begun early on the Friday morning and she had walked down the steep hill from her shack in the village, with a friend supporting her, to the hospital. I was pleased to see her and was glad that her time had come. The bed she had been given had no sheets or pillows; her few belongings were beside her, tied in a blanket. She had not eaten all day because the hospital do not provide food for their patients. She was dressed in her day clothes - still with her blue scarf covering her hair. I went to find a nurse.

Looking around the ward, I saw five other ladies in varying stages of delivery, some with a relative looking on. The small sink in the corner was full of discarded paper and there were no chairs to sit on. The stark absence of white walls and clean linen spoke volumes. Feeling utterly useless, I stayed and held Betty's hand for a while, and we talked a little. Her contractions had stopped altogether and she hadn't had any pain for the past few hours.

Reluctantly, we said goodnight.

"I will come again in the morning Betty. Don't worry. I'll bring food and some of those baby clothes in my spare room."

"No, 'M'e, don't bring clothes for my baby. The ladies here get them stolen. Many people steal baby clothes because they have no money. I will come to fetch them when I am well again. I will need one small blanket."

Barrie was waiting for me outside. It was very late when we left the building. We didn't meet one member of staff along the miles of uncarpeted corridor. Electric light seemed rationed to one bulb per ward.

Approaching the maternity ward the following morning, an elderly nurse in a uniform came to meet me.

"You are the lady who came last night to see Mrs Majoro?" I nodded, aware that her tone was needle sharp. "We are going to send her home today. Her baby is not ready yet. She is not in any pain. We need her bed . She can come back when her baby is ready to be born."

I replied that I would prefer that Mrs Majoro remained in hospital, as I knew that the membrane had ruptured and if she were to go home, she could easily become infected.

"No, we need her bed now, for another patient. You can go and see her."

Betty was in tears. I returned to the medical room and found the ward sister. I told her that Betty was my maid and I wished her to receive good treatment. Having already decided that I would pay her hospital costs, I asked to sign the big book on the desk, showing my address, so that the doctor would know all about the arrangement. This made it official and not a matter of trying to bribe a nurse.

"I wish that Mrs Majoro remains in hospital and is cared for properly." I said firmly. "It is not a question of finance. Her pains could return soon and the baby born very quickly. She could become ill if she was sent home now and has no one to look after her and her house has no water."

Suddenly there was a loud commotion and a whole family entered the delivery room. They sat down beside one of the beds and looked set for a siege, placing their sticks and blankets down beside them. When I finally managed to get Betty to dry her tears, she told me that last night the girl in the next bed had given birth to a dead baby. These people were her family and had come to the hospital to say they would not pay. No baby- no money. They were poor and couldn't afford to pay now that the baby had died. The distraught mother was lying on the bed.

"Right Betty," I said, half jokingly, half serious, "tell that baby of yours to start moving.You are staying in the hospital until it arrives. No going home." The poor girl looked so relieved and began crying again. "It's Okay and more Okay. Betty. You do not have to leave."

A wooden locker had appeared by her bed and on top, a bowl of water. I felt sure Betty would be all right once everything started. I left her propped up in bed with one of L.H.P.C.'s pillows, a bunch of cosmos and a bottle of fresh water to drink. I prayed that this baby would get a move on. Several long sullen stares came my way from the bereaved family sitting on the floor. A white woman in this hospital was regarded with suspicion. Fearful jealousies arose between Basotho womenfolk when favours became known. Any raising of social boundaries was resented and treated with clear disapproval. The fact that Betty was receiving special treatment was sure to be noticed.

In the middle of the corridor outside, a tall wooden cot had been placed in which sat a baby girl, perhaps nine or ten months old. There was no one around. She looked up at me and I melted. Her blankets could have been cleaner but the little dress she was wearing was immaculate. She was a beautiful child. I asked her name.

"This is Petunia. She's lovely ain't she. She is waiting for someone to collect her." There was a bottle of milk in the cot which someone had been giving her, and Petunia did look particularly well nourished. It was strange that she should be sitting in the middle of a draughty corridor. The cherubic face of this baby stayed in my mind all day.

Driving to Ha Simone later that day, my thoughts swung between babies and weddings, plus the many important things I had to do before Saturday. I was greeted with great excitement by Rose and Emily who were sewing in the yard. Emily was trying on a dress and Rose was busy sticking pins along the hem.The old hand sewing machine with a bandaged middle was sitting on the table inside the house and several ladies were stitching things together.

"We are making Emily something to wear for Saturday, Nettie. She has nothing suitable for a wedding and she wants to look nice. I hope we shall finish it in time." Emily was twenty years old and very pretty. Her idea was to have something extravagant and Rose's idea was to keep it simple. Mother and daughter conflicts like these I knew all about. "But she has no shoes."

"Em, you can borrow a pair of mine. I will lend you some. What about Walter? Has he got himself fitted up for a wedding?"

"Yes," intervened Rose. "He bought himself clothes last year when he was working. He has trousers and a silk shirt. My two children must not let you down, you and Barrie. To go to an English wedding is the most exciting thing they have ever done. They will make us very proud to be chosen."

"We wish we could invite you all Rose, really. I came to make sure of their transport on Saturday, Emily, would you and Walter be able to get a kombi into Ficksburg? Barrie has sent you money for the taxi and that is to make sure you will arrive in time for our ceremony. We can't offer you transport from the camp as everyone has their own arrangements."

I dropped some money on the stoep. Some of the other guests would not understand about Emily and Walter.

"Walter knows the house where we are being married. It's Mr Bornman's house and he will make you most welcome."

Turning to Rose, I asked if she would request Walter to sing one or two Basotho songs, especially for our guests. I knew how much he loved singing. She stopped her snipping for a moment and her hand came towards mine. Her eyes were full of tears.

" It is wonderful that you are in our country, Nettie. I never thought we should know an English lady who brings us this friendship."

I had no words to say, except to walk down to their river with Bernice, sit on the big flat rock and dangle my feet in the water, waving to the children who played on the familiar hillside. They knew that I went there often and would come for sweeties if they dare. That day, I cried my own tears into the river, for the happiness which I had found in Ha Simone and for this family who had become my own. They had nothing but their love to give me. It was from them I had learnt how to belong. I looked across at Bernice who was sitting on the opposite bank. She had brought a pencil and was writing most carefully, so that her chin almost touched the page, her school book clutched up against her knees.

"Nettie, how do you write England ?"

On Easter Sunday we breakfasted early. The morning air felt fresh and the mountain slopes going up towards Pitseng were pink with cosmos. We dawdled over coffee and were consumed by holiday pictures of the Cape Peninsula where we planned to spend our honeymoon. Our journey down to Capetown next week would take us through the semi-desert of the Great Karoo. We planned an overnight stop a few kilometres from Beaufort West at the Karoo National Park. Our route then went through Western Cape Province, through the Huguenot Tunnel, beyond the grape growing country and the Winelands to the foot of Africa. I had always wanted to see Table Mountain and visit South Africa's spectacular coastline.

Then my mind turned to Betty who was still confined to the delivery unit of Leribe maternity hospital. Gathering up a small white blanket and an armful of cotton wool and soap, I walked down to the hospital to see if there was any news. Many groups of churchgoers passed by, and on the big field by the hospital, Lesotho families joined together in their Easter celebrations.

I was greeted at the main reception area by the sound of singing. Inside the big swing doors was a strange sight. The maternity wing was full of people, sitting on the floor and singing hymns. Many were patients, dressed in hospital gowns, some were visitors, others were in wheelchairs. They surged as far as the eye could see. It didn't matter that there was no priest or pulpit - they were pleased to be allowed to sing their Easter prayers in a hospital corridor. They made a wonderful sound and made me think of home.

I found Betty at last, alone in a small quiet room. She was lying on her side, cradling her tiny son who had been born in the night. Wrapped in a brown hospital blanket, this newborn African child was making his first contact with a harsh world.

" 'M'e, my son... he is born !" Betty was wreathed in smiles. "He arrived at one o'clock.in the night. He was born so quick. Only two hours. The nursing sister, she was good to me. I hope you come today."

I peered into the folds of the blanket to see a tiny brown wrinkled face. A moment of sheer delight. Suddenly I recalled the birth of my granddaughter, Abigail Louise, which took place in an English hospital, where mothers enjoyed medical help quite unknown to the African woman. How could I ever have guessed that one day I should be privileged to await the birth of a Basotho infant and asked to make the choice of an English name.

Betty looked up at me and I could see the lines of exhaustion around her eyes.

"I like the name of Oliver. I like best out of all the names you told me. Thank you 'M'e." She smiled and returned to gaze into the face of her newborn son. "Please will you tell Mrs Liliane that he has arrived safe. I remembered what she told me."

"The baby has a good name, Betty. It suits him."

The white blanket lying on the bed, looked out of place in this dingy room, which had neither window nor light bulb. I left them, knowing that they needed time to get to know each other. A spirited and plucky mother like Betty might just be able to guide this infant through the uphill struggle of grinding poverty allotted to his future.

"Please could you bring me my passport 'M'e. Oliver will be registered tomorrow at the Office. Then I will take the bus to Mapusoe to see my mother. She look after us. Please can I come back to work for you when I am well. I will send my cousin to help during that time."

"No, Betty, it's Okay, we will wait until you're in good health. Your job is safe."

The cot in the corridor was still there as I went in search of the ward sister to settle my bill. As I was waiting around for several minutes, I cooed at Petunia through her bars, seeing her gorgeous brown eyes dancing with pleasure and was drawn to hold the bottle of milk to her mouth, as there was no one else about to feed her. She sucked long and hard at the teat. Suddenly, a white coated medic appeared and spoke in seSotho, obviously addressing me and pointing at the child in the cot.

"You Mamma, you take baby, you English lady, kind - nobody take her."

I realized too late, the sad game that was being played. The staff hoped that after seeing her again, I would want to take the baby, who had probably been abandoned. It was a hard fact to swallow in a matter of seconds.

"Oh I can't....it's not possible." I broke off. Emotionally stirred, my protestations to the doctor sounded pathetically feeble. They would never understand. To them I was a rich white lady. The stab of conscience lay like a stone in my stomach. I knew I was right to walk away.

I remembered what Dentle had told me when I first arrived in South Africa. 'In our country many children are abandoned .' An easy thing to say that you understand - catastrophic when you are faced with a beautiful child with big brown eyes, sitting alone in a hospital corridor.

The burden inside me felt heavier as the evening wore on. Eventually I told Barrie. He took hold of my two hands very firmly and looked straight at me.

"No Nettie, we can't," he said gently, even before my foolish thoughts became words.

"I know we can't. But would it help - if we gave some money?"

"It will go straight into the wrong pocket. Look – this is Lesotho. Accept it honey, it's beyond us. Someone will take her, you can be sure. This child needs a Basotho home."

Petunia's cot wasn't there the following day when I took Betty's passport to the ward. Sitting on the bed with Oliver in my arms, while Betty went to register his birth, the girl whose baby had died, walked past me into the Doctor's office.

On the camp, pre-nuptial nerves were hotting up. Everyone seemed to be involved in conspiratorial manoeuvres or neighbourly intrigues. Our guest list rocketted into secretive hot-line information and we were aware of murmurings of polarisation between different parts of the establishment. Ours was a wedding which involved Afrikaners, Blacks, Europeans, Coloureds and many other nationalities. We were learning to live with undercover prejudices, and no matter how open-hearted or liberal we wanted our ceremony to be, biased uncompromising attitudes were evident amongst our guests. Our adversary was history itself.

The only person who seemed oblivious to everything was Thabo, who went round whistling all week and kept smiling to himself and telling his friends,

"I am coming, I am going, to the party of Mr Glenn and I have some food and I am dancing."

Contravening all previous traditions, we had decided to throw a party for all the cooks, canteen staff, maids, gardeners, taxi drivers and local office staff, the night before the wedding. Sophie was 'in de charge of de big party' because we were going to use her kitchen, her knives and forks and her sink. When the offer of food and drink is mentioned in these quarters, suddenly appetites increase along with the list of relatives who would like to attend. Families become larger and anyone vaguely related is promoted to status of brother, sister, or close cousin.

In order to prevent an all out offensive, we stipulated that we had invited people because we knew them well and that being the case, it was not long before complete strangers were coming to make our acquaintance. Two elderly ladies who made the tea in Barrie's office started to bring him extra drinks at odd times during the day. Usually he got it slopped in the saucer and casually deposited on the desk with a most doleful expression. Veronica and Evelyn both started to hover around his desk and once Evelyn actually smiled. He noticed his bin was emptied twice daily instead of once a week and every cup of coffee was steaming hot. Their names were added to the guest list. This action provoked an unprecedented spate of handwaving over the hedge next to our garden, from the ladies in the higher offices, whom I didn't actually know by name, but took to calling out greetings, loudly, every morning over a six foot hedge.

Liliane was the most supportive and courageous witness anyone could have had. She was my 'man on the ground' reporter of trouble spots, organiser of transport, wedding music, flower arrangements, camera crew, and Cape Town booking agent. She even enlisted the services of a beautiful Algerian dancer who was to come and entertain our wedding guests, then gave belly dancing lessons (remembered from her days in Brazil) to guests who showed an interest in learning the art, ready for the party. Her determination to make our day special will never be forgotten.

The day before the wedding was one of the hottest days of the year. Liliane and I set off to Bethlehem in high spirits to collect the buttonhole sprays for the guests, the bridegroom's new suit, pink ostrich feathers from the 'Bruidhuis', cream cakes and beer for Sophie's party and friends who had just flown in from England.

Everything went swimmingly until we were stopped at Caledonsport border on the way back into Lesotho about 4.00pm. Our English friends, who had travelled for days to get there and were rapidly showing signs of exhaustion, produced their travel documents to Passport Control. Our convoy halted while roses wilted and cream cakes slid off the seats. Pink icing sugar dripped onto the floor of the kombi. Liliane sat in the hot vehicle with Brigitte - a visiting French lady who had joined our party.

With buckets of carnations between their knees, balloons tied to the seat brackets, and pink ostrich feathers fluttering from the offside rear window, the ladies anxiously waited for the inspection to finish. The guard insisted on knowing our business. When we told him there was a wedding at L.H.P.C. he leaned inside the vehicle with a huge grin. Inwardly we groaned, with the knowledge that several dozen Castle lagers rode in the ice boxes in the boot. There is nothing a Basotho guard loves more than a party.

"A party – well do I get an invitation?"

I realized this could lead to a nasty moment.

"Lumela Ntate. My friends from Europe are feeling very tired from a long journey. They have come to see your country. They would like to rest."

Quickly, I pressed a couple of cans of iced coke into his hands and Sam put his foot on the accelerator. We breathed a huge sigh of relief.

The party in Sophie's kitchen was to begin at five fifteen.The doors opened at ten minutes past five and the partygoers started to arrive. On occasions like this the Basotho knows what time it is. The girls from the office came first, headed by Rita and Patricia who worked in Reception Then came the heavy mob - the taxi drivers and the gardeners - Kenneth, Thabo, Petros, Patrick and the hefty Bonaventa , the keep fit fanatic of Leribe. These were followed by the maids and the girls who worked in the canteen, Sophie, Anna and Valerie -and lastly, two smiling tea ladies- minus pink uniforms and ready for the knees-up.

By half past five, the plates on the table were empty and the cans of Castle had been drunk. Rita was on her feet, singing. She had more gravel and shout than Bessie Smith and Louis Armstrong put together. With the confidence of an old pro' at the Sheffield Empire, she cruised into top gear and set the beer cans rattling on the bar. Barrie went off to try and find more beer because it looked as if more people were coming in the door - no doubt near relatives of the people inside.The guards who were on duty at the gate came in, with one or two extra security - rather unfamiliar- but at this stage it didn't matter. Gabriel appeared, minus gun and teeth.

Sophie, in her dress of white feathers and bottletops, emerged from the kitchen to re-invent the wobble dance. With support from Anna and Valerie, (both larger than ample ladies) they shook themselves to the sound of high pitched wailing and shouting. Sophie writhed and swayed on her varicose veins, and with her arms in the air like windmills, beating time with a wooden spoon on a saucepan. This took the party into overdrive and the men joined in with a dance which sounded like an engine shifting underground coal.

They lunged and leapt, using sticks and umbrellas and anything that they could use as a spear, doing a warrior dance which shook the floorboards. Kenneth whose weight might have split the foundation timbers, thumped on tables and almost sent a pile of plates shattering to the floor. The dance was accompanied by rousing songs and we needn't have worried about the lack of a stereo system.

The battle cries were just the warm-up.The tea ladies were up on their feet, tapping their feet to the rhythm while polishing off the last of the cream cakes. Thabo had donned a white skirt over his blue overalls and all you could see through the melée were the whites of his eyes. Lusty voices almost lifted the roof off. Rita carried on fortissimo. Sophie's dining room was ready to cave in. The ancestors must have heard us from the hillsides.

When we were all feeling quite exhausted, the whole company led by Kenneth and Sam, beating time with their feet, launched into the dance of the *Shosholosa*. It represents the singing of the miners digging for gold and its haunting tune is so uplifting that whenever I listen to it, shudders go down my spine. Barrie and I were pulled into the middle of the room. Everyone sang and foot tapped, moving around us to form a circle. A host of voices - like an Eisteddfod army, surrounded us. The song truly inspires images of the raw brutality of miners working under the earth, combining sweat and smell of bodies toiling together and pumping hissing engines.

At the final passionate chorus, everyone stood still. The voices quietly faded away. We both felt close to tears. It was the eve of our wedding and we were not in our own country. Tonight had been a tribute to us from our Basotho friends.

"Goodnight Mr Glenn," said Kenneth as he came over to us, the sweat pouring from his glistening forehead. "We wish you a good wedding day tomorrow."

Still humming the final chorus, each in turn came to shake hands and give us their blessing, walking off into the black night to their unelectrified homes and sorghum porridge suppers.

It was true that we wished our families could have been with us on our wedding day. In the quiet churchyard in Hertfordshire, the cherry blossom would be growing in ringlets around the old trunks. It was where we had first made our promises to one another. It was our place and one day we would return. Kent had been our courtship. From there we had come to South Africa and found our happiness. Lesotho, the Mountain Kingdom, was our home now and we were never more joyful than today. Our wedding was to be held in a beautiful garden. The roses on our altar table were grown by an elderly lady called Beatrice, fondly picked from her garden, and handed to us before the dew was shaken from them.

The sun shone and our day began. The early morning border crossing was uneventful. We drove in separate cars, keeping to the English tradition of not seeing each other until the ceremony. Luck was with us at the border and there were no hitches. Liliane and I made our way to Judi's house in Fontein Street. The bridegroom and his entourage headed for Priscilla's. He was to arrive at the house before me and make sure the relayed music system was in place. The famous choral anthems sung by the choir of Kings College, Cambridge, should be playing as the guests arrived.

Priscilla was to make sure all the guests received their buttonhole sprays. She wisely kept the flowers in her fridge all night and got up every two hours to spray them with water, then, with her usual caustic charm, got them thoroughly mixed up so that everyone was given the wrong one. It only added to the rising excitement.

At 12.05 pm I departed nervously from Judi's house in a beribboned Silver Spirit Rolls Royce, chauffeured by a handsome young coloured boy wearing white gloves and military white mess uniform. My gallant Scotsman in white tuxedo, sitting beside me, as we drove through Ficksburg, reminding me - in the spirit of the moment - of my father, in another time.

The car glided to a halt in a wide avenue of trees. I caught sight of our guests lining the pathway to the house, pretty with shrubs and blossom. Our Indian Magistrate was standing by the table, serene and black gowned, under a canopy of flowers. Four year old Sean, our Mauritian page boy, held a small velvet cushion. He didn't understand why we were all dressed up like this and suddenly turned shy. Nervously, with trembling lips, he stood by the magistrate in stiff pose then bolted to his mother's side. Ian, gave me a huge grin broad and patted his pocket in which he held our wedding rings.

Bob guided me by the arm in military fashion as we walked slowly from the car up the path. At the table where the Magistrate stood, Barrie and I joined hands.

The ceremony was over far too quickly - we both wanted the moment to last. The exchanging of vows and rings. Verses chosen from Kahil Ghibran 'The Prophet' and then our Prayer of Dedication to our families. We stood close together in front of the table and our intertwined fingers trembled. The ribbons on my hat blew round my face in the mischievous April breeze as Ena's voice, soft and low, read out our promises to one another.

In South Africa, legality has it that the couple must go through a door in order to sign their names in the Register of Matrimony. Our procession turned from the brightness of the garden into the comparative darkness of the oak pannelled interior of Elsa's beautiful home. Pink and white wild cosmos filled every windowsill.

Our guests gathered inside the elegant room. On the Bornman's wide oak table, the soft perfume of lighted candles floated in bowls of rose water, like Chinese lilies. Miniature reflections sent flickering lights around the faces at the table. The Magistrate solemnly entered our names in the South African Register of Marriages. Seated together, we both signed our names, then ended the ceremony traditionally - with a kiss.

Engulfed in a tide of affection, Barrie and I sailed through a fountain of confetti into the glorious heat of the midday. The lilt of a hundred pre-recorded Scottish pipers greeted our arrival in the garden.

The crowd relaxed, the wine sparkled and the sound of congratulations in different languages came from every quarter. My hat sqashed by all the kissing and hugging, I managed to reach Emily and whisper how lovely she looked in the silk dress which Rose had made. Her black skin against the cream silk was striking. She and Walter, had arrived on the back of an open truck, minutes before the Rolls Royce.

At the point when everyone was knee deep in Priscilla's rose petals and Borrie's champagne corks, there was a hush in the crowd and Ena Swanapoel, disposed of her solemn magisterial attire, rose to her feet beside the wedding table. It was a moment none would easily forget. Everyone stood together, heads bowed, and silently offered prayers to those overseas - for most of our guests were separated from their loved ones in other time zones on other latitudes. Ena's voice came from the heart, offering a blessing on people of all nations in the light of a new beginning. Then she looked straight at Barrie and me as she spoke.

"This song is to remind you of your wedding day in South Africa and may you carry these memories to England when you return."

Dressed in a white gown, standing perfectly still beside the table, she sang in Afrikaans with a honeyed contralto more suited to the dome of St Paul's. Her singing voice, rich and powerful, belonged to a famous gospel choir. The song was delightfully unaccompanied and when she ended a loud cheer broke out. Our wedding ceremony had, for one short moment, broken the barriers of race, colour and creed

Soon the party swung into a different mood. We had been so moved by the dance of the *Shosholosa* the previous evening, that on request, Emily, Walter and Kenneth joyously enacted a repeat performance. It was unfortunate that Kenneth's itinerary that day was to drive Brigitte to Johannesburg in time for the evening flight to Paris, and barely allowed them time to stop off and see the wedding. Brigitte left us shortly after the end of the singing, in a flurry of farewells, after dragging her driver away from centre stage where he looked set to carry on for hours.

Brigitte's departure to Paris, we learned later, was fraught as she dashed into the departure lounge at Jo'burg holding crushed wedding cake and a bunch of cosmos - the last passenger on board.

Showered with confetti, we left in the Rolls Royce to celebrate Italian style at Priscilla's house. Most of our guests followed and those who had small children went home to prepare for the evening reception. A little after-breakfast liquid refreshment and more champagne induced an 'on top of the bar dangerous dancing routine' for a few of the men in the party, followed by a' let it all hang out' feeling amongst the ladies. Perspiring guests in suits and kilts cooled under Priscilla's mighty ceiling fan, hats were thrown off, gloves discarded and Tamu barked loudly from his chain in the yard, but no one heard. It seemed an appropriate moment to adjourn for our siesta.

Boschfontein Farm has its share of storms: lashing summer rain that lays the meadow grass flat and turns the ground to boggy peat in minutes. That afternoon, a storm similar to the one which Mr and Mrs Noah would have recognised, hit the skies above the Caledon River.

Still dressed in our wedding clothes, we had been hurrying through the black skies and purple lightning towards the Barretts when the puddles turned into rivers and we sailed gaily into a swamp. Nothing moved. Nothing that is until a farmer with a pick-up came by. Barrie and I spent our late afternoon siesta sitting in a field of cosmos, two miles from the farm on a dirt road, the wheels of our car sunk to the axles in the equivalent of an Irish peat bog.

A friendly voice shouted loudly, "don't move, I'll be back with a rope.!"

"Thanks" we shouted through the window. Then, stupidly, "we've just got married! It's part of the plan!"

Tidal waves of mud hit the side doors of our vehicle and we both fell back in our seats with laughter at the thought of our guests waiting for us at our evening reception party at Zevenfontein.

Quite soon, we felt the tug of a rope and chain. The returned farmer up to his knees in water, revved his engine mercilessly in the slippery ditch by the side of us and hooked us onto his bakkie. We had sunk to quite a depth by this time. Thankfully we were pulled back onto the dirt road in minutes.

Meanwhile, our English friends, who had witnessed our dilemma had gone on ahead to find help and disappeared up another mountain road, in the wrong direction. In Africa, if you don't know your way and you drive without a map, getting lost isn't difficult. Barrie left me at the farm and set out to find them.

From the farmhouse phone, I called Priscilla to inform her that we would be late for our reception and to let people know that we had run into a swamp in the middle of a storm. I thought she was never going to stop laughing. Her tears of mirth were as usual infectious. You don't have to be crazy to understand Priscilla, but it helps. She offered to come out with another truck and find Barrie. I began to realize that our evening wedding reception would be bride and groomless if he didn't return soon with our lost guests.

His trip round the mountains drew a blank. By this time, we were beginning to worry about the safety of our friends.The jagged cliffs and rock faces were not easy driving. Janet, who had followed us back from Ficksburg, heard about our catastophe and disappeared to the yard to round up a posse of women from the farm to help. If anything serious had happened to them the local black families would be the first to know. Janet drove the big truck into the yard. Barrie leapt on board and with Basotho ladies, dogs and chickens, he disappeared for the second time into the hills of the Caledon river valley- still dressed for a wedding. At the end of the phone, Priscilla's sense of humour had rallied.Yes, she would hurry to Zevenfontein and give the news that the newlyweds were stuck out in the mountains and had lost two of their wedding guests.

"What did I tell you - this is Africa!" She rang off.

Fortunately, our friends were discovered, bogged down in Charlie Barrett's huge courtyard, a few yards off the track, having completely lost their sense of direction on the un-named twisty roads.

Our siesta by now was in ruins. In the old dairy guesthouse we hurriedly washed in the sink on wheels, pouring water from an enamel jug at the end of the house and scrambled into clean clothes. Janet had laid the table with linen and china, all ready for breakfast and there were jars of flowers in every room. Dried sunflowers hung from the rafters and feline shapes curled on windowsills. Strands of bougainvillea fell in profusion over the glass roof looking in on us and sepia portraits of ancestors stared from the walls. Patchwork quilts, made from Boschfontein goosedown covered the fourposter beds, the air faintly musty from the family's war time memorabilia.

The blanketted skies were heavy with rainclouds as we approached Zevenfontein for our evening reception. We made our way slowly along the sodden track up to the house. It looked as though the storm of the century had torn through the weeping willows and there was no sign of Annie's navigational balloons. The grassy field at the front of the house was ominously flooded along one end, so we parked on higher ground nearer the house. Obviously, our matrimonial plans did not include an electric storm.

Annie's log fire and free drinks did much to alleviate the rather strenuous events of late afternoon. The dining room tables were set with tablecloths; delicate china and glassware had been prepared in readiness for our guests who were at this very moment on their way .The top table was threaded with ribbons and cosmos and we had been given a King and Queen chair to sit in. In Annie's kitchen, the banquet had almost reached delivery stage.

As we lifted the first drink to our lips, all the lights went out. This was followed by a wrinkle of purple lightning and a belt of thunder loud enough to rattle the bottles on the bar. It was a signal for the heavens to open and hailstones the size of small bricks to clatter against the windows making conversation impossible. Electricity power cuts like this are frequent in the Free State at this time of year, and most people suffer them resignedly. Annie was no different. With her generous Birminghamese attitude, she laid out two dozen candles. Wolfgang, the barman, turned not a hair and threw another log on the fire.

In torchlight and candle light, we welcomed our first determined map-holding guests, who had driven carefully along Barrie's red pencilled contours. These few brave men had managed to take the correct turnings off the Rosendal road and circumnavigate the deepening waterholes along the way. From then onwards, guests arrived in dribs and drabs - looking increasingly wet and bedraggled, but in candlelight it didn't matter. Bob Smith, turquoise-blue kilted and sporranned, in full Highland dress uniform, had braved storm and hailstones; his tartan socks spashed with mud and his white hair blown around his face like a wild man. Ian spent ages in the car park ploughing the mud, then stumbled upstairs muttering oaths about not going home for a week. He had come to enjoy himself and it mattered not if the weather prevented him from driving home, as long as the drinks held out.

Then Priscilla arrived. She had driven herself from Ficksburg in Betsie and was dressed in storm appropriate clothing, right down to her rubber galoshes and knee length plastic cycling cape. Brandishing a huge umbrella, a torch and a bag ,big enough to contain a full wash at the launderette, she fell in the doorway and shook herself like a drowning dog so that all in near distance were soaked. Her make-up ran down her face in rivulets and her black hair fell out of their combs in armfuls. She took a huge towel out of her bag and went off in search of the bathroom, while Annie ran behind her with a candle and a large gin.

The expletives at Zevenfontein entrance door that night, came in colourful French, growling German, torrid Spanish and unforgiving Afrikaans - each lot explaining how they almost saw the farm track but went on a ten mile trip round the slopes of the Witteberge mountains, just for fun. Everyone, even the mapless, made the journey through thunder and lightning and lashing rain, just to be with us on our special night. The storm galvanised everyone into a state of high excitement. Introductions and multi-language greetings were achieved affably with dripping hairstyles, wet jackets and soaked shoes. For the moment no -one worried about the downstairs carpark where the water level rose by inches when it rained.

Our wedding party was back on track and the atmosphere was charged with the most sparkling excitement, which increased visibly when the slim wide-eyed belly dancer arrived alone and bedraggled in a Morrocan wig and white plastic sheet, gripping a rather wet leather pouch of bangles and beads and veils to her tiny bosom. A few of the men turned sideways and pretended not to look, but took in her dusky features and plaited beaded locks. A clever hairdresser had given her a Cleopatra profile, added to which her dark eyes seemed to glow with the magnetic gleam of a female tiger. Her dancing might be enough to spark off a minor riot after the feasting and drinking had taken their toll.

As we took our seats at the long table, God turned up the voltage. The main electricity cable jolted back into life and the lights at Zevenfontein sprang back onto full beam. Annie's girls in the kitchen ran to douse their oil lit stoves where a dozen pans of potatoes had been slowly simmering - the only part of the meal which almost failed to appear on the menu. A loud cheer rippled along the room.

The meal was sumptuous; the speeches ridiculous; the dancing riotous. At the top table, looking fine in his full Highland dress, Bob gave us one or two tales from his extensive repertoire of flying stories, blushed with a few fanciful exaggerations. Ian toasted Barrie and I, himself , the cook, the wine waiter and the dancer all in the wrong order but it didn't matter because his heart is always in the right place. Barrie stayed awake long enough to thank everyone for coming and the only thing which kept him awake after that were the alluring movements of the petite dancer who beautifully twirled the floor with braided headdress and seductive waving veils, her body discreetly covered in a tight black costume like a second skin. Dark eyed behind a veil, she tossed her plaited locks and cleverly brought the whole company onto the dance floor - quite an achievement, as engineers are not well known for their clever footwork. Ask them to negotiate a tunnel boring machine round a ninety degree bend on a mountain road and that, for them, would be easier.

We escaped down the back stairs quietly and unseen, while the party was still in full flow. We didn't stay long enough to witness the end of the evening; the French National Anthem, the senior accountant's Russian dancing, Ian being poured into a truck and driven home, nor a sporranned guest falling head first into Zevenfontein's prickliest thorn bush. Priscilla, who would have sunk without trace if it hadn't been for her galoshes was thrown, laundry bag and all, into the seat with the driver, while all other guests rolled around in the back of the open truck.

Fortunately, Wolfgang's sobriety was legendary and he knew how to drive a four by four Bush Ranger through rivers of mud, with drunken passengers on board and one arm tied behind his back. Thus all wedding stories were bound over until the month of May when, on our return from the Cape, a full report was expected. Judi's story would be the only believable version.

Chapter 26

Rainbow Nation

Capetown is the home of the grape and the winelands. It is the place where the Indian and the Atlantic Oceans meet. And it is overlooked by the most famous mountain in the world. Through the centuries, Table Mountain in Southern Africa, has been the landmark of sailors, since the Portuguese first navigated their way round the treacherous shores of Cape Point in 1488. They named it the Cape of Good Hope. Magnificently dominating the bay, the flat topped mountain rises out of the sea like an anchor in the wilderness. On either side, rise Lion's Head and Devil's Peak.

It is said that Capetown is South Africa's most beautiful, most romantic and most visited city. The climate is sublime. The Cape Peninsula falls within a temperate weather zone and April here is as pleasant as a warm April in St Tropez .

Together we stood at the end of the African continent and looked out to the endless blue ocean. It was the kind of day that dreams are made of. Dazzling white topped waves, broke along the rocky shore and threw spray high into the air. At our feet, small mountain flowers spread like a carpet, pink and orange. The gulls soared superbly over our heads. The sign on the cliff top said 'the South-Westernmost Point of the African Continent. 34.21.25. South Latitude. 18.28.26. East Longitude.' It was beautiful beyond words.

Our wedding day events were fresh in our minds. The absence of our families was still raw and during the long journey to the Cape, we had re-lived the magic of the occasion and wondered how on earth we could describe it to them. Eight hours on the hot dry road through the desert with its wide lonely plains, sculptured granite *koppies* towering above, was a memorable journey. Then the night sky in the Great Karoo and a million bright stars.

Now, one glimpse of the Atlantic Ocean stretching out as far as the eye could see, was enough to throw me into a state of strangled bleats like a merino sheep. I felt as if someone had tied a cord across my windpipe. My joy struggled to express itself and tears splashed in spasms down my cheeks. A bunch of wild flowers and a large handkerchief turned the moment into laughter. Together we ran down hundreds of steps to the sea to be the only people between the African continent and Antarctica.

Unfortunately it wasn't the time of year for whalespotting. From June to November, whales are often seen at many places along the Cape Peninsula, where they seek out sheltered bays and swim close to the mainland. They come to do their courting, mating and then calving. A whalesighting would have been wonderful but the season was not quite ready.

However, we were rewarded later on that week by shoals of graceful dolphins, riding on the breakers close to the shore. Standing at the top of a cliff, you can scan your eyes from east to west and see literally thousands of dolphins, lifting and leaping along the entire bay, their backs glistening silver in the sun. Endless rows of sleek dolphinesque shapes, on wave after wave, like dancers in a ballet. Dolphin-watching became addictive that week, as we walked the flat sands watching the fishermen casting their lines.

Barrie had to prove to himself that the Atlantic is far colder to swim in than the Indian Ocean. The one white body in the sea was enough to convince me that I was married to a brave, but stubborn Yorkshireman. We stayed to watch the fishing boats come in and draw in their nets full of crayfish and lobster, while the skies turned orange and the shadows grew long.

Along a bleak part of the coast towards Good Hope Nature Reserve, we met ostriches on the beach. Heads down, their beaks searching for fish scraps to eat, they looked as natural in their setting as donkeys on the east coast at Scarborough, UK. In fact Scarborough is the name of the village which is the last settlement before Cape Point, with its powerful lighthouse, where, if you want to be blown into the sea, just flap your wings. When the summer South Easter's are blowing, everything is uprooted and thrown skywards, the wind cleaning everything in its path. When this happens, they call it the 'Cape Doctor' It is known as one of the healthiest and unpolluted regions in Southern Africa.

The people of the Cape come in all colours and creeds. It is a cultural melting pot and true to say that the 'Rainbow Nation' begins here in this part of Africa.

Black people have been living in South Africa for 100,000 years. San hunters, South Africa's first human inhabitants moved freely through the Cape Peninsula before being edged into the interior by the cattle herding Koikhoi people who migrated from the north. Koisan people also occupied substantial parts of what is today, Namibia and Botswana. They were not agriculturalists but were hunter gatherers and lived in small nomadic bands, following the migration patterns of wild game. They were small people and spoke in a language of clicks. In the fourteenth and fifteenth centuries, other African groups moved into the western Cape; the largest of these the Nguni, who spoke Zulu, Xhosa and Swazi and they could understand each other's language.

Portuguese mariners first rounded the Cape in the 1480's, using it as a stopping off point en route to East Africa and the East Indies. Skirmishes with the Khoikhoi were inevitable and attempts at trading with them unsuccessful.

The first European settlement was established in 1652 by the Dutch. White people arrived by sea from Europe and the Dutch East India Company set up a small outpost at the Cape to act as a refuelling stop on the sea route to India.They went to war with the Khoikoi. and brought in slaves from Indonesia and Java. Slaves at the Cape soon outnumbered the whites. This situation continued for some two hundred years and the slaves mostly adopted the language and religion of their masters The inter- marriage of Indonesian, African and renegade whites, formed a new community, known today as the Cape Coloureds

The colony also received the first French settlers in 1688, known as Huguenots, who were fleeing religious persecution.These people brought with them the valuable 'know how' of grape growing and initiated South Africa's wine industries. They were staunch Calvinists, who clung to their own language and religion. They settled in the 'French Corner' in a place called Franschoek, from where they cultivated large areas of land for growing grapes.

The Dutch called themselves Boers (which means farmers) took whatever land they pleased and treated the Khoikhoi like vermin. They later imprisoned their leaders on Robben Island. This was the beginning of South Africa's most notorious penal settlement. The Boers named them Hottentots but these terms are now no longer used.

When the Dutch East India Company was finally liquidated in 1795, British forces took control of the Cape as allies of the Netherlands. British explorers and settlers began to arrive in the 1800's when the government in London started to sponsor emigration programmes. Thousands of British emigrants were shipped out to the Cape to establish it as a British colony, establishing farms on the wild new terrain. In 1819, 4,000 families were granted land in the area near the Great Fish River, issued with basic farming tools and tents. Frontier life was harsh and uncompromising. They had to contend with raids by the Xhosa people, crop failures, drought and the resentment of their neighbouring Boers. Land allocation was a great cause of grievance.

When the first diamond was discovered in South Africa in 1866, there followed an influx of people from all over the world; some 50,000 or more, prospectors, who came in high hopes of finding diamonds at the mining town of Kimberley where the biggest man made excavation was made. The first Indian people were the Hindus from Madras, who arrived in 1860 to work on the sugar plantations along the east coast. Later, a shortage of mineworkers led to the arrival of the Chinese labourers. Today, many Europeans work and live in South Africa, people from South America have settled here, along with those from Middle Eastern countries.

In 1994 the first democratic elections were held. Mandela became the first black President. The Rainbow Nation seems an appropriate name for this country of so many diversities. It is a tapestry of extraordinary cultures and races. Shaped by its past conflicts, all the people now living here help to create job opportunities and bring new and different skills to the workplace. Somehow, this fantastic jigsaw will open up new highways and eventually the barriers will have to come down. Already it is a country of eleven official languages. There are black and white players in the sports arena. South Africa is beginning to get into step with the modern world – after all it is part of a bigger planet.

The day after our arrival in Capetown, the Tall Ships sailed into Table Bay. The stately galleons raced home on the early morning tide after a six month voyage at sea. They had departed from Southampton the previous September and after six months at sea, had completed their first leg of the Global Challenge World Yacht Race. The excitement on the Victoria and Alfred Waterfront was infectious - even if you had no interest in sailing. The sight of these huge vessels mooring alongside the jetty, the bustle of the marquees going up, the preparations for the official welcome, gave the harbourside a feeling of expectancy.

The last of the ships to sail in that day was the' Lord Nelson' which had taken part in the race with a physically handicapped crew. She was anchored out in the bay, having arrived too late to catch the incoming tide. We were invited on board a small boat by one of the South African naval officers on shore, to cruise out and meet them, as a welcome party. Barrie wasn't keen at first, as he is not a good sailor, however changed his mind after the offer of free champagne throughout the trip.

The sea sparkled as red as blood as we sailed out into Table Bay in a crimson sunset. The mood on board was one of great excitement. As we came alongside the impressive Lord Nelson, built exclusively for the handicapped to sail, several crates of champagne were swung across to the jubilant members of her crew. The exhilaration at our arrival was infectious and their loud hailer shouted its thanks in pure Queen's English - nostalgic for us as we hadn't heard English voices for months. It was a highly charged moment and affected me in the same way as the sound of a military marching band or an aeroplane on take-off. I get a lump in my throat and wobbly knees. The size and grace of the formidable sailing ship, becalmed after its long hard voyage, made a nonsense of naval battles and hostilities between countries. A volley of congratulations and cheers rang across the water. Our presence and our booty were appreciated.

Table Bay was alive with boats that evening, almost colliding with each other. The early stars were out as we sailed back into the harbour to the sound of brass bands and ships' sirens, hooting their greeting to the Capetonians who came out in their hundreds to see the line-up along the waterfront. A lively breeze was blowing as we disembarked .Victoria Dock was thronging with people.

As I turned to look for my husband in the crush, I realized that his first decision had been the right one. He had definitely turned a funny colour. It was no coincidence that the recently installed harbour lights were shaded green along the quayside and there were seats placed at intervals. Good planning on the part of sensitive nautical architects. The place was ablaze with lights, music and an enormous sense of pride that these magnificent old ships had steered safely home through the same storms and the same seas to the South African Cape of Good Hope, just as those in centuries past.

The following day we drove along the coast to Boulders Bay to see the penguins. It is one of the few land breeding colonies of jackass penguins on the South African mainland and as we sat on the granite rocks in the burning sun, we were surrounded by families of penguins. Like naughty children on the run the miniature black and white creatures bobbed around the boulders, while little boys imitated them and swimmers swam within yards of them.

Then a drive back through Simon's Town, a Royal Navy base from the time of the second British occupation of the Cape in 1806 until it was handed over to the South African Navy in 1957. A handsome town full of white porticos and pillared historical residences. It has a fine naval presence with its dockyards and Martello towers. Leaving Simon's Town, we left via the M4 (not a motorway - all main highways are called N roads) passing through Glencairn and on to Fish Hoek where we were staying. On arrival at our hotel, the manager was heartily dishing up platefuls of crayfish to anyone who wanted to try it. A boat load had just landed and a couple of barrels had come his way. It was my first ever taste of crayfish.

We learned to eat South African style. We ate squid and octopus at the waterfront cafes while listening to Capetown jazz. We tried crocodile and snoek. Black mussels and oysters did not tempt us, however. Our tastebuds were seduced by Cape-Malay spicy cooking, Indian curries and Afrikaner's *boboties*- a sweet and spicy dish of ground meat; prawns as big as lobsters were eaten out of paper bags and in the evenings we dawdled over mediterranean-style cuisine with lashings of Cape red from the local wine farms, who knew a thing or two about grapes.

One afternoon, we discovered the coastal route above Chapman's Peak. The road snakes high above the sea, where vertical sandstone cliffs rise in sheer walls above you and Hout bay sparkles blue and tranquil far below. The road has been cut into the rock and giant granite boulders perch on a pebble, looking as if they would fall if you breathed heavily. This seven mile narrow road, which climbs to 2,300 feet is known as one of the world's most spectacular scenic drives.

We fell in love with the Cape Peninsula with its wild mountain passes and seductive sheltered bays. We likened it to the moorlands of North Yorkshire, with ostrich instead of sheep. People smiled and were friendly and asked us where we had come from. Lesotho seemed a no man's land to them. No one we met had ever been there.

After taking a last look at the great mother city, we left Capetown and drove out through the Winelands on the first leg of our journey along South Africa's Garden Route. The hectic weeks of wedding preparations were now a distant memory and the little chalet we rented in Somerset West in the garden of a lovely old house, was the perfect answer to relaxation. The Scots couple who owned it looked after us well. Magnificent views over Gordon's Bay were enough to make us want to come back.

While General Election fever raged in England and peoples' homes were invaded by political forecasts and a thing called a Gallup poll which I had never understood, we were voting to stay out late and look at the stars.

The Garden Route is belt of rugged coastline, flanked by indigenous rainforests, lagoons and mountain peaks which sweeps the east coast of the Cape. Our hope was to get as far as Storms River and stay our last night at Tsitsikamma Coastal National Park, on the edge of the Tsitsikamma mountain range. It is an area of great beauty, combining thick forest land with its own natural bounty of animals, birds and coastal stretches of coves and inland lagoons.

We felt a bit cheated at having to use the N2 fast route instead of sticking to the coast but had to push on if we were to achieve our destination before dark. The detour to Hermanus Bay was very worthwhile. It is a famous whaling harbour where they have the only 'whale-crier' in the world and where you can watch the whales 'spyhopping' (standing on their tails with their heads out of the water) on a good day. South Africa has some of the strictest whale conservation legislation in the world and their numbers have increased considerably along this stretch of coast.

During the season, underwater microphones are used to pick up the eerie singing of the whales from deep on the ocean bed and the sound is transmitted to a room in Hermanus Museum. As time was short, we by-passed the hot thermal springs at Caledon, where centuries before, the Khoi people used to wallow in steaming mud holes.

We stuck to our plan and kept going until Mossel Bay. Portuguese sailors first landed at Mossel Bay in 1488 and received a bad reception from the Khoikhoi cattle herdsmen, who had territorial rights according to the wishes of their chiefs. It was a first bloody encounter with Europeans and the result was a pitched battle between them. One of the stories I loved about Mossel Bay was the story of the 'Post Office tree. Apparently sixteenth century mariners used to leave messages for passing ships in an old boot under a milkwood tree. Nowadays you can still post mail in a boot shaped letterbox and receive a special postmark and it is said that the original tree is still there. There are great white sharks in these waters and divers are warned not to swim unaccompanied. On this trip, we didn't have time to take in a 'shark cage dive'. It is a good place to observe octopus and squid and things called sea stars as well as penguins and seals. The discovery of 'snoekies', the best fish and chips on the harbourside, will forever be remembered.

It was late afternoon before we made it as far as Wilderness which is a beautiful coastal resort sliced in half by the N2 , threw ourselves on the mercy of the Tourist Information Bureau who couldn't have been more helpful and found us somewhere to stay; a house on the sand dunes looking out to sea. Below our balcony was a five mile long stretch of sand and red flags, telling people not to swim. The currents here are so unpredictable and even the shallows can be dangerous. Inland, is the real wilderness and miles of exciting forest trails. Stretches of lagoons, interlaced with marshes and reed beds and surrounding forest make it a perfect place to observe birdlife. It is the habitat of waterfowl and large wading birds and at certain times of the year, flocks of pink flamingoes come to feed.

We spent a magic day walking the Giant Kingfisher trail and discovered the silent peace and coolness of the forest. Milkwood trees, yellow wood and candlewood stood graceful and tall among the matted vegetation. The air was broken only by the birds which called from high in the branches and seemed to follow us.We wondered what a stinkwood tree looked like, never having heard the name before. It's smell is in the cutting of it, and it's use in the making of the highest quality furniture. A thriving timber industry still flourishes in these parts.

The path followed the Touw river, which glowed the colour of coca-cola, (from the harmless oxides in the water). Climbing higher and higher over boulders and plaited roots, we went on for a couple of hours, leaving the river for the tranquillity of grassy woodland, thick with proteas and arum lilies. Bulbous explosions of tangled roots were hazardous and slippery with moss. We studied the unhelpful guide map with the help of slats of sunshine which shone in stripes between the trees - and decided to go on.

Eventually, we discovered a rope bridge at the top of a wooded ravine, leading to the top of the gorge. With my feet dangling over the edge, binocular-happy, hoping for a sighting of giant kingfisher or bushbuck hiding in the undergrowth, I sat and waited. Barrie went on to the top. The beat of my heart almost drowned the captivating sounds of the forest. Thirty minutes went by in which I became a widow.

The wanderer returned at last, bearing the same expression as Livingstone, no doubt, after his quest for the source of the Nile in darkest Africa in 1859.

"I made it!" came the voice crashing through the undergrowth.

Late in the afternoon, at the bottom of the valley, the famous 'Outeniqua Choo Tjoe' passed through on its journey between George and Knysna on a miniature train track. The steam locomotive, built in 1928, runs along the coast giving the passengers an old-fashioned ride between lagoon, forest and sea. It seemed strange to see an animal as unusual as a train, chugging white steam into the forest canopy.

The following day, our destination was the coastal town of Knysna, a wild rugged resort, set between wilderness and lagoon, which is almost cut off from the sea. It is famous for its hand crafted furniture made from the many different African hardwoods, culled from the nearby forests, and its oysters. Dominated by sun, moon and tide, it is connected to the ocean by a narrow strip of dangerous water, flanked by two high sandstone cliffs known as 'The Heads.'

We climbed downwards to the beach to watch the fishermen. Bathed in light from the glowing sunset, they stood on the rocks and threw their lines on the incoming tide- as men on horesback used to ride into battle. The white wind-tossed spray spewed hard against the rocks and the fishermen, hardened by the salty climate, stood only just out of reach, ready to pitch their hook in the swirling water, at risk of being plunged in themselves. Deep rock pools filled with water and then emptied, sucking the water in through every crack with vicious strength. We watched until we almost feared our retreat could be cut off.

Knysna was founded at the beginning of the nineteenth century by George Rex, who was rumoured to be the bastard son of George lll, bestowing upon it a few romantic stories. He took up with a coloured mistress, thus offending his friends in Britain and came to Knysna to live, then one of the few white settlements out of Capetown. He started a trading company, which sent African hardwood from the Knysna forests all round the world.

Knysna is a Khoi word meaning 'hard to reach'. The town's atmosphere is about eating houses and oyster bars. Seafood restaurants jostle for supremacy and the trendy tapas bar at the jetty is right on the lagoon. High quality shops and hotels line the pavements. It looks clean and cared about and pretty. Money is being spent in Knysna and the locals informed us that South Africa's legacy of crime was very much lower here than in Capetown. Flourishing businesses are enjoying the upsurge of wealth from overseas visitors and it is still a nice place to live. Conservation is on everyone's lips and people flock continuously to explore the waterways and the birdlife; to walk the forest trails to try and catch a view of the colourful but elusive Lourie bird which is famous here. And to have an unforgettable ride aboard the *Outeniqua Choo-Tjoe* steam train, which leaves from Knysna every day. Others enjoy a bar stool and a plate of champagne oysters.

Barrie and I discovered Jazzbury's Restaurant on the main walkway, hidden behind a few other buildings. It had a cobbled yard where you could eat under the stars on a fine night. The homecooked food was delicious and we counted it as the best ever value for money during the whole two weeks of our honeymoon.The oysters were on the house.

Two hundred years ago herds of elephants were known to roam through the forests around the southern Cape, but persistent hunting throughout many years has reduced the number to seven.This tiny herd is thought to exist still in the forest area around Knysna and is by no means easy to locate. Three young elephants were introduced in 1994 to extend the herd, but one died and the few remaining animals are so wary of mankind that only the patient visitor may be rewarded. Just in case you may think you are imagining things, there is a sign on the road between Knysna and Plettenburg Bay telling you to beware of elephants crossing.

As we searched for somewhere to stay, we came across a tiny apartment in Plett just a few miles away, exquisitely furnished, with the most comfortable bed I have ever slept in. Its windows looked over the sea where the dolphins swam every afternoon. The price was ridiculously low and we felt so welcome. It was easy to fall in love with this part of the Garden Route and never want to leave.

Below our balcony, tiny white sails dotted the sea and above us, the autumnal April skies blazed impossibly blue. By now we both felt totally relaxed. England seemed like another lifetime. It was time to think about our return to Lesotho. We had only two days left.

A trip out to Keurbooms Bay to the north of Plett, left us with memories of a wide sweeping bay with little roads climbing up the cliffs where we said goodbye to the dolphins. It was good timing. The afternoon was a little hazy at first. Then the mist cleared and from our vantage point high above the sea, those bottle nose dolphins came diving between the rollers. My binocular eyes saw them, like tiny silver tadpoles dancing between the waves. Another month and the whales would be swimming into these waters and the clifftop would offer a grandstand view. How I wished one would arrive a little early.

We headed for the Tsitsikamma Mountains. Our friends in Ficksburg had stressed that we simply must make a stop at Storms River Mouth in the Tsitsikamma National Park at the end of the Garden Route, taking the good tar road via Natures Valley. A fresh morning winding through the draping vines of Bloukrans Gorge brought us to the beautiful golden sands of Natures Valley. It was like being in a time warp of secret garden leading into secret golden bay, which curved in a horseshoe around the languid lagoons. The sea was like a warm bath and we swam in slow motion in the heat of the day. Pink shells for Abigail were gathered once more and again we promised ourselves to return .

At the gates of the National Park we were told we could have one of the log cabins for the night which overlooked the ocean, for about the price of a hairdo. Officialdom at its best; a stamp on a card with your name on and very pleasant game wardens operating from a hut with flowers growing over barbed wire. Inside the forest, miles of tall trees, wonderful smells and flowers we didn't know the names of, emerged through the foliage. Vervet monkeys hanging like umbrellas from the trees, squealed and chirruped as our car passed underneath.

Storms River Mouth is the most dramatic estuary on this part of the coast. Beginning at Keurboomstrand, the National Park stretches 68 kilometres along the coast. It combines rugged coastline, deep river gorges and ancient hardwood forests. The scenery is exhilarating. A famous five day Otter trail attracts many people. The walk starts from the mouth of Storms River and ends at Natures Valley. You may see dolphins, whales and seals and even a rare sighting of the Cape clawless otter which lives along this coast. The walk includes crossing the Bloukrans river at low tide by wading or swimming and at night you sleep in log cabins. We would both have loved to do this trail, but had to tear ourselves away all too soon.

We managed to stay long enough to enjoy the stupendous view across the mouth of the river by walking the suspension bridge to the other side of the gorge, to a tiny beach full of pounded white pebbles, so lovely, I longed to carry them home to put in my garden. My husband swam out to a floating raft which was anchored out in the mouth of the river and dozed in the warm breeze, while I stayed and watched the river surging through the gorge.

Later, in the coolness of late afternoon, we strolled the boardwalk above the beach to see the old men of the forest; ancient yellowood and candlewood trees some of which are said to be 800 years old, leaning gracefully amid the tangled vegetation. This route takes the walker higher into the forest, where the fantastic views of glinting ocean and 40 miles of unspoilt shore, mark the end of the Tsitsikamma National Park.

It was a day of lazing and sunning and walking; of saying goodbye to the beautiful southern Cape coast. Storms River Mouth lies 18 kilometres south of Storms River Bridge, the boundary between the Eastern and Western Cape and is a natural ending to the Garden Route.

We felt blessed that our marriage had experienced a beginning never dreamed of, a few months before. Our log cabin on the beach, looking onto a wide stretch of the Indian Ocean, was the ultimate ending to our honeymoon in the Southern Cape. Today, we must face the long journey back across the Karoo Desert, heading towards Graff-Reinet, then east to Blomfontein, the Orange Free State and the borders of Lesotho, which was now, our home.

Chapter 27

The Concert

Life on the camp in Leribe was, after our time at the Cape, an emotional gear change. Soon after we returned, I flew to England to see a doctor about a long term problem in my spine. Three weeks after my marriage, I was lying in one of those awful tube things in a London clinic, trying to breathe in an enclosed metal chrysalis. I panicked and asked to be taken out. At the second attempt the nurse threaded me back in, feet first. My blood pressure shot up and I almost fainted. It wasn't the doctor's fault. I'm just one of those feeble patients who can't lie still in a metal tube - even if I go in upside down.

"Couldn't you knock me out?" I suggested, "Chloroform – anything!"

Pleading with a nurse had no effect. Feeling a complete idiot, I rang Barrie at his desk in Leribe to tell him I couldn't go ahead with the treatment. At this point, something miraculous happened and my spine stopped causing pain. Whether it was the shock of that experience or the African sunshine , I shall never know - but the condition healed itself during the next few months and my mobility recovered completely.

I must have undergone a dramatic change after living eight months in Lesotho. Joyful though I was to be back in England to see my children, hug Abigail, visit my friends, and walk in the bluebell woods, I couldn't wait to get back to Lesotho. English newspapers were full of football hooligan headlines and post election euphoria. No one seemed interested in the fate of a third world country called Lesotho, once a British Protectorate. No one in fact knew where it was on the map of South Africa and quite suddenly, I knew I had to write this book.

Then I met a man of a different sort. Richard Syms is the Priest-in-Charge of All Saints Church, Datchworth. He is a full time actor and appears in films when he is not in his pulpit. His parishioners are used to his dual role and local gossip has it that when he misses a Sunday, he could be playing God somewhere else. Richard fulfills both positions remarkably well and his congregation likes having a theatrical vicar who enjoys a pint. On one of his rare off duty moments, I asked if he would give some thought to the idea of a link with a church in Lesotho. Our short meeting in May, 1997 gave me hope. A modern device called a pocket microtape which I had taken with me on my travels, introduced the voices of my friends in St John's Church, Ha Simone, into Richard's quiet study. He was good enough to listen. With a little caution, for this was village politics, Richard agreed to introduce the idea to that brave band - the Datchworth Parochial Church Council, who would be meeting in two months time. For the moment, I would have to be patient.

Johannesburg was in the middle of a blizzard when my flight arrived on 27th May at 6.30am. South Africa time. Barrie had been held up by a snowstorm in Lesotho and was stuck in a freezing car waiting for the sleeping guards to open the border post.

He arrived two hours late and very cold. It was in fact, the loveliest homecoming and my first as a wife. If I had felt like a lost soul in England, I now sensed there was an important role for me in Leribe. I was overjoyed to be back in the mountains and realized how much I had longed to see them.

The month of June is harvest time in Lesotho and the roads everywhere are frequented by overloaded ox-carts driven by children, sometimes dangerously, and at cost to drivers of fast company cars. As for the farmers - their technology is simple. Call in the whole family to help. Pray for a long fine spell between the summer rains. Spend the week gathering in the mealie, throw them onto the cart, pile as high as possible, then drive home scattering the road with fat cobs to be picked up by starving children. The remaining stalks will feed the cattle until October.

Walter had promised me that I should be allowed to help with their harvest. He had also promised me a ride in the ox cart. On the morning after I arrived from England, I went to Ha Simone to discover that the whole family had departed for the mealie-pick. Only Emily was at home. We abandoned the four wheeled transport and set off on foot to see how the pickers were doing. It was a long walk over the fields to find them. The sun was hot and the ground slippery with mud. Emily was pleased to hear news of the family, especially of Abigail. We talked non-stop, as we thrashed along the fields of the now fully grown maize, hopping over channels of water-logged ground.

Compared with the efficient combines and mechanical balers of an English corn harvest, this agricultural landscape was very different. We passed women with children on their backs, making their way to the fields, and lines of donkeys, heavy with sacks, ridden by young boys. The beasts of burden and their riders stopped to stare at a white lady in a long skirt, silly sandals and sunglasses.

We arrived to find Desmond blessing the crop. Desmond was Stephen's right hand man at St John's, who helped out in all the services. Walter threw his arms around me and yelled loud greetings in my ear, while Desmond walked around the edge of the field waving his cross, ardently shouting prayers to the Almighty.

"Welcome home, Nettie We have missed you so much. How was your England?"

"Walter you look too thin – you haven't been eating properly."

" Oh come and look at our field, we have had so much rain we are flooded." He pulled me along to speak to Desmond.

"We have begun the harvest - but this year, our crop is not that good. Unfortunately, the rain has ruined some of it. We are trying to dig out the channels for the water to drain. Come and see."

Walter was in charge of directing operations in the field. Augustinus, Petros and Bernice were collecting the cobs and were covered in mud from head to toe. Someone's ox had slipped into the mire and the boys were trying to pull her out. Emily and I stood helplessly at the side and saw that the lines of maize, evenly spaced, were separated by ankle deep water. It was pointless wearing anything on your feet and my Marks and Spencer crossover sandals had developed a serious break. I hung them round my neck like a brace of pheasants.

We were sent to fetch sandwiches. The field workers were hungry and had no food left. In due course Emily and I brought lunch to a detachment of troops gathered from other fields who had heard on the grapevine that food was on its way. Walter, Petros, Augustinus and a small queue, devoured the five loaves and two fishes picnic, like only starving farmers can. It was decided to wait another day or two, for the ground to dry out. Picking was abandoned for the day. The boys heartily dug more channels after the sudden rise in calorific energy and Emily and I set off with empty arms, back to base.

By the time we had walked the couple of miles home, I felt like Tess in the Thomas Hardy turnip field. My feet and skirt encrusted with mud, I sat on my familiar flat stone in their river and washed myself. Two days before, I had been sitting on the best leather seats of a London Harley Street clinic having been instructed to do absolutely no mountain climbing and no hard walking. Today, my back felt fine. Tougher mortals than me had been known to wind up in a straight jacket and collar with this condition. I hoped that freedom from tension and a sunshine diet would reduce my intake of painkillers to nil.

Up at the house, Rose was home and she and I had a most joyous re-union. She was baking bread. Her hands were covered with flour as she placed the dough in a cardboard box and covered it with straw. It was lovely to be back with the family and be able to tell them that a tiny seed had been planted in England and the Church of St John's would soon make an appearance on the agenda of Datchworth Parochial Church Council. Rose, meanwhile, placed the dough out in the yard in full sun.

"How on earth do you cook bread without an oven?" I asked her.

"First the heat of the sun will make the dough rise. Then I light the primus stove and bake my *bohobe* on top, with a small amount of heat. You must taste it tomorrow. I will save you some."

Justice was in the yard with the cows and greeted me with the news that there was a new calf about to be born. He also looked thinner than I remembered. Walter and the others came in later from the fields and Stephen arrived back from Durban in a truck wearing his best suit. He had been called by the Archbishop to perform duties in a special ceremony at the mother church.

"Ke thabela ho le bona hape (I am pleased to see you again), Nettie, welcome home!" He gave me a hug and a hearty slap on the back.

"You have a lot to tell us. What did you and Barrie think of the Cape? And now you have just been to England. We missed you!" He endorsed the family's delight at the mention of a possible connection with an Anglican church in England.

"What is a Parochial Church Council?" he asked, immensley intrigued by the term.

In the shadows, sitting on the floor in the corner of the kitchen, I noticed the bent figure of an old lady. It was Grandma Makibi. She had come down from her house on the opposite mountain to hear news of the harvest. I offered her a seat but Emily said she always sat on the floor and she didn't like chairs. I squatted on my knees in front of her, for I had waited a long time to meet this lady. She couldn't understand a word of English but when we shook hands, she held mine tightly in both hers and looked right into my face. She smiled again and again. Rose translated Grandma's words and she said she knew me because Walter had told her that I came to visit him. She was dressed completely in black, because she was still in mourning for a son who had died twelve months ago. A mother must wear black for a year afterwards.

Looking into this worn old face, I perceived the lines of hardship and suffering, yet the fire in her wide clear eyes showed that same indomitable spirit as her second son and her eldest grandson. The way she gripped my hand, I felt her strength and vigour and enduring faith. She let out a loud babble and squeezed even harder, admonishing Walter for not taking me up the mountain sooner. I had to promise to go and see her and meet her friends.

Grandma Makibi, a septuagenarian, made the journey across the difficult terrain once a week to see her family and was as light- footed as a mountain goat. All the old people lived at the very top of the heights because in the days when the marauders came sweeping across the plain, the senior citizens would have more time to go and hide themselves or to drop rocks onto the enemy, if attacked. She lived in a traditional thatched rondavel surrounded by other elders, surviving on milk from a cow and mealies from the harvest. Her only vice was that sometimes, she drank too much joala .This amused the family a whole lot and they teazed her kindly when it was mentioned. Her special brew probably kept the whole village in joala. They agreed that if Grandma Makibi had endured almost eighty years in Lesotho, bringing up a family with minimum possessions, she deserved to enjoy herself in her old age. Suddenly, this tiny figure got to her feet, prodded Walter with her stick, reminded him of his promise, then briskly walked out onto the stoep and disappeared.

Stephen walked to the car with me and saw me across the yard. I guessed he wanted to talk. My heart sank when I noticed three or four sad figures walking towards the house; they were strangers yet not strange. It was late in the day for visitors. They had probably walked for miles and were coming to ask Stephen for help. I thought of the three small loaves which Rose had made for the family supper.

"Here is another family, I don't know what we can offer them. They will have to stay outside for tonight. Tomorrow I will try and find some shelter for them. Nettie, it is so good to hear that you spoke to the Minister Reverend Syms on our behalf. I know that we will have to wait a long time for an answer, but you have given us hope. Now our whole community must pray that the Church will come to us."

"People in England take a long time to decide to do these things," I said, hoping it didn't sound too pompous."They want to learn about your church Stephen. We must sit down and write them a letter soon, and in it you can tell them what kind of Community this is and how your church has grown. Richard Syms will not let us down."

I paused a little, choosing my words carefully, not wanting to offend him.

"Stephen, I have to tell you that no one with whom I spoke, knew anything about your country. People know a little about South Africa if they have travelled, but the country of Lesotho means nothing to most English people."

"This is a surprise. We, in our country, have always felt a loyalty towards England because your Queen Victoria was the great white Queen of the English to defend us in times of war. Britain took control of Lesotho in 1884 at the request of the parliament in Cape town. We were British subjects for almost a hundred years. " He stopped and for a moment, a look of slight bewilderment showed on his face. I did not want to give him any false hopes.

"You know, we always look on English people as our friends. When I was a boy at school, English was the language I was taught first. I hope that our countries will soon have the chance of getting to know one another."

"I hope so too. Goodnight Stephen, and thank you for my lessons in harvesting."

He made the sign of the cross on himself and then gently put his hand on my arm, and wished me goodnight.

"*Khotso 'M'e.* We will speak soon."

Driving home through the fading light towards my own tempting supper, thoughts of how far apart our two countries were, almost compromised my plans. How could anyone expect middle class England to understand the needs of this poor community who held out a hand to destitute families, gave them food and shelter, when they themselves were starving? How could they understand what living without water and electricity meant to a family who had no income?

My appeal to Datchworth was fraught with risk. Even if anyone even listened to my request, drawing in help from parishioners was not easy. Why should they believe me? Richard Syms had said we must wait until the 25th July, when the all important meeting of the Church Council would take place. Until then, the vital connection would have to remain a figment of my imagination. Parochial Church Councils, those faceless bodies of the church, on whose decisions many people waited – some perhaps more deserving – would have to make their choice..

That night, Rose lit three candles in the little church by the river. The congregation of St John's offered prayers and hymns. Emily sang as she had never sung before. Hope ran high in the villagers of Ha Simone. They had a small glimmer of hope in which to believe. And Johannes was leaving the village. He had found someone to take him in. A few months ago, he came to Ha Simone destitute and broken. From an unexpected source, Johannes in his blindness, had been shown a glimmer of hope.

This tiny mountain kingdom is an adventurer's dream, a trekkers paradise, yet the precipitous Afro-alpine peaks have not carved a niche in the current world travel market. The wild flowers, the waterfalls, the snowy heights and plunging river gorges of the high plateau have not arrived on the travel pages of European newspapers. One is hard pressed to find anyone who has actually heard of the country by name. Bushman paintings, cannibal caves and dinosaur fossils are only a four hour flight away from Johannesburg, via Lesotho Airways, or two hours from Blomfontein. UK passport holders do not need a visa to enter Lesotho. And yet adventurers are few. It appears that the century will grow old before the Roof of Africa becomes a tourist's dream. The exchange of sterling to rand is tempting for westerners, yet the moment South Africa is mentioned, the soaring crime rate, paranoid prejudices and sinister rumours rise up and choke the would-be traveller and send him off to the Pacific Islands with its romantic beaches. Perhaps it will take another half century and a boost in political confidence before the English pony trekker takes to the foothills of the Malutis to seek mystery and adventure. Until this time, Lesotho can only dream of offering itself to that other faceless body, the leisure industry.

Kaizi had come up to the house to find me. He was growing so tall these days but I grieved secretly over his black teeth. He had such a beautiful face. His English had improved so much and he was able to say,

"I come tomorrow to read my book" which was more of a statement than a question. He showed me the piece of paper I had given him three weeks ago with the date of my return written down.

"Kaizi, its great to see you again. Please tell Annacleda and Heleyn I am waiting for them to come and see me. I have presents for you all."

Tourist postcards of London had been promised and would catch their imagination. Kaizi had a fascination for soldiers, so pictures of the brass and buckles of the Horseguards should please him. It would be a special moment when we could look at them altogether. His matchstick legs disappeared down the drive to tell the others, just as Esther wandered into the garden to tell me the results of her school exams, that she had taken while I had been away.

The winter sun was very hot in the middle of the day, and but there was a gusty wind around that blew mischief. Doors banged if you left them open and paper flew around if you didn't anchor it. Hercule grew frisky and tried to lift the latch on the gate with his nose. He had worked out how to get out if he leaned on it hard enough, and not many days went by when he didn't escape up to the top of the mountain to chase the cows, the herdboys and the ferocious Basotho dogs. The more battle-scarred he became, the more he seemed to want to get out and fight. Even the cooked ox tail which Betty gave him wouldn't keep him occupied for long. Barrie and I went walking with him most evenings, strictly on a lead.He was known locally as Hercules because he pulled so hard that it could sometimes take the strength of two people to drag him off his chosen whim. We took him over to Walter's that week and let him loose up their mountain paths and deliriously, he took off at about fifty miles an hour, ran amok through the crops, but eventually came back when we called. We thought perhaps he wasn't a delinquent after all.

Everything looked the same along the road into Ficksburg as I drove in to see Solomon at Tlotlisong School to wrap up the final arrangements for the choir concert, which was only one week away. The noisy taxis, the ladies selling fruit along the verge beside the hospital, the stray cows crossing the road. After England, it always took a few days to get used to being here.

People were so friendly and when looking for vegetables at the usual stall, the ladies recognised me and asked , "How is your Queen?"

Everyone assumed we were on first name terms and shared the same bus route. At the butchers, I was told that Amelia (the lady who used to serve the liver) had given birth to twin girls and they came out through her belly.The anatomical reference to a cesarean section brought tears to my eyes, as the new lady assistant drew the large knife horizontally across her apronned abdomen in a gesture of affection. I couldn't bring myself to ask for three beef fillets and ended up with a bunch of sausages the length of a football pitch, which were later given to Betty.

Life in Lesotho was rich and rewarding and our marriage had ripened our relationship.The trust and loyalty we felt towards each other, reflected in many other ways. We had both learnt how to cope better with the black versus white issues which came into our daily lives. Staff who worked on our camp were friendly towards us and we enjoyed the hospitality that eminated from the Basothos. They were lively and full of fun, and loved to hear things about England. But we noticed a difference in the attitudes of the Afrikaners. It was something we had to learn about, being newcomers.

The years of apartheid has left a legacy of racial hatred behind in South Africa.The question of whether a new democratic system can be implemented without unleashing the pent up frustrations of generations of blacks has yet to become known.

Nelson Mandela was imprisoned for twenty seven years on Robben Island and fought his own private battle against the rule of the white man. His incredible journey from herd boy to prisoner to President is almost unbelievable in one person's lifetime.

Apartheid was simply a vehicle for creating division and hatred. No longer do Africans have to live with the daunting prospect of the Separate Amenities Act whereby blacks were not allowed by law to share the white man's beaches, public buildings, cinemas, bars, restaurants, buses, railway carriages, even toilets. Not so long ago, during the years of the terrible Pass Laws, a person could be stopped at any time of night or day and ordered to produce a pass, without which he could be arrested and thrown in jail.Years of humiliation have taken their toll.

Already the levels of violence have escalated throughout South Africa. We lived on a border where daily life depended on people learning to live with new totally new principles. Violent incidents were plentiful. Some of the stories we heard were frightening. White South Africans were having to re-define their lives under the new government. There were those who found it hard. Tensions, disruption and change make people jumpy. No one knows their boundaries any more. Trust has to come from trust.

Barrie and I had made friends with both blacks and whites and discovered an uneasy feeling in hearing two opposing viewpoints, which were often contradictory. Conversations in a white man's bar were sometimes laced with hostilities and feelings of disquiet would come over us. After one or two drinks, someone would throw a comment at the bartender, meant for everyone to hear, that was so derogatory it made us both tremble. We were newly arrived '*Uitlanders*' and our opinions had to be silent.

Robbing the white man was madatory here. Good people we knew in Ficksburg had been robbed several times. Some friends who went fishing up at Katse had all their equipment stolen on a quiet day by a lake. One man had his wheelchair stolen. No matter what the history books tell us, such enormous transitional changes are more than a little painful.

We were living with white man's privileges, in the heart of a black country. The only white people in the mountain region were temporary contract workers belonging to the Highlands Water Scheme, members of the American Peace Corps who taught in remote villages, and a handful of Priests or church workers. Yet, personally, I felt safe; I had no qualms about working in an all-black school and travelling to and from Ficksburg, despite the stealing incident. We had befriended our black family at Ha Simone and regarded their hospitality towards us as truly Christian.The unpredictable encounter with Walter on the road in Ha Simone had opened up a path for giving and receiving. We could only follow along that road. Our new friendships were built on respect for fellow human beings and a genuine desire to learn how the Basotho people lived. We could not possibly have the same feelings as those who were several generations deep and had been affected by wars or bitter violent events. In our daily lives, we both felt the legacy of unbridled retribution, like a veil of darkness penetrating the future. The one alternative was not to let it affect our lives and to keep our own frame of reference uppermost in our minds.

I hadn't seen Solomon Malebo since before our wedding and my trip to England. When I arrived at Tlotlisong School, he greeted me warmly and took me to see the newly arrived photocopier - a rather oversized antique looking machine which clanked noisily. It was the first and only electrical gadget in the school and constantly drew crowds of onlookers who were happy to stand and watch it clank.

"Solomon, I would like the final list of choir members who will be travelling on the bus to Butha-Buthe, to take to Patrick at the border, so that he will ensure our safe passage on the evening of the concert."

A piece of paper bearing the final list of passengers was fed into the mouth of the photocopier. Everyone stood quiet and watched. The 'on' light glowed and the silence was awesome. Solomon closed his eyes and muttered heavenwards. It was a tense moment. With a sound like chronic indigestion, the belly of the machine laboured loudly , then spat out the all-important document. This piece of paper would be the key to our success in crossing into Lesotho. Solomon put his name to it and handed it over.

The next day was spent waiting in queues at both borders, finalising the detailed plan with border control officials. Both parties knew that on Friday 13th June, a group of singers would be travelling on a bus between Ficksburg and Butha-Buthe, without passports, on condition that the vehicle returned within a few hours. Our papers were all in order, permission had been granted and all details written down- in triplicate. By the end of the day, my piece of paper had more stamps on it than a United Nations International Agreement.

At Butha-Buthe camp the big hall in the English school was being prepared and the team of men who were building a stage were instructed to have it ready by Friday morning, so that the children could rehearse during the day. At the French school there was great excitement where the music teacher breathed confidence into budding soloists, who would perform for the first time in front of an audience. Mrs Hughes gave out concert tickets to sell, which on the night must be shown to the guards at the gate. No non- ticket holders would be allowed in. Posters went up all over town.

Then there was the question of refreshments. L.H.P.C. was providing a free supper for our South African visitors, to be served after the concert. Nia knew from experience, that if the Basotho children in her class went home with a letter inviting families to an evening concert, each child would suddenly gain a few extra siblings along with a string of aunties and uncles, who would all turn up early on the off-chance of free food. So tickets were limited to four for each family and hopefully all the people who came would be aware that we would be asking for donations towards musical instruments for Tlotlisong Choir. I was left with the quandary of where to buy the food, how to transport it and of course, where to hide it.

The transport manager at Butha-Buthe camp and I, had endured an on off relationship since the beginning of this 'joint venture'. Whenever I wanted to speak with him, he had gone off camp. It was questionable whether he had given us the best vehicle for the job. I had informed him that we needed seating for more than fifty people. He said he had given us his most reliable bus for the night of the 13th . I was not convinced.

On the day of the concert, Augustine, the company driver and I, drove over to Connie's Cafe in Ficksburg, to fetch sixty plates of prepared food and bring them in by truck. It was still early and the roads were empty. As we drove past the garage in Leribe, the little old man who slept there behind the petrol tanks was enveloped in blankets and attempting to roll his newspaper bed into a neat pile. Whenever we drove by at night, we used to notice the sparks from his small fire where he sat warming himself by the side of the 500gallon tank. He was a well known local character and seemed undaunted by his nightly proximity to potential disaster.

In front of us, a bakkie full of field workers lurched onto the road with half a dozen pairs of boots hanging over the edge.The twelve passengers were all standing and as the truck went round the corner, they all leaned dangerously over the side. The driver was reluctant to use his brakes- probably because he had none- and the bakkie skidded across the mud, landing in the ditch at the other side of the road.

"Drunk!" said Augustine solemly.

"At this time of the day?"

"At any time of the day. He is a man who drinks the beer too much. He is a stupid Basotho taxi-driver. I know him. He used to be a good man before he drank the beer."

Augustine wasn't called Mr Mafia for nothing. There wasn't much he didn't know about this town. A conversation with Augustine was as good as a daily newspaper. He knew who was in favour, out of favour, out of a job, in jail or about to capitalise on his misfortunes. I liked his company and was most glad of his presence, when we crossed back from South Africa into Lesotho and the guards became interested in my sixty plates of hamburger rolls and three crates of coke.

" 'M'e is bringing de food to de special party. Many people will be waiting to count all de food when it arrives in Butha-Buthe at L.H.P.C. Mr Darcy himself will be counting de food." (Mr Darcy was the project director of L.H.P.C. known to the Basotho as '*Ntate Boss*').

Augustine was not short of confidence and with a steady hand kept the engine running while the guard sniffed around the boxes. We got through without a delay. During the 40 kilometres journey to the camp, Augustine dictated my concert speech in seSotho and I practised saying the words.

On arrival at the English school we were given instructions to take the boxes of food down to a classroom at the far end of the corridor, cover them with sheets and then lock the door. The keys were taken to Mrs Hughes and the caretaker sent onto guard duty. The atmosphere at the school was electric. Men with hammers were still banging away under the stage and the voices of the children could be heard singing in another part of the building. Even the guards at the gate were smiling and knew their duties for the evening. I went home to get ready.

All the engineers and their wives were coming to the concert. Liliane had been busy commandeering people to come and help with the seating or to shake tins. Noi would be bringing the video camera. Barrie was to go to Ha Simone to pick up Walter and Emily and bring them to the school and then organise the money side of things. My job was to go to Tlotlisong School and travel with Solomon and the choir, across the border, and make sure they arrived safely at their destination in time to sing at seven o'clock.

The atmosphere at the school was one of unparalleled excitement. At precisely five o'clock Solomon was ticking off the names of the choir members who had presented themselves for a full uniform inspection. Every pupil must be in possession of a clean shirt, pressed navy blue trousers or dress, the school tie, long socks, and a pair of polished black shoes - to be laid out before him. I had no idea how much this mattered to Solomon. His school must look the best - even if these kids did not own a farthing. Somehow, each pupil must find a uniform which reflected his standards. No uniform - no concert.

The choir was assembled in a squalid room under the eagle eye of Elizabeth and Miriam. Solomon showed me in and I crept quietly to the back of the room to listen to the final rehearsal of their final song. My heart was pounding and my hands shaking. The sound of their voices was heaven to my ears. I can only descibe the sensation as one of the most emotional moments in my life. Their faces glowed nervously and every eye was upon Elizabeth's baton.

Miriam took my arm and led me to the front. Racing through my mind were thoughts of the years of apartheid not so long ago when black singers would not have been allowed to perform before a white audience. Tonight was an extremely special occasion. I looked from the broken windows and cracked walls of the room to the eager faces of the singers from the squatter camp up the hill.

"I want to wish you good luck for tonight's concert. Your songs are very special. Your voices are beautiful when you perform all together. Everyone at L.H.P.C. is looking forward to hearing you sing. There will be children from two other schools there tonight, English and French. They will sing first - then it will be your turn. I shall be listening."

I saw Solomon from the corner of my eye motion the line of kids out of the door to the waiting bus.

Mr Mapetuani sat in the driver's seat of the most decrepit looking vehicle I had ever seen. The sides looked crumpled and the lines of rust stood out like ribs of beef. The body listed to starboard and the bumper almost escaped recognition. The transport manager's promise held a clear message.

As the bus spluttered into life, everyone claimed a seat and settled themselves. Solomon and I sat at the front, along with the geography mistress, the language master and the two music teachers. In my hand, I clutched the vital list of pupils. Solomon beamed. It was the first time his pupils had been across the border into Lesotho. To them it was a very unusual journey. To me it was the highlight of my journey to South Africa.

It was the time that we call dusk in England, which happens very quickly here. The light was fading as Mr Mapetuani coasted along on his bald tyres, towards the South African border post, taking in the generations of potholes destined to ruin the most capable suspension system. It was fifteen minutes to six. As we drew to a halt by the guard, I spotted the tall figure of Patrick standing by the barrier. He was dressed in casual clothes, holding in his arms, his son of four or five years old. The little boy was dressed in pyjamas, arms clinging around his father's neck as though about to fall asleep. I was so touched by this gesture of respect from Patrick. Even though he was off duty at this particular time, he had taken the trouble to come to the border to see the choir safely through. Solomon stepped off the bus to go and shake his hand. It was such a lovely moment. I wanted to cry. Then heads were counted, papers exchanged in seconds and an enormous rubber stamp placed on top. We were through.

The atmosphere on the bus was riotous. Fifty kids shouted with joy as we drove across the Caledon River Bridge and out of South Africa. So far, things were going so smoothly. At the Lesotho border our vehicle came to a halt. Solomon motioned everyone to stay quiet. The woman on duty came to the barrier. Our driver stopped the engine and climbed out.

"Passports please, " I heard a voice exclaim loudly.

"We are the Tlotlisong School Choir. We have the permission of your border office to travel to Butha-Buthe to sing at L.H.P.C. tonight. I think you are expecting us. Our papers are in order."

"Where are your passports?" she snapped. "I have no instructions to let you through. I did not expect you."

Solomon put his head in his hands and start to pray. The other male teacher got out and slowly went over to the barrier. All the lights in the bus suddenly dimmed. Not a sound came from the singers.

"Annette, this is terrible news," said Solomon in a dead voice. "What has happened to our plan? I must go and see. Please don't get off the bus. Stay here."

For ten minutes the discussion raged. Heated voices between the woman and our driver.Then a long wait. Solomon disappeared inside the building. The kids started whispering and someone burst into tears. Jacob appeared and came to sit with me. He wasn't a member of the choir but he had helped to organise the whole event. He looked very tense. Behind us, a long queue of vehicles had piled up and started pushing their horns. It was a quarter past six. We had only just enough time to get the the camp by seven, even if we flew.

Suddenly, we heard the sound of voices and shouting as the barrier was raised and a tall bearded man waved at us. Solomon appeared clutching a whole sheaf of papers which he threw onto my lap. He looked angry. Apparently, no order had been left indicating our arrival and the duty officer said she knew nothing about us. In the end she could see our problem and agreed that we should be given permission to travel - on the absolute guarantee that this bus came back through before eleven.

The elderly engine shuddered into action. Mr Mapetuani threw his whole weight into the dilapidated gear box and a pillow of black smoke followed us like a garden bonfire.

Up the hill into through Maputsoe we roared through the dark street. Leftover vegetables littered the pavements and market traders were starting to light their fires along the edge of the road.

We were about three minutes from the border post, when all the lights went out in the bus. There was a terrible judder from the bowels of the engine, and we came to a dead stop by the side of the road. Everyone fell into a deep silence. The driver raised himself from his seat, drew a small carpet from a box by his feet and limped down the steps of the bus, with hunched shoulders. Slowly, we watched him disappear under the engine. Only his boots could be seen. I could hear the kids whispering behind me.

Solomon was beside himself. The incident at the Lesotho border had been bad enough and this was the final straw. With his knuckles showing white, he clasped his hands together and sent messages to the Almighty in a wail of grief. The other staff members did the same. I hardly dared to look at my watch. As the minutes ticked by, we heard loud clanking noises coming from underneath the bus. All I could think of was the sixty waiting children and an expectant audience. Like some kind of lethargy, a silent gloom descended. ......I could not believe we had actually broken down after surmounting so many obstacles.

Then, like some kind of apparition, Mr Mapetuani - carpet rolled tightly under one arm- emerged up the gangway, his black face all shiny with sweat. He looked straight at me. Solomon stopped praying for a moment.

"Teacher - where you want to go?"

"Butha-Buthe camp - by seven!" I spluttered..

"Right. We go. It will be Okay!"

After one or two loud rumbles and groans and a multiple double de-clutch, the animal reared up roaring like a lion going for the kill. In fourth gear, the worn old system leapt into life, scaring all the chickens and the bleating sheep on the outskirts of Maputsoe so that feathers and legs flew in all directions as we passed. The inside lights came back on and with this, all the pupils started to get undressed and put on their fine uniforms. We careered at top speed through the countryside, scattering everything in our path. The only lights now on the road between Maputsoe and Butha-Buthe were the stars.

Newly ironed shirts, trousers with creases you could slice bread with and shiny shoes were taken down from the racks and put on. The inside of the bus was sticky with hairspray and Brylcreem. Make-shift curtains were erected and lots of giggling and wriggling went on. The gangling limbs of the triumphant teenagers were flung from one side of the aisle to the other, but gradually emerged in navy serge and pale blue cotton. Old clothes were stuffed into bags and replaced on the rack above. The bus whistled along the dark roads, past the sleeping cows and the terrified donkeys while everyone was thrown around in a mahem of excitement. Solomon's eyes shone with happiness. The geography mistress had stopped wailing and was standing up in the aisle, beaming like a Cheshire cat.

At five minutes past seven, the devoted Mr Mapetuani, with veins standing out on his forehead like purple tramlines, coaxed his reluctant vehicle past the guards at the Butha-Buthe school gates who stood to attention and cheered our arrival. I thanked him heartily and promised him supper after the concert. The faces of the kids were thanks enough, as they streamed off the bus and into the waiting auditorium. They needed no introduction.

Solomon and I took our places at the front of the hall where a crocodile of small children were mounting the steps onto the stage and while Tlotlisong Choir arranged themselves nervously on the empty chairs. The school hall was packed. No one there knew anything about our journey, though Nia whispered to me as I passed, " I am so relieved to see you. When you didn't arrive by seven, I knew something must have gone wrong."

"The driver made history," I answered."Maputsoe to Butha-Buthe in thirty five minutes! He's gone to get another bus."

Earlier that week, on the site of the Highlands Water Scheme looking out over the treeless landscape of northern Lesotho, thirty new saplings planted by the children of the English school had been placed lovingly in the soil. Their song for the concert was about the environment. It was a bewitching performance. Little rounded tummies and thumbs in mouths, hosted the front row- not in time to the music- while willowy juniors standing at the back kept it all together with the certainty of good strong voices and aluminium tooth braces. They said a prayer for trees.

Engineers can be unconventional audiences. Some cried - others put their hands in their pockets and gave generously to our cause.

The French children came on next. Monsieur le Headmaster had drilled them well. It was as if, inside *tous les enfants*, there was a song bird. Living in Lesotho, French is not a language one hears very often. The sweetness, the crisp execution of their words, the tuneful trained voices of these happy children - to a piano accompaniment - gave such pleasure to the receptive audience. They were professional. They were charming. Their soloists *par excellence*. Another round of applause and more tears.

Within these four walls were people from many different countries, brought together in music. The choir who were about to perform had lived through the very worst of apartheid times; their ancestors had lived through wars, slavery and controversy. In their lifetime, the burning issues of black people subordinated by a white government, have taken their toll. Tonight was a chance to forget the bad times and explore the good.

The choir took their places. On the back row, an albino boy stood out from all the others. His hair was white and his skin was pink. His features were African. No amount of sympathy could make up for all the insensitivites which he will have lived through. An albino life is a painful one. Yet he was here with his friends, singing for his supper.

Solomon got to his feet. His voice was soft and gentle as he said that the occasion was overwhelming. He had never dreamt that this evening could take place. The bridge between the engineers of the Highlands Water Scheme and South Africa was about to be built - by children and by music.

On the tiny stage, the Tlotlisong choir sang unaccompanied. All they were given was one line of introduction by Elizabeth and after this they sang without direction. There was no printed sheet or baton. Just a lifting of voices in unison.

Each song told a story of some aspect of life in South Africa. One was dedicated to the life of the herdboy, wandering across the mountains, another, a prayer to the African skies which promised the coming of rain. A wonderful sound, like dark velvet, echoed out of the hall and far beyond. '*Glory to God in de Highest*' broke all previous sound barriers and we felt that the roof of the school might cave in. The geography mistress got to her feet and danced solo at the front of the house, with her blanket tied around her middle and a smile on her face which illuminated the universe. The strength of their voices was powerful; the small children put their hands delicately over their ears, but everyone in the audience loved it. Their singing could have filled a London opera house without a single microphone. Elizabeth had told me that they had already come fifth in a National Competition in Johannesburg and on their next entry, they expected a top place.

Their songs were accompanied by moving feet, beating a rhythm. First, a symmetrical formation of arms in a sea of voices , like a boat moving through water. Then a chant of swinging hips, and more foot banging on the boards. At the end I gave my thankyou speech in seSotho. Solomon and I shook hands. Supper was announced.

Still they carried on singing. It was like a mountain spring which flowed down to the river, never wanting to stop. We raised more than three thousand rands, which was topped by a donor to four thousand. Watching at the back of the hall, through beads of perspiration, was Mr Mapetuani. He had been to find another bus.

The celebrations went on and on. Solomon announced that I was his new sister and we shook hands. Flowers were presented to Elizabeth and Nia Highes and the children of many countries cheered and clapped for each other. The kids of Tlotlisong School ate their hamburger rolls hungrily and came to say thankyou. They were wild with excitement, but their social graces were not forgotten and politeness remained intact. At eleven o'clock, several boys carried Mr Mapetuani shoulder high, across the yard to his new waiting vehicle, which had magically appeared from the working site of Butha-Buthe camp at some time during the concert.

No one counted them back on board. It was up to the officials at the border to tell if anyone who had arrived in Lesotho earlier that evening did not return. Since the night of the concert, I have wondered about that. They drove away on diesel and adrenalin and as far as I know, Mr Mapetuani's coach did not turn into a pumpkin.

Chapter 28

Death of Sam

Sam's death shook everyone rigid. His body was found in his vehicle at the side of the road. It was untouched. There was no robbery. His clothes were not stolen. His keys were in the ignition.

Sam must have travelled this road to Johannesburg literally hundreds of times. Passing back and forth carrying passengers, safely and on time. He was not off his route. His vehicle was parked on the verge a few yards back from the tarmac, neatly turned. There was no sign to say what had made him drive off the road. All his documents were intact.

It was like a big puzzle.Everything about his death was just how he had been in life. Neat and tidy. No unwieldy marks or signs of violence. Just quiet and peaceful. Everyone was stunned. His family didn't know why, his company didn't know why - but he was dead behind the wheel of his bakkie.

A few weeks went by and the stories started. He had been killed by a poisonous dart. He had died in a trance. There were bound to be internal injuries. The rumours went on and on.

Violence happens every day in South Africa according to the newspapers, the farmers and the city dwellers. Photographs of the dead line police station walls and families' sitting rooms. As an individual our driver hated anything to do with violence. He was gentle and unassuming..

Sam - the quiet orderly Sam, who turned up every day for work and never had any time off. The driver whom everyone trusted. The man who never let anyone down. He looked after us ladies when he took us anywhere, made Lesotho come alive for us. He was totally committed in all he did -often doing many hours of a journey which were far outside his duty.

There was an inquest some time later. The Medical Inspector said that our driver had died of natural causes, from a brain haemorrhage. He had an old injury, which resurfaced and caused him to die, uncomplaining of even a small headache. Over and over your mind goes…..what if this...what if that....why did he stop there on the side of the road when he was alone? It didn't make sense.

I had a taken a lovely photograph of Sam when he and the other drivers had been waiting in the yard one afternoon for their pay. Sam was looking relaxed, his kind eyes were smiling. He was wearing a black shirt and a fawn coloured flat cap, good trousers, good shoes. He asked me to take a photograph because he hadn't a camera. I didn't think about it after that.

One morning- some time after the inquest - I was in my garden on the camp. A lady walked towards me; she was young - perhaps twenty five or so. I didn't know her. She smiled nervously when she saw me. Her English was poor but she managed the words,

"You have the photo of Sam… can I see it?"

She waited patiently outside and I gave her the picture of Sam, looking relaxed, smiling at the camera. The young woman stared down at the photograph. Large sad tears welled up in her eyes and fell unchecked onto her thin hands.

"Would you like to keep it?" I asked. She nodded, turned and walked slowly out of sight, her shoulders hunched. Her thinness showed through her dress. I didn't know who she was, but she was mourning the man she loved. I never saw her again.

Sam was very loved by his family. He had worked hard so that his son should have a good education. Now he was in college training for a good career. Sam's death, at the age of forty two, brought unfamiliar thoughts and strange suspicions into our lives. Something was lurking in the shadows. We would probably never know how our friend came to die on the road to Johannesburg.

I will always remember him as the quiet man with whom I always felt safe. Sam was a Basotho and proud to be one. They said his death was natural.

BIBLIOGRAPHY

APA Publications 1999 - Insight Guide to South Africa.

Mary Benson – A Far Cry - published by Penguin Books Ltd (Viking)

Karen Blixen - Out of Africa - published by Century Publishing Co. Ltd. 1985

Mike Crewe Brown - A Travellers Companion to Southern Africa - published by Southern Book
Publishers (PTY) Ltd. Johannesburg.

Josie Drew - The Wind in my Wheels - published by Little Brown and Company 1992

Kuki Gallman
I Dreamed of Africa - first published by Viking 1991- Penguin Group 1992
Night of the Lions.

Stephen Gill - A Short History of Lesotho - published by Morija Museum & Archives 1993.

Peter Green & Jeff Astley – One in Word & Work – 10years of the Lesotho Durham Link. Published for and on behalf of the Lesotho-Durham Link

James Gregory - Goodbye Bafana - the life of Nelson Mandela. Published by Headline 1995

Paul Harrison - Inside the Third World - published by Penguin 3rd Edition. First pub 1979.

Elspeth Huxley
The Flame Trees of Thika - published by Chatto and Windus Ltd London 1959
The Mottled Lizard - published by Chatto & Windus 1962. Penguin 1981
Red Strangers - published by Chatto & Windus 1965. Penguin 1999
Out in the Midday Sun – My Kenya – published by Chatto & Windus 1985. Pimlico 2000
Nine Faces of Kenya – published by Collins Harvill 1990. The Harvill Press 1997

Fergal Keane - Letter to Daniel – published by BBC Penguin Books

Peter Lanham & A S Mopeli-Paulus – Blanket Boys Moon - first published by William Collins Ltd London1953, Africasouth Paperbacks by David Philips 1984

Laserline Surrey - Lesotho Highlands Water Project. Engineering publications 1992-1995
.

Lesotho Tourist Board publications P.O.Box 1378. Maseru 100

LP Publications - Lonely Planet guide to South Africa, Lesotho and Swaziland.

Nelson Mandela - Long Walk to Freedom - published by Little Brown and Co 1994. Abacus.1995

James A. Michener - The Covenant - published by Random House, New York 1979.

Dervla Murphy
South from the Limpopo - published by Flamingo. An Imprint of Harper Collins Publishers.
The Ukimwi Road - by the same author.

Mpho 'M'satsepo Nthunya - Singing Away the Hunger - Published in South Africa by University of Natal Press, Scotsville 1988. First British edition published by Souvenir Press 1998.

Catherine Odie - ENKOP AI my Life with the Masai - published by Simon Schuster Australia.

Oliver Ransford – The Great Trek published by John Murray 1972

Brian Roberts - Those Bloody Women -Three Heroines of the Boer War - published by John Murray 1991

Olive Schreiner
The Story of an African Farm - published by AD Donker 1975. (first pub 1883 by Chapman & Hall, London.)
Trooper Peter Halket of Mashonaland - first published in 1897

Dirk Schwager - 'LESOTHO' published by Schwager Publications 1986.

Pauline Smith – The Beadle - published by Jonathan Cape 1926. David Philip 1989

Russell Suchet - A Backpackers Guide to Lesotho illustrated by Jenny Morgan. Published by Suchet 1997.

Stephen Taylor
Livingstone's Tribe - A journey from Zanzibar to the Cape 'Published by Harper Collins.1999.
Shaka's Children - A History of the Zulu People published by Harper Collins.1994

Laurens van der Post
The Lost World of the Kalahari - published by Chatto & Windus,1958.
The Heart of the Hunter - Published by the Hogarth Press, 1961

Laurens Van der Post & Jane Taylor
Testament to the Bushmen and Witness to a Last Will of Man 1984 - Published by Viking 1984.

GLOSSARY (Afrikaans words in italics)

a re tsamaeeng - let us go
Afrikaner- A south African of Dutch descent   .
Afrikaans – the language of the Afrikaner
bakkie - small pick-up truck
Basotho – the people of Lesotho.
biltong - strips of salted dried meat
boer - farmer
boerewors - large sausages
boy - a male servant of any age
braai - to grill on an open fire -usually with charcoal
bobotie- meat dish served with sweet chutney
circadas - insects (like crickets)
cheko - a childrens' game like hopscotch
Daar ver in n' Krib – Away in a Manger
dagga – cannabis
dankie - thankyou
donga - deep ditch caused by soil erosion
dorp - village or small town
fynbos -indigenous heather - like scrub and wild flowers
Goeiemore Mevrou – good morning Madam
Haeno ke kae – where is your home
ho bala - to read
Initiates – males or females who have been through the ceremony of circumcision.
Initiation School – the school which prepares males and females for circumcision.
joala- a locally brewed beer made from sorghum
highveld –open pasture of the highlands
kaffir - a black person (derogatory)
kea leboha – thank you
ke bokae - what is the price
Ke kopa ho ea ntloaneng – please can I go to the toilet
Khotso – peace (as a greeting)
knobkerrie – a carved stick traditionally the symbol of a warrior
kombi – minibus
kraal - an African homestead, or a small enclosure for animals
lapa– a small courtyard surrounded by reeds
lebitso la hau u mang - what is your name
lelapa – private courtyard
liso- a mixture of clay and dung mixed with water (pronounced 'disu')
litapole - potatoes
litema - designs used by the Basotho to embellish their houses
Litolobonya- a dance performed by women
lobola - bride price
lowveld – open pasture in the lowlands
lumela Ntate – hello Sir/ father (lumela is pronounced dumela)
lumela 'M'e – hello Madam/ mother

lumelang - hello (plural)

mahe – eggs

'M'e - mother

mealie-maize

mealie pap - boiled maize

mofifi-a twig which is used to ward off lightning

mohlolo- a miracle or a wonder

molilietsane- high pitched sound made by women when they are happy and celebrating

Moloti- legal tender of Lesotho (same value as the Rand)

morabaraba - a game played with small stone

Mosotho – an inhabitant of Lesotho

metse - village

muti - traditional medicines

NAPCP - National Aids Prevention and Control Programme

ngiyabonga bawo – (Zulu) thank you father (respectful term to an older man)

ngoan'esa – brother

khaitseli – sister

Ntate – father

popi – a doll

robot - traffic light

rondavel - a round thatched hut

sala hantle- stay well

sangoma - a traditional healer

sepetlele – hospital

setibeng – a place of water

shamba - small-holding

Shosholosa – a dance performed by miners in the gold mines.

Sjambok – to beat in punishment

slagveld- battlefield

stoep - verandah

tsamaea hantle - go well

tsamaeang – go well (plural)

township – area to which blacks were consigned during apartheid

uitlanders – foreigners (black or white)

u phela joang - how do you live (how are you)

umqombothi – beer (Zulu)

Voortrekker – person of Dutch origin who took part in the Boers' Great Trek of 1838 from the Cape Colony to Natal and Transvaal

Lightning Source UK Ltd.
Milton Keynes UK
UKOW06f1021101015

260244UK00001B/2/P